Brain To Boot

Military CQC & Self Defence
Psychological Enhancement &
Conditioning Manual

Caution

The contents of this book are for educational purposes only.
The principles described in this book can be extremely dangerous and should only be attempted under safe, controlled and legitimate Military Close Combat training conditions. Any use of self defence skills must be in accordance with the laws of self defence of the country. Exponents must fully understand the workings and dangers of the misuse of these skills. Instruction must be under the control of a qualified and professional instructor of the Todd Systems of Close Combat. The author and publisher expressly disclaim any liability from death, injury or damages the user of the book may incur. The author and publisher also expressly disclaim liability for any death, injury or damages to third parties from the use or misuse of this book.

ISBN 978-0-473-67450-2
Author: Tank Todd. Army Special Forces Close Combat Master Chief Instructor
Depot: Self Defence School, a dept. of The Todd Group
P.O. Box 5579
Moray Place
Dunedin 9058
New Zealand
Phone/Fax: +64-3-477 8902 Email: tank@toddgroup.com
Websites: www.toddgroup.com www.fighttimes.com
www.closecombatschool.com www.schoolofselfdefence.com
www.cqctimes.com www.eliteactionadventure.com

If you have not received your included audio training exercises, downloading access, password and instructions with your copy of your Brain to Boot manual, then email a request to us at coms@toddgroup.com

Foreword

I am a Family Physician in private practice. Prior to this I spent over ten years working in Emergency Medicine and Acute Psychiatry. I am also Director of Clinical Tactical Systems.

I first got involved with the Todd Group over a decade ago, after hearing of a Special Forces soldier and doctor, who had been trained in Todd CQB in the military.
I had previously been held at knifepoint on two occasions, including once at my place of work.

I ultimately met with Geoff, and have been moving up through the ranks from a basic exponent through advanced exponent to specialist proponent and instructor status. During this time I have had the chance to observe, participate and instruct on Todd Group courses in multiple countries. What has been most notable is the professionalism with which Geoff conducts training. His teaching methods and style, in my opinion, are head and shoulders above anything I have encountered through my long training and experience in Medicine. Geoff has the ability to utilise multiple teaching modalities, coupled with an innate knowledge of psychological, physiological and biomechanical principles.

This Brain to Boot package is a distillation of Geoff's more than three decades of instructing thousands of military and law enforcement personnel, and of course, civilians. It encapsulates the psychological and medical principles that will make anyone reading and working through the package the best combatant they can possibly be, regardless of their prior training experience.

Dr Steffan Eriksson 2015

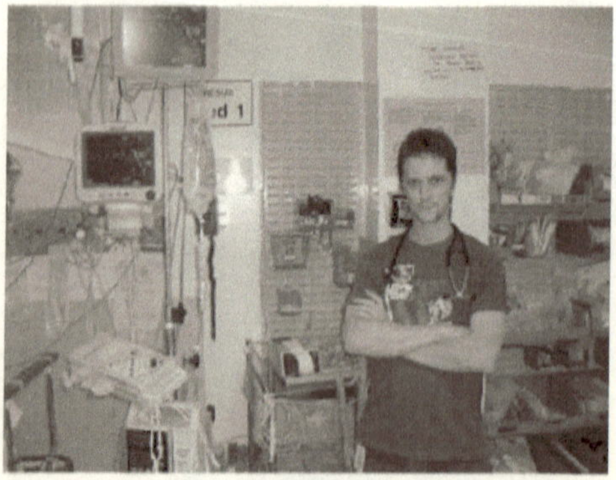

Contents

GLOSSARY

Actions on – Combative term for an assault situation

Battle handling exercises – Military practical method of training under surprise sudden aggressive shock action

Being stalked contingency – CQC term for combating an enemy stalking inside your evasive counter offensive range

Blocking back – Sliding one boot back to set or change a stance, or stepping back under assault

Body line – CQC term for the outer bodily shape

Buddy Training – Paired combative training consisting of a combatant and an enemy per

C&R – Control and Restraint

Closed stance – lead boot side in CQC stance

Combative sighting – Visual focus and assessment between ones cover guard

CQB - European military term for armed combat. Close Quarters Battle

CQC – European military term for unarmed combat. Close Quarters Combat

CQC squat – (Small squat, $^{1}/_{4}$ squat) (half squat, medium squat) (full squat, $^{3}/_{4}$ squat)

Decentralisation – Going to the ground deliberately, accidentally or by means of enemy force

Fast Mapping - Combative assessment at real time as part of threat neutralisation decision making

First look D – CQC term for on threat identification first look provisional threat neutralisation decision making

Flat line – Approximately 75percent combative output

Force protect – CQC actions of self-protection and threat neutralisation

Friendly's – The identification of non-enemy subjects

Hard Cover Guard – compact body line protection from the top of the head to the waist by means of the arms

Hard footing – Dropping ones centre of gravity to provide maximum stability and resistance combined with footing adjustments

Hard Targeting – reducing the risk of assault or injury by using preventative and counter tactics and skills

Kill Zone – The point and place of contact under assault

Making the D – Make the decision

Medium Footing – Controlled ground affinity maintaining positive control and stability under movement or statically

Mind mapping- minds eye tactical assessment and decision making

Mind's Eye – In your mind visualising threat and means of threat neutralisation

MSD – Military self defence

Open stance – Rear boot side in CQC stance

Orthodox – Primary means of combative option

Point and place sighting – CQC term for keeping a visual on your enemy and your immediate surroundings

Point blank range – In CQC body to body contact

R.W.A – TODD Systems civilian self-defence/CQC term for Ready Willing Able

Reactionary – A subconscious undertaking

Ready resistance – CQC deliberate ready status under threat

Regention – Regaining control of a situation or a weapon

Response – A deliberate undertaking

Scenario training – Civilian and law enforcement term for realistic practical training

Second look D – in expected actions on encounters time permitting taking a second look for threat neutralisation decision making

Self-Commands/Silent Commands/Mind Whispering – Silent mind constructions and commands in preparation for threat neutralisation

Sit stat - Situational Status

Soft Footing - Pre Actions on ready or rest status maintaining ground affinity with minimum physical stress

Stalking contingency – CQC term for when stalking into range to employ an assault and before you can your enemy attacks and you must counter engage

Stationary evasion – a static means of clearing the kill zone by pivoting turning one's body from front on to side on to the enemy

Threat neutralise – The employment of tactical anti encounter, escape and evasion or offensive/ counter offensive CQC or self-defence skills to prevent or stop a threat

TODD - Take Out Death Destruction.

TOET – Test of elementary training

Tool Box – Description of combatants combative tools or skills

Triune brains- the reptilian combative or escape and evasion primitive brain.

- Mammalian (limbic brain) low level capability brain

- Homo sapiens (Neocortex) high level intelligence threat assessment and decision making threat neutralisation brain

Unarmed combat – Threat neutralisation by means of using your bodily weapons and non-ballistic weapons

Unorthodox – secondary alternative or emergency combative option

W.A.R – TODD Systems military CQC term for Willing Able Ready

DEDICATIONS

I dedicate this brain to boot psychological conditioning and enhancement manual and package to three professionals in their own right that assisted me for more than three decades:
The late Col Dr Roland John Wilson, the late Grahame Reid and the late Bill Hall.
Both Grahame and John were long-term proponents of CQC and military self defence assisting me with my medical implications of close quarter combat and psychological conditioning and enhancement research and development.
Grahame was a proponent of military unarmed combat and military self defence for over 50 years and John begun his involvement with the military serving in Vietnam with his military career spanning until his passing. He was a highly respected medical Doctor and anesthetist. Grahame was a lifelong pharmacist known as Doc from his military service years who also had a diploma in herbal medicine. Both John and Grahame were lifetime friends of mine that I held in the highest regard and had the utmost respect for. Mr. Bill Hall was a true and genuine friend and father figure to me. Bill was of the highest integrity and assisted me with developing and operating the Todd Group business. He served in the army including in an early irregular force Independent Company and then in World War II in Bomber Command.

Col Dr Roland John Wilson

Bill Hall

Grahame Reid

ACKNOWLEDGEMENTS

I would like to acknowledge and genuinely thank everyone that has assisted me over more than three decades in relation to the Brain to Boot manual. I would like to thank my instructing team and exponents as well as the contract services I train for their assistance and support with the completion of this very important undertaking. I especially would like to thank Professor Timothy Crack and Dr. Steffan Eriksson for their tireless assistance with proofing and editing. I would also like to thank Graeme Wilson and Stephen Thorburn for their constant support and assistance with IT and word processing expertise. My 2IC Kowley "Cowboy" Mitchell has assisted me for decades with many of my CQC projects and this has included the Brain to Boot, His loyalty and assistance have contributed considerably to Todd Group research, development, design and product development. He is a skilled proponent and instructor of CQB as well as a very talented and innovative practical hands on man. I would also like to pay respect and appreciation to my military services friends and associates that have contributed and supported my work.

INTRODUCTION

Background

From a very young age facing bullies considerably older, bigger and more physically capable than myself, I realised the most important factors in defeating them were mental toughness and dirty tricks. I was a well overweight child that had been put in hospital in an effort to reduce weight under dietitians and physical fitness trainers. This proved less than effective, so as soon as I was old enough to seek out training to deal with my weight problems and learn new skills for taking care of the bullies, I did so.

I was committed to training in unarmed combat and self-defence no matter what it took, combined with weight lifting and physical culture. Military unarmed combat and military self-defence made sense to me considering they were not sport, had no weight divisions or gender categories, and there were no rules. Anything that was not legal, even in no holds barred, was a perfectly acceptable means in military close combat. Such practices that were considered fouls or illegal in NHB or MMA were often considered low level means of enemy incapacitation or elimination in military CQC or military self-defence. Skills like escaping holds by using weapons were a primary option, for example, over unarmed escapes.

The reality was that over-kill armed escapes were far more definite in regards to objective achievement than unarmed options. I knew that for me personally combative dirty tricks were the best way to deal with foes that wanted to hurt me. Such foes tended to be older, physically far more capable and often towered over me. I may have been well overweight and shorter than my foes but I would not give in and would do whatever it took to make sure I would win. I always wondered why I was so overweight and wanted to do something to lose weight and improve myself physically.

Many years later when I noticed that my hand began shaking while shooting my pistol it was discovered I had Graves' disease (hyperthyroidism) and I believe my considerable early weight issues were a result of hypothyroidism. Something must have triggered the swing from hypothyroidism to hyperthyroidism. After years of treatment I had to undergo two doses of radioactive iodine to destroy my thyroid. I believe if it had been detected in my early years and more had been known about it way back then things could have been very different for me. Although blood tests today are very definite and provide accurate thyroid function levels, I feel at times to have both symptoms of hypothyroidism and hyperthyroidism. This is not apparently medically possible but it is very much the way I feel. I could never understand the reason why I trained much harder than many fellow exponents, despite eating similarly, yet had weight gaining problems.

My father was more a father by title only after splitting up with my mother when I was very young. I was brought up by my mother who could be overly kind but could also be unpredictable. Often, when frustrated with her difficult single parent life brining up two children on minimal income, she would unleash her frustrations on me. I do not want to go into specific details, but know that my early upbringing did shape my life and make me physically and mentally tougher for the experiences, as well as capable of being very aggressive.

I learnt quickly how to overcome my fears facing considerably older bullies, including some of my mother's grown men boyfriends. Any fears I had of her boyfriends, or anyone that crossed me for that matter, was replaced with the best way I knew to put an end to the probable hostility and that was by dealing out some aggression of my own usually before they could.

Not having a father living or actively involved with my life was unfortunate but a reality for me. My parent's marriage ended in violence and I always had, for some unknown reason, a blind loyalty to my father and tried to make him proud of me. He unfortunately did not show me any positive influence or any appreciation with anything I did. Through my home situation and neighborhood environment I already knew it was far better to deal out rough justice than take it. My teenage years were far from happy and I was exposed to more than a fair share of bullying and harsh treatment. The threatening situations I faced influenced to a large degree my attitude to dealing with anything I considered conflict. Some of my problems were of my own doing, and contributed to my developing an uncompromising, never back down very aggressive attitude.

I hold no grudges. I just now choose my friends and understand I could not choose my family. I was a victim of circumstance that allowed some negative aspects to influence me.

My own father, in public at my workplace and in front of my wife, challenged me to a fight. At the time this really surprised me as he was a complete hands off father in every sense, including neglecting any parenting or husband duties, or showing any violence towards me.

Although he was a solidly built man who had his share of fights and had been a biker, I knew I could through my combative training beat him. I did not want to do this, but he left me no choice when in a confined space surrounded by dangerous objects, and with my wife beside me he kicked off throwing punches at me. As a last resort I knocked him out with a chin jab and had to drive him home unconscious.

In my early years I found a positive influence and made a friend for life in my mate Ben who was some years older than me. He was an excellent hunter and taught me many skills by letting me go along with him and his mates checking traps and shooting small game. I went to his house most days after school, and his family treated me so well and made me feel so welcome. I was the overweight kid that was always there at Ben's home and was trailing along behind him hunting and fishing.

I will be eternally grateful for the stability and care he showed me. The negative aspects were balanced out to some degree by the positive influences Ben provided. Ben was always a great role model and very stable, never letting anything get him overly upset or overly excited. I believe that the positive influence that Ben had on me enabled me to get back on track when I faltered, simply by thinking about how fortunate I was to have such a loyal friend, and how I needed to be more responsible like him.

The reality is that all responsible people have emotions, and if we didn't we would be very dangerous individuals, if not lunatics. I still feel emotive when I think of my childhood and some of the life changing experiences and now memories brought about by it.

I later met a friend for life in Bill Hall, a World War II veteran of Bomber Command. Bill became the father figure I did not have, and he was also my dear friend until the day he passed away. People would ask me when they saw Bill and me together if he was my father, and I would reply 'no, he is my best mate Bill' but he is also like a father to me. Bill had the highest integrity, and was fiercely loyal and courageous.

Later in my CQB/CQC exponent career, training under some of the evolutionary pioneers of military close quarters combat and close quarters battle, one of the first questions I would ask them was of methods they employed to develop psychological development in their combatants. I was privileged as a civilian to be accepted for training, not only by former pioneer experts in military close combat, but also be accepted for training and qualification by some of our allied current military master-chief instructors.

Harry Baldock had prepared me well in regards to where to find, and what to seek, in my continued pursuit of knowledge and excellence in military close combat physical and psychological tactics and skills. Harry taught me how to problem solve, as well as how to develop tactics, skills and programs. He was a realist that knew the value of hard, practical and effective training, and that there were no easy ways or short cuts. He was an expert in combat sports and physical culture as well as unarmed combat.

Harry considered military unarmed combat lethal and way too deadly for civilian usage back then. There was a considerable time until he would teach me the military armed and unarmed combat that he instructed to troops in World War II. He taught me the value of preparing and proving oneself when it came to unarmed combat; the only way, as far as he was concerned, was the military way – 'hands on'. Much of the words of wisdom from Harry, especially in the quiet times while working with him preparing to take over the facility, have proven to be very beneficial.

Harry was the ruler of his domain, The Baldock Institute, and while he trained me well, our relationship was predominantly at the Baldock institute only; his home life was his private life. This changed to some degree when he was preparing me to take over the facility. My wife and I were both part of the transition training to take over, and Harry and Mrs. Baldock even attended a combative social function we conducted.

He told me when the various martial arts crazes came along many individuals looking for some deadly secret joined the band wagon looking for some mystical, magical or easy option answer that simply did not exist. Harry told me this could certainly cause them to have an imaginary belief in ungrounded capabilities to defend themselves. As Harry would say, there is no easy way and the individual has to be mentally tough in the beginning.

He said, 'Mark my words, in your generation the true benefits and advantages of the combat sport of wrestling will again be realized, but only the mentally tough and physically committed will be able to excel in such a tough sport'. Well, the UFC has proven the capabilities provided in MMA by wrestling are needed, and the demand for our Todd Group combative and self-defence training provision has certainly confirmed military combative skills as a requirement for not only the military forces and units we train, but also for savvy civilians with the combative smarts when it comes to their safety and self-protection.

Military CQB/CQC has become more needed with time in relation to urban violence, including violence against police officers. There has been an increased need for close protection services and consequently the training provision of specialist close protection courses of instruction.

Post-World War II it was considered, or hoped, that the skills used on the battlefield would never be required again, and it was an unwritten undertaking by many experts that they would not train civilians in their methods used to defeat the enemy. How times have changed, and now more than ever before, the primary options of military close quarters combat, military self-defence and military close quarters battle have been increasingly needed by law-enforcement personnel and civilians alike to neutralise the unpredictable extreme violence that has become more common.

Most of my former instructors had some simple physical skills to enhance confidence, or a basic method of self-reassurance, or methods of overcoming one's fears and increasing one's commitment.

The important key for me was taking all the wisdom, expertise and information my expert instructors could offer, and in training, testing and on the job, evaluate the tactics and skills to identify any provided advantages or unnecessary disadvantages in these tactics and skills, and their order of execution.

I tested the tactics and skills to destruction in wide ranging circumstances to prove a particular individual tactic and skill's worth and level, or means of individual exponent psychological enhancement. The tactics and skills testing involved my HQ training team, as well as wide ranging groups of combatants from recruits through to Special Operations pers from around the world.

The tactics and skills were tested under expected combative actions-on conditions and under unexpected actions-on conditions.

Some of the best research was undertaken when subjects were unaware of my research and thought they were simply being trained or tested on course in CQC.

The Brain to Boot package development and testing needed to prove my program as the primary means of psychological enhancement as well as identify the correct and best order of execution to provide the greatest benefits and advantages.

I found most of the information I had been taught on the subject was more in relation to the reasons why individuals react and act in specific ways in close quarters combat, military self-defence and close quarters battle threat situations, over how-to methods of enhancing and improving mental toughness. The information I was taught in regards to what reactions and responses to expect in threat situations was important in relation to recognising and understanding the symptoms and effects of combative fear and stress.

My early learning on the subject included lessons on autonomic nervous system reactions to threat, fear and stress, and how the physical effects of fear, if not eliminated, controlled or kept in check could create negatives that can lead to reductions in capabilities, or to hesitating, stalling or freezing in an actions-on encounter under assault. These symptoms, or warning reactions as I like to call them, can be experienced by different individuals in different ways. Reactions may include trembling thighs, chattering teeth, sickness to the stomach, increased heart rate and heavy breathing, along with other various and varied levels of the individual's experienced symptoms of fear and stress in relation to the situation and degree of threat.

I was well aware from my instructors of the negative psychological effects of such high risk, high stress situations including tunnel vision, audio exclusion and a rapid and dramatic decline in fine motor skill capabilities as well as respiratory problems.

Prior to training under Col Rex Applegate he asked me to prepare an extensive videotape on the skills I would teach for regular force and special operations armed and unarmed combat.

When I turned up at his residence one of the questions I had for him was regarding his methods of developing psychological strengths in the personnel he trained. He replied 'looking over your teachings I can see you already have a high level of mastery of this most important part of close combat'. He went on to explain, 'I see you factor into the skills you have developed the highest levels of safety as well as preparation prior to their employment, and you have a bag of sound contingency options that all go to make the user more confident in the tactics and skills and as such in themselves'. He explained to me, as had Harry Baldock, that a major part of the individual soldier's mental toughness is achieved through trust in their tactics and skills and trust in their instructors.

Both Harry and Col Applegate explained the importance of tactics and skills being the best of battle proven, and when combatants have trust and belief in their objective achievement capabilities, through trust and belief in their tactics and physical skills, they gain in mental toughness and psychological confidence.

Dirty, deadly over-kill means of threat neutralization are physically and mentally empowering confidence-wise, and this is what I had drilled into me as an exponent and on instructor training. Arm your combatants with the best means to deal with all the likely threats and changes in threat and situation by means of complete primary option threat neutralization first, and have secondary alternative emergency and contingency options. Such wide ranging combative skills combined with the Brain to Boot psychological enhancement practices is the modus operandi of increasing mental toughness, inner-resolve and downright deep down grit and intestinal fortitude to provide the mentality to best achieve the objective.

I learnt when I instructor qualified that psychological enhancement and conditioning for battle was a subject, from a military combative master's perspective, that had plenty of scope for further development. The maximum levels of psychological enhancement capabilities that I have always factored in as part of my primary, secondary alternative and emergency skills development practices, as well as contingency options, are what considerably increases the chances of objective achievement. These are trade craft practices I naturally always include to the highest level with all tactics and skills development.

My natural inclusion of maximum combative psychological capabilities in my tactics and skills development was re-confirmed by my legendary military pioneer expert instructors;

they identified not only the importance of primary, proven physical skills selection and development to provide increased psychological confidence and inner-resolve, but also my inclusion of the highest levels of such psychological capabilities in all my skills.

Col Applegate my mentor, instructor and adviser in special operations irregular armed and unarmed combat commended me on the level I had taken this most important aspect of close combat to. In fact he said my practices were the most current and extensive he'd seen in his working lifetime on the subject of practical psychological combative methods of making the individual soldier more confident and capable from a combative master-instructors perspective. He advised me to keep working to finish a complete package on the subject. He said I had done more than anyone he knew of to prove a how-to process for the individual soldier to improve their psychological combative capabilities over the usual mainly scientific reasoning as to why we are psychologically affected by close combat situations. The gems of combative knowledge I learnt from Col Applegate from his World War II OSS research and development were truly invaluable. Much of this knowledge was developed after operators returned from Special Operations and had been de-briefed.

Harry Baldock had a wealth of knowledge and experience in matters of the body and mind. He was a WWII New Zealand army unarmed combat chief instructor. He was a pioneer tutor of physiotherapy in Dunedin, New Zealand and trained many wrestling champions on the importance of hard training and never quitting. He extensively studied the human body and the means of enhancing one's health and physical capabilities. Harry taught me so much about physical and mental toughness, and in the last several years at the Baldock Institute (now the Todd Group) when he was training me to take over, he also told me of the evolution of the human being and human body and how our brains and body function in relation to combat sports, unarmed combat and self-defence.

So after receiving endorsements and encouragement from my mentors I have continued to develop, test, prove and confirm psychological combative capabilities enhancement tactics and skills so as to be able to provide the best means of combative psychological conditioning and enhancement. To receive this endorsement for my work in progress to that date and be encouraged and requested to continue with this package from Col Applegate, a legend in military armed and unarmed combat, only strengthened my resolve in the pursuit and development of increased knowledge and excellence in the field of psychological military conditioning and enhancement for military close combat and self-defence.

Col Applegate commented it must have taken me many years to that date and stage in the development of the package. He went on to say that it was difficult for a serving hand to hand combat instructor in the military to have the time available to do such extensive work, unless they were tasked solely to spend the years required to complete such a package and that would not be likely. He said the military will be very fortunate indeed to get their hands on my finished package. He also commented that traveling around the world constantly for the last ten years plus was testament to my commitment to the dirty and deadly trade that we both had committed our working lives to.

He was extremely interested in the hours I spent and the years developing principles, tactics and skills and how I went about it. I had shown him the technique to command package I had developed as a military combative drills method of training and learning skills by name and execution. He said it was a first for military combative training as far as he knew and led the way as a great drill training means. I advised I was going to use a similar type of audio exercise phase for the Brain to Boot and explained my ideas. He provided suggestions and advice on using and modifying the whispering sneaky or creeper course methods he had shown me in armed combat training.

The endorsement I received from Col Applegate only made me more driven to include in the Brain to Boot increased related subjects content on specialist methods of overcoming the effects of threat, fear and stress in relation to close quarters combat and close quarters battle to enhance the individual combatants psychological capabilities.

The Brain to Boot was born out of an initial desire to provide those I train and instructor qualify with the best means of developing and enhancing the most important ingredient in themselves and the combatants they train; that being a means to overcome the effects of threats, fear and stress - including under extreme adversity - by means of proven practices to increase intestinal fortitude, inner resolve and combative self-confidence.

To date those I have briefed or shown draft information on the Brain to Boot package include military combative Master Chief instructors, military psychologists and doctors with psychiatry backgrounds, they have all described the package as groundbreaking and specialist to not only military close quarters combat and close quarters battle, but also to self-defence and dealing with the realities and effects of all violence.

This project has taken several decades, and as the word has gotten out through the military combative grapevine, inquiries have been regularly received from services and individuals from all over the world in regards to when the package will be released and how they can get their hands on it.

The awareness of my work in law-enforcement, security, close protection and the civilian sectors has meant my initial intended user and usage for the package has been increased to include all organizations and individuals with an interest in my work and need for my Brain to Boot package.

My field of expertise is military armed and unarmed combat and military self-defense, and I have developed the Brain to Boot package from my more than 100,000 hours and over 35 years of practical experience.

One doctor with a background in psychiatry described the Brain to Boot as the how-to of psychological capabilities in relation to conquering one's fears and increasing one's capabilities in extreme violence situations. He went on to say that during his psychiatric training, conquering one's fears was not written about or taught by military combative experts, and was not developed for combative skills applications enhancement. What was taught was more the reasoning of why and how to treat mental illness rather than the Brain to Boot's specific practices to enhance psychological capabilities for combatants facing high-risk threats—by means of combative physical and mental practices.

The Brain to Boot package has taken me more than three decades simply because of the amount of required combative specialist research development, testing and proving of the tactics, principles and skills required combined with tens of thousands of hours of participation and observation that needed to be undertaken. I needed to observe and evaluate combatants prior to exposure to the Brain to Boot package, and then again after they had undertaken the Brain to Boot psychological enhancement training. The research required me to look at current practices in relation to psychological enhancement for close combat, and I must report they honestly didn't exist as a complete correct order of execution specific skill set in many cases. This meant that although the skills instructed may have been battle proven they simply did not go into detail or depth in relation to the required psychological considerations and correct or best order of execution of combined combative physical and psychological components.

This all takes considerable time, and it was important to ensure the finished package is made up of the best of the best in relation to its proven, simple, and easy to understand and employ methods of psychological enhancement. The methods and order of execution must provide the individual combatant psychologically with the capability to manage psychological combative effects, and employ psychological self-enhancement means to provide the best means of dealing with the effects of sudden aggressive shock action and extreme violence.

Such psychological conditioning practices when employed in a controlled, aggressive and correct manner proved to enhance the individual combatant's mental toughness and psychological capabilities by a considerable amount. The fact of the matter is much of psychological enhancement and conditioning is a result of battle proven CQC tactics and physical skills components.

The Brain to Boot package is nothing mystical or magical and is all based on simple and proven combative fact. The higher the stress level, the lower the skill level and lesser the reaction time. This dictates the need for simple, immediate and effective means of maintaining the highest levels of psychological and physical capabilities, and this is what the Brain to Boot is all about.

The old saying ‘less is more’ is very true and more has been discounted and discarded than has been adopted through thorough and extensive research development and testing to destruction, in and under, military combative extremes. Everything that has been adopted has proven its worth, and identified itself as the best, safest and most effective primary, secondary alternative and emergency contingency means of providing the best combative winning chance, and that is as guaranteed as it gets in the unpredictable world of real life or death CQB/CQC and military self-defence.

To be contracted and respected by the military elite of the elite as a civilian primary provider of specialist military armed and unarmed combat training provision for more than two decades is the greatest reward and recognition for me personally. I have a total commitment to the people I train and to setting and maintaining my highest possible professional standards as lives depend upon it. I spend my entire working year every year ensuring the military services, groups and units I train have the very best of physical and psychological combative skills I can provide to ensure they can achieve their objective as safely and effectively as humanly possible.

The Brain to Boot psychological practices are the most important and major part of being capable of objective achievement in high risk and often sudden aggressive shock action extreme close quarters actions-on encounters. All the skills and equipment in the world amount to very little if you do not have the means to overcome the effects of exposure to extreme violence. When the combatant is armed with the means to maintain and enhance their inner resolve and intestinal fortitude when up against a formidable, unpredictable extreme violence threat, they have the best combative chance of objective achievement.

The elite forces personnel I train globally are highly motivated, highly determined individuals with wide ranging skills sets. They have passed extreme selection courses and training cycles and proved themselves every day of their working lives. They understand the importance of over-kill gross motor combative skills capabilities, as well as the attention to detail requirements with specific deadly skills employments. They very much understand the importance of dirty and deadly proven practices that prey on human reaction to action as part of disarming enemy capabilities, combined with combative enemy disabling and disposing of the threat completely. Combining their high levels of mental toughness and commitment to objective achievement with battle-proven tactics and skills, aided by dirty tricks and deliberate tactical proven practices that cause psychological confusion and hesitation, all increase chances of objective achievement. These important masking and deceptive practices that break the enemy's mental focus and point and line of sight can be the difference between victory and defeat when up against a formidable foe. These personnel also understand the extreme treatment they could be in for, not only in actions-on encounters, but if taken prisoner. The importance of psychological requirements is evident in everything they do, every day, whether it is training, or meeting, maintaining and surpassing required physical and battle fitness standards, or staying current in tactics and skills and maintaining the highest proficiency levels. They also have a commitment to their comrades and confidence in their comrades, knowing they have undergone the same selection and training as themselves. The strength of unity is psychologically empowering to the strong of mind and physically capable. While these elite forces personnel understand the importance of over-kill, they can also conduct themselves with complete control and composure, and with controlled aggression levels to ensure combative competency is maintained, especially in deadly skills employments where minor errors, including reductions in confidence, can cause self-injury, injury to others, or can be fatal.

They also have a respect for humanity and a firm understanding of humility.

The reality is we are all human and experience varied levels of the same, or similar, effects in relation to facing violence and aggression. Whether it is in a civilian self-defence situation, on the battlefield or a special usage role, although the risks and dangers may be very different and varied, the need for the means to make oneself as psychologically ready, tough and prepared as humanly possible is the same.

Over the past ten years, the brain-to-boot practices have been instructed on Todd Group civilian, police and military courses. Those that have been exposed to such training have given completely positive reviews and endorsements as part of post-course comment in relation to this very specialist and specific training. They have commented that their personal capabilities to overcome what is going on within them, and around them, have been increased significantly, and as such, the execution of their skills have been enhanced considerably. They have also commented that they can now keep the effects of fear and stress in check better, and maintain a higher level of vigilance, employing better decision making. They can also control combative physical outputs and, if required, maintain controlled high output combative skills employment for extended time frames compared to their previous efforts. Additionally, they were surprised at increases in combative endurance.

Most important, the unanimous agreement has been that, through the psychological and physical combining of the brain-to-boot practices in the correct execution order, the likelihood of them achieving their combative objectives has been enhanced considerably. Both their real-time situational awareness and their recollection of their actions post-encounter have been remarkably enhanced. They can maintain a controlled level of aggression, and as such, have more situational control in relation to themselves and neutralizing the threat situations they face. They have found they are physically more capable of executing high-level controlled aggression while maintaining the means to adapt to changes in threat and situation.

Positive feedback revealed that, regardless of the physical skill selection, the brain-to-boot psychological practices enhanced the levels of control and output levels in skills employments, and as such, enhanced the likelihood of objective achievement. Comment has included that, although the package has a primary order of execution, it also allowed for human order of execution error without completely affecting the individual's chance of objective achievement. Knowledge of the primary correct order of execution, through extensive and intensive primary order of execution training, provides the combatant with the ability to identify personal error and make corrections in real time.

In the realm of unpredictable unorthodox armed and unarmed combat, Murphy's Law really does apply—what can go wrong may go wrong. Any tactical principles and skills must therefore allow for an individual's specific assessment, decision making and means of execution, whether it be considered textbook or flawed, to provide objective achievement capabilities.

Live by the sword; die by the sword

The following is a brief but very serious outline of what the business of dealing with violence can cost.

I have dealt out my share of rough justice over the years, always for the right reasons and never looking for trouble but always finishing it. I am well aware of the realities and consequences of living by the sword in relation to the serious personal consequences of such actions. The reality is that in an instant, by a single action, one can lose their life or take a life, can be wounded or can seriously injure their foe.

Outside of the effects of death or injury to oneself or the aggressor, you can find yourself arrested and charged with serious offences which may cost you your livelihood, break up your family or even destroy your professional reputation.

If you live by the sword you must be prepared to die by the sword and the consequences must be accepted as coming with the territory.

I have had to face many such instances, and fortunately have always not only defeated my foes, but have maintained control to ensure my controlled aggressive actions were commensurate with the threat and laws of the land.

I will outline the most serious consequences of my living by the sword and fighting on the street. If you decide to go down this path as a part of your on-the-job realities, you must be well aware of the triggers, dangers and negatives that can come as a result of yours or others actions.

My wife and I had to endure the loss of twin unborn baby boys as a result of my living by the sword. I would have given my life to ensure my babies were born safe and healthy, but these are not decisions mere mortals can make.

While working our business in the early hours I had a monster of a man turn up with only one motive, and that was to challenge me to a street fight. I assessed his demeanor and determined his intentions, including identifying that he was of considerable physical stature, and was aggressive and determined to fight. I identified that he was big, strong and prepared to fight. I had to make the decision whether to take him out by means of overkill methods instantaneously or to take him on. I decided with so many citizens present to take him on rather than take him out, by means of destruction of the integrity of his knee joint, destroying his ability to stand or move. This decision, based on reducing the risk of witness hysteria, and the likelihood of prosecution, cost me dearly.

I ended up in a violent struggle having to endure considerable, extremely violent, physical contact over several minutes. The encounter (or encounters as it turned out), in total, took a considerable amount of time for a fight on the street, around three minutes initially, and another two minutes when he decided to have a second crack at the title.

Everything in Murphy's Law that could have gone wrong in the early hours of that morning went wrong on that fateful occasion. It was raining, we were in the middle of the road, cars were backed up with their passengers out looking, and a crowd of bystanders all watching, chanting and cheering. I lost a shoe in the early seconds of the blue which was considerably problematic. My option to go toe-to-toe bare knuckle quickly proved a massive error. I had to endure and weather a torrid storm of power punches, head butts, knees and elbows.

Through training, battle inoculation and combative conditioning - including toughener and sickener phases - I was able to hardcover myself close-in at point blank body contact CQC kill-zone range and restrict my foe's capabilities considerably. 'Fast time at slow time' was a reality of this encounter through my training kicking in and my ability to stay ready and in control. My prior training and preparation for such unpredictable top-end extreme violence is something that has always provided me with the capability to reduce risk and maintain sound steady situational control. I was aware of every action I undertook and I was aware of my foe's attempts at causing me grievous bodily harm.

I employed every aspect of my psychological conditioning to endure and neutralise this serious life-threatening actions-on encounter. I remained in total control utilizing all my senses and my definite physical and psychological required components, starting with controlled combative respiration. Even though this was a furious, constantly changing and continued actions-on extreme violence encounter, it was like everything was happening at slow time, and was clearly visible and obvious to me through my prior training kicking in.

I had to fast map after my wrongful decision to take him on with bare knuckles, and thus go combative, employing dirty and potentially deadly methods to neutralise the threat by incapacitating him. This encounter ended up being two separate encounters, several minutes apart, as a result of not neutralizing the threat during the first encounter. For a moment, after the first encounter, I thought I had killed him or at least paralysed him.

Then, he regained his footing and initiated an assault against anyone he could get his hands-on. I went to the aid of a mate that he chased a hundred yards or so down the road, and in this second encounter when he again tried to do me grievous bodily harm, I showed no mercy. Apart from some cuts, bruises and deep bites which made me look worse for wear than I actually was, I was in okay shape considering it all. I went back to where it all began and told my wife I was okay but that he was not so lucky.

Minutes later he staggered back, picked up some plates and threw them at us. This was his last stand and I went outside and left him spark out on the footpath. I returned to see if my wife was all right, and without going into too much detail, we ended up at the hospital. She lost twin baby boys dangerously late in her pregnancy.

We have a strong marriage and got through it but it reminds me always of the terrible price we both paid for my living by the sword. Every now and then my wife will say that our twin boys would have finished University now, and it makes me think long and hard about the consequences of my living by the sword; in this sad and unfortunate situation the loss of the lives of twin sons as a result of living by the sword.

This devastating consequence only made me train harder and change my modus operandi in relation to dealing with serious threats including the old adage I was informed of in my early days it is better to be judged by twelve than carried by six.

Life goes on, and although we were told at the time my wife may not be able to have children, some years later our daughter was born. She has made us so proud through her sport of wrestling, being a multiple national champion and international competitor, graduating from University with honors and securing a good job as a computer software developer.

In my years after that encounter, working as a minder and bouncer, I made sure every outcome was favorable to me and my team without exception. I picked the time, place and means, and determined the outcome. I treated every threat as potentially life-threatening and reduced the threat level by every means at my disposal. I only went combative when forced to, and when I did it was with an uncompromising commitment to winning by any means necessary. When forced to, I dealt out some ruthless justice.

It also made me decide that as soon as I could achieve the objectives I wanted, I would give away the full-time minder and bouncer work and dedicate myself to instructing military close quarters combat, close quarters battle and military self-defense.

What I've just revealed has, up until now, been known only by people close to me. However, I thought it very important for the reader to understand the realities of real life and the subsequent loss of life because of me living by the sword. In that encounter, my decision making was affected by my business and customers, and not wanting them to be witness to my primary ruthless controlled aggression and the outcomes of it. I was confident in my capabilities to take this giant on and beat him, knowing that if the going got too tough, I could resort to my take-out combative capabilities which I did in fact do.

I have seen more violence than most over more than forty years. I have been punched, kicked, head butted, bitten, bludgeoned, bottled and cut, as well as being set upon by multiple attackers. These are the realities of fighting on the street and bouncing at pubs and clubs. I become more hard-nosed, more aware and ready to deal with anyone that crossed me. I have learnt the hard way that there is usually more than one way to achieve an objective, and often by using my brains to outsmart my foe, rather than letting my brain getting rattled (as the late Charles Nelson told me), my safety was increased.

I became a lot more deliberate, and a lot less instantaneous, but at the same time more unorthodox. I knew I could be difficult to live with or associate with because of my unwillingness to forgive and forget when someone had taken a liberty against me. Once bitten, twice shy has been very much my modus operandi in relation to family, friends, associates or unknowns that have tried to cause me grief or harm. I may not have been able to choose my family but I certainly chose my friends as loyalty means so much to me. I do not care whether they are combative capable or not, but I do expect them to show the same loyalty that I show to them.

Some people never have had to fight in their lives and that includes people that train in fighting or martial arts. By not fighting, I mean never fight on the street against formidable aggressors trying to cause them grievous bodily harm. I had plenty of experience fighting on the street and in pubs and clubs, which was a great means of learning about myself and what needed to be done to win, as there is no second place on the street - only a winner and a loser.

I once got Repetitive Strain Injury (RSI) from restraining and extracting belligerent punters from a major night club and this was before I even knew what RSI was. I was restraining and moving dozens of such individuals down stairs and through crowds three nights a week, and apart from the RSI, this was a great learning experience and means of testing tactics and skills.

Some of my fights as a youngster were tougher and I learnt more from them than when I was an adult working as a bouncer and a minder. I can recall so many fight situations and incidents but a few hold strong in my memory bank. This is mainly because of the skill, guts and difficulty of these likely lads.

The first was a simple spat with a lad I knew little about. When we got down to it he proved to be very formidable at wrestling, and the pressure and leverage he inflicted on my head and neck respectively with a well applied headlock up under my cheek bone, got me motivated. I initially resisted, and then I tried to escape the headlock with dirty tricks that he appeared to be well aware of and countered out. I took my time, maintained stability, and set up position. I made sure I had a Plan B before going to plan C.

Plan B was to lean on him and make him wear my weight, making him think I was unconscious so that he would release his fiercely secure hold. If that didn't work, plan C was to resort to using an implement to escape the dirty old head lock.

Well Plan B suckered him, and when he released his grip I unleashed my fury on him. See, less is often more, and lazy skills require a lot less physical effort; in this case it caused confusion by deception, and as a result preyed on his human decency (and probably his concern of the legal consequences of his actions) and likely secondarily his concerns with seriously injuring me.

Then there was another local lad, confident and mature for his years, a real hard-case who was capable on the street and formerly a formidable wrestler. He was well known for his capabilities back in the neighborhood when it came to street fighting. For some reason we ended up in the park next to my house going at it toe-to-toe. This proved to me at that young age that I could go toe-to-toe and hold my own with formidable adversaries. Years have gone by, and while we do not see each other that often, when we do it is good to catch up and recall times gone by, mutual respect.

There were the occasional likely lads that fancied themselves and wanted to take me on and have a crack at gaining a reputation. Recently a long term combative training member of the Todd Group recalled an incident that had slipped from my mind in relation to the challenger.

This was back in the late '70s when the martial arts craze was truly running high. We were training at an old warehouse up an alleyway when a tall, broad shouldered, blonde headed guy entered through the small tradesmen door looking for me. He had traveled from another city to have a crack at me. He proclaimed to be a skilled stand-up martial artist that hadn't been beaten in the street, and he had heard about my unarmed combat training, my reputation on the street and as a bouncer. I am very careful in picking the time and place and means to take care of business. I informed him that no one interferes with my exponents' training, and that if he cared to wait ten minutes until the end of training, I would gladly oblige him. I also informed him that if he did not agree to do so, I would order the thirty or so exponents in attendance to use him for a boot party.

I was psychologically weakening his resolve, and after the training ended I ordered the exponents to form a circle, and said to him 'let's go'. I could see in his eyes and from his body language he was less confident than earlier. Now with his confidence lower I decided to completely change his thought process by setting up and telegraphing an escape action leg stamp, combined with verbiage which if I remember rightly was something like 'f--k this, I'm out of here'. As I used the deception of escape action and he orientated towards me, I slid back in with a leg stamp right below his knee joint. His turning and closing in on me only increased the contact impact by means of two moving colliding objects, and as such increased impact force levels. End of story, he was down, a dislocated knee, in shock and incapacitated.

Years later several of those in attendance let me know just how confidence building to them personally it was to witness their instructor demolish such a formidable looking, physically impressive fighter that towered over their instructor, with such ease of effort and with such a decisive and definite outcome.

Another aspect of living by the sword is the fact that you must protect those in your care, and your understudies, and you must perform with confidence in achieving your objective decisively. The reality is that often, when in such positions of authority or seniority, and when faced with potentially dangerous situations, your motivation to get the job done is increased considerably both subconsciously and consciously. The unfortunate reality can be that by living by the sword under such situations in a leadership role, where you are expected to neutralise the threat, you must do so by means of deliberate over-kill methods of the highest level, and as such, the outcomes can be most destructive and produce dire after- effects.

I worked as a bouncer with some very powerful and formidable men, and I never backed down or failed to back them up on the job. We would often train together bare knuckle, and I not only had street fights, but also the odd arranged fight. In those early years I just wanted to train and test myself as often as possible, and did not really think of the consequences because all that mattered to me was winning. I knew some tough street fighters as friends, and through my work and training. My training life style and work situation very much revolved around training for, and facing, violent situations, and dealing with violence and some extremely violent people which all came with the territory. I stood back to back with the best street fighter in town fighting against gang members and we won. Unfortunately it was a topic on radio talk back the next day, grossly exaggerated by callers, and we were then known as 'the gang busters' way back then.

On another occasion I again fought alongside a very formidable street fighter, this time against most of an entire footy team, and again we were the winners.

I have seen the effects of violence close-up and in real life on more occasions that I can account for or choose to remember. So many victims of violence, beaten, bludgeoned or stabbed over my years involved with the business of violence. While many would run for cover, or cringe at the actions-on realities and outcomes, to me it was just part of life on and off the job back then.

My real life experiences and my training testing and qualifications in military armed and unarmed combat, along with being trained by leading military combative pioneers, have made me the instructor that I am, and it is with this background experience, expertise and qualification I consider myself well qualified to author this most important manual and package. I have more combative instructing time than any of my military instructor colleagues, in fact, over 100,000 hours in my trade spanning more than 30 years. I am the last instructor-qualified CQC/CQB descendent of the late great Harry Baldock and Col Rex Applegate, as well as being instructor-trained and qualified by Charles Nelson.

This combined with the support and assistance I have received from medical experts including Grahame Reid, known as Doc when he was undergoing his military national service training, the late Col Dr. John Wilson, Dr Steffan Eriksson and Dr Clive Dreyer.

I know now I have been over-engrossed in my training, working and fighting. At times, to those not directly involved, associated or interested in my lifestyle, it could be perceived as concerning or less than desirable to be around me. Fortunately I had other interests and pastimes, and a stable happy married life. Personally what mattered most to me was being the best combative proponent and instructor I could be, and others opinions matter little to me.

Later when I started training elite forces, a former course manager introduced me as someone 'who lives, eats, sleeps, farts and shits CQB', as I had focused all my real life experiences as well as my training, testing and qualifying as an instructor to being the best instructor I could be. One of the first magazine articles published about me in the Australasian Fighting Arts by Kevin Brennan was titled 'A Brilliant Mind for Dirty Fighting'. This paints a picture of the thoughts of those in-the-know about me and what I do. I would have to agree they are fair descriptions of my training and working life.

'Never start it, always finish it' was my modus operandi, and when I say never start it, I do not mean you cannot initiate the action. By this I mean that if someone threatens you or the like, it would be up to you whether you kick off first or not. This would depend on your assessment of the situation and threat level, and the decided best and safest option to neutralise that threat.

Even though we live in constantly more violent times, violence is not an accepted means for the responsible citizen to deal with threats to their personal safety. However, the villains are getting more violent, armed, and are training and getting more skilled in many instances.

This was a wakeup call for me to change roles, from operating in dealing with violence, to instructing full-time on how to avoid being a victim of violence, or how to counter or combat formidable foes. My methods as a bouncer were downright effective, but were becoming a less accepted means of problem solving, and I was not prepared to increase risk by not using primary methods of threat neutralization. So it was time to hang my bouncing hat up and engross myself in tactics and skills development, and full time military, police, close protection and civilian instruction provision.

This final live by the sword decision was made after a gang attack where we had to defend ourselves or risk serious injury or worse. The reality was that there is no easy or nice way of neutralizing such a threat of serious violence, and winning is all that matters and win we did. These foes had changed dramatically from the type we faced in the decades before, where they accepted the outcome if they wanted to have a crack at you.

I can always remember the saying I first heard from a former Special Ops mate of mine when someone was pushing their luck, that goes like this 'don't let three little letters stop you from having a crack at the title' This always made me laugh, but he used it to psychologically weaken his foe to either prevent the fight before it started, or reduce their confidence.

We were starting to face back then not only extreme violence, but also gangsters that would use the law to get even if they could. They thought they were unbeatable on the street, and they were armchair lawyers that would use the police as a means of getting even and removing people that could, would and did beat them. By doing so they could potentially remove the last means of protection for the punters at pubs and clubs by getting rid of the bouncers. This made our job difficult, if not impossible, by means of the hands-on, unorthodox but extremely effective approach we employed if no other option was available to neutralise the threat. The reality is that if you accept jobs where you must live by the sword, you must win at all costs or your reputation will be lost, and you will become a target against any likely lad or gangsters looking to make a name for themselves on the street.

The unwritten laws of the street of times gone by included the best of three street fights decides the best fighter, and when it's over, it's over and you never get the law involved. The scumbags, after losing, were becoming more prone to getting the Old Bill involved to do their dirty work, as they were not capable of doing it themselves. So after more than twenty years of living by the sword, week in, week out, I gave it away without ever losing an encounter, and committed my efforts and enthusiasm to instructing.

The other negative of living by the sword is that by winning you may be breaking the law through your actions and may be perceived as similar or the equivalent of the foes you are dealing out. Police could be perceived as being on the one side, and those that live by the sword, by the nature of their actions, being perceived as being on the other. While some police were happy to have handy lads around to take care of problems, there were some new generation cops that believed in everyone having rights, and knew bouncers were easy targets that would not assault them unlike the scumbags. There was becoming a new mentality where police had to respect everyone's rights and vigorously investigate, even complaints made by gangsters and villains against those that rightfully beat them.

Looking back now with all the questionable ethics and actions behind me, I can see clearly that it is very much a case of black and white, and you are either on the side of the law or you're on the other side against them. It has been described as the Wild

West back in the '70s and '80s where I come from as a bouncer. Becoming a full-time instructor and instructing specialist police units and police instructors I find far more rewarding and far more beneficial than putting myself at risk living by the sword and dealing out rough justice to lowlifes. I also realized that the older you get the more you increase your chances of losing on the street so that was another reason for changing roles.

I have also trained some fine exponents that are serving police officers and instructor qualified them. I know that most police rank and file are not highly trained in combative capabilities like the civilian and military combative specialists I train. They are at war with the criminals on the streets, and I will always do my best to give them the best tactical chance of staying safe and neutralizing the threats they face, like I always have with the military.

I am proud of not having a single team member of mine defeated, or for us to fail in our duties over more than two decades in some of the roughest bars and clubs in my city, and doing it without a badge back up and all the resources the police had at their disposal. We were using specialist tactics combined with unorthodox skills when they were simply not heard of in our city back then. This was a great time of skills development, in training, testing and proving tactics and skills on the job. The unsuspecting foes were often unwitting lab rats for our proving of tactics and skills.

Mentality, as well as physical, proven deliberate actions is very much required if you are going to live and potentially lose by the sword. I have had close friends commit suicide, and a close friend was killed in a street fight when he went to the aid of another, only to be set upon by multiple thugs. He was left to die on the street, and he left behind a partner and a little girl starting school the next week.

My dear friend, the late Bill Hall would always say to me in relation to major problems, 'Oh boy', then he would say 'now let's set about fixing the problem'. His wisdom and advice is something that brought me strength and solutions when faced with adversity, dire situations and problems. I remember Bill's words of wisdom, and apply it to threat neutralization, keeping me in a deliberate controlled state of objective achievement. I have seen my share of death and serious injury, and this has only increased my personal resolve to ensure I do everything, and anything, to win and not merely survive.

CQC MSD joining training testing and qualification facts

Through my associations and connections with military qualified combative instructors, I was offered an instructor position for upcoming military training courses back in 1990.

As a civilian who had a lifetime's commitment to CQC and self-defence training this was a very special opportunity, privilege and honor for me.

This prospect was exciting to me, but something I could not accept unless I had undergone and completed an instructor qualification course the same as the military personnel I would be training. This was at a time when allied forces were preparing for a major upcoming deployment. I can remember being told it was not necessary for me to instructor qualify as I had such an extensive background of training and qualification in military CQC. I was told I had proven myself many times over and had been trained and qualified by legendary experts of military CQB and CQC that none of them had. I was adamant, however, that I must undertake the same hand to hand combat instructor qualification course as the personnel that I would be training.

This led to me going to Fort Bragg for familiarisation and meeting the Chief hand to hand combat instructor with the 5th Group there at the time, Lawrence Jordan a then U.S. Army Special Forces Master Sergeant and now a U.S. Army Special Forces Sgt Major retired. This was the start of a lifelong friendship between the two of us.

After familiarisation and pre-instructor qualification course preparation training, I went to Thailand where I underwent my hand to hand combat instructor qualification course.
I successfully completed and passed my instructor qualification course and also achieved back in the 90s Master instructor

qualification, certified by Lawrence Jordan. I insisted on and accepted the challenge for my hand to hand combat instructor qualification course because it was the right thing to do. I was 30 years of age was just recovering from a serious ankle injury but nothing would stop me proving myself on my instructor qualification course. This was because those that count are people that have all been there and done that in training, testing qualifying and proving themselves and this is what I wanted.
I knew to be accepted and respected you must earn it.

I have met all too many people that claim to be subject matter experts that have never had the intestinal fortitude to even accept the challenge of partaking in training courses undertaking qualification testing and proving themselves.

The instructor qualification course was not easy and I had to up skill in things like long distance swimming and become accustomed to heavy load bearing long-distance pack marching.

I had to improve my cardio strength and endurance, but most importantly my mind-set was what got me through and was the biggest asset in achieving my pass. Not completing and not passing my instructor qualification course never entered my psyche. I spent several months running, pack marching, swimming and pushing myself with multiple daily PT sessions. I stepped my personal combative training up to several hours every day, including inoculation training under medium to high intensity unarmed assault. I did everything I could, utilised every available hour of the day and addressed every area of weakness to ensure I would have my best chance of performing at peak performance levels. My ankle was a major concern and I was advised not to go because of the state of the ligaments and tendons. But at 30 years of age I simply knew time was running out for me and the circumstances that had made this qualification course opportunity available to me may not be repeated again.

The runs were excruciatingly painful to the point of my ankle joint becoming locked up, but that was not going to stop me.

The hours of swimming as a result of not being able to kick, because of my ankle injuries, meant I had to cover the required long swimming distance using only my arms. With 200+ pounds in a pack that was uncomfortable to the point of painful, I covered the 12 and a half miles inside the required time. I never over thought anything and did not try and think about what was going to happen next.

I accepted each challenge as it was presented and did my very best to achieve the objectives every day all day on every challenge. On completion, even though my ankle injury was excruciatingly painful along with most other parts of my body, leaving me walking wounded, the satisfaction and feeling brought about by completing and passing this major combative and physically demanding challenge is hard to describe. I was a civilian, I had volunteered and I had passed and qualified; this was very special indeed. It was my mental toughness and inner resolve that had enabled me to achieve the objectives, pass and qualify.

While I had got myself as physically fit as I possibly could, this would never have been enough by itself, and I reiterate that it was my mental preparation and mental toughness that got me through the very challenging requirements. My modus operandi was blatantly simple, let nothing stop me, give it my all and do what I had to do to achieve my objectives. Failure did not enter into my mind-set. Thinking back now, if I had failed, I would be able to accept I done and given my best and that it was not good enough.

The instructing I do on military CQC courses where exponents are there because of their duty requirements and as a result of previously joining the armed forces and meeting all the joining and training requirements is very different to civilian CQC courses of instruction, application and joining. I run the Todd Group in the same way I run my military courses of instruction. The main concern is about setting and maintaining the highest combative standards and providing the best training and chances of the highest level of objective achievement for all the exponents on course, without favor or prejudice.

Firm, fair and unfriendly with a commitment to providing combative excellence in training and testing is the standard operating procedure of Todd group combative training provision. There are many civilians that enquire or apply for courses that simply do not have the mental toughness to either front up or accept the challenge and complete our courses of instruction. It can be frustrating with these time wasters and dreamers with their copious questions and then failure to meet the course joining requirements after application.

Many like the sound of the training but simply do not have the mental toughness to sign up turn up and commit to self-improvement and achievement and advancement. I have met many individuals over more than three decades of traveling, training and instructing that have built a self-image of being a combative expert but on checking they have never even completed a military CQC basic course of instruction let alone an advanced or specialist course or been tested and qualified. They may have convinced the uninformed or gullible, but facts are facts and to be qualified you need to have been trained and tested.

The Todd Group business model being a model of setting and maintaining combative standards often scares off paper hounds and the less than mentally committed applicants just by the nature of the requirements of the official joining instructions. The types that excel are those that realise the best of battle proven military unarmed combat and military self-defence is what they need if they are to be confident and competent in the neutralisation of formidable threats. Such individuals are quietly confident grey types that apply, turn up are fully committed in participation without question or excuse.

This demeanor and commitment to self-improvement and advancement is what the Todd Group rank-and-file have been built on over the past 88 years. You can get most people physically fit, but making them mentally tough is a different story if they do not believe in themselves or if they are not prepared to accept challenges. The lads and lasses I have trained are what the future of the group is all about.

They self-select and identify themselves as committed realists. They do not want any easy or political passes as they know to be confident and competent requires commitment, inner resolve and a realist attitude. The realist mentality is most important in military CQC and military self-defence, especially understanding everyone can be defeated and no one is undefeatable. Psychologically the candidate's mental toughness requirement starts with applying, meeting the joining instructions requirements followed by participating on course with realist smarts and maximum mental toughness. Only the psychologically weak make excuses for withdrawing or failing to achieve the required objectives.

Military CQC training and testing, just like its employment in actions-on encounters, is as close and revealing as it gets and there is nowhere to hide. The weak like the strong self-identify by their commitment inner resolve and practical smarts or lack of the previous. There is no mystique in CQC or MSD it is just a simple matter of applying, attending, committing and proving oneself to one's self and to your instructors.

Mental toughness begins with decision-making on undertaking the best training available, and giving your training and testing your very best.

I personally accepted the challenges of training and testing and only wanted to be trained by those that had been there and done that themselves and that were highly qualified experts in the field of military unarmed combat and military self-defence. Settling for close cheap or easy options in CQC and MSD training says a lot about the individual's respect for their personal safety and for themselves. There is no easy soft options but objectives are achievable if you have intestinal fortitude, inner resolve and commitment to being the best combatant you can be. Then there is the need to remain current by continuously self-evaluating and asking yourself if you are maintaining a satisfactory level of competency and physical capabilities.
Military CQB/CQC and MSD are living packages that need to ensure combatants have the best chance of neutralising threats, staying ahead of enemy capabilities and as such proponents need to remain current by keeping up their combative training.

Those that think combative training is something to be completed are fooling themselves, as to remain current and be the best combatant you can be is very much something that must be continued. My former expert instructors that were very clear, blunt and to the point on this, always reiterating combative training needs to be continued not completed.

My dear friend, the late Bill Hall would always say military self-defence training and military unarmed combat training are the best insurance you can hope for when there is no out option available to you when at the sharp end facing a serious threat. Always be realistic with yourself making sure your instructors and their instruction provide the very best and safest of battle proven tactics and skills.

Do everything you can to be as best prepared as you can mentally, physically and skills wise. Don't settle for anything less than the very best of psychological and combative training when it comes to your self-protection and safety. From the rest come the best is very true and always strive for being the very best you can be in self-defence and close quarters combat. Psychologically, post an actions-on encounter if you were defeated but gave it your very best, after the dust settles you will be able to live with yourself knowing you gave your all psychologically and in combative and self defence capabilities. You will learn from your mistakes just like you learn from your successes and this will make you more formidable should you face same or similar threats in the future

Overview of the Todd Systems

The Todd Systems instill in their exponents and instructors the importance of the combined understanding and employment of psychological and physical combative proven practices. These practices start from the ground up, having an affinity with the ground in order to maintain your footing stability, and a ready status to employ expedient combative actions or counter actions.

This is a primary example of the importance of your sense of touch and feel.

Simultaneously these primary practices and other important components are employed from the head down. They include your sense of sight by means of tactical vision and combative sighting as well as your hearing and sense of smell combined with combative respiration and more.

These primary state-of-readiness and personal safe-guarding practices include everything between the helmet and the boots in relation to utilizing your sense of touch feel and hard cover guarding maximum safety tactics and principles.

These very important methods of maintaining mental toughness and personal safety will be detailed later in this brain-to-boot manual, not only in relation to the execution of these physical and psychological performance enhancers, but also in relation to the correct and best order of execution.

It is crucial to keep the entire body, including all the involved limbs, joints, muscles, tendons ligaments and organs as ready and protected for the rigors and realities of close combat, whilst remaining the least stressed, tense or fatigued while in the ready status. Then, during actions-on encounters, being able to control aggressive output and reduce risk to the lowest possible levels by being psychologically and physically in total control will prove to make a considerable difference when up against a formidable enemy. The required combination of both the physical and psychological components that must jointly make up combative actions or counter actions mean that the brain-to-boot package consists of deliberately employed, major primary components, and minor but very important performance-necessary enhancement components. These major and minor executed components in relation to the employment of specific physical combative skills when combined and included in a correct order of execution with commitment, confidence and skill competency, provide your best combative chance of objective achievement in relation to your decided skill employment.

Proficiency and competency of execution is achieved through prior training, including high repetition drilling of skills, and factor-of-confusion practice, achieved through battle handling exercises or scenario training. Utilising a CQC Test of

Elementary Training assessment (TOET) will identify proficiency levels, and identify correct order of execution of skills components, as well as identify errors and missing components. These skills components increase the individual skills executions output considerably in relation to proficiency, performance, safety and objective achievement. Through high repetition practice and with gains in proficiency, gradual increases of speed of execution and intensity will develop skills components cohesion, and performance enhancement, including increased velocity. These deliberate included components will become a single action employment through high repetition practice and through muscle memory.

A low level of psychological empowerment or a less than highly committed controlled aggressive physical combative output results in increased risk and danger levels, and of course decreased objective achievement likelihood.

Failure to include major or minor skills components or incorrect skills execution order will certainly reduce capability and increase risk. The advantage of employment of battle-proven military combative gross motor skills with high-level controlled aggression is that they allow for human error and are over-kill by a considerable margin. This does increase the likelihood of objective achievement, even in skills employments where minor components are missing, or the order of execution is incorrect.

Combative reactions are subconscious and automated to a degree when compromised by means of self-preservative autonomic reactions to the stimuli of sudden aggressive shock actions. Actions are definite decisions executed by making a definite and deliberate threat neutralization decision, and are born out of the need for immediate self-preservation and threat neutralisation. So the misconception of achieving threat neutralization by reaction is more unlikely than likely. You would have to be most fortunate to react to an unexpected assault by lashing out in a defensive reaction and somehow contacting with the assailant's bodily delicate vitals to such a degree that you neutralise their capabilities. Such a fortunate outcome would be based more on luck than the combatant employing a ready-set-go primary combative definite primary practice skill employment.

You will find in the employment of counter-engagement that it is more likely that the autonomic reactive response as a result of the sudden aggressive shock action was the initial subconscious automated reaction, immediately followed by a deliberate combative responsive counter-action, giving a perception of the reactive automated reaction and the responsive counter-action being a single action.

High repetition, combined reactionary and deliberate counter engagement training, and practical battle handling exercises that provide unexpected factor-of-confusion practical training, increase practical combative proficiency and reduce hesitation in making the D (making the decision) in executing the counter engagement option post-reaction. Self-preservation reactions, combined with lashing or reaching out, instead of making fast, factual assessment and definite deliberate decisions, increase risk and reduce the likelihood of threat neutralization. Self-preservation reactions, combined with immediate non-definite and deliberate executions of non-primary options (including rushed execution, panic reaction counter-actions) often lack in the required individual physical skill primary components, as well as the required physical components correct order of execution, and as such may increase risk and reduce output effect and safety. The level of physical output capability in rushed, reactive, less than deliberate employed combative actions will be considerably reduced if you do not assess, decide and make necessary adjustments as part of the skills employment.

About Brain to Boot

The following program formation began for me with my personal observations and training from military combative experts and pioneers in the fields of close combat and psychological conditioning for battle. I would always ask my instructors to instruct me in their toughener, sickener and mental development methods. The practical information provided in this package comes from my more than thirty five years as an exponent and instructor of armed and unarmed combat, as well as being a crowd controller, minder and close protection specialist instructor and operator.

When I became the chief instructor at what had been the Baldock Institute, it was my time to continue in the footsteps of my former superiors, and this package is a result of that work in the field of combative psychological development and enhancement. I had the privilege of being instructed by World War II experts in close combat, the late Sergeant Major Harry Baldock, the late Platoon Sergeant Charles Nelson and the late Col Rex Applegate. I would listen to these and other current military instructors and veterans, in relation to methods of developing and increasing an individual's level of inner resolve or mental toughness and of the realities of real life situations.

US Army Special Forces Sergeant Major retired Lawrence (Larry) Jordan was a next generation Master-Chief instructor of military hand to hand combat that provided me with considerable battle proven knowledge that has been beneficial to my work including the development of the brain to boot. I was Master instructor qualified by Larry and we have been close friends since 1990. My association and friendship with captain Ben Mangels a Chief unarmed combat instructor formerly of the South African military dates back to the mid-1980s. Ben contributed to my knowledge through working with him as part of our International Close Combat Instructors Association duties as well as assisting him delivering training. He freely showed me his military combative skills.

Charlie Nelson

Harry Baldock

Col Rex Applegate

Lawrence Jordan

The personnel of the military units I have trained have also contributed considerably to this subject matter, along with my Todd Group exponents and instructing team. They have provided the opportunity for me to undertake research and to observe, evaluate and develop skills and principles based on their natural human actions and reactions to violent threats, and the effects of such threats in relation to fear and stress. This research and development has taken several decades, and has included on the job evaluation as well as training-related evaluation, including battle handling exercises and combative testing. The battle handling exercises my assistant instructors and exponents have partaken in under my control have contributed considerably to the development of the brain-to-boot package.

The most important benefit of this package is that the user can self-assess, and compile a personal profile, in relation to their individual physical attributes, capabilities and disabilities, as well as their combative and self-protection skills and their psychological strengths and weaknesses. Then, through the teachings and instructions in this program, the individual can improve their combative mental confidence by means of definite physical and psychological tactics and practices that will provide a means to achieve, and maintain, the highest levels and state of readiness, to go combative if and when required. The reality is that the best chance we have and can expect to have is a combative chance; nothing more and nothing less.

Protecting the nape of your neck, orifices of your head, your throat and sides of your neck, and your brain is psychologically beneficial to reduce risk, and as such, improves mental confidence by initiating and maintaining hard cover, hard targeting practices and knowing that your hard cover and hard targeting provide the best and safest capabilities to reduce risk to the lowest level humanly possible.

Hard targeting of internal organs is by means of your cover guard. This includes cover guarding against strikes, or the deflection of strikes, or hard cover counter-stamp kicks. These all provide wide ranging emergency threat neutralization capabilities. Changes or adjustments of your cover guard and stance can provide specific bodily vital protection. Such hard cover protection is a last line of protection when evasion is not an option. You need to ensure your airway is protected and unrestricted, and tactical breathing is maintained, blood circulation is maintained and all immediate specific bodily target threats are neutralised.

Maintaining a primary state of combative readiness and ensuring you are as safe and protected as humanly possible with all your combative physical capabilities primed and at the ready is required to increase psychological confidence and combative performance.

In extreme actions-on situations where primary options cannot be employed through injury or situation, through prior knowledge you will employ secondary alternative or emergency options to reduce risk to the lowest level possible, and increase your safety and chances of achieving your objective.

While we can take for granted our ability to function without consideration under normal, everyday life conditions, the reality is that when stress and fear levels increase, and danger comes into the equation, combined with the necessity to go combative, there must be both physical and psychological components employed in unison to reduce risk and ensure confidence and a state of readiness and willingness is maintained.

Outside natural autonomic reactions to perceived or actual threats, I firmly believe that it is the individual that makes a decision to engage, counter engage or escape and evade. The unfortunate freeze reactionary response where an individual does nothing is testament to a lack of intestinal fortitude and capabilities to overcome the effects of the situation and employ methods to self-protect, neutralise the threat, or escape and evade. The reality is the difference between an individual that does act against such threats and one that doesn't is based on the individual's mental toughness, tactical skills, and physical capabilities—as both individuals are made of the same flesh and bone.

The psychological capabilities are the most essential capabilities, as even with less-than primary combative options employments the objective can be achieved, but with no self-confidence or skills confidence, and a lack of combative mental toughness, the individual is weak and doomed to become a victim of assault.

This program is focused on practical methods of initiating skills to get and remain physically and mentally ready. This program will provide the means to deal with expected physical violence, and when engaged with an unexpected actions-on situation, employ skills to hard target oneself, and take control of the situation as quickly and safely as humanly possible, by means of emergency skills employment.

BRAIN TO BOOT

About the program

The Brain to Boot package, with over three decades of evaluations and input from combatants, instructors and experts in related fields, has ensured it enables the individual combatant to overcome effects of human error by having a constant means of assessing, deciding and, where required, changing one's tactics in the execution of the best means of threat neutralization, and as such, objective achievement. The Brain to Boot package provides the means to overcome human error when combined with a principle-based combative system so that decision making, or changes in decision, can effectively be employed while maintaining positive combative psychological control of oneself and one's situation in real time while being on the move.

Through training in the Brain to Boot package and practicing the correct order of execution, individuals soon learn how best to employ the principles, tactics and skills, as well as helping them to overcome human error with the least impact on their personal safety and the outcome. Through high-repetition practice and confidence in the advantages provided, it will be very much a case of initiating the first component, either combative respiration in an expected actions-on encounter, or hard cover guarding self-preservation in an unexpected contact situation combined with simultaneous combative respiration.

Through high level Brain to Boot practice under battle handing extreme conditions, once the initiators of going combative are deliberately switched on, the components primary execution order will follow. This is by means of definite and deliberate decision making, combined with mental and muscle memory, brought about by practicing the components in complete and cohesive combination over individual components.

The Brain to Boot was never meant to be just a book. It has always been designed and developed to be a training package to provide the means to psychologically enhance an individual's combative capabilities. Developing such a package to be used by global self-defence, close quarters combat, close quarters battle and law enforcement defensive tactics proponents has taken considerable time, and has been problematic because of the need to ensure that it is easily understood and that there is no confusion as to the why and how.

The simple primary order of execution for expected and unexpected combative actions-on encounters had to be definite and deliberate with no possibility for decision making error. I have also backed it up with expanded detail in a simple and easy to understand expansion of the fact and reasoning behind the components and their order of execution.

The objective of the Brain to Boot is not to encourage proponents to change systems or styles but is meant to enhance the execution employment of the skills of their system or style. Obviously if through exposure the Brain to Boot identifies weaknesses and dangers in an individual's system, style or individual skills, then it's a no-brainer, and those with the combative smarts will certainly seek the required training.

However, the aim is that regardless of the Brain to Boot user's style or system, by incorporating the Brain to Boot package principles, tactics and skills with their style or system, they will achieve psychological enhancement that will improve their fighting or combative capabilities. I have used the Todd systems of military armed and unarmed combat as the subject system for description and reference purposes so the reader can understand how the Brain to Boot practices apply to combative and self-defence tactics and skill employments.

The problematic aspects of developing an interactive generic mental toughness program for combative use have included the following:

- Considerations in relation to methods of practice, safety practices and precautions to reduce the risk of injury in practice.

- The audio training exercise components have been developed to provide progression from the basic static clock exercises, through to offensive and counter-offensive exercises covering ground at a later advanced exercises stage.

- Paired or buddy training comprising of a combatant and enemy per were problematic in relation to the audio training exercises, simply because of the need to ensure both the combatant and the enemy per's execution cues were syncronised, in relation to executing commands, orders and instructions needing to be precise and at real time.

The reality was electronic cues simply could not be guaranteed to be reliable or safe timing wise, and as such, giving both the combatant and the enemy parties orders, instructions and commands proved to be a far more reliable method of providing practical and safety enhanced exercises. Sometimes good old-fashioned basic manual methods are superior to high-tech methods, and this was the case with developing the audio training exercises components of the Brain to Boot package.

Developing both the expected actions-on and the unexpected immediate actions-on training exercises took considerable time to ensure the process allowed for the individual proponent to combine their own physical skills with the Brain to Boot components. Having to complete both the text and the audio practical training exercises components has added to the considerable time taken to complete the Brain to Boot package.

The following program formation began for me with my personal observations and training from military combative experts and pioneers in the fields of close combat and psychological conditioning for battle. I would always ask my instructors to instruct me in their toughener, sickener and mental development methods. The practical information provided in this package comes from my more than thirty years as an exponent and instructor of armed and unarmed combat, as well as being a crowd controller, minder and close protection specialist instructor and operator.

When I became the chief instructor at what had been the Baldock Institute, it was my time to continue in the footsteps of my former superiors, and this package is a result of that work in the field of combative psychological development and enhancement. I had the privilege of being instructed by World War II experts in close combat, the late Sergeant Major Harry Baldock, the late Platoon Sergeant Charles Nelson and the late Col Rex Applegate. I would listen to these and other current military instructors and veterans, in relation to methods of developing and increasing an individual's level of inner resolve or mental toughness and of the realities of real life situations.

The personnel of the military units I have trained have also contributed considerably to this subject matter, along with my Todd Group exponents and instructing team. They have provided the opportunity for me to undertake research and to observe, evaluate and develop skills and principles based on their natural human reactions, responses and actions in relation to violent threats, and the effects of such threats in relation to fear and stress. This research and development has taken several decades, and has included post actions on reports as well as training-related evaluation, including battle handling exercises, CQC inoculation and combative testing. The battle handling exercises my assistant instructors and exponents have partaken in under my control have contributed considerably to the development of the brain-to-boot package.

I thank all my former instructors and the units and services that have given me the opportunity and support with my work as well as my instructing cadre and exponents, for without such assistance, this outcome would not be possible. Respect and loyalty, always.

The most important benefits of this package is that the user can self-assess, and compile a personal profile, in relation to their individual physical attributes, capabilities and disabilities, as well as their combative and self-protection skills and their psychological strengths and weaknesses. Then, through the teachings and instructions in this program, the individual can improve their combative mental confidence by means of definite physical and psychological tactics and practices that will provide a means to achieve, and maintain, the highest levels and state of readiness, to go combative if and when required. The reality is that the best chance we have and can expect to have is a combative chance; nothing more and nothing less. Psychological conditioning is the result of practical usage of the tactics and skills against formidable enemy pers under realistic threat conditions.

You will be informed of the important combination of physical and psychological components working in unison to achieve the desired objective. This includes everything from the ground up to the top of your head including skeletal, muscular and internal organs and one of your most powerful primary weapons: your mind and the power of your mind. I will now outline the importance of the use of all of these components.

Your feet, through your boots and more specifically, your toes, balls of your feet, arches and heels are all vital components utilized for such applications as the sense of touch with the toes while stalking or going covert, and immediate and explosive expedient movement via the balls of the feet. The arch of your boot encapsulates the lower leg in stamp kicks, and the heel of the boot is for delivering a sound means of ground incapacitation or elimination.

The ankle, knee and hip joints prior to any action must maintain a (soft) slight cocked status, and ensure instant readiness, but not a position of excessive stress or fatigue. A combative (medium) status by means of a natural increase in expedient movement will enhance positive action but not slow movement through over tension and excessive loading of the legs.

A combative (hard) status is necessary in actions-on encounters against a formidable enemy as part of requirements such as resistance to hold position, or to physically dominate your foe. Maintaining the element of surprise in a covert neutral stance with the feet shoulder width apart is less stressful than when already compromised and therefore maintaining a hard cover stance and guard.

A situation where the priority is to maintain the element of surprise would see the shoulders, arms, wrists and fingers joints in a covert neutral at-sides position, reducing stress and fatigue. However, when already compromised, employing an on-guard position that makes you the hardest target possible, offers the smallest window of target opportunity to your enemy, and gives you the highest level of safety. As such, confidence is a priority without creating overdue stress on the muscles joints, tendons, ligaments and limbs. Ensuring your back and neck are not held in a position of tension or stress before any actions-on, and that they are well protected by hard cover and increased resistance if required, is a priority. For expedient combative entry and evasion footwork, ground cover or ground clearing, medium-plus footing is required.

Fluid extension and retraction from the ground up and out when employing physical striking skills and remaining centered by constant alignment to your target, adjusting your position by pivoting on your lead boot to orientate to your enemy over turning, twisting or rotating your back while maintaining rigid footing, will reduce stress and injuries. It will also increase target contact impact velocity and accuracy. In the execution of stamp kicks, range, target alignment, set up and stamping from high to low diagonally through the knee joint or below the knee joint is the required direction and means of power and velocity transfer.

I have seen shooters on steel plates hit the first few plates then miss the next plates with multiple rounds through holding ground and keeping their footing locked in the same start direction. Not pivoting or adjusting their footing and orientating to the target can increase tension and stress on the spinal column and other joints. Age, injury, physical capabilities and medical conditions can all have negative effects when rigid, locked-stance footing is employed instead of target orientation. Minimum tension at the weapon holding end could mean being inches out at the target end. In unarmed combat, if your boots are locked in an opposite or opposing direction to your executed combative skills, then velocity, power and accuracy will be sacrificed, and self-injuries can be inflicted that may incapacitate you or at the very least will affect your combative capabilities. Through prior training, and repetitive and varied practice, the human bodily weapon chosen, if employed correctly in relation to target alignment and correct and controlled aggressive skill execution, will reduce risk of injury. Through training and muscle memory, when employed in a combative situation, there will be less likelihood of self-injury and increased confidence.

In CQC protecting the nape of your neck, orifices of your head, your throat and sides of your neck, and your brain is psychologically beneficial to reduce risk, and as such, improves mental confidence by executing and maintaining hard cover, hard targeting practices and knowing that your hard cover and hard targeting provide the best and safest capabilities to reduce risk to the lowest level humanly possible.

Hard targeting of internal organs is by means of your cover guard. This includes cover guarding against strikes, or the deflection of strikes, or hard cover counter-stamp kicks. These all provide wide ranging emergency threat neutralization capabilities. Changes or adjustments of your cover guard and stance can provide specific bodily vital protection. Such hard cover protection is a last line of protection when evasion is not an option. You need to ensure your airway is protected and unrestricted, and tactical CQC respiration is maintained, blood circulation is maintained and all immediate exposed specific bodily target threats are cover guarded.

Maintaining a primary state of combative readiness and ensuring you are as safe and protected as humanly possible with all your combative physical capabilities primed and at the ready is required to increase psychological confidence and combative performance.

In extreme actions-on situations where primary options cannot be employed through injury or situation, through prior knowledge you will employ secondary alternative or emergency options to reduce risk to the lowest level possible, and increase your safety and chances of achieving your objective.

While we can take for granted our ability to function without consideration under normal, everyday life conditions, the reality is that when stress and fear levels increase, and danger comes into the equation, combined with the necessity to go combative, there must be both physical and psychological components employed in unison to reduce risk and ensure confidence and a state of readiness and willingness is achieved and maintained.

Outside natural autonomic reactions to perceived or actual threats, I firmly believe that it is the individual that makes a decision to engage, counter engage or escape and evade. The unfortunate freeze reactionary response where an individual does nothing is testament to a lack of intestinal fortitude and capabilities to overcome the effects of the situation and employ methods to self-protect, neutralise the threat, or escape and evade. The reality is the difference between an individual that does act against such threats and one that doesn't is based on the individual's mental toughness, tactical skills, and physical capabilities—as both are made of the same flesh and bone.

The psychological capabilities are the most essential capabilities, as even with less-than primary combative options employments, the objective can be achieved, but with no self-confidence or skills confidence, and a lack of combative mental toughness, the individual is weak and doomed to become a victim of assault.

This program is focused on practical methods of initiating tactics and skills to get and remain physically and mentally ready. This program will provide the means to deal with expected physical violence, and when engaged with an unexpected actions-on encounter, employ skills to hard target oneself, and take control of the situation as quickly and safely as humanly possible, by means of emergency skills employment.

Important information and usage instructions

The brain to boot manual is part of a psychological conditioning and enhancement package for military CQC, CQB, and MSD. It is vital that the user understands the importance of achieving proficiency and competency in the brain to boot primary principles, tactics and skills, including all major and minor components.

The correct order of execution is essential before the proponent can confidently utilise the brain to boot principles, tactics and skills under increased intensity sudden aggressive shock action battle handling exercises and for real-life actions-on encounters to threat neutralise.

For this reason, this manual must repeat and reiterate important tactics and skills as well as minor and major required components constantly. This is a training manual part of a training package not just a book. The individual parts of the brain to boot proper order of execution must be utilised in a cohesive correct order of employment. The requirement in training and drilling to repeat components that join to other components is essential so proponents not only learn the reasoning in relation to why and how but also understand the correct order of execution performed with coordination and cohesion in unison.

The brain-to-boot physical and psychological combative tactics and skills are made up of major and minor components. These major and minor components, executed cohesively in the correct employment order, provide the best chance of combative objective achievement.
The primary options include the following: threat detection and recognition, combative respiration, hard cover guarding, heightened senses, first-look visual threat detection, and preliminary decision making, second look decision and option confirmation, initiating CQC set up adjustments, and CQC actions employment.

Compromised unexpected actions-on pre-contact stationary counter engagement:

- Medium to hard cover guard and hard stance footing, employed simultaneously with combative respiration.
- Real time actions-on threat assessment and decision-making of combat or counter-engagement options.
- Alignment to the enemy and set ready status adjustments to go combative.
- Decided option employment off of a small half or full squat combined with CQC respiration.
- Threat neutralisation fast map assessment and threat neutralisation confirmation.

Unexpected actions-on, unarmed offensive assault skills employment attack the attacker:

- Prior to contact last millisecond enemy threat identified in the kill zone.
- Simultaneous hardcover cover guard and medium to hard footing stance risk reduction combined with CQC respiration.
- Fast map assessment, decision making and immediate combative pre-execution adjustments.
- Small to medium squat combined with combative respiration employment of unarmed offensive assault decided option attack your attacker.
- Fast map assessment confirmation threat neutralisation.

Unexpected actions-on unarmed evasive or stationary counter-offensive assault skills employment prior to actions-on contact:

- Self-preservation hard cover guarding and medium to hard footing ready status stance combined with simultaneous CQC respiration.
- Assessment, decision making, adjustments, small to medium squat and CQC respiration initiated decided unarmed counter-offensive assault evasion if time and distance allow or if not stationary counter engagement or stationary evasive counter engagement, evade assess make adjustments and counter engagement employment.
- Fast map assessment.
- Confirm threat neutralised.

Unexpected actions-on unarmed counter-offensive assault skills employment immediately post actions-on contact:

- Self-preservation ready resistance hard cover guarding resistance, hard stance footing ready status setting, simultaneous CQC respiration.
- Fast mapping, assessment, decision making, adjustments squat respire and employ stationary counter engagement.
- Fast map assess confirm threat neutralised.

In an expected actions-on unarmed offensive assault skills option employment, the following is the correct major and minor components order of execution:

- Threat identification and recognition.
- CQC respiration.
- First look visual threat assessment and initial decision making.
- Enhanced senses.
- If compromised, ready status medium to hard footing stance and hard cover guard setting.
- Enemy alignment.
- Ground affinity ready status set.
- Continued assessment and unarmed offensive assault option decision-making and confirmation.
- Decided option visualization.
- Decided unarmed offensive assault option pre-employment adjustments.
- Self-reassurance: Ready, Willing, Able; Willing, Able, Ready.
- Emergency contingency option confirmation and visualisation to be ready if engaged prior to the decided confirmed combat option employment.
- Constant checks and re-checks of the enemy, situation and environment as well as your ready status.

- Constant adjustments at real time to maintain a primary ready status.
- Controlled calculated stalking into range combined with constant fast mapping assessment to detect changes in threat and situation.
- Small to full squat and combative respiration ready-set-go unarmed offensive assault option employment to provide the highest level of expedient action, risk reduction, as well as enemy deception and confusion in your combat actions on execution.
- Continued fast mapping assessment throughout the execution of the decided unarmed offensive assault option, to detect changes in threat and situation, and make decisions on required contingency options employments.
- Confirmed threat neutralised.

Expected unarmed evasive counter-offensive assault options order of execution:

- Threat identification and recognition.
- CQC tactical respiration.
- First look visual threat assessment and initial decision making.
- Enhanced senses.
- If uncompromised maintain a neutral status.
- Enemy alignment.
- Break an evasive option primary reactionary distance.
- If compromised set a ready status, medium to hard footing stance and cover guard.
- Ground affinity ready status set and hold ready.
- Continued assessment, second look, and unarmed evasive counter-offensive assault option decision making confirmation.
- Decided option visualization, evade, assess, adjust, counter engage.
- Tactical assessment, evasive counter engagement decided option re-confirmation and visualisation. Evade, assess, adjust, and counter engage.

- Maintained combative sighting between your cover guard if compromised or un-compromised neutral status point being the enemy and place being the threat environment visual sighting.
- Maintaining Evasive counter engagement stability and expedient action ground affinity footing ready status.
- Continued checks and re-checks of enemy threat situation and environment as well as your ready status.
- Stationary emergency contingency option if engaged and unable to evade confirmation and visualization.
- Self-reassurance: Ready, Willing, Able; Willing, Able, Ready.

Common required pre-actions on employed contingencies.

- If required real time fast mapping assessment of changes in threat and employment of pre-actions on contingency options, such as the maintaining of a primary evasive reactionary range, by controlling distance and edging back and away from the enemies master side if possible.
- If required prevention of enemy stalking inside your primary counter engagement evasive range by engaging your enemy before they can assault you with a being-stalked deceptive fake high attack low unarmed offensive assault option.

Unarmed evasive counter engagement execution:

Evasive counter engagement employment initiated off a small to medium squat with combined combative respiration, CQC evasion sighting, evasive action employment, post-evasion fast map assessment counter engagement decided option adjustments in position, range, stance and guard, and counter engagement decided option employment. Confirm threat neutralised.

The previous are outlines of major and minor components of unarmed offensive and unarmed counter-offensive assault expected and unexpected actions-on encounters physical and psychological major and minor components. When employed with confidence and cohesion, and in unison, these will considerably increase your combative capabilities, both physically and psychologically.

These major and minor physical and psychological tactics and skills employed in the correct and logical order of execution are extremely important to confidence and competence enhancement in training, testing and in actions-on encounters.

The practical training exercises you will undertake after completing the important personal physical, psychological and skills capabilities checklists, and thoroughly reading, understanding and becoming familiar with the brain-to-boot manual, will include the previous major and minor required components to increase your personal safety, and maximize your chances of objective achievement, psychologically and physically.

The brain-to-boot package comprises a lot of expanded information on the major and minor required components to combat or counter actions-on assault as well as related subjects. Knowledge is power and you must believe in yourself and your battle-proven knowledge to enhance your combative capabilities, including knowing you have the required physical combative competency, mental toughness and psychological confidence to do what must be done, and to ensure that what must be done is employed with controlled, calculated aggression in the achievement of your combative objective.

While this is not an exact science, it is a military combative science comprising primarily of medium to gross motor skills practices, executed from a neutral status, or a state of hard cover and hard stance combative readiness. Read and digest the entire content of this manual, and practice the required unison of physical and psychological tactics and skills at slow time and low intensity until proficiency is achieved. Always remember that when learning new skills, 'slow is fast and less is more'.

Increase intensity with proficiency, and always train with safety in mind. Expect nothing; assess and decide on everything. Make the decision based on hard facts, set up your decided option and go combative with ruthless, controlled, aggressive confidence and an open mind, eyes open and senses at high alert, fast mapping and making changes and adjustments where required, in relation to changes in threat and situation. Maintain your highest levels of combative capabilities by the employment of the brain-to-boot tactics and skills.

Believe in yourself, believe in the tactics and skills, and never underestimate any enemy. But never allow prior reputation, appearance or intimidation to weaken your resolve. Focus on an enemy target's form rather than the enemy's features.

Occupy your mind and physical assessment and ready status actions with preparation, checks and re-checks, adjustments and maintaining a ready status prior to going combative, leaving no time for self-doubt, anticipation or perception. Factual assessment in real time and continuously making yourself a hard ready status combatant will remove any time for psychological capabilities reduction or weakening factors.

Comply with all safety information in relation to training practice and the training exercises provided with the brain-to-boot package.

PHYSIOLOGY AND EVOLUTION

Evolution of the combatant

The earth is estimated to be 4.5 billion years old. When you compare this with the estimated 200,000 years existence of the modern human species, this suggests that a number of varieties of primitive species contributed to the genetic makeup of modern man.

The ancient evolution of modern human beings to a great extent occurred in Africa between 2 and 6 million years ago. Our ancient ancestors migrated to other continents and parts of the world between 1 and 2 million years ago. The human evolution has taken over 6 million years, and has been brought about and shaped by nature, natural disasters and necessity of survival and self-protection. This would have meant that combative capabilities were essential for self-protection, protection of one's family colony, obtaining food and primitive assets required for survival. Much of our evolutionary progress has been made possible by genetic changes passed down from generation to generation. The biological evolution over more than 1 billion years could well be derived from a single common ancestor. Interestingly around 99 percent of the genes in chimpanzees and humans are the same. This does not prove that humans evolved from chimpanzees but does indicate that we share common ancestors.

It is believed that dire climate change and temperature drops that destroyed forests forced our ancient ancestors from the trees to live on the ground, and later into a nomadic lifestyle following game and food sources. 1.9 million years ago human ancestors began to migrate from Africa to other continents and the oldest Europeans date back 780,000 years. Neanderthals date back approximately 250,000 years and are believed to have died out around 40,000 years ago. Modern human's presence in Europe is believed to have begun around 40,000 years ago.

Our common ancestors could date back as far as 5 million years. Primitive human beings could well-be the result of a split in primate species. Scientific evolutionary evidence points to genus Homo existence 2.5 million years ago and Homo erectus

2 million years ago with Neanderthals and Homo sapiens between 200,000 and 250,000 years ago.

Homo sapiens' evolution brought about considerable change in anatomy, including increased brain size as well as skeletal changes to the skull, pelvis, legs and feet. The human brain is twice the size that of a gorilla or chimpanzee. The increase in brain size has been responsible for many of the behavioural and intelligence changes from our primitive ancestors. Increases in the size and complexity of all parts of the brain have provided modern man with considerable sensory advantages, as well as coordination and problem-solving advanced capabilities.

It is believed that our ancient ancestors possessed a higher level of the sense of smell than that of vision. Modern man developed sweat glands to aid in dealing with climatic changes and lifestyle differences, including following game and gathering vegetation foods required for a nomadic existence.

So, between 4 and 8 million years ago, after splitting from our primate ancestors, Homo sapiens have changed considerably to meet changes in habitat, deal with natural disasters and develop the required skills to survive, including hunting and protecting oneself and one's family. About 1.8 million years ago it is estimated changes in the bone structure of the hand and metacarpals brought about the capability to make complex tools and weapons. Modern humans were very much nomads surviving as hunters and gatherers up until 10,000 years ago.

It takes many sciences combined to analyse and come to probable decisions in relation to some complex aspects of human evolution that are very much based on small pieces of evidence combining to paint a picture of human evolution.

The development and progression of combative capabilities in armed and unarmed combat has been very much as a result of striving to be superior to enemy's unarmed and armed capabilities.

While all civilisations possessed fighting and self-protection capabilities, it is the ancient European methods of formalised military combative training specifically for military usage that have been my primary interest, and especially from a historic perspective, the ancient Greek, Roman and Celtic forms of military close combat.

My primary interest in current battle-proven methods of armed and unarmed combat is in the European military methods, specifically from World War 1 until current. My training and qualification has been in the methods of European military combative skills, specifically those used in World War I and World War II, and up to and including the present.

New Zealand has a long history of CQB and CQC training, and arguably established some of the earliest irregular forces, in the bush and forest rangers. New Zealand the colony is renowned for our 'number eight fencing wire' mentality, where we make do with what we've got, we are very good at mastering the basics, and we have extreme commitment and inner resolve in objective achievement.

Military unarmed combat is very much a last resort option when all other capabilities have been lost. That is, if your primary weapon and secondary weapon capabilities are not available, then you must rely on non-ballistic weapons, improvised weapons or unarmed combat skills for objective achievement. A good analogy is with navigation, where if your GPS and compass are destroyed or lost, basic navigation is essential. Military unarmed combat is also for specialist-role employments where silent killing is required.

We take a very military science perspective in relation to CQC, removing ego, emotion, style or sport from the equation. We look at it from a military combative perspective; we eliminate any skills that are tactically flawed or could get you killed against a superior enemy combatant including an armed enemy. You don't want to grapple with a razor sharp dagger, or against a gut gun, and you do not want to employ skills that require high-level, fine motor skill capabilities or extreme athleticism when only your gross motor skills are the best options. You don't want to be rolling around on the ground under battle conditions where the environmental terrain can be as deadly as the enemy. You don't want to be thinking take-on or submission; you want immediate incapacitation or permanent elimination in relation to the threat situation and your rules of engagement or the laws of self-defence. You always want to presume your enemy is bigger, stronger, physically fitter, faster, highly skilled and goal driven, bent on killing you and probably armed.

Even for the physically capable and mentally tough realist with CQC smarts, taking someone on in CQC or self-defence is not a primary option and is possibly suicidal. Rather, taking them out in kill-or-die military CQC or threat neutralisation inside the laws of self defence for civilian self-defence are the primary means of increasing your combative chances of winning.

The most formidable enemy can have their capabilities reduced, including their intestinal fortitude affected by means of overkill, controlled, aggressive ravaging, and destroying of life-support systems such as the spinal cord, respiratory system, the brain and internal organs by penetration. Such silent deliberate human destruction demoralizes and destroys even the most highly trained enemy combatant.

The following provides some information in relation to ancient combative warfare training.

Some skills dating back to the ancient Greeks, Romans and Celts are still primary options in military CQC today. They've stood the test of time and have proven to be effective in battle against all enemies.

Obviously military CQC and military CQB are living practices of war. Just as in evolution and survival of the fittest, the psychologically toughest, and combatively smartest in unarmed combat and armed combat in relation to weapons tactics and skills have had to change to ensure superiority, and the best combative chance of victory over defeat. The short club would become less effective than the long stick, staff or spear that provided increased safety range and scope, and the long stick, staff and spear would be out-ranged by the bow and arrow, and so on. Today modern high-tech weapons capabilities are always under development to provide superiority over one's foes.

Psychological capabilities in primitive times, where killer instinct was responsible for survival, as well as with unarmed combative and weapons capabilities being extremely primitive and elementary, meant superior mental toughness must have been a great advantage.

European CQC Evolution

It is true that every early civilisation had methods of fighting, but the history outlined here is of a structured warlike military nature. Ancient Egyptians practiced close combat over 6000 years ago. The Celts records revealed their practices of close combat date back a century before Bhodidharma, regarded as the founder of kung fu. Competitive forms of deadly combat sports were being contested at the ancient Olympics as early as 688 BC. Training at this point in time was structured and evidence can be found of ancient Celtic engravings and etchings showing combat training in various armed and unarmed practices as well as performance enhancing exercises. Christianity destroyed much of the records of ancient European close combat in belief that it was non-Christian. The ancient Europeans had the ultimate test of effectiveness in life or death competitive battles. Swords being utilised in combat had been depicted in detailed drawings as early as 1200 BC. For over 300 years the Roman Empire conducted gladialanical combat where combatants would kill or be killed.

It was the advance of weaponry that they eventually saw the decline of many unarmed practices. European close combat has largely been forgotten due to the secrecy it was surrounded by through history. Ancient artifacts like chalices and sword scabbards dated back to the fourth century BC and depict soldiers practicing close combat. Greek Pankration dates back to the first Olympics in the seventh century BC.

The Galatian Celts were employed in early close combat to combat the Greeks as they fought their way through Greece into Anatolia. Many Greek soldiers who trained in early close combat and fought Galatians were Celtic mercenaries. When Alexandra the Great's Empire extended to India, the considered birthplace of eastern martial arts, his soldiers' instructing would have been continued by those they trained. These early European warring factions practiced every detail of close combat as their lives depended upon the skills and training. The early Europeans produced countless weapons to supersede enemy weaponry and fighting skills.

British Captain William Fairbairn, considered the grandfather of European modern military close combat, was proficient and well versed in the early European methods of military close combat. He and his US counterpart Colonel Rex Applegate were given the responsibility by their prospective governments to learn all they could of fighting methods of the world, both enemies and allies.

Fairbairn's role was to analyse the methods and practices from the late 1800s onwards and as such he became well versed and proficient in many Eastern systems giving him a vast knowledge in the mastery of fighting arts of the world. This insured his programmes, practices and principles were the best for the times in real life or death military unarmed combat. It was with this vast wealth of knowledge that Fairbairn, Sykes and Applegate trained the most elite operatives of the Second World War.

With military close combat's history dating back from ancient Europeans and the Celtic warriors through to the great wars its history has been born out of life or death military combative training.

CQC analogy

The following is a CQC analogy utilising a military combative structure to detail the required reactionary responses requirements of the triune brain (explained later) and the autonomic and somatic nervous systems. These systems are considered our combative means of threat identification, reaction response, and deliberate action through a complex combination of the three brains and connections and links between the autonomic and somatic nervous systems.

- The cranial cavity is the command headquarters.
- The bodily senses, nerve endings and receptors are the external threat detection and signal support capacity.
- The torso is the military base engine room.
- The extremities are the external base protection capabilities.
- The reptilian brain is our ready reactionary force.
- The mammalian brain is our threat evaluation and commensurate reactionary response force.
- The autonomic and somatic nervous systems are our headquarters support, advance warning, and reactionary responses capability.
- The neocortex is our high-tech strategic combative planning command and combative deliberate response control centre.

The triune brain and the autonomic and somatic nervous systems have individual and combined roles to play depending on whether the combative actions-on encounter is expected or unexpected, and the level of threat, combined with time and range considerations to effectively combat or counter the threat, as well as the option of escape and evasion.

In the following outlining of the triune brain and the autonomic nervous system I will outline how they apply in a combative sense, as well as providing a basic brief on capabilities and capacities in relation to close combat and self-defence.

Triune Brain

For around 65 years now, for many, it has been the belief that we have three inter-connected brains or command centres rather than the previously proposed single brain. These three brains are inherited and evolved to operate in wide-ranging functions required for life existence, intelligent undertakings, and combative needs (e.g., fight or flight). Dr Paul Maclean was a mastermind and pioneer of this triune brain theory, and current neuroscientists are still debating it. In any case, it illustrates nicely the psychological concept of CQC.

In relation to CQC and self-defence, I believe that we have four brains; the three in the cranium and the fourth in the torso:

- The Reptilian Brain
- The Limbic System or Mammalian Brain
- The Neocortex
- The Gut Brain

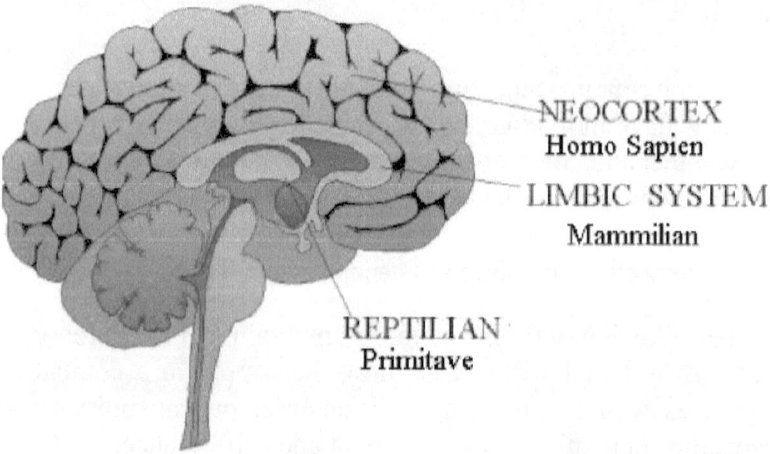

The oldest of the three cranial brains inherited from our evolutionary ancestors is the reptilian brain, located in the brainstem and cerebellum. The reptilian brain is not exclusive to Homo sapiens and is the oldest brain type found in animals as well. The reptilian brain is a not a thinking brain, but is a self-preservation survival and combative brain that is reactive and responsive under threat. It has not changed over millions of years, and it is very much a killer instinct brain that may be the difference between life and death, especially in unexpected violent actions-on encounters where the first indication of the assault is when contact is made.

The reptilian brain was 'programmed' by nature, and developed by evolution, to enable our ancient ancestors to protect themselves and their assets vital to their survival and existence, including their food sources. The reptilian brain must have been our ancient ancestors' primitive but primary and best means of self-preservation and survival especially under unexpected sudden aggressive shock action threat, by providing reactionary combative capabilities, including physical escape and evasion capabilities against an undefeatable threat.

The reptilian brain is still very important in modern day CQC under unexpected actions-on encounters. The reptilian brain is also important in relation to expected actions-on encounters against a formidable enemy, where deadly combative actions are required, especially in relation to Murphy's Law. The neocortex brain, discussed below, has the capabilities of threat and situational assessment, thought and consideration leading to tactically correct decision making to neutralise the threat. The neocortex drives controlled ruthless aggression, but when that is not enough, the reptilian brain's killer instinct is needed. Even in the most calculated, controlled combative employments such as covert threat neutralisation, the reptilian brain's killer instinct, reactive responsive, disconnected from conscience or remorse capabilities provide the required levels of killer instinct to neutralise a formidable threat. In any combative situation where dominant momentum is lost, and the threat level and risk is increased, the killer instinct of the reptilian brain is essential. The reptilian brain is also needed any time when the threat risk and danger escalation levels increase, and personal safety as well as objective achievement is in jeopardy. The reactionary responses of fight, or in combative terms, enemy take out, is initiated by the reptilian brain. The flight response (in military terms this is escape and evasion) option is more decided or by majority influenced by the mammalian brain over the reptilian brain in the face of probable defeat.

In the case of the fight decision, the reptilian brain provides the killer instinct required in a life and death combative actions-on encounter. The flight decision response is brought about when the enemy is considered superior, and no means of immediate threat neutralisation capabilities are available. Thus escape and evasion is the safest and best option.

Our reptilian brain may have been inherited from our ancient ancestors and may not have changed since then but it may be our best means of combative survival when the first awareness of an actions-on encounter is physical contact. The reality of an individual freezing under threat or assault can be a result of either a lack of mental toughness, or being completely overwhelmed and so being rendered psychologically as well as physically incapable of any combative or escape and evasion option at that point in time.

A combatant, through surprise sudden aggressive shock action, can be wounded, injured, decentralised or incapacitated, but if they are strong of mind and combatively confident, they can reduce risk, recover and go combative. Those that do nothing but are capable simply do not have the resolve, intestinal fortitude and possibly the prior training and combative capabilities to protect themselves and neutralise the threat.

The reptilian brain is also important for life-support bodily functions. These include respiration, controlling our heart rate and blood circulation, and controlling body temperature. These in turn are essential for tendon and muscle actions as well as for maintaining or regaining stability under actions-on combative options employments.

The brain-to-boot package has been developed around my research and findings in relation to unexpected and expected actions-on encounters. The reptilian brain may not be a thinking brain, but it is very important when there is no time for conscious thought, and the requirement is immediate reactive and responsive counter engagement or self-preservation escape and evasion. The reptilian brain can be problematic, however, because it lacks any assessment or decision making capability, and has no memory capability to learn from previous errors. In unfamiliar situations and environments under the factor of confusion, or when surprised, the reptilian brain therefore may wrongfully react to stimuli deemed threatening when they are not, and may also lead to overreaction.

The reptilian brain utilises predictable, limited option, subconscious reactions incorporated with a reactive, responsive, self-protective counter engagement under perceived threat. The most important factor is the human combative competency and confidence of controlled capabilities required to neutralise a formidable enemy foe that, through training, instill commensurate or overkill threat neutralisation capabilities. The reptilian brain may provide the human reactive self-preservation killer instinct response, but the individual combatant must have required physical capabilities, combative competency and inner resolve under threat against a formidable foe to neutralise such a threat, in a controlled and calculated manner. The reptilian brain is, however, incapable of emotion or actions based on intelligence.

While the reptilian brain may not have a thinking or memory capacity, its reflexive reactions which include physical, mental and muscle memory reactions (from prior reactionary executed combative skills) will apply to future reactions employed against the same or similar threats.

To a large degree our killer instinct capabilities have been very much dumbed down in modern society and rendered dormant, but not made totally obsolete, by being less required. Killer instinct is required considerably less often today, as a result of the modern, civilized times we live in. We have become very much a society based on negotiation and conflict resolution, out of a belief that we can talk our way out of anything. Obviously this is not the case in kill-or-be-killed modern day warfare, but it does represent civilian life.

Interestingly the reptilian brain is positioned high at the back of the nape of the neck where wild animals often choose to inflict fatal injuries on their prey, and even civilised human beings dispatch small game. The very much outlawed foul strikes to the back of the neck in pugilism are known as rabbit punches to the back of the head and neck.

The nape of the neck and the spinal cord entry to the brain are well-known for being susceptible to injuries of paralysis and fatal outcomes. These injuries target the reptilian brain area.

Civilization has truly slowed down our reactive responsive killer instincts but has also developed superiority in cunning, planning, resourcefulness and the major reduction of the need for the use of our killer instincts. Evolution and development of the brain has led to increased combative options and capabilities, but this also requires training in the means to control external and internal factors affecting the individual's combative capabilities and combative psychological enhancement.

With a higher level of the use of sensory capabilities, and with distractions such as emotions and feelings entering into the equation, we are less likely to instantaneously reactively respond by means of combative combat or counter engagement. This can be a negative in life or death encounters.

In training, especially in hot climate environments, I have learnt the importance of cooling body temperature by regularly pouring water into my jungle hat, bending forward, putting the hat on and then standing up allowing the water to slowly run down from the top of my head to the back of my neck. This is just another indicator of the importance of the reptilian brain and its function of temperature control. The opposite effect is when you have eaten an ice cream and get an immediate headache. By rubbing the nape of the neck and producing a warming effect, the headache can be quickly eliminated.

The next formed brain in relation to evolution is the mammalian brain, more correctly known as the limbic brain. This is the brain responsible for our feelings and emotions. The limbic brain is very much in the centre of the brain mass.

The limbic brain is very sensory in relation to feelings and emotions, and this capability in a high risk, high stress combative environment, can provide situational information by heightened awareness. While the limbic brain is not a planning, thought and combative actions decision-making brain, it is, like the reptilian brain and autonomic nervous system, capable of rapid threat recognition. In unexpected actions-on encounters the limbic brain along with the reptilian brain and autonomic nervous system can be the first detection and reactionary response systems.

Much of the limbic brain's capability in a combative situation is as a result of previous exposure to combative threat situations and scenarios. This is why realistic CQC combat and counter training is so important. Being a brain that is high in sensitivity, feelings and emotions, it has the capability to reduce the killer instinct response of the reptilian brain.

Part of the limbic brain includes the autonomic nervous system, consisting of the sympathetic, parasympathetic and the enteric nervous systems. The sympathetic system is a reactive and responsive system in combative actions-on encounters and the parasympathetic system is like a control system to ensure reactions and responses are commensurate with threat and threat related neutralisation requirements.

Obviously human factors such as intestinal fortitude and skills capabilities, as well as controlled aggression, factual assessment and tactically correct decision making are major factors in the best option decision-making being made to neutralise threats. The autonomic nervous system provides constant vigilance and surveillance of external environmental factors, and as such, can detect threats before the actions-on is initiated.

The autonomic nervous system also includes the enteric nervous system responsible for regulating internal functions such as digestive requirements. It acts to regulate gut and digestion functions positively for combative requirements as well as ensuring physical requirements for escape and evasion are provided. While it is not as well-known as the sympathetic and parasympathetic nervous systems, the enteric nervous system is an inherited part of our autonomic nervous system from our animal ancestors and it has evolved with changes in lifestyle and living requirements. Being involved with matters of the gut could well be an indication of the importance of obtaining immediate food for survival of our ancient animal ancestors and not ending up in the gut of a bigger and more aggressive predator. A logical theory could be that when animals needed more intelligence than they previously possessed for just eating and drinking, the intelligence process in their gut was added to with one in their cranial cavity.

It could be considered a mid-section and internally linked nervous system that has complex capabilities to process information and send signals to the central nervous system. This is so especially in relation to danger and risk as well as assisting in setting a state of primary combative readiness. Combatively the enteric nervous system is known as the ‘gut brain’.

The control of digestion and excretion is very important in an unexpected as well as an expected combative actions-on encounter. Feelings of sickness to the stomach, and butterflies are common warning signs under threat generated from your gut brain.

The autonomic nervous system, as its name suggests, automatically and in real time constantly scans, via our external sensors and receptors, our immediate surroundings for threats and risks. The autonomic nervous system in a sudden aggressive shock actions-on encounter will initiate responses and reactions through its link to the reptilian and mammalian brains, in relation to fight or flight. In military terms this means going combative or escaping and evading the enemy.

The reptilian and mammalian brains, depending on the degree of surprise and sudden aggressive shock action, may take individual or joint control. For example, the reptilian reactionary brain may initiate subconscious reactive survival reactions in the form of a combative counter engagement action or escape and evasion.

However with recognition and evaluation time being available, the mammalian brain and the reptilian brain may well be overridden by the neocortex thinking brain in relation to threat assessment and threat neutralisation decision making. It is reasonable to believe that, in enemy unexpected unarmed offensive assault first warning contact situations, the reptilian brain could well be the first capability to neutralise the threat, independently or jointly with the mammalian brain. Under such threat, the reptilian brain, being a combative killer instinct primary option reactionary decision maker, would be the dominant brain. It is likely in escape and evasion option decision-making that the mammalian brain would be the dominant deciding brain as a result of its ability to sense or feel dire situations, and as such, recognising helplessness by means of a combative option against an overwhelming formidable threat.

These two brains in a sudden aggressive shock action situation can provide a joint response, or influence or dominate each other, depending on the individual and the threat specifics, including the degree of threat. The reptilian and mammalian brains will very much combine to provide the best means of threat neutralisation for the individual, whether it be combative, or escape and evasion as an immediate first reactionary response capability. The individual human factors are the important variable and all the training in the world is valueless in extreme actions-on encounters if the individual does not possess the intestinal fortitude and inner resolve to overcome their fears and utilise their skills capabilities. A highly confident, and mentally tough, untrained combatant with practical smarts committed to winning and self-preservation, would have a greater chance of threat neutralisation than a highly trained individual with a low level of, or no intestinal fortitude. Conversely, a highly committed and confident individual up against a formidable, equally or greater mentally tough, highly trained combatant would be disadvantaged by having low level or no battle-proven skills capabilities.

The neocortex, being the most recent of the three brains to develop to a high level of learning and understanding, fills approximately three quarters of our cranial cavity, and is responsible for the highest level assessment decision making and ultimately providing our best chance of threat neutralisation, whether it be by combative or escape and evasion means.

The neocortex is not only a large brain, but it also is divided into different divisions responsible for very different roles. The thinking part of the brain is at the front, often referred to as the frontal lobes immediately behind the forehead. This section of the brain gives us the ability to assess and evaluate information, and make definite and deliberate decisions to solve complex and complicated issues and problems.

Combatively, the neocortex enables us to decide on a deliberate plan of action to neutralise the threat based on all information, prior training and experience. The decision-making is not only based on prior experiences from the memory bank, but more importantly enables the combatant to utilise their principle-based skills, adjusting and changing them to effectively combat or counter the enemy threat.

The neocortex also comprises of two sides that are connected. The left side is the more 'regular force' drills and commands part of the neocortex. It is the language centre very important to the drill instructor and giving combative drill technique to command's instructions. The left side is very important in an immediate actions-on encounter where the operator must fast map, evaluate threat and situational realities, and verbally give situational reports. Within training or operationally, this left side of the brain provides direct line combat and counter options based on prior training and practical assessment and decision-making.

The right side of the neocortex is more perceptive and based on possibilities over probabilities for combative decision-making. The right side of the neocortex is highly intelligent and extremely connected with higher capability problem-solving capabilities. Being over-technical, traditional or sporting for self-defence or military close combat can, however, prove to be a major downfall.

So, the right side of the brain can be described as a brain less controlled by fact, prior training and previous experiences. For close combat and self-defence, however, such thought outside the combative memory bank and toolbox can complicate issues and increase risk. The left side could be described as the provision of military specific battle-proven practices based on the military science of CQC and CQB and military self-defence, while the right side could be described as the more open to suggestion and theory proposal, less formalised and highly creative side of the neocortex.

The reality is military CQC is a military science, not an exact science, and relies more on prior training and battle-proven experience from the memory bank of previous combative threat actions on including threat neutralisation.

A valid description or comparison between the two sides of the neocortex is that the left side is more your conscious, deliberate and definite self-defence and combative side of the neocortex and the right side is your more subconscious, expansive thought outside the primary, secondary alternative and emergency options combative memory bank and toolbox. So the right side is very important for higher learning and complex problem solving, but less relevant to immediate combative actions-on encounters where the best of battle-proven methods of threat neutralisation are required.

Combatively the neocortex is utilised in unexpected actions-on encounters that are not immediately neutralised, and when a higher level of thought and decision-making is required to neutralise a continuing threat. In expected actions-on encounters where there is time for detailed assessment and tactically correct decision making, it is likely to take control as the major means of deciding on the best means of threat neutralisation. In unexpected actions-on encounters that have not been neutralised immediately by the reptilian brain or combined reptilian brain, mammalian brain and autonomic nervous system, the neocortex can override the more primitive brains, and provide the best possible tactically correct means of threat neutralisation. This is again dependent on the individual combatant having the mental toughness to take control of themselves in the situation, and utilise the higher capabilities the neocortex provides.

The neocortex makes decisions based on high-level thinking and problem solving supported by memory capabilities from training and from previous combative actions-on encounters. There is nothing more valuable in relation to tactics and skills employments than the experience of prior learning and threat exposure. This, our most sophisticated brain, provides unequalled capabilities when we are faced with extreme risk and danger that requires highly skilled and tactically decided means of threat neutralisation. In prolonged combative encounters against a formidable enemy, especially when on the back foot as a result of the enemy's greater physical capabilities, the primary complex neocortex brain thought and problem-solving capabilities, aided by its memory bank of prior training and prior related experiences, are required to neutralise the threat as safely and effectively as humanly possible in relation to the individual combatant. This is our highest-level means of threat-specific information assessment and combative problem solving decision making.

The neocortex provides the capability to be combatively ready and capable in relation to fast mapping on the move, under threat, in real time, in ongoing required combative actions contingency options employments. Contingency options employments are based on prior battle-proven training and combative real life experiences. To utilise such a human computer to assess and decide on the best combative means of threat neutralisation requires extensive and intensive prior combative training experience.

The neocortex may be the most recently evolved of the three cranial brains, but it has grown in size and capability to meet our modern day, considerably wider and more varied combative requirements. This is especially important when you consider how we have become considerably more verbally orientated and capable of extreme cunning and deception in the set up and delivery of wide-ranging methods of assault both armed and unarmed, covertly and overtly.

The highly trained and mentally tough combatant, through employing hard targeting tactics, should reduce the risk of being compromised and taken by surprise considerably. In doing so, they will reduce the risk of the reptilian brain, or the combined reptilian and mammalian brain, overriding the neocortex.

The neocortex starts developing well before we are born. It provides us with wide ranging capabilities applicable to neutralising violent threats, by sound assessment and tactically correct decision making, and well timed and controlled, aggressively executed, combative options of threat neutralisation. In law enforcement hostage negotiation, or suspect interviewing, the neocortex is utilised to employ strategies including unorthodox means and methods to achieve the objective. It is also the verbal or language centre of the brain.

The neocortex is the required brain for elite operators who must be in control of their emotions, and who must be able to reduce fear to as low a level as is humanly possible. Taking control of their internal self and external environment, while conducting themselves as an individual and as part of a small specialist team requires very special attributes. Sudden aggressive shock action, confusion, environmental uncertainty and unfamiliarity require a high level of confidence and competency, self-belief and trust in one's comrades. Being able to think on the move, maintain all senses at high alert, while communicating and performing individual and team required tactics and skills under threat, requires a very special individual indeed. Through training and copious amounts of repetition, as well as exposure and inoculation to the faced threat and the threat environment, the selected and highly trained combatant will overcome the urge to break from tactics and go reactionary, and will instead utilise the neocortex to the maximum.

Through tactics training, battle handling exercises or scenario training, the military combatant or civilian training in self-defence or unarmed combat, utilising their psychological conditioning and enhancement, can override the primitive reactionary responses, and utilise their most developed brain, the neocortex, for effective threat neutralisation.

Our reptilian brain and our mammalian brain have the capability to initiate reactionary physical responses under threat individually or jointly, preventing our most advanced brain, the neocortex, from being part of the immediate reactionary physical combat, counter, or escape and evasion option. Immediately the reptilian and mammalian brains become aware of an immediate impending or initiated threat, they automatically and subconsciously turn on the fight or flight capabilities. It is the individual under threat, through a lack of intestinal fortitude, and possibly combined with a lack of capability to neutralise the threat, that allows the threat situation to overcome them and assume the negative threat status of static helplessness.

Unfortunately, often when the dire nature of an assault wound or injury registers, and the reality of the encounter is suddenly recognized as being life-threatening, the individual endeavors to overcome their fears by allowing their reptilian brain to kick into self-preservation fight or flight mode. Unfortunately, it may well be too late in relation to the physical wounds or injuries received when static and under assault.

Your senses are critical in ensuring continuous information signals are transmitted to your involved brain, or brains, in the combative threat assessment and decision making, and combative skills employment execution control and command centres. Sight and hearing are especially important, along with your sense of touch and feel to maintain balance and stability. These all assist with combative skills employments in low light or restricted or eliminated vision situations.

This information needs to be based on factual, actual real time threat assessment, and not on perception or speculation. This is very important, as your brain's higher thinking and decision making capabilities are reduced by the effects of adrenaline and endorphin dumping. Whereas such releases are important to provide increased physical capabilities, they can also restrict or negatively affect sensory physical assessment and decision making capabilities.

Physiology

All of the physiology that I have learnt over the past three decades in relation to military CQC, MSD and CQB has come from military Master-Chief instructors and medical doctors that are proponents of military close combat.

The following is a basic brief in relation to the physiology in regards to the effects of expected and sudden unexpected aggressive shock action as it relates to military self-defence and military close combat.

Especially in sudden aggressive unexpected shock action, flinching is an autonomic nervous system reaction to reduce risk and self-preserve. Flinching is not something that can be completely eliminated and nor should it be as it is a natural mechanism of self-preservation. Flinching is an involuntary automated reaction that reduces target mass and increases stability by lowering the centre of gravity. As with the ready-set-go status of the small to medium squat, flinching prepares and places the combatant in a position conducive with expedient action from a cocked, loaded, primary ready status position. The trained combatant by means of a continuation of the flinch can increase and reinforce stability to counter enemy resistance, and set a state of increased readiness for dynamic expedient action by a considerable amount. Techniques that oppose the natural mechanism of self-preservation, that is, flinching, are negative practices in relation to commonality between involuntary automatic self-preservation reactionary responses, and primary deliberate means of combating or countering the threat post flinching.

In unexpected, immediate actions-on encounters flinching is a common initial reaction to sudden immediate threat situations, even before the effects of adrenaline and other hormone are experienced. In unexpected sudden aggressive shock actions-on encounters, once your bodily senses and receptors have sent a signal of the external dire threat to your brain and the reactionary requirement for an immediate reactionary response is determined, that reactionary response will be initiated instantaneously, normally under such an actions-on by your reptilian brain or a combination of your reptilian brain and your mammalian brain and autonomic nervous system. In expected actions-on encounters or in encounters where there is the luxury of time and distance, the higher level neocortex brain thought and problem-solving can reduce the effects of fear and stress and through prior training suppress the effects of dumping of adrenaline and other relevant hormones. In a first knowledge being contact shock aggressive actions-on encounter, however the immediate priority is an autonomic nervous system response combined with the two more primitive brains' reactionary responses. The trained combatant, by means of the neocortex, can override the more primitive brains reactions, after benefiting from the early warning that the more primitive brains provide by their reactionary responses.

Often the effects of stress and fear are adrenaline and a multitude of other stress reaction hormones being dumped into the bloodstream are a result of the effects of impending or imminent threat situations. If there is time for negatives such as self-doubt, anticipation or perception to creep in and weaken the combatant's resolve, and if they do not know how to eliminate or control such effects, the result can be dire. Combative respiration should be deliberately employed immediately the actions-on situation is recognised, identified or encountered. Combative respiration should also be employed with every skill execution, as well as to negate the effects of close contact including ground impact. Doing so will hard target you. It may also prevent or reduce the effects of undetected adrenaline and other hormones dumping under unexpected assault, but this is difficult to determine. The effect of adrenaline dumping however in expected threat situations is very real and needs to be countered by combative respiration. While adrenaline dumping has some positive effects such as constriction of blood vessels to minimise blood loss, in an actions-on encounter, combative respiration will reduce other more negative effects. Flinching and the small through full squat continuation of the flinch is an effective means of hard targeting risk reduction and making ready to go combative. Combative respiration is similarly the primary means to reduce the effects of adrenaline dumping and keep your senses at high alert as well as maintain primary skills levels. Expected threat situations to a lesser degree may not involve flinching but certainly the effects of adrenaline dumping will be experienced.

Flinching not only reduces target mass and increases stability but also increases ground holding resistance by systematic muscular, tendon, skeletal and core rigidity, and tensing increases, providing high level resistance capabilities.

There are varying degrees of flinching in relation to the individual combatant and the degree of sudden aggressive shock action including the nature of the shock action that includes at extremes, throwing oneself to the ground as in explosive battlefield life or death threats. My dear friend the late

Bill Hall a veteran of RAF Bomber Command told me that when he first came back from World War II, upon hearing a car backfire in the street, he threw himself to the ground by means of his falling skills taught to him in his unarmed combat training in the United Kingdom.

Medium to deep flinching continuation to a crouch position is a common response to immediate shock action. This is especially true if the momentum and velocity of the assault is considerable, and to maintain one's footing and hold your ground, considerable increased stability and resistance is required.

In my experience, observations and research I have identified that the initial flinch reactionary movement in relation to the depth of the squatting action, including moving off the confrontation line or completely self-decentralising, is in relation to the sudden aggressive shock action stimuli, degree of shock, surprise, force, impact risk and danger. In situations and under conditions of the effect of extreme level incoming threat, including the effects of heavy contact as well as the combatant's instant recognition of extreme danger, I have identified that it is a combination of an automatic reaction and a deliberate response to the sudden aggressive shock action and determined risk and danger.

In situations of immediate unexpected sudden aggressive shock actions-on encounters, a combatant can increase their safety and likelihood of threat neutralization if they can identify the threat in real time and combine their deliberate response action with their subconscious automated reactions. Prior exposure or practical smarts, under immediate threat, can in real time help to identify the threat which could be an incoming dynamic movement, sound, flash of colour, vibration through incoming threat assault, or simply the effects of downright aggression. Success in this situation may involve combative or escape and evasion means.

I have observed and identified that the continuation from the initial flinch subconscious status, by means of a deliberate continuation action in recognition, and as a response to the force of the threat and the need to self-preserve (including preparation to neutralise the threat or break away from the threat), is a common continuation for the trained combatant.

Multiple continuation reactions and combined deliberate actions to extreme sudden aggressive shock action may well include an initial subconscious reactionary flinch, followed by deep crouching through to self-decentralisation. I have seen many instances of this while instructing military CQB and when working crowd control and close protection as well as on firing ranges.

The human senses and receptors that provide our brains and our autonomic nervous system with a warning signal, including information in relation to the nature of the immediate threat before contact, prove just how constantly alert our subconscious methods of threat detection and threat identification really are. In my twenty plus years as a bouncer at some of the more popular and less savory bars and clubs, I have seen many an occasion on a dance floor or in a dark area where some thug or bully has decided to cowardly, from the side or rear flanks, king hit an unsuspecting target. The low light or even flashing lights including strobe lights, the loud music, people all around dancing, speaking loudly, including being less than in control under the effects of alcohol, and the unsuspecting target victim immediately prior to impact, reacts to the king hit by means of self-preservation and often combined with pre-learnt safety and combative actions.

The reality is that fully committed assaults of maximum force, by means of that maximum force can be identified by your subconscious brain and autonomic nervous system as a result of your external sensors and receptors being superior to human physical actions-on incoming movements and assault actions. The difference I have identified is that the untrained are less likely to combine, with their subconscious reactions of flinching, moving away or downward off the confrontation line, deliberate responses of increased self-preservation safety combined with threat neutralisation counter engagement.

I have observed boxers, when assaulted without warning, immediately slip, cover and counterpunch, and I have seen wrestlers flinch and shoot under the punch, clinching with their attacker and taking them down.

Personally in my time as a bouncer in pubs and clubs as well as on the street when taken by surprise, I have employed my combative skills from the subconscious automatically initiated reactionary flinch or combined emergency evasive reactionary response off the confrontation zone combined with the reactionary flinch. The enemy, or in self-defence threat situations, the aggressor's degree of discreet or covert initiation of assault or their level of contact and momentum in completely unexpected actions-on encounters will determine your degree of subconscious reactionary timing, and the timing of counter engagement, for the trained combatant.

In high intensity unexpected actions-on encounters where heavy contact is the first indicator of the assault, and through your subconscious automatic self-preservation reactionary capabilities, flinching and immediate increases in self-preservation occur, there may be several seconds delay for the trained combatant prior to going combative, due to having to absorb, resist or redirect the enemy's momentum, combined with making adjustments, fast mapping, assessment on the move, and setting up and initiating their decided counter engagement. The reality is that my findings, through my decades involved with dealing with violence, is that the combatant with the highest level of mental toughness and the most proven practical self-protective and counter engagement skills has the greatest chance of not only increasing personal safety, but regaining control, even off the back foot, and turning a bad situation into a front foot situation of dominance by means of their battle-proven skills of threat neutralisation.

Those combatants who are highly trained and have been involved with battle handling exercises and scenarios where they must fast map, assess on the move and make decisions to counter unexpected threats and sudden aggressive shock actions, are considerably more skilled at taking control and achieving threat neutralisation in real life actions-on encounters than those who are not.

Stand-up fighters, wrestlers and grapplers as well as mixed martial artists that are accustomed to contact in training, especially contact to the head (the primary target of most aggressors) have far less difficulty in dealing with such threats. I have seen traditional martial artists sparring with boxers and kick boxers and finding out the reality that they are not prepared to deal with common violence in relation to head punches, head butts and dirty fighting. I have seen traditional martial artists employ definite blocking techniques and get it wrong against direct action head punches and punches employed with deceptive feints. Individual blocking of individual strikes studio or dojo style can be less than effective against unpredictable, unorthodox aggressors determined to cause you grievous bodily harm.

You must have proven skills that have commonality with your subconscious automated reactions to unexpected sudden aggressive shock actions in order to reduce counter engagement threat neutralisation combative timings. If unaccustomed to the realities of real life violence then through exposure and gradual inoculation increasing the degree of speed, force, velocity and intensity by means of the best of battle-proven practical skills, you will develop in confidence and competency. Individual blocking or defensive actions are high risk, as they only provide a 50 percent chance of getting it right in relation to the nature of the threat.

Battle-proven skills provide principle-based primary practices that will provide hard cover protection and deflection capabilities as well as setting up counter engagement against wide-ranging threats.

The Todd System of CQC breaks the body into two components; from the waist up and from the waist down. Hard cover guarding and straight line striking deflection capabilities provide body line cover from the top of the head to the waist, and stationary pivoting evasion combined with lead leg stamping provides cover and counter engagement from the waist down. The reality is in a high risk unexpected actions-on encounter post subconscious automatic flinching, your small through full squat continuation will increase stability, reduce target mass, and combined with your hard cover guard and deflection capabilities, as well as the pivot stationary evasion and lead stamp kick, will enable you to effectively neutralise wide ranging unarmed offensive assault actions-on threats.

The body is an amazing machine and in the face of aggression, whether it is an expected or unexpected actions-on situation, will dump adrenaline which, when secreted into the bloodstream, has the effect of aiding you in going combative or in your escape and evasion. However, if not kept in check and under control, like too much of anything, it can have negative effects.

The importance of deliberate primary combative offensive or counteroffensive actions having commonality with the subconscious automatic reactions of sudden aggressive shock action, especially in posture and positioning, is very important for self-preservation safety and counter engagement threat neutralisation. The negative practice of expanding or increasing bodily mass under assault, as opposed to dropping one's centre of gravity to increase stability (while also reducing target mass), can be the difference between life and death.

Never confuse flinching and increasing stability by crouching and resisting, with freezing. The reality of keeping the effects of sudden aggressive shock action in relation to released adrenaline under control are required to prevent hesitation or freezing under assault. The status of freezing under assault can be caused by more than just being unable to control the effects of adrenaline dumping. It can also be caused by the individual being low on intestinal fortitude and inner resolve as well as simply not knowing how to counter the threat. A situation of being overwhelmed by one's subconscious automated reactions to the threat, combined with a feeling of helplessness under assault out of a lack of mental toughness and not being trained in how to neutralise such an assault, can see the individual simply give up.

Under such a dire situation the overwhelmed victim may well simply turn their back on the threat under assault, fall to the ground and assume a foetal position where they are simply an easy static target. Often all too late, when the reality that their aggressor wants to do them serious harm becomes apparent, they will try and fight back or get away, that is, if they are physically capable.

The reality is one or more of your senses will identify the threat initiating the flinch reaction and simultaneously send the information to your brain. Your brain, upon identifying the threat risk and danger level, will release adrenaline to give you the ability to go combative or escape and evade. In addition, endorphins, which are naturally produced painkillers, will be automatically released to dramatically reduce the effect of pain through injury or wounding. The immediate combined effects of adrenaline and endorphins are increased respiration and a rise in blood pressure. There may be other effects depending upon whether the target of the actions-on encounter has time to recognise and experience lesser effects, usually the result of impending but not immediate actions-on encounters. These effects include perspiration, chattering teeth, trembling thighs, feeling sick to the stomach including stomach cramping, or butterflies.

Through actions-on experience and realistic actions on encounters simulated scenarios training and battle handling exercises the combatant can become accustomed to the effects of adrenaline, endorphins and other hormones released and they can learn to control and keep such effects in check.

The fact that all three brains and the autonomic nervous system are connected provides us with a high level dire situation emergency threat recognition identification and emergency threat neutralisation capability. In unexpected assault the combined reptilian and mammalian brains working together can provide primitive combative or escape and evasion capabilities. The trained combatant can take advantage of the primitive brain's warning indicators and override the primitive brain's reactionary responses with deliberate higher level, combative threat neutralisation capabilities utilising the neocortex. In situations of imminent but not immediate actions-on our neocortex—our highest thinking and problem-solving brain—will maximise the confident and competent combatant's capabilities of threat neutralisation.

Being able to control the effects of hormones dumping under threat is vital. Whereas adrenaline and endorphin levels when dumped into the bloodstream provide the capabilities to physically perform and self-protect at combative actions-on extreme levels, they also can interfere with human senses. This means they can reduce your ability to threat detect and execute combative skills accurately and with optimum coordination and cohesion, as well as reducing the ability to focus on the immediate threat and your situational environmental and additional threats (e.g., tunnel vision and audio exclusion). The effects of such threat stress and risk situations is a considerable reduction in your fine motor skills; hence, any battle-proven military combative program should promote gross motor skills as the primary means to neutralise the threat, over fine motor skills that are affected adversely by the bodily release of adrenaline and endorphins under sudden aggressive shock action. The best of battle-proven gross motor skills provide maximum human destruction, with the minimum effort required, in kill-or-be-killed battlefield combative actions-on encounters.

Relating the brains to CQC

The brain to boot package is a result of my lifetime's research and development in combined combative physical and psychological tactics and skills to assist with psychological conditioning and enhancement for military CQB/CQC and military self-defence. This is from a CQC Master-Instructor perspective.

The widely considered evolution of the human brain from its primitive origins to its modern Homo sapiens makeup of the combined reptilian, mammalian, Homo sapiens and gut brains provides a lot of reasoning and understanding of how we have evolved in capabilities to deal with fear and stress. The gut brain, a very primitive means of our primitive ancestors to identify the need to eat or drink has been taken over by our cranial housed brains since our primitive ancestors came down from the trees and through natural disasters had to learn how to search for food and water. The oldest brain in reactionary self-protection being the reptilian brain is a non-thinking reactionary brain that when a subject is taken by surprise can provide instant reactionary counter engagement or escape and evasion.

The mammalian brain, although not a thinking brain has the capability to call on prior experience and as such has a more responsive over reactionary means of counter engagement capability. The mammalian brain is a more emotional brain and will often influence or override the reptilian brain. Both the reptilian and mammalian brains have a limited range of options in relation to threat neutralisation. From reactionary combative reptilian counter engagement brain through the mammalian brains reactionary response based on prior experience and exposure to same or similar threats, the options are either very primitive basic combative options or escape and evasion if the threat is perceived to be too great.

The autonomic nervous system plays a major role via sympathetic and parasympathetic reactions to identified threats. The human senses have amazing capabilities to identify a threat even before we physically realise or recognise it. Incoming information signals in relation to the threat and return signals in relation to preparing our bodies to deal with the threat include unconscious automated reactions and responses. Combine this with somatic sensory capabilities to sense external threats and the capability to identify and recognise threats for the combatant is considerable.

The trained combatant through training and threat inoculation in relation to overriding or controlling fear and stress effects and understanding the importance of utilising the best and safest means of threat neutralisation must override reptilian and mammalian reactionary responses. The combatant must draw from the most intelligent brain, the modern man Homo sapiens brain, the warrior's most intelligent threat neutralisation decision making capability. This most highly intelligent tactical brain has the capability to problem solve and draw on recollections from our prior and previous experience memory bank. Combining our sensory and central intelligence systems with the best of battle proven skills that have commonality in employment and cohesion with natural human self-preservation reactions such as flinching increases our speed and means of threat neutralisation.

The employment of our highly intelligent Homo sapiens brain in relation to making sound assessments and decisions on the best and safest way to neutralise the threat also includes our capabilities to recognise the effects of fear and stress including hormonal release bodily reactions. Understanding and accepting that the bodily effects of hormonal dumping should be considered as early warning signs in relation to possible risks and dangers of the faced threat is a positive. Reactions include increased heart rate and respiration, trembling extremities etc. The brain to boot methods of reducing or eliminating such effects enable the combatant to set a state of readiness to go combative or escape and evade.

Understanding that principle-based tactics and skills required to neutralise both expected and unexpected threat situations by combat unarmed offensive assault or counter unarmed counter offensive assault reduces the risks of confusion in decision-making under threat. The brain to boot logical order of execution of tactics and skills both psychological and physical components provides the best and safest means of setting up and employing your best means of threat neutralisation.

In an expected actions-on encounter on identifying and recognising the threat, the logical order of requirement to best make ready and be willing and able to neutralise the most formidable threat is as follows. Threat recognition and identification combative respiration to reduce the effects of fear and stress and take positive control. Senses high alert. Immediate first look, assessment and decision-making. Threat alignment and setting a state of readiness.

Second-look threat assessment decision-making confirmation and mind's eye visualisation of the execution of the confirmed option. Constant checks and rechecks of the threat the environment and your state of readiness. Confirmation and visualisation of your emergency stationary contingency option to threat neutralise if engaged prior to your confirmed option being employed.

Self-reassurance in your mind's eye WAR willing able ready, RWA ready willing able. Making of adjustments in range target alignment position and any ready set go required combative adjustments. Timing and employing your combat or counter engagement execution from the small to medium squat ready set go expedient action status combined with syncronised CQC respiration. Constant immediate post execution fast map assessment and the employment of any required adjustments and contingency options. Confirmation the threat has been neutralised.

In unexpected actions on encounters either by immediate pre-contact threat recognition or first recognition as a result of combative contact the following order applies. Hardcover guarding and simultaneous combative respiration. Real time threat neutralisation assessment and decision-making. Enemy alignment and adjustments in range position and setting a ready status. Immediate execution of the decided threat neutralisation option from a small half or full squat status combined with CQC respiration. Fast mapping real time assessment and the employment of contingency options if required to ensure the threat is neutralised. Threat neutralisation confirmation.

The previous outlines the primary principles and order of execution of neutralising expected and unexpected threats and can be employed for both unarmed offensive assault and unarmed counter offensive assault or armed threat neutralisation employments. Keeping the mind busy with required positive tactics and continuous threat and situational assessments as well as checks and rechecks of the threat, threat situation environment and your setting and maintaining a ready status is a most positive means to prevent one's mind slipping into the negatives of anticipation, perception and self-doubt. Everything must be based on factual threat assessment and the best of battle-proven decision-making to quickly, quietly, safely and effectively neutralise the threat. Important primary major principle components of the brain to boot tactics and skills such as the employment of the small squat half and full squats provide risk reduction increased resistance capabilities and the setting of a state of readiness. The deliberate set state of readiness for expedient offensive evasive or escape and evasion responses and actions increases mental toughness by reducing risk in making the combatant a hard target who is ready, willing and able. The priority option of combative respiration immediately on threat identification recognition and utilisation of combative cycled respiration in the execution of all combative skills enables the maintaining of the highest immediate and extended levels of combative physical capabilities. This is vital to maintaining mental toughness. Executing skills not only correctly but powered by around 75 percent plus commitment combined with cycled respiration will enable increased accuracy, endurance, reduce telegraphing actions and compromising yourself, and will provide more than enough power and velocity to destroy enemy primary delicate life-support bodily targets.

Combative respiration is considerably different to physical fitness respiration such as running where you do not have to time cycled respiration, or single repetition core strength required respiration such as in power and strength practices. Combative respiration is important to combative objective achievement especially neutralisation of a formidable foe where extended continued combative physical requirements may be needed to neutralise the threat.

Non-conscious human reactions of self-preservation, having commonality with combative hardcover hard targeting self-protection skills and setting a status of ready set go threat neutralisation capability increases safety and the chance of objective achievement by considerable. To maintain mental toughness requires the usage of the safest and most effective tactics and skills that provide the highest level of risk reduction in the setting and employment of the most effective means of threat neutralisation.

Combining the brain-to-boot physical tactics and psychological enhancement practices to set and maintain a state of ready willingness to go combative with combative skills that are gross motor skills that provide the simplest means of threat neutralisation will increase the combatant's inner resolve considerably. Being able to recognise symptoms of fear and stress and switch on combative capabilities by means of initial combative respiration will reduce or eliminate adverse reactionary effects and will for the trained combatant provide the best means and chance of threat neutralisation. The combative respiration switching on and visual recognition human sense capability will turn all other human senses on to the required degrees.

Deliberate increases in the extent of additional senses required to identify specific threats can be achieved simply by focusing that sense in the detection and direction of the considered threat. Through high repetition training of the brain to boot tactics and skills in unison and in the correct order of execution they will become primary means of setting and employing combative actions and counter actions. Utilising the same tactics and skills in sudden aggressive unexpected shock actions on encounters like battle handling exercises will provide the means to utilise the skills in their most reduced primary order of execution to neutralise a threat under contact or immediately prior to contact in the kill zone at real time.

The brain-to-boot principles tactics and skills allow for human error in execution or order of execution error by means of being ready willing and capable of identifying at real time what is required to neutralise the threat by real time fast mapping assessment. The brain-to-boot combative and psychological principles tactics and skills have commonality with all the Todd systems employment requirements from threat detection through threat recognition to fast mapping assessment and threat neutralization decision making. This commonality extends to making ready and setting a primary state of combative readiness to go combative or escape and evade depending on the decided best option.
Combative executed skills employments combined with the brain to boot practices in unison in the correct order of execution provide the best and safest means for a primary combative employment in regards to the individual combatant's physical combative and psychological capabilities.

Knowledge is power, and understanding the evolution and workings of our reactionary and intelligent brains provides reasoning and confidence in our means of threat assessment and decision-making in relation to threat neutralisation. Regardless of evolution being accepted or not the brain to boot practices provide a logical order of proven combined psychological and physical combative tactics and skills that reduce risk as much as individually possible and increase safety and threat neutralisation based on required combative needs. Having tactics and skills that increase safety and reduce risk enabling the combatant to set and maintain a status of primary ready and willingness is psychologically empowering. Combining the brain-to-boot psychological conditioning hard targeting practices with a knowledge of destruction of the human anatomy by the most dirty and deadly means further adds to the combatant's mental toughness and as such self-confidence to threat neutralise the most formidable threats.

Combining the brain-to-boot methods with the simplest gross motor skills that utilise every advantage provided by battledress boots, primary, secondary and improvised weapons enables mental toughness to be maximised. The single most important component of threat neutralisation physically and psychologically is the earliest initiation and maintaining of combative respiration. This enables factual real time assessment and decision-making as well as maintaining mental focus and post-employment, higher accuracy recollection.
The timing of combative respiration with the employment of unarmed combat or the usage of non-ballistic weapons employments is the most important component in being psychologically and physically best ready and prepared in close combat. Inhaling via the nose immediately pre-unarmed combat skills employment or in an armed option sighting phase combined with exhaling via the mouth during the execution of the unarmed skills or armed option employments has proven to increase proficiency and accuracy remarkably. When the combatant knows their threat neutralisation skills provide high level safety and the best chance of threat neutralisation confidence is increased. Combining the set up and employment brain-to-boot psychological and physical tactics and skills enhances the best of battle proven skills employment chances of threat neutralisation.

Somatic Nervous System

The somatic nervous system is part of the peripheral nervous system, and unlike the central nervous system and spinal cord, it is not protected by bone. The somatic nervous system by means of a very complex process is responsible for sending sensory and motor signals to and from the central nervous system. For the somatic nervous system to be able to do this it requires nerve connections under the skin that can transmit contact signals information to the central nervous system.

The somatic nervous system is faster than we can see or think and not only detects contact and sends information signals to the central nervous system and brain, but can also send the required signals back to ensure self-protection and counter engagement physical actions are executed to neutralise the threat. Somatic nervous system nerves can be sensory capable only as in some of our human senses or solely motor actions capable, as well as being sensory and motor action capable.

This form of peripheral threat recognition and identification and subconscious reaction to reduce risk and increase safety for CQC ensures that when we are taken by surprise, covertly or unexpectedly, our subconscious defence capabilities kick in. This in turn reduces the effects of contact prior to our responsive, deliberate, physical capabilities being employed to neutralise the threat or in an escape-and-evasion option removing us away from the threat. The reality of close quarter's combat actions-on encounters or in training is that through the rough and tumble contact impact unprotected nerves can be damaged.

Reaction and response signals from the central nervous system to the muscles involved with combative or escape-and-evasion physical actions are transmitted from the central nervous system to the required combative or escape and evasion bodily parts. These physical combative or escape-and-evasive reactions and responses can be both subconsciously reactionary and consciously deliberately responsively executed or a combination of both.

Under assault the combatant may well react to an unexpected incoming striking action as a result of contact impact. This may be a subconscious reaction such as flinching or removing the bodily target area from the impact contact zone, followed by deliberate responsive hard cover guarding, real time threat assessment and decision-making. These may then be followed by the set up and employment of combative skills to neutralise the threat, or if the threat is deemed overwhelming, initiating tactical escape-and-evasion.

The somatic nervous system has signal pathways to and from our human sensory capabilities such as our primary combative sensory capability of eyesight. Being a peripheral nervous system with nerve endings all over our skin surface it is very important that we use our sense of touch, in relation to maintaining an affinity with the ground, to ensure that balance and stability is maintained or corrected. Then we can, through deliberate employment of footwork capabilities that include subconscious muscle memory, achieve expedient combative actions.

In combative foot work and in an escape and evasion, without such important sensory nerve endings even simple physical skills capabilities like maintaining a stand-up posture and movement would not be possible. In the execution of combative actions, nerves connected to our skeletal muscles make the execution of combative skills possible. The somatic nervous system's signals capabilities provide direct lines to and from the central nervous system, with the combative and self-protection required bodily capabilities.

The reflex reactionary actions of the somatic nervous system in relation to contact happen without brain-decided action being initiated. This is achieved by means of nerve signal connections directly to the spinal cord. This reactionary signal achieves muscle movements that are not brain decided.

For combative counter engagement, without having the capability to subconsciously connect our muscles and skin as well as all other bodily organs and parts required in self-protection and self-preservation with our central nervous system, we would find ourselves when taken unexpectedly in extreme danger of being incapacitated or eliminated.

MILITARY CQC PHYSIOLOGY

Fight or Flight Reactionary Response

The hypothalamus is a vital part of the mammalian or limbic brain in relation to combative or escape and evasion capabilities. It is located just above the brain stem and is roughly the size of an almond. The hypothalamus is responsible for kicking off the sympathetic nervous system and the adrenocortical system. The sympathetic nervous system transmits along nerve signal lines while the adrenal-cortical system uses the bloodstream to release hormones such as adrenaline important to going combative or escape and evasion. In simple terms these two combined systems comprising of electrical and plumbing enable us to neutralise threats by combative means or escape and evasion.

The hypothalamus enables all our combative required bodily systems to go from a stand down status to a combative status instantaneously. Everything is increased in speed and intensity as well as rigidity, achieving a state of combative readiness. Relaxed muscles, tendons and joint ligaments become tense, hard and ready to provide resistance and expedient action. Our sympathetic nervous system sends out signals to not only our combative required skeletal muscles, but also to our adrenal medulla of both our adrenal glands.

The two adrenal glands sit on top of the kidneys and include the adrenal medulla and the adrenal cortex. These two parts of the adrenal glands perform very different functions. The adrenal medulla is the inner part of the adrenal gland situated in its centre and it is essential in combative encounters and escape and evasion under threat. The other part of the adrenal glands is the adrenal cortex which is the outer part of the gland responsible for the production of hormones essential to maintaining human life.

The adrenal medulla produces hormones including adrenaline, which is very important to combative and self-defence capabilities. The sympathetic nervous system is responsible for the release of adrenaline into the bloodstream. The hormones released into the bloodstream by the adrenal medulla, including adrenaline, provide increased energy and capabilities in combative and self-defence situations. Your heart rate and blood pressure increase along with your oxygen intake.

While these changes and increases do provide enhanced and increased physical capabilities, it is important to remember that such effects must be controlled, and that this control requires from the outset combative respiration. Too much of anything can have negative effects, especially in timing of combative actions, accuracy and determining of range.

In combative situations where the threat is not neutralised in the first 1 to 3 seconds and the actions-on encounter extends to 10 or more seconds, the effects of adrenaline, if not controlled, can adversely affect combative performance capabilities.

In combative and self-defence actions-on encounters of between 10 and 30 seconds, where the combatant has not employed continuous combative respiration to control the effects of adrenaline dumping, they could well find themselves rapidly deteriorating in their physical combative capabilities. The dumping of adrenaline is a chemical means of ensuring the combatant automatically is put on high alert, achieving a high state of readiness and dramatically increased assistance in the achievement of high intensity combative capabilities under threat. Instant or increased combative energy is also enhanced by the added effect of adrenaline ensuring the liver delivers more glucose into the bloodstream, which in turn converts into immediately available energy.

Fear or Stress effect

You will read in the brain-to-boot package of the importance of not only the union between physical combative skills and combative psychological enhancement components, but also the importance during actions-on encounters of maintaining a state of combative readiness with the entire body ready and capable of achieving 75 percent plus combative output.

From the balls of your feet via your combat boots, up through your lower legs, thighs, buttocks, hips, torso, shoulders, arms, neck and head, maintaining a state of readiness prior to any actions-on encounter where you are ready but not putting any part of your body in an overstressed status is vital. In actions-on combative skills employments, being able to protect the integrity of all parts of your body, while achieving high-level output, is also equally vital. In a pending actions-on encounter, fear and or stress can be increased by the release of adrenaline and a multitude of other hormones. This is known in CQC as 'self-induced stresses'. This fear or stress factor effect also manifests in positions of increased bodily tension and rigidity.

The dumping of adrenaline can have physical effects on muscles and tendons, ligaments and joints. The combative terminology of 'hard,' 'medium' and 'soft' bodily parts such as 'hard knees,' 'soft knees' refers to the status of the joint. If the knee is not being held under any stress or tension it is referred to as a soft knees status. In a close quarters combat body contact, clinch, resisting enemy momentum where the knee of the lead boot is over the toes of the lead boot and rigidly resisting the enemy's forward momentum, the knee will be referred to as a hard knees status. When stalking into range or employing expedient entry assault or evasion a medium bodily status would be utilised. This is a deliberate and responsive employment of specific bodily parts increased levels of rigidity tension and resistance.

Under unexpected sudden aggressive shock action as a reactionary means to the threat and as part of subconscious automated reactionary responses including under adrenaline and other hormones dumping into the bloodstream, a hard body status is a common occurrence. The trained combatant under involuntary flinching or immediate counter resistance, to hold, or regain position, or dominance out of self-preservation, may well subconsciously or deliberately utilise such hard body tactics.

The important thing is that the trained combatant knows when to resist and yield as part of threat neutralisation, and will not allow such subconscious effects to overcome them to the point of freezing in place under threat. The fear or stress factor as a reflex as a result of threat and hormonal dumping will effectively reduce muscle and tendon length as part of natural automated self-preservation and preparation to go combative or escape and evade. The danger is in becoming stuck, or holding a fear factor status that can have a negative effect by increasing stress, tension, pain and interfering with combative employment performance capabilities. The combatant that mentally checks by feel, and where necessary adjusts in relation to ensuring they are maintaining the required ready set capabilities without adding negative levels of tension stress or fatigue, will ensure they are in control constantly. Knowing the feel of maintaining a primary ready combative status prior to any actions-on encounter, as well as knowing the feel of effects of the negative fear factor, including the deliberate prolonged holding of a self-imposed stress position, must ensure adjustment is undertaken. Simply reducing tension and or resistance by adjustment of stance and or guard to a controlled primary readiness status, over a negative employed hard body status will ensure the effects are reduced before they become problematic.

The brain-to-boot package conveys the importance of employing a state of readiness, from the top of the head to the soles of the boots. This means of maintaining a pre-actions primary status ensures minimum stress and tension is applied to any part of the body. The fear or stress factor effects apply to the entire body, from the top of the head to the soles of the boots and through the entire musculoskeletal system, and combatively especially to the extremity's muscles, tendons, joints and ligaments.

Over my instructor lifetime of involvement in CQC, I have observed exponents' reduced performance and kick off expedient action capabilities as a result of allowing the subconscious effects of stress and fear to adversely affect their combative performance, and this is worsened by the dumping of adrenaline and other hormones. While as a means of subconscious or deliberate resistance to hold ground, or regain ground or dominance, a hard body status is positive, it certainly is not positive in any pre-actions-on encounter or for extended periods in any combative actions-on encounter.

Being able to resist, yield and employ expedient combative actions-on skills is important if controlled, or as part of subconscious self-preservation immediately prior to deliberate threat neutralisation, but it is not a primary combative practice prior to an actions-on encounter or for extended duration under actions-on encounters. An individual that does not possess the inner resolve and awareness capabilities to identify and overcome the effects of fear or stress factors may end up with the dire result of freezing under assault.

Maintaining a state of combative readiness includes ensuring your senses stay at high alert. Your senses must not only be used for threat detection and situational awareness, but also to identify, by feel, fear and stress effects. Staying in tune in real time with your bodily status will enable recognition of the effects of unacceptable levels of personal fear or stress. This will enable you, by adjustment, to reduce such negative effects. In situations where increased resistance is required to maintain or regain ground or dominance, the opposite applies by adjusting up your level of hard body resistance and tension.

Combative stances, guards and footwork in relation to holding a ready, hard cover guard status must be of minimal duration and the cocked expedient action kick off must be a minor to medium physical set up and positional change, instantaneously executed.

The primary combative stances have commonality with automatic human self-preservation reactions, and are a natural same direction continuation of movement under threat, so as to reduce risk, increase safety and also to ensure the combatant is in a natural ready set status to go combative, like a runner out of the blocks. This will not only decrease deliberate response timing, but will also ensure, through prior training, the ready-set-go combative execution is immediate and deliberate thus eliminating the likelihood of freezing in place.

From the subconscious risk reduction and self-preservation flinch, to the ready set to go combative status, the entire body from the balls of your feet through your boots upwards, to the top of the head and outward to your bodyline and bodily extremities will be employed, not only with the achievement of maximum expedient action, but also with correct bodily alignment to ensure maximum speed of direct line movement, as well as medium power and velocity of the combative skill is achieved. Primary combative skills having commonality and being cohesive with natural human subconscious reactions under threat is a must. Combining this with real time mental assessments in relation to the feel of adverse effects, and making immediate adjustments in relation to the feel of stress, ensures combative skills executed with correct timing and skills competency are positively enhanced not negatively affected.

Combative positive and negative heart rate ranges

There are many variables in relation to individual's heart rates while resting and in combative actions-on encounters. However there are general heart rate ranges consistent with positive and negative effects in relation to combative actions-on encounters.

The following heart rate ranges are in relation to the trained and motivated combatant up against a formidable foe in an actions-on combative encounter.

- Fine motor skill range between 50 and 120 bpm: the range required for specialist combative roles skills employment, where the combatant must be in control physically and psychologically.

- Detailed motor skill range between 50 and 180 bpm: to employ CQC skills inside this range requires prior training, and importantly, ensuring in actions-on encounters controlled tactics are used.

- Gross motor skill range between 50 and 220 bpm: for high risk CQC encounters against formidable foes, skills that are able to be executed within this range producing threat neutralisation are primary options under such conditions.

- CQC proponent primary heart rate range between 115 and 145 bpm enables the execution of CQC skills ranging from detailed through gross motor skills.

- There is an increased likelihood of non-conducive behaviour and actions including submissive behaviour freezing under assault or blindly fleeing above 175 bpm.

- Above 155 bpm detailed motor skills can begin to deteriorate.

- Above 115 bpm fine motor skills can begin to deteriorate.
- Resting heart rate between 50 and 80 bpm.
- Optimum CQC heart rate between 115 and 145 bpm. At this level the combatant's sensory cognitive and responsive capabilities are at a primary level to ensure the best combative chance of threat neutralisation.

By utilisation of full cycle controlled low intensity combative respiration the combatant can maintain 75 percent plus committed skills employments, maintaining a heart rate conducive with combative endurance that would exceed any, if not every, combative actions-on encounter requirement. By employing this form of respiratory and combined other brain-to-boot physical and psychological combative components, maintaining a heart rate that provides extended endurance capabilities in the execution a gross motor skills ensures the maintained heart rate meets all the combative requirements of threat neutralisation.

The best confirmation of optimum combative performance levels is the individual combatant's personal demonstration that they can operate at the 75 percent plus range of skills employment commitment for durations of several minutes. This duration far exceeds the general time-frame in actions-on CQC and CQB, dirty and deadly enemy neutralisation requirements.

Under varied training and practice conditions the exponent should practice combative respiration to employ single stamp kicks, striking combinations, combined with evasive counter engagement actions, deliberate self-decentralisation, ground counter engagement recovery as well as point-blank body contact clinching with a training partner, and employing unarmed combat skills to achieve enemy secured seizure by means of controlled combative respiration and employment of skills to end an encounter.

The control component to ensure that both your heart rate and respiration level allows you to maintain 75 percent plus continuous combative output is simply to employ every stamp kick by means of a single respiration cycle, employed throughout the complete execution of the stamp kick. Striking skills numbers of strikes per single combative respiration cycle will depend upon the individual combatant's respiratory capabilities, ranging from a single strike through to several strikes per single combative respiratory cycle.

Confidence is gained through competency and the knowledge that you have the capabilities to threat neutralise with a single combative action, or can maintain that same physical outputs capabilities level for multiple combative skills executions.

Understanding fear

Fear can take hold in a fraction of a second when an individual is faced with an immediate frightening experience that may well be unfamiliar and seem undefeatable. Add to this the dark of night, unexpected frightening sounds, shadows, movements, scents, shapes and the risk and threat stimuli amplify the perceived situation. The individual can be psychologically affected before any threat has materialized, or any hostility has been directed at them. To prevent this, they require immediate situational control and management. If this is not undertaken, the fear and stress of the situation in their mind can render some individuals incapable of self-protection or combative actions employments.

The effects of fear can be immediate and continuous if allowed to increase in intensity. Individuals that are not proficient in psychological and physical control procedures to reduce or eliminate the effects of shock, fear and stress can fall victim to an ongoing and often increasing 'long line effect'. This long line effect is an overloading of sensory central nervous system capabilities as a result of identified or unidentified threat via autonomic electrical impulse and hormonal dumping; it needs to be controlled to be combated. The combatant must remember such effects as a racing heart, increased respiration, trembling thighs and chattering teeth are all autonomic reactionary responses that require deliberate manual control and management.

The subconscious fear reaction is completely autonomic; however, the combatant fear response is completely self-inflicted, and it is in the hands of the individual combatant to take control of their situation and set a state of combative readiness and willingness.

To understand fear you must understand that we have a primitive and intelligent means of dealing with the effects of fear when faced with threatening situations. The primitive or reptilian means comprises of a low level of intelligence option in the form of a reactionary attack. If the threat is overwhelming, however, the primitive response is to run away.

The combative intelligent means to deal with the threat is by detailed assessment, controlled thought and deliberate methods of threat neutralisation to ensure self-safety is maintained at the highest possible level. The threat is then neutralised by the best and most proven means.

In shock, fear and stress situations, often the primitive means and the intelligent means of threat neutralisation will be opposing each other. The individual combatant must then take control and utilise high-level intelligent reasoning, decision making and employment of the best and safest skills to neutralise the threat.

Our brains include several different parts that are involved with the realities of fear and controlling fear. The thalamus is responsible for sending signals comprising of bits of information from our sensory capabilities to the required reactionary and responsive parts of the central nervous system.

The sensory cortex is responsible for evaluating incoming bits of sensory information.

The hippocampus not only files and makes available when required prior experiences in the form of memories from a memory bank, but can also differentiate between prior experiences from that memory bank and the faced immediate threat information perspective.

The amygdala can make sense of all the bits of information received in relation to feelings as well as threat characteristics storing fearful experiences and memories of fear.

The hypothalamus is responsible for the initiation of our combative or escape and evasion capabilities, in military CQC or the fight or flight reactionary responses as it is known in civilian self-defence.

It is very important that we have a memory bank of prior experiences for our subconscious brain components to call upon in threatening situations, so as to ensure intelligent combative threat neutralisation options are employed.

Managing our fears would be much faster by the primitive means but this would also be high risk against a formidable foe and would provide considerably less capability. Although the intelligent form of threat neutralisation takes longer, it provides a much better and more expansive, detailed assessment of the threat risk and danger levels, and through intelligent thought and planning better threat neutralisation options.

Our hypothalamus is utilised in our combative or escape and evasion option decision-making both by our primitive and intelligent forms of threat neutralization. The hypothalamus, in an imminent situation, will trigger our nervous system and our adrenal cortical system.

The sympathetic nervous system utilises a complex electrical signals means and our adrenal cortical system dumps hormones into our bloodstream including adrenaline. These hormones being dumped into our bloodstream cause the reactionary effects we describe as warning signals, including increased heart rate, increased respiration, trembling thighs and others.

Our parasympathetic nervous system often works as an opposite to our sympathetic nervous system aiding in more intelligent decision making.

Post immediate actions-on encounters the parasympathetic nervous system will invoke emotional feelings depending on the nature of the experience, threat and the outcome which may include guilt regret or anger.

I have personally seen an exponent, post facing an extreme combative experience, shut down and collapse with failing vital signs, having to be resuscitated and through positive dialogue, encouraged to maintain a state of consciousness and recovery. The reason behind this individual's shut down was that he had been through a grueling and realistic combative testing process far beyond anything he had experienced before, and he had to resort to deliberate actions that were in relation to a brutal intensity far different and beyond what he had ever employed before. His parasympathetic reactionary responses firing on overload had overwhelmed him with emotions and feelings not common to him, and as such the psychological effects caused him to lapse into an unconscious state.

The Todd Systems of CQC are well known for their very self-revealing testing phases, and for our means of training an average individual with inner resolve and combative smarts to be the best combatant they can be. This is achieved through the individual's inner resolve, intestinal fortitude and commitment as well as by provision of the best of battle-proven tactics and skills training practices that enhance mental and physical combative capabilities.

In order for an individual to overcome shock, fear and stress they need to be able to identify the warning signs or effects of threat risk and danger as early as possible and initiate the brain-to-boot practices to control and manage them.

Over 30 years ago I personally developed a military combative drills package called Technique to Command. This technique-to-command package was developed to ensure exponents were familiarised with their combative skills by title and in execution.

Outside of gaining skills proficiency it also provided a valuable means of ensuring they kept their sensory capabilities at high alert even when fatigued during or post experiencing extreme combative realism. Under Todd Group Phase 1 test conditions, the candidates undergo technique-to-command drills early in their phase test, and then again after they have completed all modules including the combative phase and battle handling exercises. The reasoning behind this is to ensure they can control their emotions, including the effects of shock, fear and stress, remaining alert and aware of their immediate surroundings, as well as being able to listen to instructions and perform the required skills to a high level on command.

Being able to keep all senses on and under control is important, not only for combative enthusiasts under technique-to-command drills, but also for operators whether military, police or close personal protection specialists. They must keep all senses open and alert, taking in information, orders and instructions, and transmitting information orders and instructions while conducting themselves at the required level of combative or tactical competency and commitment.

Training the combative way provides psychological and physical means of setting and maintaining a primary combative threat neutralization capable status. This status ensures factual threat recognition and identification, while enabling elimination or control and management of the effects of fear and stress, all while maintaining an alert and aware status.

This alert and aware status includes being combative ready, willing and able to employ primary, secondary, alternative or emergency combative skills to neutralise faced threats including employing escape and evasion if it is judged the safest option against the threat situation.

Combative skills employments at a controlled 75 percent plus flat line continuous employment level will ensure deliberate controlled tactics and skills are intelligently decided and deliberately executed. An individual that is not capable of taking control of their emotions and setting a primary ready status of combative competency in capability stands to increase risk and danger to themselves personally.

While you do not have to be an expert in the complex components, mechanisms and capabilities of the human brain in relation to shock, fear and stress, it is important that you understand the basic reasons behind experiencing effects of shock, fear and stress and how to manage, control or eliminate such effects.

Once you understand by recognition and identification the warning signs or symptoms of shock, fear and stress, and know how to control and manage them by means of your psychological enhancement combative practices, your deliberate combative assessment and decision making in relation to the best and safest means of threat neutralisation employment will become a deliberate continuation of the recognition and identification phase. The combining of these two phases cohesively reduces time in assessment decision making and the employment of threat neutralization.

This will minimise your static target risk status in relation to time, and will on execution of your combative tactics and skills of threat neutralisation, ensure controlled deliberate aggressive momentum is maintained until the threat is neutralised.

If you understand shock, fear and stress, understand the required primary practices to control and manage them, and combine this understanding with your best means of threat neutralisation, then you have the best combative chance.

Maintaining a 75 percent plus flat line combative commitment level enables constant, real time, fast mapping assessment and decision-making to deal with changes in threat situation including an awareness of environmental risks and hazards, and ensuring such dangers are minimised to the lowest level humanly possible.

While we may not have high-level understanding of all the complex workings of the human anatomy and central nervous system decision-making, by understanding the effects, reasons and requirements provided in the brain-to-boot package we can perform at a primary combative capability.

Military CQB/CQC/MSD for the confident, competent combative proponent is not an exact science, but it is a military science made up of gross motor skills methods of threat neutralization. The proficient, competent proponent must know themselves, in relation to their physical and psychological makeup, and their levels of confidence and skills competency. They must know how to conduct themselves under extremes, in a controlled, deliberate state of readiness and willingness, utilising definite mechanisms and measures of deliberate, controlled, combative, aggression employment, setting and maintaining primary threat neutralization capabilities.

Combative proponents may not have a high-level understanding of human biology and the complex workings of our central nervous system's brains, but as doers they must learn how to destroy threats while maintaining personal safety, and this is what matters most against formidable foes.

As human beings, if we did not experience fear, understand it and know how to control and manage it, we would be far less than best prepared to deal with high-risk violent threats. An individual who claims they have not experienced fear is either a liar, stupid or a lunatic. An individual that has not experienced fear and emotion would be an extreme, uncontrolled danger to themselves and to others.

Having an intelligent means of overcoming shock, fear and stress by means of mental toughness and proven combative physical capabilities is what makes us capable of overcoming our fears and defeating formidable foes.

Post actions-on control and management

The importance of psychological enhancement capabilities and control mechanisms, combined with high level, controlled aggressive combative output under training, testing and operational conditions have been detailed in this manual. Now I will cover another very important combative control requirement: the coming down or cooling off post training, testing or after operations, in regards to the physiological effects of dealing with violence.

I developed a CD for my combative exponents titled 'Combative Code of Conduct'. This CD is to give them an understanding of the after effects, risks and responsibilities when coming down from high intensity training, testing or real life self-defence situations. It is equally as applicable and important to military operational combative or law enforcement defensive tactics post actions-on encounters.

The effects of operating at increased but controlled heightened senses, combined with controlling and managing the effects of hormonal dumping into your bloodstream during training, testing or real life actions-on encounters are very real even though the combatant may not realise these effects.

Now I will outline the most important post encounter factors. This is based on a post actions-on encounter that is psychologically manageable by the combatant in the long term, but which requires deliberate management immediately post encounter. At this time the combatant is still coming down from the effects of the actions-on encounter, and as such needs to know how to make and keep themselves safe.

Post actions-on physiological effects in post extreme actions-on encounters can last for between 30 minutes and an hour. However, physiological and psychological effects can make an individual's demeanour and behaviour considerably different to normal for many hours post encounter. The number of hours varies widely in relation to the individual, and also the degree and nature of the actions-on encounter and their role.

Achieving and maintaining a controlled deliberate primary combative flat line 75 percent plus combative commitment, while maintaining heightened sensory capabilities, is psychologically and physically consciously (and subconsciously) demanding.

Add to this the effects in relation to facing risk and danger under imminent expected actions-on conditions or unexpected sudden aggressive shock actions-on conditions, and you will understand that such a state of intensity does not end when the threat is neutralised.

The parasympathetic nervous system effects, post actions-on encounters, are very real and can affect individuals a lot more than they realise or want to accept. Obviously the effects vary from one individual to another in relation to their attitude and demeanour, as well as their understanding of the continued effects post actions-on.

During the encounter the combatant will be conducting themselves at a state of controlled aggression that enables them to do what must be done, and overcome the effects of shock, fear and stress as well as pain. After the encounter they will not be able to immediately return to a pre-actions-on non-combative status.

The flat line level of the controlled state of tactical readiness will subside slowly with time post actions-on, unless methods to quickly reduce the effects and reduce the recovery time to a normal status are known and utilised. During this period, individuals, even though still in the flat line controlled aggressive zone, may experience a feeling of mental and physical fatigue. Often they will have a blank look on their face, and their body language will show signs of being almost completely distant from themselves and everyone else around them.

A lack of alertness and awareness, signs of fatigue, and a very different appearance and presence to their previous high level combative ready and willing status will be very apparent. Their previous on guard ready status in footing, stance and guard will have changed considerably, and the individual may well look like they are simply spent and their mind and senses are focused on something else.

The shoulders back and chest out, firm knees, ready footing, sharp eyed pre-and actions-on status may be no longer; however, they are still under their physiological and psychological effects of their post combative actions-on encounter. It is during this post encounter period that the combatant needs to be in a safe and risk-free environment. They need to be around comrades, friends or family who understand them and what they have experienced. They need to be away from any triggers that could cause them to adversely react.

To remain in a hostile environment post encounter while still under the effects of coming down from an actions-on situation can leave the combatant in a physically and psychologically weakened state. Under such conditions it is important that they are away from the threat situation that includes negative elements. They need to be given every opportunity to quietly come down from the effects of their experience in safe company.

They will be experiencing after-effects as a result of the parasympathetic nervous system. These effects in relation to emotions and feelings are psychologically draining, and often combatants have difficulty in not only dealing with the realities of their prior actions-on encounters and experiences, but also a feeling of difficulty in understanding exactly how they feel post encounter.

The last thing they need is to be around unsecured environments. I have personally seen individuals that look expressionless, have nothing to say and simply look blank and spent post actions-on encounters. Then there are others that are still experiencing the effects of hormonal dumping that are wired and can't stop talking about their experience.

As part of my combative code of conduct I highlight the risks of being in an unsafe environment after such actions-on experiences, in relation to external triggers that can set off a chain reaction of over or under reaction. I encourage my lads to stick together in their own safe environment away from outsiders and especially socialising with unknowns.

I encourage them to refrain from drinking alcohol or if they must have a social drink with their mates limit the amount of alcohol consumed. It is important that individuals understand that post actions-on encounters they are in a state of continued arousal physiologically for up to an hour, and psychologically they may be affected for many hours or days post encounter.

Some individuals with the blank and fatigued look, if in the wrong place may to a thug or bully, have a look of helplessness and be targeted. Others, while still in that increased state of arousal, may be easily agitated and react aggressively to adverse attention.

The buddy system is very important so that your mates know the likely affects you are experiencing, and can be a responsible influence keeping you away from potential triggers and dangers. You need to be around those that are trusted and can be trusted to take care of you, including pointing out potential risks and errors of your ways. While still aroused and possibly anxious and in an agitated state, it is important that you are in a safe environment away from external negative effects.

Being able to, in a quiet manner, come down from the high-level state of combative capability is essential. Some individuals will experience a feeling of emptiness, while others will consider the encounter to fall well below expectations depending on how formidable the threat was, and how quickly and easily it was neutralised.

The reality is a formidable, highly competent and confident combatant that neutralises their foe in seconds with over-kill controlled aggressive ease, may well consider the real life actions-on encounter far less demanding and intense than the high commitment and intensity of realistic battle handling exercises or intensive combative training. Nonetheless they will still be under the influence of post actions on effects from hormonal dumping and a status of sensory high level alertness.

Ensuring you come down and cool off in a safe and comfortable environment, where you can come to terms with your experience and then ensure you get rest relaxation and sleep, is the safest and best way to handle this coming down cooling off period.

In addition to avoiding negative external environments post actions-on, you also need to avoid the company of individuals who do not understand your post encounter status and your need for a quiet and safe recovery period. Individuals that are not understanding or accepting that you need to be in safe company in a safe place away from potential triggers should be avoided.

Military Physiology Mindset

Military base analogy of the CQC human body and mind:

- Headquarters - cranial cavity.
- Base – everything inside the outer body lines.
- Base CQC engine room -Torso
- Base external CQC force protection capabilities - The bodily extremities
- HQ external voluntary threat warning and signaling capability - Somatic nervous system.
- HQ internal involuntary threat determined reactionary responses capability-autonomic nervous system

- Base emergency ready reactionary force protection - Reptilian brain.
- Base commensurate emergency response threat neutralisation - Mammalian brain
- HQ strategic high level response task force - The Homo sapiens brain (neocortex)

Example:

Expected CQC actions-on encounter.

HQ and base all systems alert and ready.

Torso internal engine room and bodily extremities ready and willing to threat neutralise.

External voluntary threat detection signaling capability standing by.

Internal involuntary automatic reactionary capability initiated.

Base emergency ready reactionary force protection capability and basic commensurate threat response capability ordered to stand down by the HQ strategic high level response task force.

Mind and body ready, willing and able.

Constant sensory capabilities in ensuring adjustments in safety and security are made to provide maximum hard target capabilities.

Decided deliberate option confirmed and visualised.

Deliberate option set up tactics and skills including psychological requirements undertaken in unison.

Combatant ready willing and able to threat neutralise, range skill commitment primary status confirmed deliberate actions-on all systems go.

Mechanisms of self-preservation

Over more than thirty-five years I have observed many individuals in high stress situations. These individuals range from civilians to elite forces personnel. These situations include CQB/CQC training courses and test phase's toughener and sickener training, battle handling exercises, battle inoculation and familiarization with high risk, high stress encounters that identify a combatant's every individual reaction and action under such specific sudden aggressive shock action stimuli. This experience has provided a very good research source, as you cannot simply hide your psychological reactions, weaknesses and strengths under such sudden, aggressive, expected and unexpected shock action encounters.

The reality is that you can't cancel out completely, or change, human natural reactions to the stimulus of high-risk threats and sudden aggressive shock action or extreme danger. If you try to employ skills contrary to human natural reactions you may get away with it in a controlled unrealistic studio environment, or against a less than formidable enemy, but when in a foreign or very real, high risk, high stress threat environment and the first overwhelming danger indication is felt, human reactions replace any unnatural practice.

The Todd Systems, like the European military systems I have learnt from my former military combative Master Chief instructors, have been developed to have commonality with natural human reactionary responses to sudden aggressive shock action. They are very much logical, natural, correct responses and continuations of autonomic reactions to sudden aggressive actions. These mechanisms of human self-preservation, including flinching and increasing stability and resistance under threat, reduce risk and have commonality with making ready to employ combative offensive or counter-offensive actions. Increased safety through reduced target mass and increased stability, by centre of gravity dropping or lowering, ensures that the combatant is in a safer position and ready status to employ expedient actions that can be achieved through simple, deliberate continuations from the automatic human reaction flinch status to the ready position. Minor adjustments post the autonomic reactions to change stance, position, alignment, range and make ready to employ the decided combative option will be simple, easy, minor adjustments that will be obvious through prior training in regards to specific skills primary set up requirements. Such adjustments may occur naturally to the trained combatant that has executed thousands of repetitions of the employed skill in practice and be aided by muscle memory. Such an underlying subconscious automated skill adjustment process to achieve your maximum output, maintain stability and safety by such automated adjustments, can naturally occur in the execution of the skill for those that, through high repetition and factor-of-confusion type realism training like battle handling exercises, have developed the sense of understanding in regards to making major or minor adjustments to ensure maximum destructive contact is achieved.

Skills that increase target mass, reduce mobility or sacrifice stability have the complete opposite principles to battle-proven skills that have been developed, tested and proven in battle training. Such skills in battle are high risk, and reduce not only objective achievement but safe objective achievement. One, they oppose natural human mechanisms of self-preservation and two, even though they may have been practiced in a traditional or sporting environment, the reality of real life or death sudden aggressive shock action will usually override such non-primary non-combative practices by immediate autonomic reactionary responses of self-preservation.

There is a reason why your mechanisms of self-preservation override hobby- or sport-practiced actions when you are exposed or overwhelmed. That reason is because they are risky and could get you killed. Your subconscious mechanisms of self-preservation know the difference between what will increase your safety and what will increase danger.

If someone somehow managed to override natural human sympathetic reactions to the stimuli of sudden aggressive shock action in relation to self-preservation by employing dangerous methods, then they would really be increasing the risk of defeat by somehow instilling unsafe practices—probably by a lifetime's repetition of methods that could get them injured, wounded or killed. When you find yourself in a reactionary, natural position of human risk reduction and self-preservation, through autonomic reactive responses to sudden aggressive shock action danger, and this position is foreign to your primary practices, the risk is increased by not being proficient from such a real life reactionary status. Stalling or changing position and the realities of either having to execute your primary actions from an unfamiliar position, or taking the time to change position and extend the likelihood of being contacted, are negatives and could be fatal negatives.

It's much too late to find out when you most need primary methods and means of self-protection that your techniques simply are not effective against a formidable, ruthless aggressor or enemy that knows no rules, and is bound by no morals, code of conduct or ethics, and will show you no mercy.

Finding out under assault that your primary practices are negative practices in regards to risk reduction and achieving a primary ready-set-go counter engagement status will be devastating to say the least. Not being able to employ your primary proven skills from a natural status of human reactive self-preservation, and as such finding out that your primary practices are foreign and contrary to self-preservation, will leave you exposed and vulnerable. Anything other than primary practices that have been battle tested and battle proven for risk reduction, safety and fast objective achievement, and that have commonality and cohesion with normal natural human reactions to sudden aggressive shock action, simply reduce your capability of achieving your objective and, as such, maintaining personal safety.

Psychologically you must be prepared to do the unthinkable, endure adversity and override pain; combine this attitude and never-consider-defeat mentality with the best of battle-proven skills that have been honed through extreme high repetition training, including factor-of-confusion sudden aggressive shock action realistic battle handling exercises, and you are most capable of victory. Always remember that being physically adversely affected under assault, either injured, wounded or when you lose ground, or when you are decentralized or your balance and stability is compromised, is a psychological negative that can weaken not only your physical counter engagement capabilities, but also affect your inner resolve to protect yourself, regain control and neutralise your enemy.

The brain-to-boot combined physical and psychological components require constant physical as well as mind's eye checks, to maintain maximum safety, and a real time state of readiness. Keeping all your human senses alert, and by doing constant checks and re-checks, reduces the likelihood of the danger of your mind drifting into self-doubt or perception over tactical assessment and factual threat and situational determinations. Once you allow yourself to consider the enemy threat as undefeatable or focus on enemy strengths over their human biological weaknesses you are reducing your resolve considerably. If you have the slightest thought that you do not have the capabilities to neutralise the threat, then you are already all but defeated, and all but the victim. Threat and situational guessing over employing tactical assessments only adds to the risk and danger.

By employing primary tactics and practices of hard targeting and constantly remaining ready, willing and able, performing all the real time checks, re-checks and required adjustments, you will reduce the likelihood of dwelling in the negative realm of self-doubt and threat perception over tactically correct threat assessment. You will also ensure all the ready status physical foundations such as stability maintenance and a ready status for expedient action movement are maintained by a positive combative ground affinity footing status.

Making the D and being definite in your decision and steadfast in your inner resolve is important. It is equally as important, however, to be able to fast map on the move in real time remaining and being prepared, ready, willing and able to initiate constant fast mapping assessment, determine and decide changes and adjustments that provide the best, safest and most proven means to neutralise the threat.

While you must be definite in your decision making, you must also be ready and capable to execute contingency options to deal with changes in threat and situation. Maintain a flexible and willing attitude and demeanour in regards to dealing with changes in threat, and as such, making changes in your tactics and skills. Never underestimate your enemy or their capabilities, and employ any and every primary tactic and skill to neutralise their capabilities, never allowing yourself to rate or consider the enemy as undefeatable.

Overlook your enemy or aggressors features by focusing on their bodily mass or form, including their bodily extremities and actions over physical features, or known information such as reputation that can psychologically weaken your resolve. I personally had many street fights working the doors over more than two decades, and always believed that any aggressor was only as good as their last fight, and that fight was not against me, and that I was not going to fight them, but was going to neutralise them. I never took them on; I always stopped them and was prepared to do anything and everything to win.

Employing constant checks and re-checks of your personal position and state of readiness as well as your kit, weapons, the threat, situation and environment provides a high level of physical and psychological preparedness and willingness to do what you must do to neutralise the threat based on fact. I trained a large team of crowd controllers that never failed once in the achievement of the objectives, or were beaten in a single encounter, simply because they were combatively trained in tactically correct options for the role, duties and responsibilities. We trained together and worked together as a team, and made sure we were never beaten. This was at a time when most crowd controllers were individual fighters, or big lumps that really did not train in crowd control tactics to reduce risk to the lowest common denominator. We took our role and duty seriously, and anything less in any combative or self-defence situation is simply physically and psychologically unacceptable if you want the quickest quietest safest and most effective outcome in your favour. We also knew that the groups of thugs we faced were not made up of a full gang of highly trained combatants, and that once the King Pins were sorted, the less than formidable headed for the hills or were stopped with little resistance. Loyalty to one another, training, testing and working together employing the same individual tactics and skills as well as having set standard operating procedures (SOPs) and team formations, tactics and skills ensured the highest levels of confidence in oneself and fellow team members.

Going tactical and being combat ready, willing and able, and employing all the previous tactics, principles, checks and re-checks as a process acts as a constant reminder of the situation you are in, and the priority of remaining at peak readiness. It also reduces the opportunity to drift into self-doubt, anticipation or perceived threats over actual factual threats determined by factual tactically correct assessment.

Keeping your mind and body in a state of utter readiness will ensure your best combative chance at victory over defeat. The reality of the effects of extreme sudden aggressive shock action, violence or impending expected violence, where psychologically the combatant will experience the following autonomic reactive responses to facing such threats includes initial flinching and blinking as well as tremors, perspiration, feeling sick to the stomach an increased heart rate as well as breathing heavily. These are the realities of facing violent threats and will be addressed later in detail.

You may not be able to eliminate such reactions completely, so you must know how to deal with such realities by stopping such effects as soon as identified, or reducing the effects dramatically as quickly as possible. Such effects are usually experienced prior to an actions-on encounter immediately that the threat has been recognized or identified. They are usually experienced pre-actions-on, but can be experienced mid-encounter depending on stops and starts or lulls in action, or when an individual, rather than staying combative and pro-active, checks their injuries, wounds or simply gives up the fight mentally and becomes a static target. Psychological submission such as when decentralised and being assaulted on the ground, simply getting into a foetal position with no plan and execution of escape or counter engagement, can lead to the psychological effects or physical contact injuries that take away your means to neutralise the threat and leave you at the enemy's mercy. Allowing oneself to be put into and stay in such a state of helplessness is a combative negative, and if you cannot eliminate, reduce and control the effect of fear and your negative thoughts of helplessness are having upon you, you simply have no hope of threat neutralisation. The reality is that if you are feeling pain you are alive, and there is a good likelihood you have the physical capabilities to go combative but just need to know how to do so psychologically and skills wise.

First aid is important if you are wounded or injured but not while still under assault. To focus on wounds or injuries under assault makes you a static target and can weaken your resolve as a result of the visual effects of the wound or injury. The best rule is to go combative to escape or neutralise the threat then get medical treatment.

Similar effects can be experienced post encounter as pre-encounter when the realities of one's actions and the results of one's actions are clear. I have seen combatants endure extremes under test conditions and exceed their physical and mental capabilities considerably, and then on immediate post situation reflection go into a state of shock and virtual shut down. I enforce in my rank and file the importance of treating pre-encounter symptoms of fear and stress such as tremors and increased heart rate as positives in the sense that this is a warning sign that you are in a risky situation, and that you need to take actions to reduce the risk by immediately stopping or controlling such effects. These are natural human reactions, and a human that does not experience natural human reaction and emotions and claims to not experience fear is dangerous, not only to others, but also to themselves; such a person may well have a mental illness but is most likely a liar.

As an instructor I find it very frustrating when instructing drills or high risk skills in a controlled manner, at an enabling level when an individual states they are not capable of any other positioning, pulling or placement of skills other than fully contacting with the target.

My response is 'how many people have you killed or have you never had a fight?'. The reality is, controlled aggression provides capability to focus on contact with the target in relation to accuracy, power and velocity. I explain 'train and test the way you intend to combatively operate', but remember you are only training and testing on your enemy party training buddies. Keep the 75percent plus high commitment, aggressive contact for the enemy or safe and robust training equipment.

Both cowards and heroes are made of the same flesh, blood and bone. The only difference is that one has the ability to overcome their natural fears, psychologically and physically, and go combative while the other does nothing and is a victim of their own failure.

Whether it be going through a door and facing the unknown, or your senses in a high risk environment being alerted to subtle warnings of danger, you must use your trained mental and physical abilities to increase your chances of victory. The undeniable realities of being compromised, and the effects of unpredictable, unexpected sudden aggressive shock actions may well change some of the primary components execution order you need to employ, in relation to your required physical and psychological requirements needed to neutralise the specific threat.

The important order of major and minor combative required components such as immediate hard targeting, combative tactical respiration and visual assessment must always be components that are initiated immediately when the unexpected actions-on encounter is identified, or when first contact is experienced. The sooner combative respiration is initiated the better; this will keep in check psychological effects of fear, stress and sudden aggressive shock action. Combative respiration is a first consideration and component employment, unless taken by surprise and your automatic reactions to sudden aggressive shock action kick in, followed by your immediate initiation of physical skills to hard cover protect yourself. Under such an unexpected, immediate physical threat situation post your automatic self-preservation reactionary responses, your combative respiration would be initiated simultaneously with, or immediately after, your cover guarding before any counter engagement evasion, or stationery evasion, holding ground and self-protective hard targeting and counter actions.

Reaction over definite action

I hear many exponents and instructors proclaim that X amount of practice equates to skills capabilities that are reactionary. This is something that is debatable. Whereas human autonomic reactions to sudden aggressive shock actions born out of self-preservation are factual, I believe that in large part most combative skills employments will be decided, definite, deliberate actions in relation to the threat, and based on the individual combatant's decided means to neutralise the threat. That is not saying that muscle memory does not play a major role in the execution of decided deliberate combative skills executions. Muscle memory to me is more of a combination of cohesive proficiency, and combining the required skills and physical and psychological components correctly and in unison. Having a high proficiency level, and certainly mastering any skill, will increase the level of automation in the practice or execution of the skill, however it is the master of the skill that initially deliberately decides to execute the said skill. You could compare it to driving a car where you cannot always see where your wheels are in relation to the curb; however through driving competency as a result of repetitious employment you can control distance and proximity to the curb.

Simultaneous counter engagement, like counter reacting to a punch with a slip and punch or the like is a combination of deliberate action and muscle memory proficiency, but the reality is there is some degree of decision making in relation to the choice of reactionary counter. The reptilian and mammalian reactionary counter responses are the only true subconscious counter re-actions

Even in unexpected, immediate actions-on encounters post the flinching reaction, you will utilise your senses to identify the threat, make an immediate assessment and decide on your means of counter engagement or escape and evasion. The reality is though, the higher the level of repetition in practice, and the greater your exposure to realistic battle handling exercises and scenario training, the more capable you will be of quickly quietly and effectively neutralising the threat it however is still a deliberate decided action.

Primary point of focus combined with combative respiration requirements

The danger of visually focusing on the enemy threat only is that your ability to recognise additional threats, changes in situation, environmental risks or terrain hazards is reduced considerably or eliminated. The trained combatant must be able to employ point, as in the primary threat vision, and place, as in the immediate threat, surroundings and environment vision. Focusing on only the immediate enemy-presented danger combined with holding one's breath is a sure way to fall victim to tunnel vision and audio exclusion, and as such, increases the danger from not only the 'focusing only on the enemy' threat, but also obstacles, terrain, hazards and additional enemy threats and deprived respiration.

I have, on training phases and combative test phases, identified individuals that are fixated to the point of being unable to hear commands or warnings, see additional threats or assess, fast map and change their tactics and options to meet required changes in the threat situation. Interestingly individuals suffering from tunnel vision, audio exclusion and restricted respiration have difficulty in identifying or remembering a lot of information in relation to the actions-on situation, including their own combative actions. I have demonstrated many examples of this in relation to CQC. The usual demonstration on identifying a subject that fails to employ combative respiration, and is oblivious to audio instructions or warnings, focusing only on a singular threat and usually set on one means of dealing with the threat, is performed as follows:

On identifying this combatant, I will move in, and just out of his line of fixation but staying inside his 140 plus degrees of peripheral vision, make hand signal gestures or unusual subtle suspicious or definite actions including coming close to or even crossing his path. This can be combined with simple threat actions, like standing in a covert manner and then going for your pocket, or walking towards the combatant with your hands behind your back. I have also utilised assistants wearing brightly coloured clothing to be inside the combatant's normal 140 degrees of peripheral vision. After the combatant's execution of their decided skills I will ask them what additional factors they noticed leading up to, and during, the execution of their decided combative option.

To a great degree, they have difficulty in remembering anything other than the enemy target that they had concentrated their total line of vision or point of aim on. They often are unable to clearly detail on request their decided combative option execution, and often they can't even remember what specific option they executed, or any specific aspects or components of their skill execution. Standing on a 45 degree angle diagonally forward of them when they are supposed to have their senses at high alert ready to detect any definite or subtle movement or change in threat situation, and on making anything from masked covert, through to deliberate definite actions, signals or warnings is a great way to identify the individual combatant's actual state of readiness and awareness.

I have developed methods of enhancing a maintained state of readiness over the years of instructing to ensure that while exponents are practicing CQC, they remain ready, steadily alert and aware of what is going on around them as well as the primary threat. Simple distractive verbiage during combative training in relation to non-combative related subject matter, or cracking a joke during unarmed offensive assault and counter-offensive assault practice, is a means to keep the exponents' senses alert, open and focused on the primary point, being the enemy per, and the place, being the immediate environment. Sometimes I see that look on their face of 'why the hell is he going on about current affairs, sport or cracking a joke while we are training in CQC?' The confident tradesperson can multitask and remain aware of not only the job at hand, but also others around them and their surroundings by remaining focused and vigilant. The same or a similar requirement applies to the trained and capable combatant.

I have trained individuals in the past that have a tendency to blink in relation to subtle or direct actions targeted towards mostly, but not exclusively, their upper quadrants. The blinking of the eyelid is another automated mechanism of self-protection and self-preservation protecting the eyeball against penetration. I can assure you the twig that flicks towards your eye in the great outdoors is not a highly trained combatant, but by nature of the unexpected action (normally under or outside your peripheral vision), the speed of action and the size of the twig, your blinking eye lid becomes your last means of protection for your eyeball. While preventing blinking completely may not be possible and is not recommended, you certainly can in a combative situation, by inoculation training, reduce the tendency to blink to the extent of repetitious blinking. I utilise methods of focus on other components of CQC rather than directly trying to instill in the combatant the need to reduce and control involuntary blinking.

Give the combatant another task to focus on, or by starting with slow, low intensity threats in high repetition practice, and only increasing the speed and intensity when the individual becomes accustomed to the level and comfortable with the action this will make the threat stimuli feel more routine or normal, and can have effects such as reduction in blinking. I utilise a volleyball, soccer ball or basketball contained between the combatant's cover guard during cover guarding and deflection practice, to test and true their cover guard capabilities.

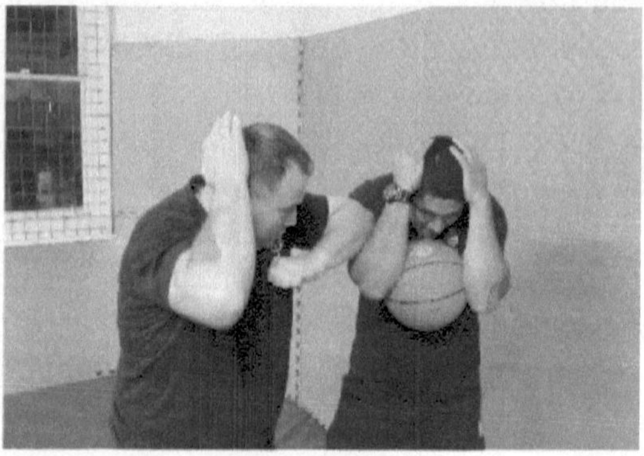

Utilising a ball for safety competency and confidence enhancement in hard cover guarding

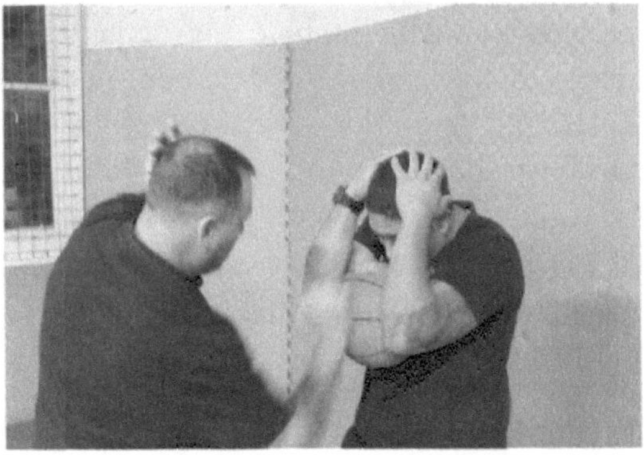

The requirement is that the combatant must focus on keeping the cover guard in place, retaining the ball between their forearms against their chest and under their chin. Reminding them to execute combative respiration every time they cover against or deflect a strike, and now the major focus is on the previous components being maintained, and the visual components become mandatory recognition of the striking limb and its incoming direction of travel. The stress and fear factors, to a considerable degree, have been reduced or removed from focusing on the threat and means of countering the threat, by the inclusion of the ball and needing to retain it in position. I have achieved excellent results through starting out at slow speed and low intensity with slapping roundhouse actions against the cover guard, and controlled palm striking actions inside the cover guard, utilising combative sighting between the cover guarding forearms to detect incoming strikes that need to be deflected. The focus on maintaining retention of the ball in position with the cover guard, and the safety aspects of the contact being against the ball having little adverse effect on the subject, improves visual focus and controls effects such as blinking by distraction, in relation to having to consistently focus on the requirements of cover guarding and retaining the ball combined with deflection.

I'm often asked to describe the difference between in general terms the civilians I train and the elite forces personnel I train. My answer is that the elite forces personnel that I have trained from around the world have a high level of expertise in a wide range of tactical specialist skill sets and they self-select through their ability to be able to maintain high levels of control in extremely high risk situations. I explained they can, under the multiple effects of special operations or battlefield close combat encounters, perform their required individual and team tactics with the factor of confusion ever present. The sound of live fire and muzzle flashes all around them, including the effects of close proximity explosions must be overcome, and tactics and skills employed while load bearing.

Being able to listen through an earpiece, speak in a microphone if required while assessing on the move, evaluating information and making tactically correct decisions under life-and-death threatening situations requires a very special and skilled individual. Basically, apart from being highly skilled in a wide range of specialist subjects, they have a high level of inner resolve and intestinal fortitude, and a commitment to objective achievement that makes them very special indeed. While many athletes in the civilian world are extremely high achievers in their chosen sport or sports, the difference is that special operations personnel have high levels of expertise in a wide range of specialist tactical and combative subjects.

I regularly instruct on the effects of stress and fear to wide ranging sectors of society, including advising of the importance of keeping adrenaline and endorphins under control especially in expected actions-on situations. Failing to do so can lead to nervous reactions such as smiling or uncontrolled shaking, involuntary bowel motions or urinating under extreme threat situations. Freezing in place being incapable of self-preservation or escape and evasion are common realities of allowing the effects of fear, stress and the release of adrenaline and endorphins to overcome your ability to assess, decide and execute a means to neutralise the threat situation. The realities of adrenaline dumping as a result of a high risk encounter is that there is a risk of an immediate overload of information via your senses that can, in turn, result in total focus on the threat, and as such, reduce your 140 degrees of peripheral vision capabilities, perhaps all the way to tunnel vision, making it difficult to identify additional threats.

Audio exclusion is something that I see all too often on basic courses initially, where under combat milling or pugil stick fighting, exponents simply cannot hear instructor commands, even with a megaphone or the sound of a piercing whistle. Freezing in place removes the ability to execute expedient, evasive escape or combative action by leaving the subject flat-footed with extreme tension throughout the musculoskeletal framework to the point of virtual paralysis.

The effects of expected actions-on situations where time and distance can work against you psychologically by focusing on your enemy strengths over identifying enemy weaknesses and targets to be destroyed, as well as anticipating or perceiving negative effects or outcomes, all stand to weaken the combatant's inner resolve and intestinal fortitude. Highly trained military combatants, through selection, training, testing and importantly battle handling exercises and operational experience, become well aware of the necessity to go tactical and employ controlled, ruthless, deliberate aggression, and never allow the effects of sudden aggressive immediate shock action or impending actions-on encounters to adversely affect their ability to maintain the highest levels of combined physical and psychological capabilities.

Some effects can be minor such as feeling dry in the mouth or sweating. Through exposure to the stimuli, the effects of impending probable and delayed exposure of aggressive shock action can be experienced, and the means to overcome or manage such effects need to be employed. Instruction from experts in military close combat that provide factual information and controlled exposure to the effects of such threats and threat situations, combined with training in the best means to eliminate or control such effects will ensure the combatant is not overwhelmed by such adverse effects. Confidence will be increased once the experienced effects can be controlled, and as a result, tactics and skills competency maintained at the highest level individually humanly possible.

My instructors always told me that natural bodily produced endorphins were many times stronger than morphine. They said that adrenaline, like we employed it to prevent bleeding, provided a natural means of wounds bleeding control. The physiological and psychological reasoning behind the medical facts in relation to the central nervous system human hormones and mechanisms of identifying danger, transmitting messages and initiating sympathetic reactions followed by the required deliberate decision-making, overcoming the effects of the situation and executing combative or escape and evasion, are indeed complex in reasoning.

The practices needed to control the effects (e.g., adrenaline dumping) of aggressive, violent, high risk situations are simple, and by understanding the warning signs and employing simple control measures immediately, you will be able to achieve and maintain your primary state of combative readiness over losing your control of the situation.

The human body is an amazing machine in relation to providing capabilities to perform and achieve in high risk high stress situations. Extreme physical actions including physical strength exceeding an individual's normal capabilities and expedient dynamic speed of movement and physical skills employments can be employed, and objectives can be achieved against adversity and formidable enemies. Simply by means of threat triggered reactions, responses and deliberate decisions being made as a result of careful assessment, maximum physical combative capabilities can be achieved.

The human body also has the amazing ability to produce and deliver natural painkillers in endorphins, when and where they are needed, and in the dose needed to overcome the pain of the wound or injury at that immediate point in time. This gives a combatant the ability to continue with the achievement of their objective. I have spoken with soldiers that have been wounded in combat and they have conveyed to me the fact that at the time they were wounded (and some seriously wounded), apart from an immediate initial sharp hot or hard hitting impact sensation, the extent of the wound was not fully apparent to them. Some were amazed, on receiving post-contact medical treatment, at the extent of their wounds or injuries in relation to the level of pain at the time the wound or injury was inflicted. They also were clear that through prior training and realisation of the effects of wounds, especially post actions-on, the effects were not foreign and they knew and understood the realities and likely outcomes. Being instructed by and speaking with veterans who explained the realities of when they were wounded in relation to bodily reactions, changes and functions, ensured soldiers were armed with knowledge and a sound understanding of what was happening to them, and as such, it was not unknown territory. The kind of relief of pain the body produced immediately on being wounded was described in line with instructors' words, as superior even to morphine. They were very clear that once they were out of immediate actions-on danger the increase in pain could be considerable

The Flinch Reaction

The flinch factor is something that from as early as I can remember, I identified as a common reaction to shock action, whether it be without warning, or to a lesser degree when in a state of readiness. Obviously the degree of flinch reaction is reduced when in the state of readiness, especially if the enemy actions do not threaten one's safety to a major degree.

The first reality of the flinch factor against unannounced, instantaneous shock action post flinch is a fraction of a second's hesitation, possibly immediate shock or disbelief. Call it what you want, but there will be a post automatic flinch reaction, and if the threat contact is immediate, there will be physical self-preservation responsive defence/hard targeting and a fraction of a second's time lapse. This is when you must initiate tactical, controlled combative respiration immediately or simultaneously, before assessing the nature, extent and direction of the threat and determining and employing your decided action.

The flinch is a natural human reaction to sudden aggressive sudden shock action that is best described as an involuntary automatic self-preservation reaction. Components of the flinch may include blinking, tensing, dropping your centre of gravity and in the span of an instant, opening all your senses in an effort to determine not only the threat and its location but also your best means of neutralising it. Changes in posture, lowered centre of gravity, employing your arms and hands as protection or for improving your balance are all common characteristics of the flinch. In extreme threat situations such as explosions, the flinching and dropping of one's centre of gravity may be continued to ground decentralisation.

Through training in the best of battle-proven tactically correct options in a spontaneous actions-on encounter the combatant can reduce the effects of sudden aggressive shock action and decrease the time lapse between the initial shock factor, the assessment and decision making phases, and the employment of the decided option.

Post flinch factor decided options are not always offensive enemy engagements, and may well be evasive or escape actions depending on the assessment of the threat, and taking the best and safest option in relation to the threat and objectives.

By training in physical skills that have commonality with the reactionary direction and characteristics of the flinch that reduce target mass, increase stability and achieve a cocked position, ready to deliver expedient action, you increase your chance of combative threat neutralisation. Human self-preservation reactions must have commonality with autonomic reactions to sudden aggressive shock action.

The flinch factor, a natural human reaction, will be clearly apparent in battle handling exercises training, if such exercises are realistic and include a high level of sudden surprise shock action. In an immediate actions-on encounter you may well be reacting to sudden aggressive shock action that can be initiated as a result of one or more of the following triggers: a flash of colour, sudden movement, or sound.

In a high stress situation where you are in a ready status you will have a higher level of alertness and chance of early threat detection. Even in an expected actions on encounter, a degree of deliberate response will be an automatic involuntary reaction to this sudden aggressive shock action. The subconscious reaction combined with the conscious response will more than likely make you physically flinch, crouch move out of the kill zone or even fall to the ground depending on the level of the sudden shock action as previously outlined. In some cases it will be an initial automatic reaction immediately followed by a physical decision to continue with the initial responsive action in relation to the threat. Take for example, when unaware, the involuntary flinching in the face of an unexpected explosion. The initial reaction would most likely be one of flinching statically or away from the blast in reaction to the sound of the explosion. An immediate simultaneous continuation of the flinch in relation to the initial sound and the possible feel of the ground tremble and blast may well be a continuation to a crouch position, making oneself a smaller target or possibly throwing oneself to the ground or scrambling for cover.

In an unexpected assault where the impact of contact knocks you off balance, your subconscious reactions can include both flinching and crouching down and away from the contact combined with an instantaneous decision to resist decentralisation and hard cover guard.

If the assault momentum is high a deliberate panic decision might be made to self-decentralise out of helplessness, increasing risk and danger of being static on the ground under assault. The confident competent combatant will employ a deliberate decision to resist recover and counter engage or escape and evade. The contact impact force and the combative capability of the combatant and their inner resolve will determine their deliberate decision making and decided option employment.

Exploiting human reactions and responses

There are sensitive parts of the human anatomy that if targeted on a majority of individuals will achieve a common subconscious reaction and deliberate responses. In the ancient sport of Greco-Roman wrestling, 'tweaking' employed to improve the chances of securing a primary grip as part of a lifting maneuver is well-known. Simply digging the finger tips in below the belly and above the pelvic bowl area will often get an immediate up and away movement from the digging action, and this will enable the wrestler to secure an underbelly compound grip.

Post tackling an opposition player by applying downward palm pressure on the tailbone and by positioning the tips of the bent fingers immediately behind the anus, prevents easy footing recovery and reduces the likelihood of the tackled player reversing out of the post tackle secure position.

There are some reactions and responses that can be effectively achieved by targeting and exploiting delicate vitals including the genitals and eyes as part of the setup of decided combative options employments. A surprise slap or strike to the genitals can effectively cause the subject to bend forward, moving them closer to the ground and into a position where specific combative skills can be employed.

In the execution of some combative skills where the enemy is employing methods to prevent the skill being employed, having an understanding of how to create a reaction that will open them up to your specific skill employment is advantageous. Often by targeting a delicate life-support or intensive pain generating bodily target your enemy may well cease in their efforts as a result of their mind following the effects of pain and their efforts will be directed at stopping the pain.

Individuals who have phobias or adverse reactions to targeting of the genitals, closing off the airway, or executing other dirty or deadly actions may, as a result, panic allowing their primitive reptilian reactions to take charge. Similarly, they can be overcome by such effects to the point of panic, responding with other than controlled aggressive deliberate combative skills, which will reduce their chances of threat neutralisation. Unceremoniously pulling down the enemy's pants, or pulling out their genitalia, will certainly invoke definite reactions and responses that can take the fight out of anyone lacking in the capabilities to neutralise the enemy, or overcome their fears or phobias in relation to such actions.

The trained combatant, as well as being knowledgeable in the medical aspects in relation to CQC and the most important psychological enhancement practices, will also be well aware of how to exploit weaknesses in relation to delicate bodily vitals or exploiting body mechanics by leverage. What I am saying is that you can interfere with even a determined aggressor's intentions by exploiting soft targets, and you can take away most of their body weight advantages by exploiting soft targets.

Combative stress positions are a perfect example of an immediate and effective means of preventing enemy combative actions by exploiting body mechanics that relay the danger or helplessness of the situation to the central nervous system. The central nervous system, identifying that there is an extreme risk or the likelihood of the loss of life or limb if the enemy resists or goes combative, will cause the vulnerable enemy to go into static lockdown. The sympathetic reaction often seen in relation to such combative stress positions of helplessness and hopelessness is what I call the death kick, where the extremities give a minor reactive kicking motion, as if to indicate a final reaction and determination of no means of reducing or preventing the threat.

In unarmed combat, often weapons are used to render the enemy helpless of self-preservation, and helpless in preventing the setup of the fatal finishing armed skill employment. The terminology 'disarm, disable, dispose' applies to a formidable enemy that cannot be neutralised with a single primary disposal action, but must be relieved of their combative counter capabilities and incapacitated by disarming and disabling prior to elimination. The understanding of skills that will definitely incapacitate or eliminate the enemy if deliberately and correctly applied is psychologically empowering, and increases the individual combatant's mental toughness by belief in the skills they possess to threat neutralise combined with the knowledge of the human weaknesses of the enemy target.

Having knowledge of the medical implications of CQC, knowing how to target and destroy enemy capabilities by means of an aggressive confident demeanour provides the combatant with increased chances of objective achievement enhanced by mental conviction and combative competency.

I have heard people speak before of Fairbairn's 'blood clock' in his books being medically incorrect in relation to timings. This is because they are looking at it from a civilian perspective in an environment where access to immediate medical attention may well be possible. Col Rex Applegate, the World War II combative pioneer responsible for training OSS operatives in World War II worked closely with Fairbairn and his assistant Sykes, and he told me the following:

The blood clock timeline determinations were decided in relation to the battlefield and the time the combatant would be able to maintain life prior to falling victim to fatal wounding effects without immediate emergency medical treatment. While the individual may not expire in 30 to 60 seconds and it may well take 3 to 4 minutes, the reality on the battlefield is that without immediate emergency medical assistance after those 30 to 60 seconds the likelihood of self-surviving would be unlikely in relation to fatal wounding. This is just another example of the power of combative knowledge, medically, combatively, physically and psychologically. Knowledge combined with mental toughness provides the individual with the highest combative chance of winning and objective achievement; nothing more, nothing less. Conversely, not being armed with knowledge and not having a high level of inner resolve considerably reduces the chance of threat neutralisation and saving one's life.

Multiple movements per single respiration cycle

It is possible, once proficiency has been achieved, to execute multiple strikes per every CQC respiration cycle. Two or three strikes can be executed per respiratory cycle depending on the combatant's physical capabilities. Inhale via the nose a single intake immediately prior to your skills employment, and employ an evenly split flow exhale cycle in relation to the number of strikes. Time-wise, combative respiration should comprise of 1 to 2 seconds in the inhale component of the respiration cycle and 3 to 5 seconds on the exhale component of the respiration cycle.

Be sure to employ controlled and regulated power and velocity output, ensuring each strike is approximately 75 percent of your maximum capabilities, but less than 100 percent to ensure controlled aggression is maintained, and to reduce the likelihood of being countered through telegraphing your action. 100 percent fully committed actions can not only telegraph your intention, but increase the risk of injury if you miss your target—and on missing the target you are vulnerable and exposed to counter assault.

Over-cocking and telegraphing in the setup and execution phases of striking, respectively, increase the likelihood of failure to achieve your objective. I have seen, in prize fighting, a fighter dislocate his shoulder through overcommitted overextension—rendering himself temporarily incapacitated as a result. Always execute your strikes from the small squat through full squat and ground upwards and outwards setup execution to ensure your strikes are powered by your full body commitment. Employing multiple strikes per single CQC respiration cycle, with every strike being executed with a small squat, will increase power and velocity and also reduce risk by ensuring during the execution of the multiple strikes that you are not a static target. Multiple strikes per CQC respiration cycle that include only an initial small squat executed with the first strike and then the second and third strikes being executed from a more upright status, have less power and velocity being thrown from a more static upright stance, than from the small through full squat ready-set-go upward and outwards strike enhancement option. Multiple strikes per single CQC respiration cycle, including the small squat incorporated with every strike, combined with a non-striking arm sound cover guard, reduces risk considerably and as such increases psychological confidence in the striker's capabilities to safely achieve the desired objective.

Stamp kicking requires a single CQC respiration cycle per stamp kick. The reason for this is that the legs carry the body's weight, and it requires considerably more physical effort and time to load and execute a kicking action over a striking action. Making range, setting up, loading and executing your stamp kick requires considerably more physical input and output than striking, and as a result requires a single complete respiration cycle per stamp kick action. The inhale respiration component is executed simultaneously with the small to medium squat stamp kick execution set up, and the exhale respiration component of the cycle is executed entirely throughout the stamp kick execution. The level of the exhale component of the respiration cycle should be an even flow throughout the stamp kick execution, to ensure controlled aggressive output is maintained from the ready-set-go timing in relation to the small to medium squat status, through to the completion of the stamp kick execution. Mind and body work in unison, ensuring controlled combative respiration to achieve maximum controlled aggressive output.

It is important that you do not try and execute more strikes per combative respiration cycle than you are physically capable of, or that you do not throw a volley of strikes that consist of over and underpowered individual strikes. Controlled, even, aggressive output powered by controlled, even, combative flow cycled respiration are required to ensure your best chance of objective achievement, the maintenance of your highest levels of safety and the important ingredient of psychological confidence in your striking capacities. Knowing your strikes are executed with controlled, aggressive cohesion and belief in yourself and in the capabilities of your strikes is psychologically empowering. Your single combative respiration flow cycle in relation to the execution of stamp kicks will ensure the stamp kick is also executed with controlled, committed aggression. The confidence in your stamp kick capabilities from high repetition and varied situations scenario training, utilising the same set up and execution ready-set-go practices, combined with your controlled combative cycled respiration will build confidence in your stamp kick capabilities and your ability to safely and effectively neutralise the threat.

Combative controlled respiration flow cycles in relation to striking and stamp kicking are very important not only for achieving controlled 75 percent plus output, but also for maintaining physical capabilities in relation to formidable threats or changing situations where continued combative actions are required to neutralise the threat. The employment of controlled, aggressive, cycled combative respiration will enable you to continue to execute combative actions at 75 percent plus commitment for extended periods of time. Multiple strikes per single combative respiration cycle can also include range maintaining or closing range foot work. Fast mapping on the move to ensure you continue to not only employ all the respiratory components off the ready-set-go small through full squat setup execution, but also maintaining your momentum and making range, comes with proficiency. Such proficiency by means of fast mapping and making adjustments on the move, combined with the execution of skills and timing in relation to controlled combative flow cycled respiration, increases your chances of objective achievement and ensures you maintain your highest levels of physical capabilities should you be required to continue your combative actions to neutralise the threat. Multiple strikes per combative flow respiration cycle should never leave you short of breath if you are executing such skills within your physical capabilities.

Confidence in your capabilities will demand that your strikes are within your repetitions capabilities in relation to maintaining your physical capabilities and achieving 75 percent upwards controlled aggressive committed output. Always employ the repetitions in relation to your physical capabilities and in relation to the threat neutralisation requirements. Maintaining physical capabilities requires cycled combative respiration made up of striking numbers within your physical capabilities. You can execute multiple combative strikes, 1 to 3 strikes per combative respiration cycle. Executing more strikes than you're physically capable of will only serve to deplete your physical capabilities and as such can cause weakening of your psychological capabilities. Operating within your 75 percent plus commitment and the number of strikes per combative respiration flow cycle in relation to your physical combative capabilities will enable the setting and maintaining of a primary combative status. The same 75 percent plus 'controlled combative flat line output level' applies to all combative output throughout the execution of any threat neutralisation—enabling continued and maintained primary physical and psychological capabilities.

Sensory reduction

Over several decades as the Chief Combative Instructor at the Todd Group (formally the Baldock Institute) I have conducted research observations of exponents I have trained in relation to the effects of shock, fear and stress in relation to combative actions-on encounters.

There are definite positive advantages in relation to autonomic system reactions in actions-on encounters when they are recognized and regarded as early warning signals. The result of such threat stimuli reactions, if known and understood, combined with the brain-to-boot tactics and skills to control or eliminate adverse effects, can enable proponents to quickly achieve a primary combative ready status. These effects or warning signals if not controlled can be definite negatives, reducing combative physical and psychological levels.

After conducting my own observations and research I spoke with my now late instructor and first combative mentor Harry Baldock—a pioneer of military unarmed combat, combat sports physical culture and physiotherapy. My findings were in line with his, which dated from the 1920s right up until the 1980s.

I was putting exponents through rigorous intake intensive training and grueling testing phases year in, year out combined with training regular force and elite forces personnel in CQB/CQC, giving me considerable and excellent research opportunities. I had noticed under battle handling exercises and training, some exponents would not only get tunnel vision and audio exclusion, but also their cognitive skills capabilities were dramatically affected under extreme shock, high stress conditions, including when affected by fear. While audio exclusion and tunnel vision were two commonly recognized effects of shock, fear and stress, they were very much considered to be individual effects.

I have observed individuals under high stress and sudden aggressive shock action encounters who, when the individual's line of vision becomes fixated on one point of focus (that being the primary enemy threat), were affected by audio exclusion, and their cognitive and physical combative capabilities were considerably reduced. In some cases, the individual's senses of balance and feel in relation to maintaining a ground affinity or stability recovery, respectively, were also compromised.

During my research, I would conduct pre-actions-on testing while the candidates were unaffected by any fear, stress or physical fatigue. I would have them undertake coordination, accuracy, stability and combative physical skills executions, measuring their performance levels. I found undertaking this research covertly was far better than if the individuals were aware they were being used as lab rats. The candidate's performance would then be measured under extreme, sudden aggressive shock actions-on encounters as well as post encounters. The evaluation would include measuring differences in their combative physical and cognitive capabilities, which could then be compared to pre-actions-on and full actions-on findings.

There was a dramatic reduction in visual and audio awareness, especially in relation to their immediate situation and environment outside of the immediate enemy threat. Even more concerning was when candidates allowed the actions-on encounter to overwhelm them to the point of reduced sensory capabilities, and their threat neutralisation decision making was very slow, one-dimensional, and often lacked in the required physical and psychological components execution levels to be effective.

Over the years of being involved with combat sports I have seen many coaches screaming and yelling instructions at their charges, simply because the contestant becomes single-minded and single-focused on their opponent to the point of being oblivious to anything else. Often they were unaware of the out zone on the mat, could not recognise their errors, were oblivious to the referee and simply could not hear the coach's instructions. They even had difficulty in understanding the referee's simple instructions and their facial expressions were that of confusion. When the stress of the match exceeded limits they could handle, they often performed considerably below their capabilities. When they were completely overwhelmed and overcome by the opposition, they often resorted to mimicking their opponent's actions.

I personally considered this to be a sign of being psychologically affected by the match and their opponent to the point where they recognise and accept that they are losing. They then make the subconscious decision to mimic their opponent's moves as they consider them superior to their own.

Similarly with combative test phases and battle handling exercises, I see individual exponents unable to hear instructor's commands and instructions, as well as being unable to recognise environmental hazards as a result of being fixated on the enemy party. Their usual training competency and confidence levels are dramatically reduced.

My findings were that all sensory capabilities were reduced and affected by fear, stress and shock, if the individual combatant did not know how to eliminate or control and manage such affects.

In highly confident and competent exponents, I found the initial effects of sudden aggressive shock action, through the brain-to-boot provided training, could be controlled or completely eliminated. In these proficient exponents the brain-to-boot training kicked in to make the situation and threat very clear to the point of seeming like slow motion.

Some exponents experienced a feeling of having been there and done this before, which I put down to the extremely high repetition training, including a high level of exposure to very realistic, unpredictable, aggressive shock action training.

I have read that some people consider seeing everything in slow time accompanied by a sense of having being here and done this before as a weakness. I cannot understand why, when this status is a testament to having all the required attributes to identify and neutralise the real time threat by primary means that are proven and provide a sense of familiarity. I have identified that it is in fact a complete positive as a result of the individual combatant being highly trained, and familiar and accustomed to sudden aggressive shock action encounters.

To be able to control your sensory capabilities from condition overload, and your autonomic nervous system from reducing or eliminating your combative capabilities, you must achieve a state of mental and physical unison. This status will enable you to set and maintain a state of readiness and willingness to go combative. This primary combative status will enable clear threat recognition and identification, through the processing of bits of information without system overload. The combatant that experiences their training kicking in under aggressive shock, actions-on encounters, making everything clear and controllable, has achieved a high level of combative competency and confidence capabilities.

The brain-to-boot package is about recognising the warning or danger signals, controlling or eliminating the effects of these warning signals, and utilising combative physical and psychological practices in a correct order while maintaining the highest levels of mental toughness and physical combative capabilities.

While the adverse effects of the early identification warnings of risk and danger need to be controlled or eliminated, it is very important that your sensory capabilities are maintained at a primary 'on' level to assist with not only the primary threat neutralisation but also in the identification of additional threats hazards and dangers. This includes conducting mind's eye and visual checks of not only the enemy threat, but also the entire threat situation and environment.

Utilising all your senses to undertake threat and situational related checks and re-checks is a very positive means to ensure your sensory capabilities are activated and remain at a state of primary alertness and awareness.

By utilising the brain-to-boot physical and psychological practices, commencing with combative respiration to control the effects of shock, fear and stress, the individual combatant will be able to recognise and identify the threat specifics, and decide on and execute primary threat neutralisation as quickly as is humanly possible, thereby reducing delay time. This immediate recognition and setting of a state of combative readiness and willingness, combined with employing combative tactics and actions at approximately 75 percent of full commitment, enables the combatant on threat recognition and identification to reach and maintain a state of primary combative capability quickly and for extended duration, if required.

This deliberate controlled flat line or level of combative capability needs to be maintained. The recommended 75 percent plus commitment level assists in maintaining control over psychological and physiological effects as well as providing extended combative endurance capabilities if required against a formidable foe in a prolonged actions-on encounter. Combative skills-wise, by the employment of gross motor skills that require less pinpoint accuracy and provide considerably more threat neutralisation capabilities than required to neutralise even a formidable enemy, combined with the brain-to-boot psychological enhancement practices, the individual combatant's chances of threat neutralisation are considerably increased.

When we face sudden aggressive shock actions-on situations, our sensory capabilities are often operating at overload, sending to and receiving bits of information from our brains, as well as dumping hormones that have a major effect on immediate threat recognition identification, threat neutralization decision making, and decided combative options employment capabilities.

The more mentally prepared and physically combatively capable the individual combatant is, the lesser the effects of shock, fear and stress will be, and the quicker the combatant will put in place measures to reduce or eliminate the effects and confidently go combative.

The brain-to-boot combative respiration is the first and most important component of controlling or eliminating the effects of fear and stress, including high level effects in sudden aggressive shock action extreme violence encounters.

The normal human resting heart rate of 50–80 bpm is not practical in a high threat, self-defence or combative situation. So, being able to control the heart rate to around 100 bpm will ensure effective employment of battle-proven gross motor skills that, at 75percent plus commitment, provide effective threat neutralisation of the most formidable foe. I refer to this as the ‘controlled combative flat line level’, essential to the required output under extremes and with the reality of required combative endurance being a possibility in an extreme combative encounter against a formidable foe. The competency and proficiency of the combatant in the brain-to-boot practices to overcome the immediate effects of sudden aggressive shock action, recognise and identify the threat, and employ commensurate threat neutralisation, is what makes the highly trained, aware, ready and willing combatant far different from his hunter-gatherer ancestors or lesser trained fighters with low-level intestinal fortitude.

Controlled combative respiration immediately on threat recognition and identification will reduce the combatant’s heart rate, keeping them in the medium to gross motor skill primary actions-on combative skills controlled primary flat line output range.

When the heart rate is between 100 and 120 bpm, gross motor skills capabilities are manageable, especially for short duration threat neutralisation for the physically capable combatant. Maintaining this higher heart rate level for extended periods of time against a formidable foe will, however, have considerable negative physical effects that, as a result, increase psychological negative effects and can weaken the combatant's inner resolve.

The higher the heart rate is allowed to increase above 145 bpm, the more dramatic the negative effects will be. These effects will not be singular sensory reduction, but will include all senses being affected, reducing the combatant's awareness, alertness, physical capabilities, motor skills and mental resolve.

The brain-to-boot package enables fast mapping, threat recognition identification and the implementing of physical and psychological practices in a correct order of execution and in unison that will prevent or reduce negative effects, including providing reduction of the timeframe between threat recognition, going combative and threat neutralization.

The importance of utilising gross motor skills over fine to medium motor skills applies not only to offensive and counteroffensive actions, but also to economy of movement in remaining aligned to an enemy target.

Pivoting and adjusting footwork to stay aligned to your enemy, combined with gross motor skill 75 percent plus over-kill destructive combative actions, reduces the need for pinpoint accuracy.

Under my combative research, simple accuracy, coordination, physical output, as well as awareness and alertness capabilities were reduced considerably when compared with the same individual's capabilities in situations such as training or practice, where they were not affected by shock, fear and stress.

The hunter-gatherer needs to be trained in the most primary and proven combative threat neutralisation skills, and must be accustomed to sudden aggressive shock action training, in order to be confident and competent to neutralise a formidable threat in a real-life actions-on encounter. They need to know how to quickly recognise and identify the threat, utilise their brain-to-boot skills to control and enhance psychological and physical capabilities to set their primary flat line deliberate controlled level of combative capabilities output. Doing so ensures that they can effectively neutralise even formidable threats under extremes and go combative for a continued duration if required.

Arming the combatant with knowledge in relation to understanding the psychological and physiological effects of shock, fear and stress, combined with providing the means to control or eliminate such effects, and through fast mapping, threat assessment and threat neutralization decision making, the duration between threat recognition and immediate actions-on threat neutralization execution can be reduced to the lowest level humanly possible. The combatant then has the best combative chance of threat neutralization.

My research was conducted under wide ranging threat levels, under extremely realistic conditions and in some very tough and demanding environments. Utilising stimuli such as darkness, disorientation, exposure to a high level of the factor of confusion, as well as high-risk and constantly changing violent threats identifies the combatant's real capabilities. Negative realities of facing and overcoming such violent encounters and extreme effects can dictate outcomes considerably if the combatant is not well trained and accustomed to such realities.

Even some of the most physically capable fighters, athletes and sports persons, under such dire adverse combative conditions facing such extreme threats, find that their physical and psychological sporting capabilities are not what is required to combatively neutralise a formidable violent foe that knows no rules. They find that their less than battle-proven, competitive physical and mental capabilities deteriorate quickly. The neutralisation of extreme violence requires a specific and specialist combative psychological skill set to enable fast, efficient threat neutralisation and maintained combatant safety.

Knowledge is power and arming the willing and capable combatant with knowledge will enhance their capabilities. They must understand how shock, fear and stress work and how it affects them, as well as how to control and manage the effects and maintain a deliberate primary combative flat line level of threat neutralisation capability. They must understand the effects and side-effects of facing extreme violence before, during and post actions-on encounters. They must have experienced the most realistic of training where anything and everything can be expected at any time.

They must also be able to take control and employ deliberate psychological and physical tactics and skills under extreme conditions, and in the face of sudden aggressive shock actions-on encounters.

There are many individuals that are physically capable and have high-level traditional martial arts or fighting arts training, but have never experienced sudden aggressive shock action where they have to manage their psychological and physical self, and take control of the situation and neutralise the threat.

The side foetal position; consciously and subconsciously

The side foetal like positioning employed during decentralisation is a means of immediate self-protection and self-preservation. This is because it being part of CQC side falling reduces ground impact and enables quick recovery. It not only increases deliberate combative action to reduce risk, thereby increasing safety, but also enables continuation of cohesive counter engagement.

Combative side falling and CQC rolling has been developed to not only reduce ground impact to major bodily vitals, but also to protect primary weapons during decentralisation and recovery. Preventing the muzzle being driven into the dirt, or an edged weapon causing self-injury during a falling or rolling and recovery movement is vital in CQC/CQB. The retention of weapons is also increased with decentralisation skills that enhance weapon retention, and weapon safety, through commonality of position and movement.

The important thing about deliberate falling and rolling in relation to your bodily positioning in a side foetal position is that it is an immediate temporary status only. Risk is increased considerably on the ground while under assault, both through increased duration of assault and the potential for more enemy pers to join in on the assault.

Immediate effective recovery and counter engagement, or ground evasion as part of recovery, counter engagement or escape and evasion, must be cohesive immediate continuations.

The side foetal position, correctly employed with a rocking motion, transfers ground impact from the side of your boot along the side of your body line to your outer buttocks to the outside back of your mid to lower shoulder blade. This side falling and rocking action keeps the nape of your neck, back of your skull and your spinal column away from ground impact.

Having confidence in your capabilities to safely and effectively fall on difficult terrain, reducing the risk of any injury other than soft tissue bruising type injury, enables counter engagement without hesitation.

One of the important factors of combative falling and rolling is the ground skimming action; falling or rolling from as low to the ground as possible, with speed and without hesitation, to prevent excessive ground impact. Combine this with the return rocking motion post side falling, providing a cohesive ground executed stamp kick capability, and confidence is further increased.

In a situation where immediate recovery or escape and evasion is not possible, a reverse land crab, flat on your back, ground pivoting capability, is required to orientate to a moving enemy; it is just a matter of rolling over from your side foetal position to a three point of ground contact position, on your back with both knees bent, and the soles of your boots in contact with the ground. This position allows you to push through the soles of your boots, while pivoting on your buttocks, to stay centered to an upright enemy. This can then be combined with oblique kicks to counter enemy kicks or stomps. Recovery from this position by means of rolling back to a side foetal position, increases recovery, safety and counteroffensive capabilities during and post recovery.

Through practice of effective, deliberate decision, or unexpected decentralisation employment of a side foetal initial falling action under wide ranging and varied threat conditions - including on varied terrain - confidence will be gained in the capability to reduce impact and risk, and to set up recovery and counter engagement, or ground executed counter engagement, as part of footing recovery. Knowing that the potential for serious injury is minimised enhances mental toughness.

There are some human reactions that are unconscious reactions to assault, such as reaching out under stand up assault, or under armed threat, reaching out, that can lead to the negative reality of defensive wounds. Assuming a foetal position under ground assault is another reactionary, subconscious means of self-preservation. The danger of continued holding of a foetal position under ground assault is that a determined foe will identify exposed vitals and gaps in your foetal position defence capabilities and exploit them.

I have seen even experienced practitioners of fighting arts, when overwhelmed and decentralised by a formidable foe, assume and maintain a foetal position or even worse a foetal position with your back turned to the foe under assault, with no execution of counter engagement, recovery of footing, or escape and evasion. The initial advantages of the foetal position soon become advantageous to their foe, by means of their grounded target maintaining a static position of helplessness. Primary proven combative skills must have commonality with subconscious self-preservation and self-protection reactions under threat, but with minimum hesitation or stalling.

A confident and competent combatant will take advantage of momentum when falling, enabling the quickest recovery and counter engagement, or ground employed counter engagement, as part of recovery or escape and evasion. They will ensure they are not a static grounded target if at all possible. Their side foetal position should be part of one cohesive, increased self-protection, counter engagement deliberate action, or deliberate recovery continued counter engagement, or escape and evasion action.

Combining decentralisation with second wind timed combative respiration will reduce ground impact injuries, including being incapacitated by being winded on ground impact, and will enable cohesive recovery and counter engagement transitions. This enables maximum utilisation of time and fast mapping assessment in relation to your best means of threat neutralisation. Not having to focus on multiple components under threat and being able to employ immediate cohesive transitions from risk reduction and self-protection to threat neutralisation is the difference between threat situational competency and situational vulnerability and helplessness.

Having a single means of maximum safety, and setting and maintaining a state of combative readiness (such as the small squat) and combative foetal side falling that has commonality and cohesion with your combative threat neutralisation capabilities, provides economy of assessment and economy of threat neutralisation employment.

Not being confident and competent in your capability to tactically, deliberately self-decentralise under a threat situation that may injure or incapacitate you on impact, puts you at increased risk. Under unexpected forced decentralisation, you must be able to employ without hesitation, using muscle memory, safe combative ground falling or rolling to enable fast mapping, continuation, assessment in decision making, and consequently, cohesive counter engagement, or escape and evasion capabilities.

Through prior high repetition drilling, and unexpected actions on battle handling training, where you have safely and effectively employed your combative ground falling or rolling capabilities, combined with threat neutralisation, you will have achieved psychological confidence and skills competency that transfers into real life actions-on psychological and combative skills empowerment. This confidence through competency will ensure that when you most need increased safety and threat neutralisation capabilities, they will be executed without doubt or hesitation. An individual that is not confident or competent under such adversity may not only end up in the foetal position under assault, but may also turn their back on their foe. This is a dire position, and one of helplessness, where they are at the mercy of their foe.

Your 6th and additional senses for life and in self-defence and CQC

While the general belief is we human beings have five senses in sight, hearing, smell, taste and touch you only have to think hard and dig a little deeper with research to find the human body to function, self-protect and heal comprises of a mass and maze of internal automated processes we never even give a second thought.

Balance and stability maintenance for example is something we require for all movements in everyday life that is a subconscious sense undertaken process.

These human computer processes by means of complex situational and threat recognition capabilities clearly identify both a conscious deliberate means of threat recognition and threat identification as well as a subconscious automatic human recognition capability to aid in self-preservation and self-protection.

Often our eyes will identify and transmit information in relation to a threat considerably faster than we can threat identify. In fact the human eye can transmit approximately 10 million bits of information per second.

The brain-to-boot in relation to threat focuses on the common threat categories of expected and unexpected actions on combative encounters.

The sixth sense applies mainly to an expected actions-on encounter where the combatant is focused, alert and possibly feeling uneasy in regards to a probable or impending actions-on encounter.

In an unexpected actions-on encounter usually the enemy compromises themselves and it is their shape, sound, movement, smell or the employed unarmed offensive assault actions themselves that provide the combatant with threat recognition immediately prior to contact. It is difficult to determine the level the sixth sense plays in threat recognition under unexpected actions-on assaults.

Through the mammalian brain and its capability to store recollections of prior experiences and the autonomic nervous system's capability through subconscious mechanisms of situation and threat recognition there is an increased capacity of threat recognition and identification before you are even consciously aware of it.

In expected actions-on encounters where there is extended time, range and safety and security layers present prior to any actions on encounter your most highly capable human computer the Homo sapiens brain, may well override your reptilian mammalian brains as well as take charge over your autonomic nervous system in relation to processing sensory information and controlling automatic effects of threat and danger.

In unexpected actions on encounters when compromised and taken by surprise by subconsciously reacting and consciously responding to the threat stimuli, the combatant increases the chance of threat neutralization. This prior form of threat recognition and identification could be physical contact or kill zone flashes of aggressive incoming shape, action, color, sound or movement. It could be by means of your enemy compromising themselves by the nature of the set up and executing of their highly committed aggressive actions. The combatant through subconscious automatic mechanisms of self-preservation and conscious deliberate self-protection responses at real time has the capability to self-protect and threat neutralise.

We have the capability to subconsciously react and respond to many forms of threat before they have been fully identified.

Subconscious reactions to loud noises, gunfire, stun grenades or, in unarmed surprise assault, last fraction of a second threat recognition of committed incoming attack, are by majority initially subconscious reactions.

In expected actions-on encounters in a self-defence or combative situation where the threat is probable or imminent, discrete movements or movement related sounds are identifiers of our predominantly conscious sensory but also subconscious automatic means of threat recognition. Threat identification and threat neutralization by means of our highest thinking brain, the Homo sapiens brain, is the primary method of controlled calculated threat neutralization under a managed threat situation and by deliberate threat neutralization options.

I have observed thousands of individuals under battle handling exercises when surprised by sudden aggressive shock action that can through going combative, and by means of the subconscious and conscious capabilities combined, neutralise enemy party sudden aggressive shock action pre-contact. They do this by being ready and via prior knowledge of likely common threat categories.

In my combative instructor qualification course I was introduced to theory on the 6th sense in relation to reducing your chance of being compromised as part of the point of no return stalking of a sentry.

Some of this information to me was hard to understand and even harder to prove especially “thinking of the color black” to reduce your likelihood of being detected.

However through my research and development and testing of tactics and skills under covert sentry stalking has identified some deliberate practices that have proven to be beneficial to covert stalking.

Reducing your bodily mass by stalking in a crouched position, mimicking your enemy pers’ movements, using them as a rear flank concealment against their own sensory capabilities and visually focusing on one or both shoulder blade to detect movement has proven positive, proactive and effective in covert sentry stalking.

My reasoning for visually focusing on one or both shoulder is the fact that when I have found myself subconsciously alerted in relation to being stared at I have identified the subject was always looking at my head, face or center line.

With the spinal cord and central nervous system running up the center of the back through the nape of the neck and with the known high number of nerve endings and connections to sensory capabilities I have identified the best means of neutralising any subconscious sensory detection capabilities is by visualising on a shoulder blade and responding or mimicking your foe's movement or actions in relation to that shoulder blade identifying the direction of bodily movement.

Such stalking contingency options to reduce your chances of being detected require covert specific economy of movement tactics and must be drilled in training and practiced under realistic scenarios training to achieve high level proficiency in competency and as such confidence.

My association with other military instructors and operators has provided access to very specific information in relation to specialist role combative skills employments and this information supports the methods and measures I have developed to maintain a covert discrete status and reduce the risks of being detected by either the five major senses, the 6th sense, or any other of the many internal subconscious human sensory capabilities.

I am not convinced that the thinking of the colour black to reduce one's aura has any proven fact combatively and believe it is more important to focus on the specific combative undertakings requirements and your physical tactics and skills to reduce the likelihood of being compromised than focusing on the unknown. What I can prove is that you must have a strong and focused mind, and alert sensory capabilities combined with hand-eye-foot coordination to be able to maintain a covert status in the set up and execution of specialist combative skills while maintaining anti and counter capabilities if compromised.

I do believe the reality is when a combatant is aware of a potential threat and their conscious and subconscious senses are at a state of high alert, there is a greater chance they will detect and identify the threat prior to an actions-on encounter.

The untrained often believe that the sole primary means of threat identification is their eyesight and while visual capabilities are the primary component in the execution of combative capabilities they are only one of our sensory capabilities in relation to detecting threat.

As a crowd controller often operating in a crowded environment with many distractions including low light, darkness, flashing light, loud music and masses of human verbiage, I found when alert and aware and going tactical I was capable of identifying unexpected aggressive shock action assault prior to contact.

Interestingly I found my sense of hearing could reduce major background sound working in such an environment and that my sense of hearing could pick up threatening danger sounds related to sudden assault.

Just because you cannot see internal subconscious threat recognition and identification capabilities you should not discount that they are there constantly working to assist in everyday life including in threatening and dangerous situations.

An important factor is the level of confidence and competency of the combatant in relation to conscious means of threat recognition specific threat identification and decision-making by means of processing fast mapping information at real time and neutralising the threat.

Even an untrained individual will be provided by means of sensory information and subconscious reaction a level of self-preservation.

For the highly trained combatant with a memory bank of prior exposure information and deliberately trained responses to combat recognized and identified threats, their training will kick in and through real time fast mapping assessment and decision-making it will seem you have all the time necessary to make deliberate decisions and skills employments to neutralise the threat.

Through muscle memory and your sensory capabilities in the deliberate decision-making of combative skills employments between initiation and target contact, your senses and sensory capabilities combined with muscle memory provide a subconscious capability of target zeroing.

There are many actions and activities we perform in everyday life by sensory capability and muscle memory. Our central nervous system receives and sends signals all over our bodies to initiate and regulate subconscious reactions as well as support deliberate responses. The signals are turned on and off automatically in relation to required reactions and responses to our external environment.

The military combative way of high repetition drilling of skills and tactics as well as realistic battle handling exercises in relation to surprise sudden aggressive shock action ensures a central nervous system through prior experience and exposure is familiar with the threat and as such when called upon when needed in the future can react and respond with maximum speed.

Just like gaining physical proficiency through prior training our subconscious reactive and responsive nerve signals will be familiar and strengthened in relation to decreased reaction response time. Just like our five major senses your nerve signals capabilities become strengthened, enhanced and increased in speed of reaction by being familiar through prior exposure to the threat. Prior exposure and familiarization enhances physical sensory detection capabilities.

While you may not think about it there must be millions if not billions of pieces of information both detailed and non-specific in relation to expected and unexpected actions-on encounters that are sent via our peripheral nervous system networks including through the spinal cord to our brains.

Without this constant source of sending sensory information to the brain and returning signals to operate required bodily parts and functions the brain would not be able to provide the combatant with any means of self-protection and counter engagement or provide any unarmed offensive assault capabilities. Your brain may be your Homo sapiens computer, but without interconnected sensory and signaling capabilities it would be combatively redundant. In combative threat situations it has become obvious to me that it is primarily movement that triggers your sixth sense that enables the earliest possible threat detection and recognition and increases your chances of combative neutralisation or escape and evasion neutralization.

The human body being aware of the space it occupies in relation to external dangers constantly transmits millions of bits of information in relation to threat recognition and identification. While we are not consciously aware of these millions of bits of information we are capable of conscious awareness of tens of bits of more definite information at any given time. The subconscious internal processing of millions of bits of information constantly at real time is a primary means of human self-preservation and combative self-protection.

Combative competency not only in skills capabilities but also in maintaining a positive ground affinity, stability and balance status has positive enhancement capabilities in combative skills executions by reducing required levels of focus on setting and maintaining a primary stable balanced platform for combative skills employment. Your nervous system will constantly be checking movement and stability considerations and you won't even be aware of it. Movement, balance and stability are major continuous areas of focus undertaken subconsciously by means of our central nervous system external sensory awareness capabilities that require considerable mental focus and power.

High-level combative proficiency reduces the required levels of detailed skills employment focus and as such frees up more power capabilities to enhance combative options employments. Freeing up as much power in capability to control the effects of stress and fear as well as enhance real time factual assessment and primary combative option decision-making increases your chances of threat neutralization. If you are unable to set and maintain the highest level possible of awareness and combative readiness, your sixth and additional senses capabilities as well as your five main senses capabilities will be operating at their maximum levels of capability. When you are relying on your automatic mechanisms of self-preservation alone your chances of threat neutralisation are reduced to only your reactionary reptilian brain capability.

The nervous system sending electrical signals and initiating the release of chemical agents such as adrenaline into the bloodstream under threat requires combative control measures to reduce warning effects that if not eliminated or kept under control can interfere with primary senses and your sixth sense and alternate senses capabilities.

The trained combatant must be able to go tactical and turn on deliberate conscious sensory and combative skills capabilities, managing and controlling subconscious alerts and levels of chemical releases, to aid in going combative or escape and evasion to ensure the highest level of combative capability and state of readiness is maintained. Your autonomic nervous system is your body's major subconscious reactionary mechanism to external threat stimuli. Interestingly I have discovered under battle handling exercises with the reality of surprise sudden aggressive shock action likely that the moment that the trained combatant goes tactical in readiness for combative encounters the autonomic nervous system kicks in and requires immediate deliberate control measures to ensure the combatant is not psychologically overwhelmed and weakened by the physical warning effects and responses in relation to the detected impending threat.

When instructing sentry neutralisation training where the combatants find themselves psychologically and physically drained by the practice of such skills. The reasoning behind this is the effects of not only the inhuman act they are training to undertake but also the realities of the consequences if they are compromised.

This sets our sensory mechanisms and central nervous system racing and as such the combatant must control the effects of hormone dumping to maintain the required level of motor skills to perform the covert and deliberate requirements of the sentry neutralisation task.

Even though sentry neutralisation may not be a highly physically demanding undertaking in relation to the covert stalking phase, combatants find they perspire as much as in high level physical output the mental focus is as physically and psychologically draining as in extreme physical endurance or prolonged close quarter combat high intensity training.

Your subconscious and conscious sensory capabilities continuously receive millions if not billions of pieces of information, evaluating that information and storing it, providing the capacity to utilise it when next exposed to the same or a similar situation you must also discard a huge amount of unnecessary information. The kept information must be filed in similar threat situation files in a compressed format for later situational information evaluations based on comparisons from this available information.

I have had the privilege of working with elite forces instructing CQC for more than 20 years as well as working with and being trained by some of the evolutionary pioneers in the military combative field and have benefited greatly from the wisdom in relation to factual information of post encounter subject material.

I spoke with one highly determined and skilled combatant that was wounded and through his prior training and instruction was able to understand the extent of his wounding and this increased control over his psychological coping capabilities.

He told me he felt after being wounded that this was not the end of the unfortunate encounters for him or his team at this time and on this day.

Call it a premonition but possibly more an alert awareness of potential risk and dangers during medical evacuation and while having to remain close to where he had been wounded. Combining this with the prior enemy contact made him think more of the increased risks of the situation and as such understand and accept the potential risk realities.

His uneasy feeling turned out to be founded as there were problems with the emergency evacuation and the wounding of another member of his patrol.

Often in training and especially under surprise sudden aggressive shock action battle handling exercises I've experienced a feeling of déjà vu that I put down to the familiarity of the drilling and training in the required skills to neutralise the threat.

Obviously these threat situations, including the actions and reactions of the enemy party, are somewhat similar and predictable along with the required deliberate responses and combative actions to neutralise the threat.

This can post-actions-on threat neutralisation give a feeling of I knew this was going to happen and I have been here experienced this and done this before.

This is an extremely positive determination of combative threat neutralisation epitomising factual assessment fast mapping at real time decision making and correct primary skills neutralisation of a formidable but predictable enemy threat. Simply by employing primary proven tactics to hard target oneself increases threat recognition and threat identification capabilities and by means of extensively practiced threat neutralisation primary practices the entire threat and threat neutralisation encounter can feel familiar and predictable.

In conclusion, in combative situations in the employment of combative threat neutralisation the faced threatening situation enemy actions and the combatant's deliberate means of threat neutralisation practiced thousands if not tens of thousands of times in training and under sudden aggressive shock action battle handling exercises should feel familiar as well as should feel previously experienced. The most common sixth sense experience of being stared at and is not exclusive to combative encounters as I'm sure most of the population would have sensed before whether it be an admirer or an aggressor.

On recognition by means of their sixth sense or one of their primary senses information in relation to the subject will be transmitted to their brain and quickly determined as acceptable or not acceptable in relation to the processed information on the subject.

Military combatants and civilians in unfamiliar uneasy surroundings and situations often feel uneasy as a result of bad vibes. These bad vibes to a degree are influenced by conscious knowledge that this type of environment or situation could present risks and dangers.

The dark of night, a bad part of the city, deadly silence can trigger feelings of unease.

Not only do suspicious movements, shapes and sounds increase a feeling of bad vibes but so too does being in a bad place or situation. There does not need to be any physical sounds shapes or movement to get an uneasy feeling. The unknown in relation to what is known as deadly silence or dark of night can invoke feelings of a bad place or bad situation.

I put this down very much to prior exposure and experience and your central nervous system relating it to such prior stored information and sending return alarm warning signals.

You must remember our minds can fool us and especially in unusual situations can unnerve us by sending alarm and warning signals in relation to similar but not the same previous experiences. Just like controlling hormonal dumping to maintain a state of combative readiness you must not allow alarming mind signals in relation to the unknown to weaken your resolve or interfere with your maintaining a state of readiness to go combative or escape and evade. Such psychological interference can affect your combative cognitive capabilities as well as your mental resolve.

Performing assessments and coming to logical determinations in relation to the immediate external environment threats and dangers is a positive practice over the negative dwelling and focusing on the unknown or not known yet information.

Often tactics to improve threat detection capabilities such as positional changes taking cover or concealment and utilising specific senses to identify the direction and nature of the possible threat will identify that it was nothing sinister and of normal or natural causes. In sixth sense awareness situations maintaining a false perception status of unawareness while utilising your peripheral vision and heightened other senses to identify the threat is a powerful means of taking control and reducing the fear and stress effects of the unidentified or unknown.

Allowing your foe to believe you are oblivious to their presence and intentions and that they have not been compromised will allow you to strengthen your position and status by employing hard target tactics including anti-encounter tactics by means of clearing or moving out of the danger zone. Our primary senses capabilities enable prior threat recognition and threat identification in advance of threat materialization as a result of external advance awareness capabilities sending pieces of information for processing. They can take in massive amounts of pieces of information, decipher it determining threat specifics, and relay reactionary and responsive signals to the required bodily parts to aid in the neutralization of the threat.

Perception just like anticipation is dangerous if allowed to consume your brain's capacity required for tactically correct physical assessment and factual determination and decision making.

Just as in the detection of improvised explosive devices where you need to simply stand still eyes shut and remain silent employing your primary senses of smell and hearing in an effort to locate any suspicious scent or sound you need to utilise similar principles in darkness in a likely risk environment. The differences for self defence and combative purposes when you feel you are being surveilled you need to employ anti-encounter surveillance tactics making yourself as discreet as possible and as hard a target as possible while you physically and mentally focus on the direction and position of the threat as well as the threat characteristics and specifics.

Command and control your mind and your mind related reactions and responses to ensure everything you do and all your time is positive and geared towards achieving your maximum safety setting and maintaining of a primary ready combative capabilities state.

Before you discard the reality of a sixth sense and many other internal subconscious senses that are constantly involved with our life health and well-being you need to consider the following. We seldom think of maintaining balance and stability in our everyday lives when walking and running sitting or getting out of a seat.

The constant maintaining of balance and stability requires complex mechanisms of external environment awareness and internal self-monitoring systems to be able to subconsciously be in control of our upright status.

Our bodies and bodily organs receive sensory signals constantly to perform life maintaining undertakings that we are oblivious to.

These complex automatic control mechanisms must be as regular as our heartbeat to ensure that internal functions are continuous or when problems are detected means of fault or error correction are undertaken. I can remember talking to a doctor close friend who was also an army officer and an avid supporter of military close quarters combat training in regards to the sixth sense and him adding our immune system is another additional sense with interconnections with the central nervous system. This is something that the late great Harry Baldock also told me of in relation to his being a pioneer in physical culture, health and well-being as well as a physiotherapy tutor and massage therapist.

While in close quarters combat our primary consideration is with factual threats that can kill you ,we are well aware of the dangers of allowing our subconscious and conscious minds to combine in uncontrolled negative thought factors of anticipation and perception over externally factually determined threat detail. If we did not control perceived and anticipated thoughts we could overload our subconscious and overwhelm our conscious status reducing our combative capabilities.

Just like in the brain-to-boot major and minor components as well as in combative skills executions comprising of major and minor components so must our internal automated less obvious combative minor components play an important role in our self-preservation and self-protection.

The following is a simple outline of how our senses conduct, evaluate and process information and is merely an overview of a very complex body of systems and networks required for human existence.

We have specific sensory receptors to detect specific external and internal stimuli including threats and health-related issues.

Our eyes are sensitive to light and provide visual imaging capabilities in relation to threat and combative situations.

Our ears provide hearing capabilities including the capability to block out background sound and focus on the detection of even discreet indications of threat. Our nose provides the capability to detect various smells including unknown unfamiliar less obvious scents when turned on and turned up. Our taste sense originates from our taste buds of our tongue.

Our sense of feel or touch applies to not only our finger tips hands toes and soles of our feet but also to our entire skin with all our nerve endings and sensory receptors.

Going covert as in sneaking or ghost stepping requires all senses to be utilised and at high alert.

To avoid being compromised visually checking ground to be covered and then using tactical ghost stepping to detect potential terrain hazards that could compromise you is a specialist role employment example of using your sense of touch and feel with your toes and specific parts of the sole of your foot through your boot.

Maintaining balance or moving in darkness navigating unfamiliar or uneasy terrain requires your senses to be at high alert and the need for your sense of touch to assist in careful movement and balance maintenance.

Our bodily sensory detection systems including the five major senses constantly send signal transmissions along our sensory transmission networks to our brain. Our brain from the memory bank of exposure to similar or same situations combined with the piece of current information received can initiate the determined best course of action sending signals back to the specific parts of the body required to neutralise the threat.

Some of the difficulties in going covert, especially in darkness in an unfamiliar environment and uneasy terrain in a situation of probable danger, is the requirement to not only remain uncompromised but also to move covertly maintaining a status of maximum balance and stability. Our sixth sense is very much the major factor in providing subconscious balance and stability maintenance. One of our additional external awareness sensory or self-preservation capabilities combined with our additional internal sensory capabilities possibly number 6,7,8 and so on are very much subconscious means of monitoring the immediate environment and maintaining a constant state of situational and environmental awareness by detecting potential dangers, hazards and threats often before we can consciously identify and recognize them. These additional sensory capabilities operating prior to threats materializing send signal transmissions to our central nervous system setting off a human computer recognition response to neutralise the threat.

On many occasions over the years I have personally experienced a feeling of a sense of danger or threat that has not been by visual or other major senses detection. While I really do not know how to explain it, I cannot discount it. I believe through a heightened state of awareness and readiness combined with prior experience and exposure as well as an understanding of the common and likely threat to be encountered, it makes me ready and less surprised which provides increased capability in relation to the earliest likelihood of threat recognition providing more time for factual detailed assessment and decision making in relation to threat neutralization. This provides a feeling of familiarity and through physical and psychological sensory control and management capabilities being familiar the effect and outcome is far more controllable.

I relate this directly to prior experience and exposure and an understanding of how things should be in specific situations.

Recently while deerstalking after tracking an animal for over 1 $^{1}/_{2}$ hours I came to any area where I could no longer find fresh tracks. I stood silently closed my eyes turned all my senses on but could not locate the deer I'd been tracking.

I put my rifle against a tree and turned around to relieve myself, keeping my senses at high alert while I did so.

Something made me detect a presence to my rear flanks that wasn't obvious in relation to sound, movement or shadow so I cautiously turned my head and detected the deer via my peripheral vision. It must have leapt amongst a patch of bush and poked its head up and was staring directly at the back of my head. While maintaining peripheral vision I recovered my rifle and slowly aligned to the deer and shot it.

My determination of this was that even though I was relieving myself I remained vigilant and subconsciously detected a presence focused on me.

Over more than 20 years involved with bouncing at some of the rougher establishments I had my share of incidents where the cowardly king hitter would try and take me out from the side or rear flanks.

Through maintaining a state of alertness and awareness and always endeavoring to employ hard targeting tactics I found that even under the most cunning and calculated unexpected assaults my last millisecond reactionary threat recognition and response always reduced risk enough for me to hard cover guard or employ evasive hardcover guarding self-protect, fast map assessment, make counter engagement required adjustments in range position combined with deliberate counter engagement option set up requirements and employ my counter engagement.

I can remember one such incident in the middle of a crowd fight where I had limited side and rear flank protection capabilities. Some big lump of a likely lad decided to try and take me out diagonally from my rear. Even though there was action going on all around me, limited light and loud music, immediately prior to getting knuckled something made me flinch and my training kicked in by means of dropping my center of gravity reducing my target mass hardcover guarding with my chin lockdown inside my shoulder as I had practiced thousands of times in realistic training.

This coward and his cunning punch got inside my cover guard and my means of negating the effect was to pivot and deflect the punch with my inner upper arm and shoulder. I had matching joining bruises on my chin and inner shoulder joint but considering this coward tried to take me when I was occupied with other foes and cunningly from outside and behind my peripheral vision capabilities my subconscious reactionary and then conscious responsive counter engagement led to his defeat.

In conclusion I believe we have far more than five or six senses and they include our major external sensors and many more important life-support and like protecting internal sensory control and response capabilities.

I believe you should not discount or disregard the unknown or not understood but you must ensure it does not affect your factual physical capabilities required for self-protection and threat neutralization.

By employing all your brain-to-boot tactics and skills both physical and psychological as well as the highest levels of risk reduction hard targeting capabilities and maintaining a state of high level awareness you will increase your chances of threat detection and as such threat neutralization.

Wounds and injuries realities and effects

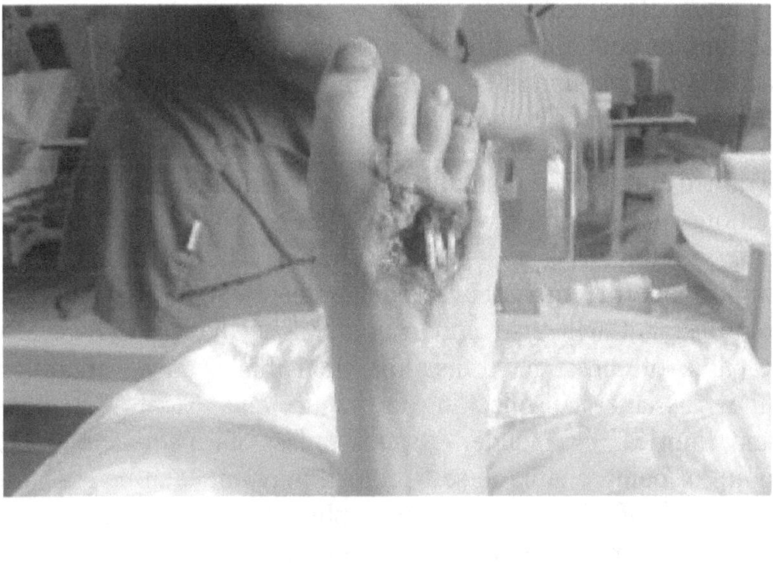

The outcome of a 12 gauge shotgun wound

There are many variables in relation to the pain and effects of actions-on incurred wounds and injuries. These include the individual's inner resolve, intestinal fortitude, pain tolerance, mentality, the specific wound and the individual's capabilities to overcome pain sensations. The extent of physical wounds or injuries in relation to still being able to self-protect, go combative and threat neutralise, or escape and evade are another matter apart from the pain factors.

Continued threat risk and danger in an actions-on encounter when wounded will require the combatant, without hesitating or dwelling on the extent of their injury, to neutralise the threat by the best and safest means available to them.

The following are general realities of wounds and injuries, based on my personal experience and extensive research, in the form of interviewing individuals that have been wounded or injured in military operations as well as civilians that have been wounded or injured in self-defence or street fight situations.

There is a considerable difference in effects and general outcomes between expected actions-on encounters, and unexpected actions-on encounters in relation to wounds and injuries. The required means of combative responses and actions to neutralise threats, in both expected and unexpected actions-on encounters will vary, in relation to threat categories, threat levels and situational specifics.

Trained formidable mentally tough combatants in an expected actions-on encounter will do everything possible to increase safety, reduce risk and threat neutralise. They will realise the importance of emergency medical treatment for wounds and injuries, but will also understand that if they are physically capable of threat neutralisation, then this is more important under assault than checking the nature and extent of wounds and injuries. Pain under assault, unless incapacitated to the point of being unable to self-protect, may not even be felt; this is a result of adrenaline and endorphins being pumped through your bloodstream and the combatant mentality taking over.

The highly motivated, determined and capable combatant can override the effects of pain, maintaining a level of control, psychologically and physically, to enable the employment of threat neutralising capabilities.

In an unexpected actions-on encounter, where the combatant's first knowledge of any actions-on is contact, the risk of being injured or wounded is increased considerably. Under such realities the priority is self-preservation and self-protection, to reduce risk and increase safety (including reducing the nature and extent of wounds or injuries).

Pain under assault is an expected and accepted reality of an actions-on encounter, and will motivate the mentally tough combatant to quickly neutralise the threat. Pressure is a specific type of pain that motivates the utilisation of immediate methods to stop the pressure related pain, by escaping, or countering, the specific form of hyperextension or crushing. In situations where immediate counter engagement or escape is not possible, out of self-preservation, the combatant will employ methods to relieve the pressure; this is achieved by resistance and/or yielding, followed by threat neutralisation.

In street fighting, or under an unarmed assault, the effects of punches to the head cannot only cause blunt or stinging type pain, but also concussion. If the combatant is unprepared to deal with blows, a momentary blackout effect may result, or the complete opposite with head snapping blows that can cause an electric shock effect. Under some circumstances the effect can be both an initial electric shock effect, followed by a dull, partial blackout sensation.

When someone is not completely unconscious, recovery can include a complete lack of recollection of what has happened. A trained fighter conditioned to head contact can show few effects of concussion, whereas an individual unfamiliar with such effects can experience severe head pain, visual problems, ringing ears and nausea. This could be because they did not expect, and were not prepared for, head contact, whereas the trained fighter will be aware and familiar with how to reduce the level of impact of head contact.

There is an old saying in bare knuckle fighting; when your opponent has a tight guard- ‘kill the body and the head will die’. This means, employ body punches to the torso, winding and causing your opponent to drop their hands, thus leaving the head exposed to punches. Severe abdominal winding is difficult to overcome, especially under assault, because of pain and extreme difficulty in breathing. If you have not experienced such effects previously, immediate recovery and increased self-protection during recovery and initiation of counter engagement can be very difficult.

The pain from scrotal contact can be incapacitating, especially if you do not understand the likely consequences and requirements to self-protect and threat neutralise. Your subconscious reaction to the groin contact will be to bend forward, moving your groin back and away from your attacker. The pain sensation is identified and increased in intensity when you stand up from the subconscious bent forward crouch position. Having a knowledge of this will enable the trained combatant needing to neutralise the threat from the bent forward crouch position, to seize and secure their attacker, making them wear their weight and, depending on the level of pain, either from a point-blank bodily contact bent forward crouched position employ counter engagement, or if necessary fall on top of their attacker on the ground and target their attackers delicate bodily vitals.

The importance of minimising stand-up, extension movement related pain, and targeting the attacker's most vulnerable bodily targets, is vital in controlling pain and neutralising the threat. When a combatant is wounded, and loses the use of a striking or stamp kicking limb by injury or excruciating pain, they must maintain mental toughness, employ real time, fast mapping tactical assessment, and decide on another means of threat neutralisation. This may be by escape and evasion or combative methods.

It is very important, in cases of striking or stamp kicking limbs being rendered incapable of combative actions, that the combatant can utilise another limb, or part of a limb. Severe hand injuries may require the use of stamp kicks, the other hand, or the elbow of the injured hand. Being able to think, assess, decide and utilise unaffected limbs, or limb parts of the injured extremity that are not affected by the injury, is necessary in order to maintain momentum, and achieve the objective of threat neutralisation. This should be planned for, and practiced in training, so as to ensure you are familiar, and able to change option in an actions-on encounter, in relation to pain, and when specific human bodily weapons are rendered disabled.

Changing limbs or parts of limbs to enable continued combative capabilities is important, but knowing how to reduce effects of wounds and injuries is also extremely important. Keeping arm wounds high and tightly against your body, utilising your unaffected arm or stamp kicks will reduce blood loss. Being able to utilise your free arm to apply pressure to opposite arm wounds, and then employ stamp kicks, is a positive practice under such dire situations. Employing hand pressure to control the bleeding in relation to body or abdominal wounds, while increasing self-protection by cover guarding with your free arm, and employing counter engagement stamp kicks, provides not only threat neutralisation but also emergency medical treatment.

The effects of pain and injury can be considerably reduced when you have a determined, committed attitude and the combative smarts and know-how to utilise the best and safest means of threat neutralisation.

Knowledge and competency training for not only primary, but also secondary, alternative and emergency means of threat neutralisation is the difference between being best prepared, and only being partly prepared.

Understanding the nature and extent of risk, in relation to the reason why you are feeling pain as a consequence of real-time enemy assault, through fast mapping, assessment and primary option decision-making, means that self-preservation, self-protection and means of threat neutralisation options are based on the best and safest options.

In the case of pain, through pressure or leverage, knowing how to resist and yield to decrease the immediate effects, and set up escape and threat neutralisation, without having to compromise bodily parts or jeopardise your personal safety is a priority. Minor through major positional changes, combined with resistance of the crushing or hyperextension forces enabling pain, and incapacitation reduction will enable threat neutralisation by counter engagement, or secured seizure escapes and counter engagement. Mental toughness and proven combative methods of risk reduction self-preservation and self-protection, combined with the best of battle proven threat neutralisation capabilities enhance safe objective achievement.

Highly trained combatants in situations where wounding or injuries are unavoidable, as a last resort will employ hard targeting, hard cover guarding with their body parts that are less likely to cause incapacitation, or life-threatening wounds or injuries. Although they may have an awareness of being wounded (and related immediate contact or penetrative pain), in regards to sacrificing non-life threatening body parts to protect against life-threatening wounding, this will not stop the threat neutralisation actions of a mentally tough and combatively capable individual. The reality is, the requirement is to self-protect and threat neutralise, and there is no time or place for over-thinking about wounding risks, or checking on the effects of inflicted wounds or injuries under assault. Non-life threatening wounds may not be realised, as a result of adrenaline and endorphins, combined with highly committed combative actions employments. Contact may be avoided by means of your human senses, and or your peripheral nervous system advanced detection capabilities. Such subconscious reactions may well include reactionary threat avoidance prior to contact.

Even on contact your subconscious pain receptors will react by instantaneous removal of the bodily target away from the threat.

The highly trained combatant, aware of the realities of actions-on encounters, in relation to risks and dangers in the case of unavoidable contact, will accept the need to reduce risk to as low a level as possible, even if that means accepting low, or lesser level injury in relation to self-protection and threat neutralisation.

The highly trained combatant must be able to control reverting back to untrained human reactions that increase risk by leaving major bodily vitals exposed, or reaching out and sacrificing tendons and arteries. Having confidence in the most proven and safe combative skills, even under contact, in the knowledge that although you may be wounded or injured, the effects will not be life-threatening, and you will be able to neutralise the threat.

Having such an understanding and awareness of pain related to immediate contact, the need to immediately self-protect and threat neutralise to prevent further wounding is a must. The requirement to increase safety and neutralise the threat combines psychological and combative positive actions, and is aided by knowledge that comes from understanding the dangers of not doing so.

Primary combative practices of self-protection, reducing target mass, clearing contact kill zones, and setting a state of readiness for expedient combative, or escape and evasion action, are combined psychological and physical skills practices in relation to self-preservation and threat neutralisation.

The importance, reiterated throughout this manual, of your deliberate tactics and skills having commonality with subconscious reactions and responses to sudden aggression and contact can be the difference between preventing or reducing wounding and life or death.

Reduced risk, pain through unavoidable wounding, or through sacrificing a non-life-threatening cover guard, and shielding outer extremities must be an accepted reality, including any pain related immediate sensations that must never cause hesitation, or assessment of a wound while under assault. Emergency medical attention is important, but not during an actions-on assault, where any reduction or loss of momentum or commitment to threat neutralisation can be fatal.

Contact and any contact pain sensation must motivate and ensure momentum is not only maintained, but also increased if necessary, to as expediently as possible neutralise the threat. The reality is that if you feel the effects of non-life-threatening pain, you are alive and capable of employing a required means of threat neutralisation.

Hard cover guarding, protecting tendons and arteries, and absorbing of impact or deflection of unarmed blunt force trauma, increases safety and reduces risk and injury. High repetition training in hard cover guarding and deflection of strikes inside the hard cover guard, including practicing such skills in unexpected actions-on encounters, will ensure through deliberate response and muscle memory that the chances of full powered contact are reduced considerably.

Against penetrative wounds, as in emergency static, last resort, actions-on encounters, reducing target mass and making every effort to clear the contact zone, and cover guarding to prevent access to major bodily life-support vitals is an immediate priority. Such hard cover guarding against penetrative threats requires keeping tendons and arteries against one's body, leaving them least exposed to wounding. In unavoidable wounding situations, only an outer extremity's muscle and tissue should be sacrificed, if being wounded is unavoidable. Reducing risk by exposing and sacrificing least life-threatening and least incapacitating outer surfaces of extremities, when there is no other option available, must be followed up by immediate threat neutralisation, including escape and evasion, or disarming, disabling and disposing of the threat.

Understanding the likely effects of non-life-threatening wounds, as a result of reducing risk to the lowest level humanly possible by sacrificing non-life-threatening bodily cover shield outer surfaces of extremities, will enable maintained or increased inner resolve. Another reason, and reality, of accepting unavoidable contact as part of hard cover guarding protection of major bodily vitals, is that it is the best way to increase safety, and chances of threat neutralisation when clearing by evasion or escape, and evasion of the kill zone prior to contact, is not possible.

Any pain related to real time actions-on encounters in relation to wounds and injuries, incurred in regards to self-protection requirements as part of threat neutralisation, will be minimised by high level commitment, inner resolve, and expedient action and movement.

Controlled safety tradecraft practices, contact in training, both by means of unarmed and armed options develops the mentality, tactics and skills, to enable immediate threat neutralisation over hesitation or freezing.

I advocate on my courses training without unrealistic protectors other than battledress and modern body armour. It is very important that you train the way you will go combative, to ensure everything is as relevant and realistic to real life actions-on encounters as possible. Once my exponents achieve proficiency, and are preparing for test phases, the utilisation of real training weapons is important, including training aids that encourage evasion and avoidance, disarming, and threat neutralisation to avoid contact realities, including deterrent shocks. It is important that during such training, realism and safety factors are adhered to, such as the training knives' edges being dulled, and the tip slightly rounded.

In days gone by, metal heated training knives were employed to ensure exponents took them seriously, and that they did everything to evade, disarming, disabling and disposing of the threat rather than being contacted with the equivalent of a hot poker. Today we use such equipment (an example is shock knives) that are safer, do not burn, and are more convenient.

Pain is safety and performance inspiring, compared to training knives that often can be taken for granted simply because there is no pain or risk involved. There are combatant required, major and minor methods, of preventing or reducing the effects of unarmed, blunt force trauma.

Through a maintained state of readiness to counter, or reduce, the effects of unarmed contact to the lowest level individually possible, as quickly as possible, including the need to make adjustments and employ changed options, or contingency options by constant fast mapping and real-time decision making, this can increase safety and reduce the effects of contact.

In training in methods of counter engagement, against unarmed combat striking contact, it is better to have the enemy party test, and true up the combatant's cover guard protecting bodily vitals, over deliberately targeting and contacting with high level impact of the bodily vitals.

Slow speed, low intensity testing, and truing of the guard and cover guard, and deflection capabilities, will enhance confidence and self-protection competency, and when such confidence and competency is achieved, the intensity can be increased, commensurate with proficiency levels of the exponent.

Contact impact on the cover guard protecting bodily vitals, physically and psychologically allows the combatant to experience close proximity contact impact realities without risk of injury. Such contact impact on the cover guarding extremities will mean minor blunt force pain sensations, and this is important for preparing the combatant for the realities of contact. I have trained many combatants that have later declared to me that in real life actions-on encounters, the realities of contact were nothing compared to what they had experienced in training.

Maintaining a constant state of readiness and preparedness to do what is needed, and overriding fears and pain sensations, can be the difference between life and death. An understood and accepted level of non-life threatening wound or injury related pain must have no adverse effects on threat neutralisation.

Timed combative respiration, by exhaling immediately prior and throughout contact, positively reduces the effects of non-life threatening wounding and instantaneous related pain. This is a result of maintaining a controlled, ready and willing status, to endure and overcome the effects of contact, including wounding and injury pain through constantly committing to threat neutralisation.

Hard cover guarding, pivoting stationary evasion, turning your body from front on to side on and so reducing required bodily cover requirements, and aiding in deflection and counter engagement employments, increases safety and threat neutralisation capabilities as well as maintaining confidence.

Keeping your chin tucked in, eyes on the incoming threat, and making adjustments in hardcover guard and stance to effectively cover or deflect strikes, and counter knees or kicks with stamp kicks, increases safety and chances of threat neutralisation.

Through high repetition extensive and intensive prior training in such threat reduction and threat neutralisation capabilities, the combatant will have confidence in the employment of such skills in real time, real-life actions-on encounters.

Having hardcover guarding capabilities that provide protection from the top of the head to the waist line, and stationery evasion stamp kicks that provide counter engagement protection from the waist to the boots, is a psychological confidence booster. Even when a pain sensation is experienced as a result of contact injuries and wounds, confidence can be maintained or increased, simply by the knowledge that the effects are not life-threatening, and you have the capabilities to continue without losing the momentum of threat neutralisation.

In actions-on encounters, in real time when immediate threat neutralisation including clearing the kill zone is not practical or possible, having simple primary practices to provide hard cover against upper quadrant and lower quadrant threats that have an immediate counter engagement component is a confidence booster.

Less is more and simple is best, as in having one means of upper quadrant hard cover self-protection and one means of lower quadrant self-protection and counter engagement, that provides the required capability to overcome the effects of contact wounding, and related pain, as part of uninterrupted threat neutralisation. Combine this with minor adjustments that increase safety and reduce risk, such as keeping your teeth clenched, locking your jaw closed, and your chin tucked inside your cover guard, will reduce the effects of contact.

Prior exposure and inoculation to specific threats in high repetition and surprise unexpected sudden aggressive actions-on battle handling exercises, will prepare the combatant through familiarity and competency, and proficiency and understanding of the realities of contact, including the immediate pain experience related to blunt force trauma and penetrative wounds.

Having knowledge of dire wounding risk reduction, by means of maximising protection of life-support vitals, through training for such actions-on emergencies means the combatant is mentally and combative physically prepared to employ skills to increase safety and expediently neutralise the threat.

Primary proven military combative hardcover guarding against unarmed and armed threats will provide protective cover of major vitals such as the carotid arteries, cervical vertebrae and major internal organs including your heart, liver, spleen and aorta. Employing maximum protection of your side and rear flanks, keeping the enemy to your front, and maintaining enemy alignment, reduces rear and side flank risks.

Understanding the importance of utilising the required level of squatting to cause your enemy to miss you, by remaining focused on the incoming threat, is a primary contact preventative practice. This increases the likelihood of your enemy missing you, their intended target. If contact is unavoidable, keeping your hard cover guard on (acting as shock absorbers), with your head and neck held rigid and protected, enables hard cover guard contact absorbing or deflection. Your hard cover guard status, from the top of your head to your waistline, provides body line protection, and when combined with combative squatting or pivoting stationery evasion, removing your torso down or off the contact zone not only is preventative, but is also proactive in the setting of a combative ready set to go status.

I have had a lifetime involvement in not only military close combat and military self-defence, but also in training fighters. Through this and through owning fight magazines, I have been privy to wide ranging combat sports competition. I have observed tens of thousands of military combative exponents and instructors, as well as wide ranging codes of combat sports fighters in training and competition. My more than 20 years as a crowd controller provided involvement and exposure with hands on and observed street violence. This combined with my research and interviewing of military combatants, law enforcement personnel, fighters and bouncers, has provided the following information.

The effect of unarmed blunt force trauma in relation to pain is usually dull, numb, and localised. If there are cuts, lacerations, or fractures involved with blunt force contact impact, the pain sensation is likely to include both a localised dull feeling, and a sharp deeper stinging sensation.

Broken noses, fractured eye sockets, cheekbones, jaws, cut lips, and eyebrow cuts through impact, are likely to cause a sensation of external, dull, localised pain, and internal sharp stinging pain.

When contact is expected, and the effect minimised, the trained, highly committed combatant may not experience any pain sensation, as a result of expediently employing threat neutralisation. However, an unexpected actions-on encounter injury can instantaneously incapacitate, or eliminate the combatant, through having no awareness, and as such, no means of prevention or self-protection.

In unexpected contact where the target is incapacitated but not eliminated, decentralisation and the realities of surprise and shock, including increased effects in relation to pain as a result of having no means of self-protection or reducing such contact impact are likely to be increased considerably.

Under such adversity, the effects include high levels of pain sensations, and the combatant must be mentally tough and tactically prepared to reduce risk, by self-protection and without hesitation, employ threat neutralisation combative or escape and evasion options.

Blunt force trauma from weapons generally produces similar, but usually increased, combined dull external impact pain to unarmed contact impact, and when cuts and lacerations, fractures or internal injuries are also involved, there will be also sharp stinging or burning internal pain sensations.

The effects of penetrating wounds with edged weapons depend upon what internal injuries are incurred in relation to bodily vitals. The effects of penetrating major life-support internal organs are devastating, and the pain can be sharp, burning and deep. Some penetrating wounds can appear minimal externally, and there may be little or no internal pain sensations; however, the wound may be life-threatening.

I have spoken with victims of stabbings and slashing wounds, where there has been little or no pain as a result of nerves being cut, or simply because adrenaline and endorphins considerably reduced or eliminated pain, especially when combined with non-stop employment of threat neutralisation. Slashing wounds may well appear more life-threatening than a small knife penetration wound; however, such slashing wounds on muscle and tissue are generally considerably less life-threatening than penetrating internal wounds, that may well have penetrated major bodily internal organs.

My research has also included talking with veterans that have been shot in combat, as well as civilian casualties of ballistic wounds, including head, abdominal, and extremity wounds with high-powered rounds and shotguns. They all described the wounds as either like having a bucket of boiling water thrown over them, being stabbed with a red hot poker, or being smacked with a sledgehammer. Some described ballistic wound pain sensations as being a combined blunt force trauma and burning, stinging sensation.

The difference in thought and actions when wounded or injured, under threat, in comparison to injuries from accidents, are very different. Pain effects from general accidents, like falling off a ladder, are more about doing nothing immediately on ground impact. Common post-accident responses include lying in a foetal position, suffering silently, or cursing, letting out pain related sounds. Profanities, moaning and groaning with the pain effects, followed by seeking help and assistance are common.

This is very different to being injured or wounded under assault, where you need to self-protect and threat neutralise; to do so means overcoming the effects of incapacitation and pain. The trained combatant is well aware of the importance when wounded or injured, to immediately continue with tactics and actions of safety and risk reduction as part of threat neutralisation. They also are committed to not only their own safety, but that of their comrades.

A friend of mine, and ex special operations soldier and medic, provided me information in relation to his duties dealing with mates that were ambushed. He arrived to a situation of dead and seriously wounded mates. He previously heard the muffled, almost illegible radio communication from one of his wounded mates, and recalls he could barely understand any of it.

The wounded, on knowing that a medic was on his way, had an understanding that their medic would go to every length to treat them, and as such their situation and likely outcomes were improved. They had confidence in their medic and mate, and knew they would be provided with emergency treatment. On checking one wounded comrade, this seriously wounded comrade told the medic he would be okay, and to take care of another member of the patrol that was more seriously wounded. Loyalty, duty, comradeship and the knowledge that giving in or giving up is not an option, enables the trained combatant in an actions-on encounter to be physically capable, and able to continue even if wounded.

Street fights where there are no safeguards, rules and regulations unlike combat sports and martial arts competitions, also require those involved to continue when injured or lose. There are many reasons why injured and wounded combatants and street fighters can continue after being seriously wounded or injured: Mental toughness, a will to win, combined with the human body's incredible capabilities to endure the effects of serious wounds and injuries. Endorphins, human natural painkillers, and adrenaline and other hormones that make continued combative capabilities possible, all contribute to the mentally tough combatant's capabilities to continue to go combative even when seriously wounded. Endorphins combined with nerves being severed, or damaged, may well prevent the wounded or injured combatant from feeling any pain, or grossly reduce pain effects as a result of even serious dire wounds and injuries.

Temperature, including extremely cold conditions, can also reduce the effects of wounds, and when combined with nerve damage can completely eliminate pain. For the military combatant that has an understanding and acceptance of the realities of actions-on encounters, combined with a commitment and duty to objective achievement, pain will motivate them rather than interfere or stop them.

Having trust and confidence in one's comrades, and if seriously wounded, in your highly trained military medics and the knowledge that assistance will be rendered, enables even the most adverse and dire situations in relation to fear and stress to be understood and withstood.

While there may not be any formal rules or regulations about the way the trained military combatant should react, respond or act in relation to being wounded or injured, a combatant's mentality and demeanour in such situations is one of controlling their responses in relation to pain.

The very nature of being part of the military requires combatants to accept the realities of war, and by control and coping mechanisms overcome overreaction to wounds, injuries and pain.

A former military medic that has served and treated wounded comrades, and has also spent a long career working in hospital emergency rooms, told me that generally speaking, the wounded soldier is more quiet, and copes better with pain, than civilians experiencing pain. He was clear to identify that generally, the wounded military combatant would be considerably less likely to overreact to pain, whereas many civilian patients would not be able to cope with, or control themselves, in relation to the effects of pain.

In my world back in the late 1970s through the 1980s, working as a bouncer at some of the more popular and rougher venues, where dealing with violence was a reality, pain and injury came with the territory, and a little bit of hurt, pain or an injury was never going to stop you from doing your job and winning. In fact, pain and injuries were incentive and motivators to win and get the job done, more than threat neutralisation stoppers or deterrents. The old saying that some of the best fighters come from the worst upbringing environments and backgrounds can hold true, and if they are well accustomed to the effects of fear, stress, pain and injury it will be nothing new, and they will have developed the mentality to disregard pain effects and get on with the fight.

Likewise through the realities and rigours of military training, facing adversity, knocks, bumps and injuries, the combatant becomes familiar and accustomed with what is expected, and how to cope and deal with it, rather than allowing the effects of injuries, wounds and pain to incapacitate them, stopping them from continuing to employ the required means to neutralise the threat.

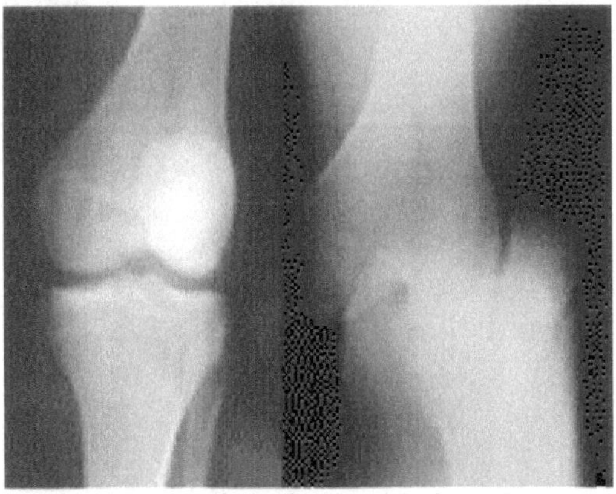

X-Ray stable knee joint pictured left and a post stamp kick dislocation pictured right.

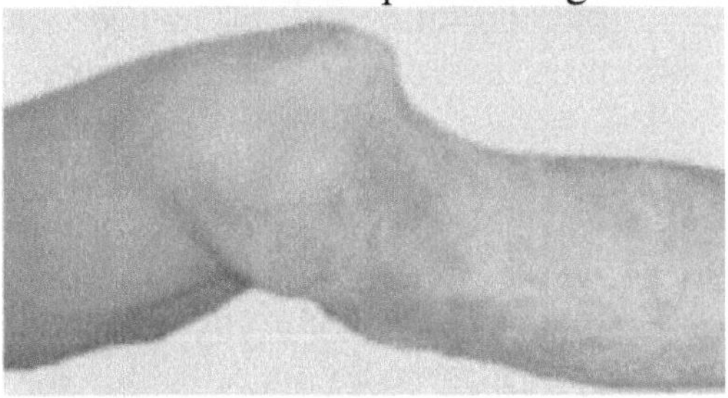

The devastating result of a stamp kick destroying the integrity of the knee joint and the knee cap.

The following are recollections from two former elite forces soldiers in relation to them being wounded.

"After taking multiple rounds I immediately decentralised myself in an effort to remove myself from the firing line. Quickly my mates were with me, and I asked them to check for an exit wound. Being informed there was no exit wound brought a sense of relief based on what I had learned from former instructors and operators I held in high regard relative to their personal experiences, including when they had been wounded. I had listened carefully to their recollections of the realities, timeframes, and bodily changes and effects in relation to their wounds.

As I was tended to by my mates, and as I waited for a medivac, I knew I would make it for two reasons; one, I would never give in, and two, because of the knowledge I had of being wounded as taught to me by those who had been there and done that, those that I trusted and respected.

I had thoughts of positive relevant things, such as how these wounds may affect my future as a professional soldier serving in my beloved unit".

This is testament to him believing he was going to live, and demonstrated forward thinking in relation to the future after the fact.

I spoke with another mate who took a round in the head and lived to tell me about it. I asked him of his first recollections, and he said it was like getting hit in the head with a sledgehammer. He said he knew he had to keep on with the job, through his training, and out of a high level of wanting to win and live.

He said that after the threat was no more, he told his mate 'I think I have been shot in the head', and it was confirmed. While he was receiving immediate medical attention, he thought of how he hoped this would not affect his future career, especially as he could not hear anything from one ear. He was most relieved when, after surgery, a wad of cotton wool was removed from the ear and he had his hearing again.

Once again dealing with the reality of a serious wound through knowledge, training and inner resolve, in short, his thought was on recovery and the effects it may have on future service and career plans over the negative thought of not making it.

I have so many hands-on and observed real-life recollections in relation to wounds and injuries as part of my bouncer days as well as post wounding and injury accounts from mates. The following are two more such accounts, one resulting in edged weapon wounding, and the second, a point-blank accidental discharge 12 gauge shotgun wound to the foot.

The first was a result of a lad going to the aid of a mate, intervening when his mate's assailant was armed with a knife. When he intervened, the armed assailants' attention was turned on him, and he received a major forearm cut, before seizing and securing the knife holding hand, losing his balance and ending up on the ground.

He maintained his grip on the knife holding hand, fighting against downward force, and the knife being forced towards his throat. With the danger increasing, he prepared and released one grip of the knife holding hand, using his free hand to render his attacker unconscious.

When he regained his footing he was surprised at his mates saying he needed to go to the hospital. He was unaware that he had been wounded not once, but had one major slash wound and other less serious cuts. Although he was aware of the knife, through adrenaline and endorphins and a determined attitude to defeat this attacker, he felt no pain and was unaware he had been slashed and stabbed.

The next account is of an individual that through an accidental discharge shot himself in the foot with a 12 gauge shotgun at close to point blank range. His immediate recollections were of the pain sensation like being hit with a sledgehammer full of bee stings. He did not let the pain overcome him, and in fact tells me he thought back to when he was training in CQC, and the advice I had given his training group on getting out of Dodge as quickly and safely as possible when wounded.

He had to take control of the situation, summon assistance, and be airlifted to the hospital.

Another common comment from many of the lads I spoke with in regards to wounds, or acts of bravery, was 'I just did what I have been trained to do, and what needed to be done, which was nothing different to what any of the lads would have done'.

Some people have a will to live and fight when up against adversity at the sharp end, and others simply do not, but the reality is the beating or wounding will only get worse if you do not have the will to fight back, or the ability to get away; this was a general consensus of my research interviewing strong minded combatants and fighters.

Duty is another powerful motivator when it comes to facing threat and extreme potential physical danger. As a bouncer, on many occasions I had to face dangerous people, armed and unarmed, and go to the aid of victims that, if I had not, could easily have been killed. The way I looked at it back then was I had a duty of care to responsible citizens and punters that were not out to get their heads punched in for no reason.

When you're in a position of authority, and have a duty no matter how frightening or threatening individuals or groups may be, you have to be psychologically strong and go tactical to reduce the risk to as low a level as humanly possible, and stand confident and ready for anything and everything always.

While you must do everything to prevent or reduce injury or wounding, you must understand and accept that it is a reality, and of the effects and possible pain of wounds and injuries.

Knowledge provides understanding, and a deep commitment to objective achievement can provide extreme capability under adversity.

The reality is, for the highly committed, skilled combatant, where there is a will and a way, the battle must go on and be won, and pain must motivate, not stop you. When wounded or injured, the difference between a coward and a hero is not in physical attributes, but is in intestinal fortitude, inner resolve and a self-belief that knows no quitting.

One of the realities of CQC instruction is providing expertise so that the combatant can neutralise the most formidable enemy, by preying on human bodily targets, that if effectively contacted, will incapacitate or eliminate the most physically and psychologically capable human beings.

There are some wounds and injuries that will simply render the most formidable incapable of saving their own lives, let alone neutralising a threat.

The reality of battle, service or civilian self-defence may see the immediate threat removed, but you may be left injured or wounded, which comes with the territory. This is when an understanding of the realities of your specific wound or injuries will provide a realisation of your status, fate and of the effects of the inflicted wound or injury.

Combine this with trust and faith in those serving with you or who come to your aid and your resolve can be strengthened considerably.

Your mind and pain

Pain affects different individuals differently in relation to pain tolerances and in relation to the nature of the effects of pain. Your mind will determine in relation to your mental toughness the degree and effects of pain as a result of combative contact injury or wounding.

Pain can be considered a sensory warning system to turn on your combative capabilities, to relieve or prevent pain, by neutralising the pain generating threat. While your mind is a major means of the transmission of the effects of combative pain, it can also work against you if you do not have the intestinal fortitude to overcome the effects and neutralise the source. Neutralising the source may include self-preservation skills in relation to immediately relieving the pain generation, as in strangulation and choking, joint locks and joint straight-line hyperextension.

Attacks on delicate bodily vitals such as eye gouging and scrotum squeezing require self-preservation methods of preventing continued gouging or squeezing prior to threat neutralisation by combative counter engagement means. In some dire situations the squeezing, crushing or gouging assaults may need to be countered, and the enemy neutralised by immediate counter engagement striking or stamp kicking skills, especially if relieving the pressure or removing the inflicting hand or leg is not possible.

Although seizure, securing or pressure type assaults can cause considerable increased danger, risks and pain by means of increased force, they are by nature of their employment considered less than immediate, instantaneous means of incapacitation. Counter engagement by means of immediate methods of self-preservation to reduce the risk of increased injury are important to enable enemy incapacitation or elimination, depending upon rules of engagement or laws of self-defence and the threat and risk situation.

If unable to employ methods of self-preservation in relation to relieving the pressure, force and pain prior to counter engagement, then the only option combatively to ensure the threat is neutralised is to employ the last resort targeting of human bodily targets that will achieve immediate disengagement and threat neutralization. Obviously some combative methods of threat neutralisation are life-threatening; however other counter engagement methods like stamp kicking hyperextension will cause incapacitation by immediate disengagement to protect the integrity of the knee joint, knee cap and related ligaments.

It is psychologically negative for the enemy to try to maintain a secure grip when the integrity of the knee joint is being destroyed by the massive force of a stamp kick.

Pain is truly an indication of being alive and vulnerable and in the motivated trained combatant, should be an indicator and motivator in relation to going combative. Your mind is very much a means of measuring pain and injury, as well as a means of neutralising pain and injury. Understanding the nature of the source of the pain and being highly skilled in how to neutralise the pain and the enemy threat is what makes those with the skills, capabilities and the intestinal fortitude to endure it different from those that give in to the mind's pain messages through a lack of intestinal fortitude and the required skills.

Just because an individual has trained in self-defence methods doesn't mean they will utilise them to neutralise pain when they need it the most, if they allow their mind to transmit pain to the point where they believe they are psychologically incapable of neutralising the pain and the threat. A practical realist with little or no skills training but with a high level of mental toughness will understand the importance of pain prevention and threat neutralisation, and will do something to stop the threat immediately.

The opposite applies to someone with skills but with a lack of mental toughness that allows the pain to overcome them to the point of helplessness. Such individuals, when they realise the helplessness of the situation may try to utilise the skills they possess, but this may be too late in relation to recovery from the effects of the assault. In any compromised situation, immediate threat assessment and decision making for threat neutralisation are essential, combined with immediate methods of self-preservation if there is risk to life or limb. Your mind is your greatest asset and is an ally in a combative situation, but if you are of weak constitution it can be your worst enemy.

Immediately the effects of pain are experienced, utilise your psychological toughness and enhancement to enable you to employ fast mapping, assessment and the safest, most effective means of threat neutralization.

It is always a reality in dire situations that you may have to accept injury as part of escaping a painful hold including submission type joint locks and bars sacrificing the bodily extremity to injury as part of threat neutralisation.

Some skills are hard to neutralise the effects of if you allow them to be applied, including escaping chokes, strangles, locks and bars and this is why hard targeting preventative skills are safer than counter skills under the effects of pain.

If no other option is available and you know that sacrificing injury will enable threat neutralisation then so be it.

PSYCHOLOGICAL ASPECTS OF BRAIN TO BOOT

Subject detailing

Never underestimate your enemy, but don't consider that their physical appearance or reputation makes them undefeatable. The reality is you are at close quarters with this enemy and the only thing that matters is victory. Desensitize and remove any personal detail from the bodily form you face. Remain focused on any action the faceless form may execute, but consider your enemy nothing more than a target form. Identify any weaknesses in their armour and exploit them with ruthless commitment, ravaging your enemy. Likewise identify any presented dangers or strengths and neutralise them, reducing the risk to the lowest level humanly possible.

You may have to step outside the normal realm of human behaviour and employ options that may well normally seem inhuman, and to do this, focusing on a target form over a human form will make your actions more acceptable from a psychological standpoint. Enemy desensitization to the point of an inanimate target form is preferred over dehumanisation to the point of considering your enemy the lowest form of human or animal life.

The Todd Systems prefer to reduce stress and anxiety by regarding the enemy as a target form that must never be underestimated. While identifying enemy potential strengths is tactically correct in relation to threat neutralization considerations, never focus on such strengths for any other reason, as to do so can weaken your resolve. Focus only on ways to achieve your objective, such as identifying and targeting faults and weaknesses, or employing dirty tricks and deception to set up your combative skill or escape and evasion. Undertake your real time, factual assessment then make the D and initiate the employment of your combative plan with ruthless controlled aggressive commitment. Never waste any time other than plain, simple threat assessment as part of your decision making on enemy strengths; instead direct all efforts to neutralizing the threat.

True battle-proven military combative skills provide the best chance of defeating a highly skilled enemy per by means of dirty and deadly battle-proven practices that are based on the military science of CQC and CQB. It is not an exact science, rather, a means to eliminate a formidable enemy threat. Ruthless, controlled dirty and deadly CQC knows no rules and has no bounds. It provides the best means of incapacitating or eliminating a formidable enemy, and is based on combative fact and proven military science.

This instills and increases confidence within the combatant who has the combative smarts to realize the probable outcomes if you employ such dirty and deadly skills with total controlled ruthless aggression and commitment.

You don't have to be a brain surgeon to realize an enemy combatant skilled in the clinch or grapple can be neutralised by armed or unarmed targeting via a cranial orifice. Or that the combat boot provides considerably more protection, and destruction, by means of stamp kicks than bare foot and shin type kicks. These are just two examples of skills that provide increased advantages and considerably higher chances of objective achievement for a combatant up against a highly trained enemy, and as such, increase psychological confidence.

You must look at your enemy's every weakness and never lock on to their strengths. Identify not only their bodily and psychological weaknesses, but also their physical faults in stance and guard etc. Look at your enemy as an inanimate object comprising of strengths and weaknesses, and employ anti counter or combat measures against their strengths, and exploit their weaknesses, faults and errors to the maximum. Use your combative knowledge of human nature and human reaction-to-action to further defeat your enemy. Use anything and everything to win from distractions, feints, dirty tricks, or anything that will give you an advantage or edge in achieving your objective.

Never allow yourself to settle into a survival mode. Victory is all that matters. Victory may mean escape and evasion or some other tactical, but not combative, option. The non-combative option may be the best and safest means to neutralise the threat, and as such, deprive the enemy of their objective achievement, ensuring you achieve your objective and are victorious.

You must remain ready and constantly scan your enemy and environment, ensuring the earliest possible visual detection of any specific actions-on, line of attack, limb of attack or employed weapon. Physical and psychological preparation, principles and practices must merge into cohesive unison to ensure you are ready, willing and able.

This starts from the ground up by having an affinity with the ground, via the balls of your feet through your boots, to ensure you maintain stability and are ready to cover ground, or escape and evade expediently. Prior to any actions-on you must maintain the required level of stability and a 'mobility ready' status. The degree of stability and mobility will vary in relation to the specific situation, encounter and combative engagement. Increased stability is obtained by lowered centre of gravity, and a slightly widened and deepened stance for clinching.

For mobility-ready status prior to offensive assault entry and engagement or during escape and evasion, you must be like a runner in the blocks. You must be ready to push off in an instant, utilizing your sense of touch in a controlled manner with the ground. You must be ready to explode in an instant, through your ready positioning loaded centre of gravity, and set balls of the feet, ankles, knees and hip joints. Your arms, hands and fingers must be in the required guard or running status for escape and evasion or neutral position if uncompromised. Your senses of sight, hearing and smell must be employed to detect as early as possible any danger, threat or change in situation or threat.

The sense of touch applies to your feet via your boots, not only to maintain stability and for efficient movement, but also to detect changes in terrain or terrain presented dangers. Your sense of touch with your fingers, thumb and palm of your hand allow you to use your sense of touch at close quarters in low or no light, to employ combative skills effectively by locating the specific enemy bodily target, and for seizing and securing your enemy prior to going combative. Your hands can follow lines or paths to targets such as the sternum leading to the throat, or the cheek bone leading to the eye socket. The toe of your boot can be used to locate the arch of the enemy boot in preparation to execute a low leg stamp kick used to destroy the integrity of the knee joint in limited or non-visual employments.

In the clinch or in ground combat because of impaired or obstructed vision, a result of a lack of light, or through physically simply being in a position where you cannot see your specific target you may well have to use your sense of touch to map your way to the target. Your sense of touch must extend to every available part of your enemy's body that could be targeted to neutralise, contain, control or manipulate enemy capability, action or reaction. This could include using your head to jam and control, or your teeth to contain and control (or as an offensive tool). Your chest, pelvis and hips can be utilised to contain, control and restrain your enemy in position. You may use your legs and feet to maintain stability and position, or to lock and secure. Likewise, your arms, hands and fingers can seize, secure, control, manipulate, restrain and neutralise your enemy, as well as to maintain balance and position, and for weapons employment. Your sense of touch applies to locating, seizing and securing webbing, combat vests, body armour or belts and then containing your enemy as part of employing combative options.

There are some important rules to remember in CQC, such as never reaching back behind yourself, except when pivoting and squeezing the genitals. Remembering such rules will ensure you do not employ practices that are tactically flawed, increasing the risk and danger and, consequently, affecting your psychological capabilities.

Your senses are truly a factor in increasing your psychological confidence and capabilities in specific combative skills employments or difficult situations. When your senses are ready and alert, they increase your combative capabilities and reduce panic and stress, which in turn increases your psychological and physical capabilities by ensuring you are combative ready and willing, less likely to be taken by surprise, and more capable of making the D and employing it. Maintaining your senses at high alert is critical to ensure you are not only ready, willing and able, but are focused on definite requirements that are positive. Having tactically correct tasks to constantly undertake that hard target you will increase your capabilities and eliminate any time for negative practices, such as self-doubt, anticipation, perception, or focusing on enemy considered strengths and advantages.

Combative skills perfection

The perfect combative skill is seldom, if ever, achieved by most combatants, but a skill as close to perfect as humanly possible in a high risk situation, against a formidable threat is hard to describe post execution. The deliberate action simply achieves the objective in an instant by means of your training kicking in, and your decided skill first action component setting off all the major and minor included components chain response in the correct order of execution, in unison, incorporating a complete components, single initiated action. It is as automated as a multiple major and minor component deliberate action gets, and is initiated and over quickly, quietly and with cohesion competency and maximum destruction. It is always a deliberate action, even though it may seem reactionary, because it is an instantaneous decided action to a natural human recognition and response to sudden aggressive shock action.

The sound and feel of impact can often be an indicator of a close to humanly perfect skill execution. High level achieved proficiency skills employments will include correct order of execution, physical and mental components making up the skill execution, as well as any automatic adjustments to ensure the individual skill achieves maximum tactical and physical employment capabilities: Respiration, closing on the target, expedient action, range, stance, cover guarding, target alignment, positioning, line of attack, rapid extension and retraction or through target destruction, constant fast mapping assessment, steadfast commitment and intestinal fortitude psychological empowerment, and finally safety practices to increase safety and psychological safety and security confidence enhancement.

The effects of fear and stress in relation to threats of expected probable or pending violence produce adverse reactions that are autonomic systems reactionary responses to the stimuli of probable or expected actions-on. When compromised in an unexpected assault encounter, where you manage to prevent yourself being incapacitated through self-preservation or enemy error, you have no time for self-doubt and must go combative and neutralise the enemy. This reality is considerably different to an expected assault where you have to contend with the effects of not only the enemy pre-actions-on, but also the time frame in relation to the time lag prior to the actions-on. If the combatant does not maintain a state of combative readiness by means of continuous positive preparatory combative practices, they may delve into and dwell on perceived enemy strengths. This can weaken their inner resolve and deplete their individual and combative confidence. Focusing on enemy strengths of any kind can reduce the combatant's intestinal fortitude and inner resolve to do what is needed to neutralise the threat. Focusing on enemy strengths and possible negative outcomes increases the effects of fear and stress, and reduces combative confidence as well as interrupting and interfering with the combatant's ability to remain ready, willing and capable. The combatant requires sound and definite methods to control the effects of fear and stress, maintaining a primary ready status, and by performing constant checks and re-checks to maintain that important ready status will ensure constant positive practices are performed and as such this eliminates time for negatives such as perception over factual assessment and self-doubt considerations.

Being armed with the best of battle-proven knowledge, and having a commitment to objective achievement, provides you with the best combative chance of threat neutralisation. All humans are made of the same stuff, but it comes down to some having the intestinal fortitude to act and others doing nothing. Psychologically being ready and prepared to act is one thing, but against an equally committed enemy, having the best of battle-proven tactics and skills makes you as formidable as you possibly can be.

When your house is in order

Iron Mike Tyson in his prime would knock out opponents with what appeared to be short punches. These punches may have been short in extension, but they came from the ground up, and the timing, placement and respiration was as close as humanly possible to perfect. For a fighter that was shorter than many of his opponents, he had to ensure his cover and constant body and head movement skills were timed to ensure he was not a static target, and he utilized angle and positional changes with exceptional timing, combined with cover guarding to make himself a difficult to hit hard target.

If you ever looked closely at his training methods on the slip bag and heavy bag, you would soon see how he executed such devastating deliveries with the entire minor but important performance components included automatically through muscle memory along with all major components, a result of years of countless repetitions. Combine this with the fact that he, and most, if not all top fighters can perform for up to 12 fight rounds and the importance of controlled breathing will be obvious.

He also had a great belief in his trainer and the training his trainer provided him with.

Having one's life in order and doing things for the right reasons makes a considerable difference in relation to the outcome. Having a mentor you respect and love as a father figure or like a brother provides direction in one's life, and under a hard, firm but fair mentor, responsibility is a must and maximum potential can be achieved. Many everyday people, in the execution of their duties protecting, saving and going to the aid of others put themselves at great risk. Many professional athletes perform way below their best when their life is in turmoil, or the important leadership or support people in their life are lost. Sometimes, depending on the individual, it can be only a small or insignificant thing in their life that is not right at the time that can affect them adversely. This can either affect their decision making performance capabilities or can create adverse or unnecessary reactions and responses.

I have spoken with many elite forces operators I have trained in relation to mental toughness and doing what needs to be done as part of a team, when there are great personal dangers and risks that are very real and dire. These lads have proven themselves time and time again, through selection, training, qualification, on exercises and operationally, as having high level skills capabilities and extreme psychological levels in relation to overcoming fear, stress and going tactical. They have also all been very definite in relation to a most important factor: looking after their mates. The bond, loyalty and trust of highly trained comrades that have each other's backs at all times is not only a strong reason for taking action under adversity, but also provides a major psychological edge and advantage that can only increase confidence, through knowing the strength gained from highly trained team members operating as a tight highly trained highly committed unit. The increased capabilities and safety and security of numbers of such special individuals combining as a tight unit is psychologically empowering. These lads just see it as their duty, and if asked about their bravery, just say 'I was just looking after my mates, and they would have done the same for me'. We can draw an analogy here between the individual combatant operating as part of a committed unit and the whole brain-to-boot philosophy of a combatant's body and mind acting in controlled unison for objective achievement.

I believe that those doing things for the right reasons in relation to the laws of the land, their rules of engagement, out of duty and loyalty to their mates or innocent victims, even at great personal sacrifice regardless of the grave danger they face, stand to improve their chances of being victorious. Those that act outside the law taking criminal actions against law-abiding citizens are only one step away from defeat of one kind or another all the time. This is also a very important aspect of the military combatant's psychological capabilities in relation to knowing that the training they have been provided with will provide them with the best and safest means of achieving the objective. Confidence in one's instructors, like confidence in one's mates, and confidence in the tactics and skills provided by your instructor is important; along with knowing what you are doing is right for the right reasons morally, ethically and legally.

You are either on the good or bad side and there is no grey area. Knowing your combative or self-defence actions are legally and morally justified and required is another psychological aspect that will enhance an individual's willingness to employ required methods of threat neutralization. When acting within the laws of the land or rules of engagement without fear of prosecution for illegal actions during any actions-on encounter, the righteous will not be over adversely affected psychologically as their actions will not be illegal or unjustified. That is not to say that they will not be affected by what they have had to do, experience or endure, but that is another matter.

Formidable enemy destruction or neutralisation

Dirty and deadly combative skills provide maximum capabilities against a highly trained and motivated enemy combatant. I have seen trained fighters fall victim to street fighters who had no respect for their target's martial arts or combat sports prowess. They had no intention of abiding by any rules, and would not hesitate in doing the unthinkable in an instant. Gouging eyes, biting the throat or the end of the nose and ears, scrotum squeezing and groin kneeing, head kicking, and head stomping as well as using edged and bludgeon type weapons are all means of destruction of even the most formidable fighters and combatants.

I was taught early in my combative career that from the outset, if you're going to attack someone's eyes or other bodily sensitive vitals, that you need to attack it multiple times to physically and mentally destroy enemy capabilities, and if they cover the targeted vital then employ multiple destructive actions against another exposed bodily vital. You need to ensure and maximize the effect by seizing, securing or containing and targeting your enemy's exposed delicate bodily vitals. Seizing webbing, combat vests, battle dress, head seizing or securing the arms in a combative clinch, or corner or contain your enemy target up against solid backdrops, immoveable objects, terrain or environmentally provided advantages will prevent or reduce them being able to avoid your targeting of their delicate sensitive bodily vitals.

Always remember when you seize or contain your enemy that is an unarmed assault in its own right, capable of neutralizing the threat. Seize and secure to incapacitate for that millisecond in time, making them unable to avoid or prevent your immediate targeting of their major vitals. Ensure containment or cornering is achieved with high impact, to incapacitate temporarily or eliminate the threat depending on your objectives, rules of engagement, laws of the land and what is possible. Good combative skills require and allow for making adjustments to increase your chances of objective achievement. You need to put your enemy physically and psychologically in a status of helplessness, where they have no means of recovery, counter actions or escape. Targeting exposed life support, major bodily vitals including delicate human senses with multiple contact impacts, moving to alternate targets when one target becomes covered or protected, with deliberate, controlled, ruthless aggression can break down and render the most formidable combatant helpless. When you know how to destroy life support systems, and damage and interfere with sensitive delicate bodily senses fully realizing the outcome of such actions, you will be psychologically more confident in your capabilities to neutralise the threat, and as such have an increased chance of objective achievement.

A formidable combatant alert and aware will employ every means of self-protection, and will persevere and endure the effects of pain and injury if at all possible as part of achieving their objective. Often a bit of pain is a motivator that will make your enemy fight even harder. Multiple, single target, ruthless, repetitive contact will injure, incapacitate, demoralize and render even a formidable fighter incapable of anything other than self-preservation—that is if they are capable of even self-preservation. Going for multiple targets in cohesive, ruthless combinations that prey on human reaction to action, is another means to achieve threat neutralisation, especially against a seasoned combatant with considerable defensive capabilities.

When I instruct unarmed targeting of the enemy's eyes on military CQC courses to ensure maximum physical and psychological destruction, I instruct forceful impact seizure and securing of the back of the head and neck that will, in itself, stun the enemy target, followed by multiple bent fork finger attacks to the eyes to reduce the likelihood of recovery and counter engagement. Combination focused upper quadrant palm heel and flat hand strikes combined with leg stamp kicks and oblique stamp kicks to the lower quadrants, or kneeing to the groin create difficulty for the subject to counter multiple targeting locations, especially if the combinations are distractive, deceptive and prey on human limited capabilities to deal with over-kill cohesive multiple target destruction. Battledress and civilian belts and trouser waistbands provide the ability to seize and secure the target at midsection, and combined with deceptive, cohesive, deliberate target destruction at upper, mid and lower quadrants increase the likelihood of threat neutralization.

Likewise point-blank range forehand and backhand executed roundhouse elbow strikes, combined with chin jab uppercut palm heel strikes can cause fatal injuries by means of targeting the jaw or airway and spinal column and cord. Ravaging your enemy by employing cohesive, combative combinations designed to prey on human weaknesses with controlled ruthless aggression is hard to defend against and harder to counter. This deliberate enemy destruction targeting delicate bodily vitals of different quadrants of the body with unpredictable, cohesive, highly committed aggressive combinations actions takes away enemy capabilities by forcing them into a self-preservation status.

Military combative combinations specifically developed to achieve the objective by such means have been developed, tested and proven to provide the objective achievement, by overwhelming enemy capabilities to defend multiple quadrants targeting, and by exploiting known normal human reaction to sudden aggressive cohesive shock action. Such military combative offensive combinations of cohesive, controlled, aggressive offensive actions that take advantage of every weakness and leave no time for enemy recovery provide a high chance of threat neutralization.

Employing such cohesive combinations from under or outside the enemy target's peripheral vision, or setting combinations up by masking them using deception, distractions or dirty tricks makes objective achievement that much easier and far more guaranteed. Seizing and securing an enemy bodily part or battle dress, then targeting exposed delicate bodily vitals with deception and controlled ruthless aggression requires far less physical capabilities, and as such, reduces the likelihood of telegraphing your actions and your enemy preventing contact defensively.

The same applies to the employment of armed combat at point-blank range in regards to seizing and securing the enemy target before drawing, making ready and employing a weapon. The most dangerous and effective weapon is the one the target is unaware of, does not see being drawn, made ready or employed, and that is employed ruthlessly in multiple destructive repetitions.

Unarmed offensive assault that is covertly employed is always going to be the most effective and safest means of threat neutralisation.

Introducing an enemy to the unknown in skills and execution means at close to point blank range increases objective achievement by unfamiliarity. Such execution aspects as broken or no rhythm and skills that seem to have no form can weaken your enemy's resolve by causing confusion.

I have trained with individuals that simply seem uncoordinated but in fact are highly committed and unpredictable. Their attack comes from anywhere and everywhere and they are hard to hit making them very much an unknown danger.

A formidable foe that is unconventional and employs skills that their target subject has not faced before can psychologically demoralise them especially if they are fully committed pushing hard forward by introducing them to the unknown unfamiliar with controlled ruthless aggression.

A jab or palm strike may not be unexpected or unpredictable. However, simply by immediately prior to contact snatching at the eyes and raking them can interfere with mental focus and cause confusion by introducing the target subject to the unfamiliar unexpected and unorthodox.

Skills execution practices that reduce counter engagement opportunities by means of execution have built in contingency capabilities. For example, if they miss on the forehand they may contact on the backhand, or upper cut type skills that if they miss on the upward action may contact on the downward raking action. Being unfamiliar or unknown they can demoralise confuse and weaken the target subject's resolve.

The reality is, most traditional or sporting practitioners practice defending against or countering expected methods of attack; however, when faced with an aggressor that appears out of control, but is in fact ruthlessly in control and extremely unpredictable, the danger level can be increased considerably. I have trained with many such individuals that may not look pretty or proper in their actions but are difficult to deal with, and when this physical unpredictability is combined with a mentality that is willing to do anything, and simply will not give up, you have an extremely dangerous individual in your midst.

I can remember conducting a combative phase test when a physically small candidate was out there unarmed battling with an enemy party over double his weight. I heard a former Vietnam veteran and Special Forces operator say 'ram your finger up his nose, that will make him let go'. That's exactly what the little lad did, combined with hooking his finger and ripping it back out of the nostril. As a result, the big lump disengaged, tears shooting from his eyes like welding sparks. He turned away and before he could recover, had been put down by means of a stamp kick and was being neutralised on the ground. The unpredictable and unexpected dirty fighting took away the 60 kilos plus advantage, and the hunted become the hunter and victor, plain and simple. Understanding how devastating such practices are not only increases your chance of objective achievement, but also is a great psychological enhancer, and provides mental encouragement to be unorthodox and ruthless. Knowing that skills, when employed correctly with ruthless, controlled aggression, are the best means to neutralise the most formidable enemy will really enhance your mental toughness in the employment of such skills.

Combining your psychological and physical combative skills in the correct order of execution and through sound assessment and decision making employing the best option of threat neutralisation in relation to the threat situation is very important. The physical and psychological components require a cohesive employment enabling controlled aggressive output in relation to the immediate threat and the decided option to neutralise the threat with the decided force level. Controlled aggression including constant focused fast mapping in real time in regards to the threat situation and threat escalation levels as well as situational changes can be dealt with by a mentally and physically prepared ready and focused combatant. This can be simply accomplished by making adjustments, increasing skills employment force levels or changing pre-decided skills options to provide the best means of threat neutralization in relation to real time threat and situational changes. A confident and competent combatant who knows how to make range, set up and engage an enemy, as well as fast map on the move, employing contingency options to neutralise changing threat situations, has the best, quickest and safest chance at threat neutralization. The need to know how orthodox CQC skills employments provide advantages over unorthodox and how the open stance in relation to stationary pivoting evasion provides increased stability over the closed stance side is advantageous.

Likewise a confident competent combatant who can hold ground, and then seize, secure, contain, control and neutralise a formidable enemy threat, or who can yield and neutralise enemy momentum and regain every advantage to take control of the situation, neutralising the threat by being proficient in and being prepared to employ the required physical skills, and being mentally fully committed to achieving the objective, will have the best combative chance of victory over defeat; nothing more nothing less.

Train the combative way

Always train the way you will go combative, or for fighting, train the way you will fight. The value of being trained by a highly skilled instructor, who ensures your tactics and physical skills are correct in relation to every aspect of their employment, makes all the difference. The military combative instructor will put you through TOETs for evaluating your skills levels. This will enable critiquing and correcting to ensure the exponent's skills are executed in training to the best of their ability, and that they meet the required levels and standards. This is the important finishing and performance enhancement that cannot be learnt and experienced from any other way than on course and under the instruction of a highly skilled and qualified combative instructor. Books and DVDs do not critique errors, nor do they provide training in every aspect of a system.

Various systems and styles specialize in, or have strengths in, either offensive or counter-offensive skills employments. This reality can create negative psychological effects on an individual exponent's capabilities if the style or system is one dimensional, or does not provide primary capabilities in both offensive and counteroffensive options.

If, for example, a system is strong in counteroffensive evasion, and every time under training conditions an exponent attempts to achieve their objective by means of unarmed offensive assault, in the case of constant failed outcomes, they tend to self-doubt or consider the offensive option unreliable. The reality is that, in this case, the combatants who both employ that same system or style are countering each other out. The reasoning for this is that the exponent going on the unarmed offensive must cover ground, while the counteroffensive exponent ready to evade simply needs to hold a ready status to employ their physical and psychological brain-to-boot practices, combined with their tactically correct physical skills executed with correct timing. Under an unarmed offensive assault (TOET), the instructor would be able to provide correction in range set up and safety practices that promote highly committed assaults, through being proficient and confident in one's hard cover guarding.

In instructing unarmed offensive assault, employing practices such as placing visually clear ground markings to the target's rear flanks provides a line of sight through the target, and consequently promotes high-level commitment thus increasing objective achievement.

Truing up one's guard increases confidence in the execution of a skill, between close range and point-blank range, without hesitation or reduction in the speed of execution.

Correcting and improving unarmed offensive assault, and the setup by dirty tricks and deceptive practices to the point where they leave no doubt in the enemy's mind and create the distraction and false reaction required to make the masked unarmed offensive assault achieve its objective.

Having the first and most important contingency option your 'stalking into range contingency option', if engaged by your unarmed enemy, squared away and at the ready will increase confidence in making range considerably. Your 'stalking into range contingency option', if your unarmed enemy engages you, must be as fool proof as is humanly possible, and must be employed time and time again in training so as to instill confidence in this contingency skills capability to neutralise the threat.

Continuously truing up exponents' hard cover guard capabilities before, during and post any offensive action employment will develop confidence in the skill, and will enable them to hard cover guard themselves under assault, make range and positional adjustments, and so set up their counter engagement threat neutralization. This emergency contingency capability will increase inner resolve if attacked while getting in range, and will therefore maximize the individual's capability to employ it as part of achieving the objective.

Counteroffensive primary, secondary alternative and emergency stationary counter engagement capabilities options, practiced in training under various threat situations and scenarios, provide the combatant with the necessary skills to deal with wide-ranging possibilities.

As part of the practice of same-system offensive actions against same-system counteroffensive actions in training, it is important to inform and reiterate to the proponents the difference and advantages of assaulting the enemy with offensive actions that are not expected by them, and that they are not familiar with. The employment of the dirty tricks deceptive and distractive set ups, combined with foreign skills against enemies unfamiliar with such skills, provides a better chance of threat neutralization. Highlighting and maintaining the factor of confusion, and the utilisation of tactics of distraction, deception and dirty tricks that are unknown and unfamiliar to an unsuspecting or unexpectant enemy changes the execution and outcome considerably.

It is most important that the individual combatant is drilled in the importance of making sure that any combative or self-defence action is deliberate and is powered by every required component, both psychologically and physically, in the correct order of execution to ensure objective achievement.

If an exponent under training and practice conditions continuously fails to achieve the desired objective in a specific skill set/role employment, then the instructor needs to perform a complete assessment (TOET) to determine the reasons, and then provide instruction in the best means to improve the specific skills employments. There may be situations where the skills simply do not meet objective achievement requirements as a result of the individual combatant's capabilities, disabilities, or psychological makeup and, under such conditions, the instructor would advise on a better alternative.

The danger of multiple exponents failing to achieve an objective during training, as a result of same-system specific options advantages countering out other role options, is that the perception or effect can be infectious. I covered earlier the offensive action against counteroffensive action objective achievement failures, through the unarmed offensive assault exponent having to cover ground, while his unarmed counter-offensive assault enemy per training partner simply has to wait and time his evasion to achieve the objective.

I covered confidence in hard cover guarding, and the use of distractions, deception and dirty tricks all enhancing objective differential achievement, especially when combined with 75 percent plus commitment and extremely close range to point-blank range executions.

Another reason for objective achievement failures in training is the concern for causing injury to one's buddy enemy training partner, or being injured as a result of having to cover ground to make range against a willing, ready and set to go enemy per training partner.

Such failed outcomes for the previous reasons and others, including seeing other formidable combatants fail to achieve the objective by means of a specific option, can cause an infectious loss of confidence and lack of trust in a specific combative practice. The best way to ensure this does not happen is through sound assessment and error correction combined with developing confidence through increased competency.

This can be achieved by ensuring controlled ruthless, aggressive employment of skills that are set up by believable realistic deceptions, distractions and downright dirty tricks that leave no doubt in the enemy per's mind that the deception, distraction or dirty trick is in fact the actual assault option and target.

Humans under repetitious combative training and practice tend to become complacent and lazy in their combative options executions. It is imperative that they are drilled in the importance of every actions-on encounter being a new and unpredictable, unorthodox and unexpected encounter that must be neutralised by the employment of all the trained principles, tactics and skills executed to the best of their ability, in the correct order of execution and with a controlled aggressive commitment required to neutralise the threat.

Variations in training include drills, stands, battle handling exercises and the introduction of effects such as low light and crowd combatives, where there are ranging possible and probable threats that must be identified and combated or countered.

Once skills have been learned and proficiency achieved, then the employment of such skills in unfamiliar environments, along with the factor of confusion ever present against unpredictable enemy pers will enhance an individual combatant's capabilities considerably. Through the necessity of constant assessment and decision-making being required in unfamiliar environments and situations, the individual combatant will learn to employ the best skills to neutralise the threat, and so will become confident to make the best (or correct) decisions and develop competency in the execution of their decided options.

I have seen individuals make negative decisions under combative test conditions, born out of failure to achieve objectives during training that was simply a result of their skills and tactical errors, as well as a lack of mental toughness as a result of not believing in themselves or their skills to provide the means to achieve the objective.

Coming up with some less than primary option that has not been tested and battle proven is tactically flawed and in the multiple combative encounter realities of testing is doomed to failure. If the skill fails in training or testing, the likelihood of it achieving the objective in an actions-on combative encounter is minimal.

Training the combative way is also important in relation to ensuring a tactically correct safe outcome is achieved in every encounter. Putting the enemy down and simulating ground neutralisation every time is a primary practice that must be employed. And when disarming, ensuring the weapon is removed from the enemy and is no longer available to them, combined with simulated ground neutralisation, is a primary means of objective achievement and safety enhancement that should be employed in every training or testing disarming encounter. In defensive tactics for law enforcement, safely and securely stowing a weapon post disarming and threat neutralisation is mandatory practice in training and operationally.

The employment of a disarmed weapon in military kill or get killed combative disarming may be the best option of threat neutralisation inside the rules of engagement. Some military units post disarming have specific tactics with a knife to ensure the threat has been neutralised.

The disarmed weapon in training may have to be secured in their webbing or body armour deposited in a designated place or handed over to an instructor.

It is important that in practice, in regards to disarming edged or bludgeon weapons or firearms, that they are not handed back to the training partner as part of repetitious disarming. The danger of this practice is the unlikely (but entirely possible) event of muscle memory taking over and the weapon being handed back to the enemy in a real-life encounter. I have heard of this unfortunate reality actually happening in law enforcement.

In conclusion, in relation to training the combative way and training the way you will go combative it is essential that the importance of the inclusion of all required tactics principles, physical and psychological skills, and their major and minor or self-defence components are included in every employed option in training, testing and operationally. There is no room for lazy training or studio training with choreography and prior knowledge of the threat, making it far from realistic in relation to being unpredictable, unorthodox and meant to cause grievous bodily harm. Obviously there has to be safeguards, and common-sense must prevail, but it is important in the development of confidence and competency that there is a high percentage of an objective achievement with the employment of the individual combatant's primary practices.

All actions-on encounters must end in achieved threat neutralisation.

Psychological advantages of primary battle-proven skills

The importance of the combatant being armed with the best of primary, secondary and alternative skills as well as emergency skills for dire, unpredictable, unexpected actions-on encounters is essential in the employment of the most effective and safest means of objective achievement against the specific threat situation.

This is why it is so important that combative training is as realistic as possible, and tests not only the level of safety and objective achievement of the tactic, principle or skill, but also tests every aspect or component of the skill to destruction. This requires formidable enemy pers with the combative smarts to employ every means of defeating the combatant's combat or counter measures. Enemy parties with the combative smarts that are tough and bent on their objective achievement are worth their weight in gold for the combatant in training, testing and proving that combatant's personal physical and psychological capabilities, and the effectiveness of their principles, tactics and skills.

This is why CQB/CQC is a military science that incorporates all the essential components such as the primary ranges for specific skills executions, the best means to effectively cover ground by expedient action, the most proven method of setting up offensive and counteroffensive actions including deception, distraction and dirty tricks that prey on human reactions and responses to such set up actions.

Direct line offensive actions, angular evasive actions, hard cover stationary combat and counter actions and weapon disarming components that provide the highest and safest levels of disarming and threat neutralization. Such disarming components include proper seizure, securing and retaining of the enemy weapon or weapon-holding hand or hands during threat neutralisation.

During realistic, unpredictable, unorthodox and unconventional training, if the combatant is provided with the means to test the individual components of their primary, secondary and alternative as well as emergency combat and counter actions skills, the likely outcomes will be blatantly obvious, as will their personal capabilities. An individual combatant's physical capabilities and psychological makeup may determine the need for adjusting or applying minor changes in tactics, principles and skills, or if the individual combatant's capabilities or disabilities simply do not lend to the employment of the specific skill, then a secondary or alternative skill may be necessary and in some cases an emergency contingency option needed.

I have identified the importance of practicing the individual combatant's primary unarmed offensive assault and unarmed counter offensive assault skills first and in high repetitions before instructing contingency options other than stalking into range contingency options.

This is important to ensure 1-3 second threat neutralisation is a primary practice of objective achievement.

Psychologically often if you give individuals contingency options early in their training or they are practiced in high repetition some individuals can decide to employ their primary option skills less than fully committed as they convince themselves that they have contingency options if their primary option fails.

The reason why their primary options may well fail to threat neutralise is because they employed them with less than full physical and mental commitment and conviction. So, I instruct 90 percent primary option practice and 10 percent contingency option practice.

Hard-testing skills through battle handling exercises and training, where the enemy pers are committed to their objective achievement and have the combative smarts, is not only the best way of proving tactics, principles and skills but also increases the individual combatant's psychological confidence in the employment of those skills. Such unpredictable, unorthodox and rugged encounters not only develop confidence in the skills, but also develop the individual combatant's inner-resolve and intestinal fortitude when faced with such uncontrolled aggressive adversity. The need to employ your skills with every ounce of intestinal fortitude, inner resolve and the correct level of physical commitment, being the basic requirements, will enhance all the required physical and psychological capabilities in the employment of the said skill to neutralise the threat and achieve the objective. Over-kill of 75 percent plus in the execution of threat neutralization should be the norm to neutralise an extreme threat.

Master-Chief Instructors develop battle-proven skills (incorporating the combative military science required in CQB and CQC) in order to give their pers the best chance of winning while never giving in or losing without exhausting all their skills capabilities. Simply surviving in CQB/CQC is a negative mind set; there is only a winner and a loser, and the loser better believe they stand to lose their life by not doing everything to win.

Ranges, methods of expedient action, evasive angles and directions, hard cover guarding and methods of quick and quiet threat neutralisation are all built into battle-proven combative adopted tactics, principles and skills. The correct tool to enable the threat to be effectively neutralised is the modus operandi of the highly trained and skilled combatant. The robustness of the sole of the combat boot, and the increased reach and power of the leg over the arm in unarmed offensive assault, generally is the primary option. However, for specific situational unarmed offensive assault employments where lower limb injuries affect mobility or there are variations in terrain and the presence of obstacles, or where an individual combatant's primary skills practices are striking over stamp kicking, then close range striking can be the best option. The arm, being lighter than the leg and essentially non-weight bearing, provides advantages in the speed of action of the arm (with velocity being improved by ground-ward, upward and outward force), where the effect can be increased considerably by the employment of multiple strikes as part of a close range combination.

In evasive counter engagement, the safety of having increased time and through safe positioning to make assessments, adjustments and destroying enemy bodily exposed targets post a diagonally forward evasion (over lateral or diagonally rearward evasion), develops confidence in the individual combatant through effective usage in training and testing. Through truing and proving of hard cover guarding and deflection for emergency stationary unarmed counter-offensive assault in training, mental toughness, physical confidence and competency develop the individual combatant's physical and psychological capabilities.

In weapon disarming, the importance of never underestimating any non-ballistic weapon and employing the most effective means to neutralise the armed threat should ensure the combatant, if able, opts for the use of their primary weapon of deadly force. If such an option is not available, or is not a legal option to neutralise a weapon's threat, then utilising an improvised weapon that is preferably longer and of hard, robust construction becomes the next most effective means of disarming and threat neutralisation. It is important to remember that just because you are armed with a primary, secondary or improvised weapon, this does not allow for the dropping of your guard, or discarding of your essential physical tactics and skills components in relation to disarming.

Your foot work and increased personal safety tactics capabilities, combined with the most effective disarming of the weapon and neutralisation of the threat, are essentially a combination of armed or unarmed military self-defence physical disarming skills and psychological confidence in disarming capabilities. True realistic testing of retention capabilities post the seizing and securing of the weapon or weapon holding hand or hands is essential to ensure safety is maintained, and the risk is prevented of the enemy being able to manipulate your grip of the weapon, regaining control of the weapon or using the weapon against you, or a seized and secured but not controlled containment.

I reiterate, train and test the military combative way, but obviously you must remember in training or testing that you are training or testing, and not in combat or real 'life and death' self-defence, and as such you must apply combative training trade craft safety practices. You must never deliberately or carelessly compromise your enemy training partner's safety in regards to loss of life or limb. True combative training and practice requires training with controlled, aggressive commitment to objective achievement and equally committed controlled, aggressive prevention of your enemy training partner's objective achievement. The psychological experience and advantages derived from unorthodox, unpredictable, full commitment training actions-on encounters is only second to using the tactics, principles and skills in a real-life combative actions-on encounter.

Facing committed, controlled, combative formidable enemy pers will certainly build confidence in your combative skills and develop mental toughness to continue with the decided option, against adversity and under extremes, until the threat is neutralised and your objective achieved. Through such training and professional instruction and insight, when threat and situational specific adjustments and changes are required to counter or combat dire situations (including considerable enemy physical and psychological advantages), in such life or death encounters the combatant will not be in unfamiliar territory. Even when losing your control of a skill employment it is essential there is a primary means of doing so that must have been learnt, drilled and perfected in training to remain as safe as humanly possible. Proven in training and proven by the individual combatant under battle handling exercises and practical training scenarios, as well as combative stands manned by formidable enemy pers bent on the combatant's demise and their own objective achievement, will only enhance the individual combatant physically, tactically, skills-wise and psychologically.

Because military CQC and CQB are principle orientated, it makes learning and retaining wide ranging threat neutralisation capabilities possible. Having individual principles to combat complete threat categories, or satisfy contingency requirements, makes it possible for the individual combatant to gain proficiency in the required tactics and skills under intensive but reasonably short course training frameworks.

I have seen too many individuals with studio only training experience who are unable to dispose of a combatant in training let alone a real actions-on encounter. Unfortunately they are unfamiliar in battle-proven tactics and skills, having never undertaken combative intensive training, and as such have never received the benefits of high intensity combative 'as close as it gets to real life' actions-on encounters. They have never faced an unorthodox, irregular, unpredictable military combative, highly trained, tested and qualified enemy per under the 'factors of confusion' of battle handling exercises.

Another unfortunate reality is that much of the unrealistic studio training practice is of cooperating with one's training partner to the point where they are assisting with the application of the training partner's technique. I have seen such studio training where individuals under control and restraint prisoner handling training apply the arm lock themselves, rather than training realistically where the operator should be employing the skills required against a formidable resisting enemy per threat. I have seen extremely dangerous self-defence hold escapes; one example being against the full nelson, raising one's arms and dropping down ground-ward. This is a suicide technique where, against a formidable full nelson application, it could produce permanent paralysis or death. Under controlled instructor's executions of this suicidal escape, where seasoned traditionalists have found the inadequacy of their technique, I have heard that the reason, or should I say excuse, is that it would work if it was not put on correctly or not with too much force. In response I advise that you should always believe your enemy means business and that their business is to cause you serious harm.

History didn't always get it right and the reality for military combative role requirements, as well as for military self-defence, is the need for the best of battle-proven skills to enable a quick, quiet and safe means of defeating a formidable, committed aggressor. A former colleague, after detailing the dangers in raising your arms and dropping down to escape a full nelson hold, clearly pointing out such dangers and how flawed and high-risk such a counter action would be got the following response: 'my Sensei said it is the best way to get out of this hold'. My colleague then offered a controlled demonstration, instructing the individual not to drop-down after raising his arms as it would compromise the safety of his cervical vertebrae and spinal cord. Unfortunately he believed what he had been told and had obviously trained the studio way where his training partners must not have applied the hold correctly, with force, and must have released the hold the moment he raised his arms and dropped down ground-ward. Fortunately the instructor released the hold when this individual decided to raise his arms and drop down against instructions. He did self-injure his neck as a result and was incapacitated on the floor and required hospital treatment. If it was not for the instructor's awareness, this stupidity could have been life changing or life-threatening.

Another reminder of history and traditional practices not getting things right is the dangerous practice of X blocking techniques against knives. You can only hope they never have to attempt to disarm a live blade in a real-life knife attack by means of such foolish, flawed and suicidal techniques. I have had individuals claim it works, or that a modified version of the X block works. To date, they will not demonstrate their X blocking prowess against my green role, razor sharp blade used in a knife combat way. You would think that if they were practicing with realism and with safe training drones they would feel and understand the outcomes of the drone making contact with their flesh as if it was a live hot blade. Slow predetermined choreography of classical non-combative un-realistic knife attacks proves nothing in the training of a combatant for combat. The reality is all knives are dangerous, and the best means of defeating one is to get as far away from the weapon as possible, never turning your back on the weapon in the process, until you are well and truly out of range of the weapon being able to make contact with you. If the use of deadly force to neutralise the armed threat is legal and at your disposal then this is a primary means of threat neutralisation if you are unable to escape. Facing a weapon threat with no out option or armed means to neutralise the threat requires extreme combative smarts, skills and inner resolve.

The need to use battle-proven practices that are as safe as humanly possible to disarm an armed enemy of their weapon and dispose of the threat takes considerable skill, and an equally controlled ready and willing psychological demeanour. It is all too late when faced with a formidable armed and dangerous aggressor to find out or admit to yourself that you do not trust, or have confidence in, your skills to safely and effectively neutralise the threat.

Always remember that you are just training, so as to reduce the likelihood of loss of life or limb under training conditions to as low a level as is humanly possible. When you know under testing conditions that your skill set provides you with the skills to effectively threat neutralise, including by means of required contingency options, and you have used your skills to achieve your objective, then you will be more willing and capable as a combatant. Proven combative knowledge increases psychological capabilities under extremes, and realistic practical training exercises against formidable enemy pers that are bent on defeating you will prepare you for what you need to win in a real life or death actions-on encounter.

You will need to make deliberate definite decisions in real time in high risk encounters where it is too late to prove a technique's worth. This must be done on training courses and in testing. Do not go your whole training life training in a non-realistic manner, and practicing unsafe techniques, as one day your life may well depend on the caliber of your skills and your confidence in them.

If you do not test and train to destruction and failure against formidable enemy pers trying to combat or counter every aspect of your means and methods of neutralising them, then you simply have a false impression of the effectiveness of your techniques, and thus false confidence. I have seen many trades people as well as bushmen, farmers and hunters that can recognise a primary practice when they see it. Yet I have seen so many people with fighting arts backgrounds that opt for unrealistic, unsafe and unproven options.

The proof of physical capabilities in training and in the testing, and the psychological advantages in training and testing the military combative way, against practical, committed and aggressive enemy pers that will stop at nothing to achieve their objective, provides an understanding of your capabilities. Such enemy pers that will put up a struggle, and will utilise anything and everything at their disposal to defeat you, demands that you must be armed with the best of battle-proven tactics, principles and skills, powered by maximum mental toughness and controlled and maintained physical capabilities.

Psychological confidence and mental toughness increases by offensive action hard cover guarding

In unarmed counter-offensive assault, evasive and stationary counter engagement employments, sound, robust economic hard cover guarding is required to reduce the risk to as low a level as humanly possible. The same applies to combat options unarmed offensive assault skills employments.

Understanding the importance of hard cover guarding, and ensuring it is utilised along with all offensive assault skills employments, will reduce the physical risk considerably and increase psychological confidence to maximum levels, by believing and knowing one's cover guard capabilities will provide safety throughout the offensive action employment.

The employment of correctly timed hard cover guarding will create interference with your enemy's mental focus. A good example of this is in the execution of a low quadrant unarmed offensive assault action where the swift and cohesive direct line hard cover guarding action distracts your enemy from focus on their lower quadrant's targets.

In military CQC where the ranges are extremely close and the entry provides little time for effective evasion, especially with the enemy target being unaware or unfamiliar with your offensive actions, the hard cover guarding can often contact with the enemy prior to the primary intended practice making contact. Such hard cover guard contact, when combined with committed expedient entry action, can in itself neutralise the enemy threat. At the very least it will open and expose them to your intended primary action skill employment.

Committed hard cover guard entries from extremely close range to point-blank bodily contact range can also affect your enemy's balance and stability, either by reaction to the extremely committed close movement, or by bodily and hard cover guard contact with them as part of your committed set up prior to your primary skill employment.

Fully committed stamp kick execution hard cover guarding at point-blank bodily contact range produces both distraction away from your intended lower quadrant target and also enhances your personal balance and stability by making contact with your enemy's body. Your set position leaning or pushing against them enhances your stability. Your enemy's natural psychological and autonomic reaction to the initial bodily contact on recognition of losing ground and stability is resistance, which will in turn increase your stability and often mask your intended target. In addition, as a result of your enemy's resistance, your intended target will be exposed to close to point-blank range maximum contact leading to maximum destruction through hyperextension of the knee joint.

Often with enough entry momentum, expedient action and commitment combined with deceptive pivoting, transitions from front on to side-on and with hard cover guarding can cause stability loss and balance destruction to the point of decentralising your enemy prior to the primary offensive action even being employed.

Hard cover guarding post evasion can achieve enemy contact prior to your counter engagement skills employments and has been proven to neutralise enemy threats as such. An expedient, swift and cohesive parry evasion against a committed incoming enemy combined with an aggressive raising of a side cover guard can see the elbow directed up under the enemy's chin. The effects of two such forces colliding and impacting can increase the effect of this means of counter striking considerably.

A CQC squat initiated, committed, forward expedient action into range, combined with deliberate throwing of objects at the enemy's face, and then raising a side cover guard out towards the enemy under their chin, simultaneously when transitioning into a side stance and guard leg stamp employment, completely masks the lower stamp kick execution. The resulting psychological and autonomic reactions can cause the enemy to lean backwards, moving their head away from you causing them to expose and hyperextend their lower leg to your stamp kick.

Both psychological confidence and likelihood of success of an unarmed offensive assault are increased, especially in the execution of low stamp kicks, when you transition from a neutral stance or a front stance and guard to a side stance and cover guard as part of your stamp kick execution transition.

Through psychological visual assessment your enemy identified you as a frontal exposed target, and then through your expedient action pivot and the turning from front-on to side-on setup of your stamp kick, combined with your best of dirty tricks brigade deliberate or fake action set up, your body will now be side on and protected by hard cover guarding. This transition reduces the risk of unarmed combat contact considerably, by reducing your target mass that is available to your enemy and also by decreasing the window of opportunity to make contact with your bodily vitals to the lowest and safest level humanly possible under such offensive actions executions.

Through extensive training and practice, and most importantly the confidence boost having used your specific offensive actions in real life actions-on encounters where you effectively neutralise the threat, your psychological confidence in your primary skills and their entry set up and execution components makes you mentally tough and physically protected by hard cover guarding and target accessibility reduction.

The savvy, mentally tough and psychologically confident combatant, through prior proven knowledge, will exploit every enemy psychological and involuntary autonomic reaction as part of setting up and masking unarmed offensive assault and unarmed counter-offensive assault engagements.

Understanding the importance of sound hard cover guarding turning front-on to side-on in unarmed offensive assault employments will increase confidence and inner resolve, and then lead to as quick as humanly possible combative skills employments. In training, by testing and truing up your hard cover guard capabilities, you will become confident to cover up against or deflect immediate unarmed enemy assault as part of your set up of counter engagement skills employments.

Trained combatant responses and deliberate actions under removed or reduced vision capabilities

The trained combatant, confident and competent to operate under low light reduced vision and no light illuminated vision conditions, must utilise their available additional senses and mechanisms of self-preservation. The loss of visual capabilities and the realities of complete darkness promote a stationary response to avoid dangers and reduce injury risks.

Just as birds and animals are transported or contained in covered cages to calm them down and prevent aggressive or panic escape actions, humans in a situation of immediate loss of vision also assume a stationary status. The human being's understanding of the dangers of reduced or eliminated vision in combative threat situations dictates that they need to apply risk reduction methods of self-preservation against assault, and that their additional senses are heightened to provide other means of threat recognition as part of self-protection.

The trained combatant with experience in employing self-protection capabilities without vision, or in restricted vision situations, will employ enhanced additional senses combined with self-protection hard targeting. Such hard targeting includes hard cover guarding and positional adjustments in relation to maintaining a position of maximum safety, usually by ensuring major life-support vitals are continuously hard cover guarded and positioned away from the threat.

Utilising any residual visual capability combined with enhanced hearing will increase sensory capabilities against assault. While impaired or restricted visual capabilities may not allow for precise visual assessment, you may well be able to pick up on outline forms or shadows, aiding in an awareness of the position and therefore direction of and detection of an incoming approaching threat.

Your hearing will be enhanced considerably, and even your sense of smell may well aid in the detection of the position of the enemy, especially by the switching on and maintaining of combative respiration.

Sound hard cover guarding of major life-support systems and delicate vitals can reduce the risk of life-threatening wounds or injuries. Having confidence in sound hard cover guarding through impaired vision situations training will ensure the experience is not completely foreign and overwhelming. Through previous realistic exposure to restricted or eliminated vision self-protection and counter engagement training, you will be armed to utilise your sensory mechanisms to locate the position of the enemy, and as such adjust your positioning combined with hard cover guarding to increase safety and hard target yourself.

Your sense of touch via your combat boots is a very important counter engagement capability that can provide the means to self-protect, causing enemy disengagement and/or keeping the enemy at bay, or neutralising the enemy threat by means of stamp kicking. This can be achieved in a close upright position, crouched position or on the ground.

Utilising your sense of touch via your boots can aid in maintaining stability and can be used to locate enemy bodily targets. Locating by sense of touch, with the toe of your boot, the arch of the enemy's boot will provide direct line set up contact as part of a stamp kick execution to destroy the integrity of the knee joint.

Prevention of being lifted off the ground from the rear flanks can be achieved by employing expedient dynamic dropping of your weight from high to low, and, by means of utilising your sense of touch with your boot when visual assessment is not possible, positioning the boot arch behind your enemy's heel combined with resisting the upward lift and counter engagement to neutralise the immediate threat.

There are wide ranging practices in relation to upright, prone or decentralised positions in relation to utilising your sense of touch as part of self-preservation, self-protection and employment of counter engagement options. You can likewise use the arch or heel of your boot to find by feel your enemies boot.

If you train the combative way and have trained for wide ranging threat categories as well as specific threats and situations, then you will have increased capabilities by means of prior knowledge and experience, and through practicing against such threats and situations.

While human beings, like many animals, may well assume a static status when their visual capabilities are reduced or removed and they are in complete darkness, the need for immediate fast mapping assessment and the utilisation of enhanced additional senses, combined with employing mechanisms of hard cover guarding self-preservation and risk reduction is the difference between a motivated, psychologically confident and skills competent combatant that is aware and prepared to operate under eliminated or restricted vision compared to one that is not.

There is a need to switch on or enhance available senses capabilities, combined with threat recognition and immediate threat locating as part of a means of self-protection and self-preservation that, if and when possible, includes threat neutralisation counter engagement or escape and evasion. Situations where a blindfold or a hood has been forcefully applied to prevent or restrict vision may well require if possible, once one's immediate situation has been made safer or the threat neutralised, the removal of the blindfold or hood. When impaired vision includes pain, whether it be from digital penetration of the eye or the effects of chemical agents, liquids or aerosols, there is a need to ensure the effects of pain do not prevent the employment of additional senses to locate the enemy, and the employment of hard cover guarding and positional adjustments to make yourself as hard a target as possible.

Heightened senses to detect incoming assault combined with hard target stance and guard

Hard cover guarding contact absorption

Pain must be considered a motivating factor in self-preservation, self-protection, enemy neutralisation or escape and evasion. The threat must never be considered overwhelming to the point of incapacitating your capabilities to utilise every bit of awareness capability at your disposal. Such awareness, combined with maximum levels of hard cover guarding self-protection and self-preservation, are important components of enemy counter engagement or escape and evasion.

Detecting enemy location by sound, smell, shadow or reflection, combined with continuous self-protection ready status adjustments in your position in relation to the enemy's immediate location, will increase your ability to neutralise the threat by the best available counter engagement means.

Gross motor skills combative counter engagement is the priority to ensure contact and maximum effect is achieved. For example, from a foetal position under assault, by barrel rolling into the enemy's lower extremities they can be decentralised through hyper extending their knee joints with your rolling body-mass. From this position, commando crawling up your decentralised enemy utilising your sense of touch, you can locate, seize, secure and assault bodily targets to neutralise the enemy threat.

I can remember a former combative master military instructor of mine telling me of a situation where a crowd was about to target a single individual in a frenzy. He recounted how the situation was prevented and the threat neutralised simply by turning all the lighting off and covertly removing the individual target of their aggression. After several minutes the lights were turned back on and the crowd, realising the target of their aggression could not be seen or found, calmed down and dispersed. That initial plunging the crowd into darkness in such a messy environment, and with all the difficulties and dangers of trying to move around in that less than familiar environment, caused them to remain stationary.

You must always remember that if you are combative confident, competent, alert and ready that your eyes are your primary means of threat recognition and identification. The threat is the source of information, and that information will be transmitted from your eyes back to your brain where your means and method to neutralise the threat will be decided. The brain will then initiate the combative action by transmitting the start-go signals to your internal and external body and bodily extremities to ensure the decided combative or escape and evasion combative threat neutralisation option is employed. Your other senses may be the initial source of threat direction and recognition, and when your sight is impaired or you have no vision, your other senses will be required to self-protect or employ combative actions. Non-visual threat identification by heightened hearing is a reality when your sight is not available; combative skills employment by touch when you have no vision becomes necessary.

Human nature and human makeup can determine an individual's tolerance to specific bodily vitals targeting. Some individuals simply have a much higher tolerance to pain in specific bodily targets than others. Whether it be increased vulnerability to bodily target pressure or impact, or little or no effect with such pressure or impact, it is important that such effects are identified as quickly as possible and your Plan B secondary or emergency skill execution is set up and employed. The right tool for the job can make all the difference in relation to targeting specific bodily targets.

A long thin forearm securing in a compound hold around the enemy's neck may well achieve a considerably faster effect than a much larger powerful forearm. Attacking human senses or delicate bodily targets by deceptive or masked skills employments will achieve a far more immediate result than loaded and telegraphed power skills that are compromised by their loading and execution (which allows the enemy target to adjust and self-protect, reducing the likelihood of direct contact).

Any required Plan B skill employment needs to fit with available target selection or set up; it is best performed when the enemy has been seized and secured, and their balance has been weakened, reducing the likelihood of the skill being countered.

In a close quarter's clinch or ground combat situation where a specific skill employment against a bodily target has proved ineffective, being able to transition to a secondary alternate or emergency combative skill execution without losing control is a primary practice. The old principle of 'never letting go with one hand until the other hand has control' stands to increase safety, maintain additional options employments, and enhance your combative chance of objective achievement. Sometimes it's a matter of changing the means of employing the combative action, especially if you are using a flesh and tissue bodily weapon to achieve your objective.

Simply using a safe transition to utilise a more pointed bodily weapon (such as the fingertips) an impact or pressure employment can achieve an immediate effect or outcome. Some larger, stronger enemy types may well resist leverage pressure, especially in lower quadrant balance and stability destruction. This is reduced by wearing combat boots and by utilising controlled initial impact combined with leverage that exploits advantages gained by immediate controlled pain generating impact shock.

Psychologically, a hard surface, painful impact shock sends a signal to the central nervous system of the nature of the targeting, which in turn sends a reaction signal in the form of an involuntary autonomic reaction of self-protection in relation to the specific bodily targets such as joints and limb.

This autonomic response reaction to hard controlled impact initiates the flexion or hyperextension, in relation to the specific means of targeting the joint and limb, which in turn increases the effect of your controlled combative skill employment.

The reality is that it is often a matter of selecting the right tool and means of application to achieve the objective effectively. Making sound first and second look assessments of the enemy threat, and deciding on skills that meet the threat neutralisation requirements in relation to the scene, enemy physical size and attributes, combined with a knowledge of the best means that you have personally available to neutralise the threat shows combative smarts and enhances objective achievement capabilities.

Contingency options

Psychologically, a combatant's confidence and resolve are increased considerably when they have an emergency stationary contingency option available. It should be one that will enable them to neutralise any enemy assault initiated on them if that assault happens prior to them being able to offensively or counter-offensively engage or counter engage the enemy with a definite pre-decided deliberate option. The stationary contingency option is also an effective means of countering unarmed assault during the stalking into range phase of an intended unarmed offensive assault action employment.

Psychologically, if the combatant has not only primary weapon disarming principles and skills, but also emergency disarming options including from stationary, then they will be more confident.

The Todd Systems provide a range of unarmed striking and stamp kicking options for the combatant to select their personal primary options in relation to their physical and psychological makeup and capabilities. The decided primary options are supported by a complete range of contingency options methods that provide the means to counter changes in threat or situation at any stage of the execution of the offensive or counteroffensive assault employments.

Knowing that the skills in relation to the military science of CQC, MSD and CQB are the most proven safe and effective for the specific roles and threat counter requirements is psychologically positive. Primary combative decided options supported by complete contingency back up options are a very important aspect of ensuring the individual combatant is as confident and mentally prepared as humanly possible.

If your enemy engages you during your stalking into range to initiate your decided unarmed offensive option, having a range-making stalking contingency will psychologically enhance your mental resolve. Under calculated controlled methodical stalking into range employment, knowing you have the physical capability to stop an enemy in their tracks should they assault you increases your combative mental toughness and willingness. To go combative in a controlled, confident, competent and calculated manner, the combatant must be physically competent and confident, and must know and believe their skills capabilities are proven safe and are the best means of objective achievement. Psychological confidence, as a result of knowing your physical contingency counter option is the best, safest, most effective, simple, direct means to ensure threat neutralization, will enhance your range making confidence and will be blatantly evident to your enemy. If a combatant cannot safely and effectively make the optimum specific skill employment range, or have a stalking contingency option that will enable them to neutralise enemy assault during the stalking phase, then they are psychologically and physically disadvantaged from the outset. Lacking in the skills to achieve the objective, or not believing in your techniques will affect your confidence from the outset; your enemy may well pick up on it and, if so, will exploit such a weakness.

Just as having a stalking into range contingency option for enemy unarmed offensive assault employments neutralisation is necessary, so too is having a contingency option for controlling range for unarmed counter-offensive assault evasive options post breaking a reactionary range, when your enemy continues stalking into your safe reactionary zone. This contingency option enhances confidence and mental toughness through physical capability. Realistic training in such practices provides skills competency and psychological confidence.

Military combative and urban self-defence ranges are very close, as a result of situation, and often battle dress and load bearing make extremely close combative execution ranges essential. Combine this with terrain considerations, fatigue, wounds and injuries, and always presuming your enemy is formidable, and you need to get close, confidently and competently. Remember, of course, to never underestimate your enemy or aggressor; always realise they could, and will, do you serious harm given the opportunity. Believe they are more physically capable, highly skilled and committed to doing you serious harm. Believe they are armed, and stay alert and aware of any drawing of, or introduction of, concealed primary, secondary or improvised weapons including terrain provided weapons. This doesn't mean you ever consider them undefeatable; it means you never underestimate them or take anything for granted.

Remain constantly ready and aware, undertaking assessments, making adjustments and fast mapping constantly. Eliminate negatives such as time for self-doubt, and instead continuously assess by maintaining a state of readiness as this is psychologically positive. Enemy and environment vision (or point and place visual as I refer to it) is essential.

Running, walking and partaking in sports (including many combat sports) requires somewhat different physical and psychological attributes in contrast to deliberate military combative or military self-defence methods of enemy incapacitation or elimination.

A highly skilled combatant with low or no commitment, inner resolve or confidence is like a firearm without a trigger finger. Likewise, a highly motivated, determined, committed combatant without the best of battle-proven skills up against a formidable enemy is not the best prepared, and in turn is not employing the best and safest means of achieving the objectives.

Against any formidable enemy in any violent close quarters encounter, or where the employment of lethal options is required, you must be mentally tough as well as possessing the physical capabilities.

Never enter into any combative encounter with a take-on mind-set; you must have a take-out mind set to neutralise a formidable threat quickly, quietly, and economically with over-kill target destruction.

Dirty or deadly proven combative tactics and skills exploiting vulnerable weaknesses in enemy defensive capabilities, and targeting of vulnerable life-support systems including human senses, reduces the required physical capabilities requirements in relation to physical output and endurance considerably. Covert take-outs, for example, being a primary operational option, are employed to cause deliberate human destruction and there will be no fight if the skills are properly and effectively employed.

In training and in personal self-defence there is also often the added concern that the extent of injury to the aggressor may lead to arrest and prosecution for assault. Legality and human factors such as not wanting to cause serious harm or injury even to an aggressor make objective achievement that much more difficult.

Combative respiration is a very specific and most necessary component to combative offensive and counter-offensive actions employments including armed variations. For unarmed options employments, combative respiration by means of a single respiration cycle (exhaling on the physical execution component), will provide the capability to employ continued combative actions at 75 percent plus commitment for multiple skills repetitions executions. A single cycled respiration per kicking action is required to achieve effective target contact destruction; for combatants in peak physical condition, however, multiple arm and hand strikes may be able to be achieved per single respiration cycle.

Based on combative observations, I can give you an indication of the importance of inner resolve as well as of the physical aspects, by giving the following proportionate descriptions of the physical and mental components requirements in CQC. More than 90 percent determination and less than 10 percent skills is an estimated description of a combative medium to gross motor skills employment requirement against a formidable enemy bent on killing you. The employment of dirty or deadly battle-proven skills ranging from medium to gross motor battle-proven skills executed at extreme close range to point-blank bodily contact range with ruthless commitment, controlled aggression and accurate targeting of vulnerable delicate life-support vitals, masked and employed with deception and/or distraction, is what gets you as close as humanly possible to a guaranteed desired objective achievement.

Skills of incapacitation or elimination will depend on situation role, rules of engagement legality, laws of self-defence and the individual combatant's mentality, assessment and decision-making.

Everything in the brain-to-boot package refers to individual combatants that are 'ready, willing, able—willing, able, ready' and unaffected by alcohol or drugs in relation to making deliberate definite decisions relative to threat situation, the enemy, and their own current physical and psychological capabilities and status.

The realities of high stress, life and death CQC, is that the higher the stress level, the lower the skill level, and the lesser the reaction time. Let me reiterate that primary skills in life or death encounters must be simple, gross motor skills and must be powered by total ruthless, controlled, aggressive commitment.

Presuming the enemy is always bigger, stronger, fitter, faster, highly skilled, armed and bent on killing you is all the incentive and motivation required to go tactical and combine with the best of battle-proven physical skills and complete combative psychological commitment to winning, not merely surviving. It is very important that the decided option and timing is as correct and accurate, respectively, in relation to the threat, and commensurate with threat levels for civilian self-defence in relation to the specific laws of self-defence and rules of engagement for military options employments.

It is important that you decide upon and execute the best option to the best of your capabilities with the sole objective of neutralizing the threat. Many people make the mistake of underestimating their aggressor, waiting too long, or employing an option that is considerably less than the threat requires, out of human decency and a blind respect of human life in relation to an enemy or aggressor that means to cause them grievous bodily harm. They look at it from the perspective that they may be able to employ conflict resolution or threat de-escalation, as well as opting for a soft physical skill option on the pretext that they could always up the ante in relation to threat escalation. Unfortunately, many fail to identify the unpredictability and ruthless goal driven violent intention of their aggressor. Then when they fail to neutralise the threat after underestimating it, and find themselves in the self-preservation mode where they are losing ground, they have lost any momentum and their chances of neutralising the threat are diminished or gone; it's all too late. This is why factual assessment and decision making that never underestimates the threat are critical.

When training a military combatant it is important that, by majority, they learn threat neutralization over peace or police officer de-escalation as life threatening actions-on requires it. There are many practices required in security and law enforcement conflict resolution and threat de-escalation that are negatives in CQC, CQB and military self-defence. These include having to communicate verbally with a possibly dangerous aggressor, and when you consider verbiage slows down reaction time, this then creates considerably more risk.

Having to be in a non-immediate combative mind set and readiness at close proximity to a potential dangerous threat is just another example of the dangers of law enforcement. Risk reduction tactics and putting barriers and layers of security between the officer and the subject become very important in such situations. Focusing on taking down information, questioning the subject all the while remaining focused on the subject and the developing situation and surroundings creates dangers.

While it is important that combatants are aware of reading danger signs, especially in body language, masked, deceptive or distractive behaviour, it is equally as important that they employ tactics to hard cover and hard target themselves by utilizing controlled range, barriers, angles and very direct verbal commands while maintaining a point and place visual. Immediate combative ready capabilities to neutralise the threat if required are a priority.

Deliberate component order of execution

My research, observations, trials and tests have identified a fault in the order of execution in relation to combative skills components to ensure the highest levels of capabilities in skill and physical performance are maintained. The reality is that anything less than the primary means of threat neutralization can increase risk and danger, and as such, can weaken your psychological resolve.

In my early days as an exponent coming up through the ranks in CQC, in an immediate sudden aggressive actions-on encounter, I was instructed in the following order of employment in relation to skills components execution:

- Visual on the direction of the incoming threat (Threat recognition)
- Alignment to the threat (Threat identification and assessment)
- Deciding on a combat or counter option followed by any set up
- Employment of that option.

I have seen this basic order of component execution instructed and utilised constantly over four decades. When I set about developing the brain-to-boot package, I re-evaluated all that I had been instructed in controlled realistic factor-of-confusion conditions to identify if, in fact, it was the best, safest and most effective order and means of skills execution. The combative respiration research and analysis of the findings soon identified that human beings, even alpha males highly trained combatively and in peak physical condition, can suffer the effects of even short duration actions-on encounters if controlled combative respiration is not employed immediately going tactical, or on immediate threat recognition and hard cover employment in an unexpected actions-on situation. If the effects of the body's autonomic reactions to such sudden aggressive shock stimuli are not kept in check and controlled, the risk and danger level is increased considerably.

Combative respiration needs to be initiated as a first deliberate option in expected actions-on situations. In unexpected actions-on encounters, it needs to be employed simultaneously with hard cover self-protection, or immediately after hard cover initiation is employed. If combative respiration is not employed as early as possible, the outcome can be that much more uncertain or difficult to achieve, and against a formidable enemy you may fail to achieve the objective.

In the pages ahead, the order of execution has proven to be most beneficial to control the effects of sudden aggressive shock action, as well as maintaining proficiency and performance achievement and endurance, including maintaining high-level combative performance for extended periods in violent encounters. Note that some of the components will be executed simultaneously as part of a combined components employment such as in switching senses on. They have proven to be correct in relation to initiating and maintaining combative proficiency, accuracy and intensity. Speed, velocity and power, as well as required endurance combat and counter actions timings were all tested and are included in the following findings. Situational and threat specifics may dictate slight changes in the components execution order as a result of decided best deliberate components order of employment, or to provide immediate personal safety, but combative respiration must be the immediate priority.

The order of execution must allow for human error, as Murphy's Law always applies, and the trained combatant must be able to overcome order of execution errors, as well as be prepared to employ primary, secondary or emergency options to neutralise the threat. Situations include unexpected actions-on encounters, where the first thing you know is that contact has been made against you, and as such you are going into immediate self-preservation mode. The hard cover, hard targeting requirements of cover guarding, deflection and stability control are a priority that must be combined with combative respiration or immediately after you have made yourself safer. Then you can fast map by means of utilizing all your automated senses and deliberate assessment and decision making capabilities.

The threat and situation combined with your D will provide you with offensive assault or counter-offensive assault options, from stationary, or by way of deliberate counter evasive or offensive assault combating of the enemy.

Battle-proven military combative training includes options to combat or counter unarmed and armed enemy threats by primary, secondary alternative and emergency methods, and as such, increases confidence and reduces any chance of panic or hopelessness when you most need to remain ready, in control and capable of neutralizing the threat by less than primary means.

Some examples are outlined below.

Evasive counter engagement:

- Primary option: diagonally forward
- Secondary option: diagonally rearward
- Emergency options: attack your advancing enemy by means of deceptive unarmed offensive assault, or as a last resort, stationary counter engagement.

Upper extremities joint locks threat neutralization:

- Seizure prevention
- Primary specific joint lock escape

- Secondary joint lock escape
- Emergency joint lock escape (including lowering your centre of gravity to a crouch, or full decentralization as part of a ground escape).

Short edged or bludgeon weapon disarming under an incoming threat category:

- Primary: evasive disarming
- Secondary: evasive option disarming
- Emergency: Stationary or retreating disarms.

Secure holds escapes:

- Primary military armed option hold escapes and simultaneous threat neutralization
- Secondary weapon hold escapes and threat neutralization
- Primary civilian unarmed hold escapes
- Secondary and emergency unarmed holds escapes to escape specific holds or prevent hold applications and to correct your errors by fast mapping in real time, and making the changes and adjustments required to escape the hold and neutralise the threat.

Psychologically you will be more enabled if you have multiple capabilities to achieve your objectives.

- Deliberate tactical combative respiration initiation
- Visual recognition and identification of the threat

- All senses activated. Eyes, ears, nose, touch and feel (as in ground affinity).
- Threat alignment, posture, position adjustments.
- Threat assessment.
- Tactically correct decision making.
- Decided option set up and employment.
- Fast mapping visual on the move to identify changes in threat and situation.

In the previous order of execution the two most important initial components are combative tactical respiration and visual assessment. Often less immediately required senses or components such as your sense of smell may well not be deliberately turned on. Although less immediate activated senses may not be deliberately activated, they will be naturally activated.

When you have initiated your combative respiration to ensure you control the effects of fear, stress and danger, and ensure you are in a ready status in an expected threat situation, the logical order of requirements follow deliberate threat visual, which will in turn initiate your assessment and decision making process. Then follows ground affinity for the required stability and mobility required for combat or counter skills employments. Adjustments to align to the target followed by real time continued assessment information processing and decision making come next. If an initial visual assessment and immediate decision making has confirmed escape and evasion is the primary best option, then adjustment, as in directional alignment and discreet or expedient escape and evasion (depending on whether compromised or not and other threat specifics) would be initiated.

In an unexpected, immediate actions-on encounter, employment of self-protection, self-preservation, personal hard targeting and simultaneous combative respiration are the immediate priority, followed by fast mapping assessment under assault and decision making to neutralise the threat. This may be through either combative skills or escape and evasion.

Under an unexpected, actions-on encounter (as with an expected actions-on encounter) combative respiration is a first and best deliberate employed action that will make all the difference in the outcome. Combative respiration will not only reduce the effects of sudden aggressive shock action violence, but will ensure sound decision making can be achieved, and physical controlled committed aggression can be maintained for maximum durations at high levels of output.

Your ears will naturally switch on with your sense of vision and will be turned up when you control the effects of the threat situation by combative respiration and so will your sense of smell. Your sense of touch, and feel as in ground affinity, or utilizing your arms, hands and changes in body position to maintain your balance and increase stability, is both a autonomic reaction to sudden aggressive shock action and a deliberate employed preparation or continuation action to hard target yourself, regain control and make yourself ready to go combative or escape and evade.

Even though the only sense you may be deliberately employing is your vision, your additional senses will also be activated. Some situations will, by the specific threat category and nature, see a specific sense automatically activated as a major sense, giving the feeling that it is the only sense being automatically utilized by sympathetic reaction to the stimuli of sudden aggressive shock action. My findings have determined that all your senses would be simultaneously activated, but the threat specifics determine which sense is the first and most utilised.

In a covert assault immediate actions-on, where the first warning is immediate physical contact, immediately following the autonomic flinch reaction would be self-protective hard targeting skills such as cover guarding, reducing target mass, increasing stability and simultaneous initiation of combative respiration as both a control mechanism and to enhance physical performance. Initiating a visual, fast-mapping assessment decision making, real time adjustments in position, range, angle, footing, and your combative employment or escape and evasion option then follow with minimal hesitation. If you have, through combative respiration, eliminated or reduced the effects of sudden aggressive shock action, then your senses of hearing and smell will be on and at high alert even if you are not aware of them being activated.

Just as in utilizing your vision, you can opt to utilize your hearing and smell any time they are required to aid in threat detection. Suppose you are walking along a street and you see a dodgy looking individual. You discreetly undertake an assessment and decision making action at the same time that a car back fires and a smoker walks alongside you. Your hearing and sense of smell will indeed identify the introduction and location of such sounds and smells while you keep a visual and prepare to initiate your decided action. Your sense of smell can be enhanced by wetting the finger and rubbing it around your nostrils. Your hearing can be enhanced by turning your ear towards the sounds direction and closing your eyes.

The order of execution of senses, and of deliberate actions and reactions may well be affected by specific situations or human error in the order of execution; however, tactical combative respiration must be employed as soon as possible or as soon as it is safe to do so.

In expected threat actions-on situations, self-reassurance ('ready, willing, able' 'willing, able, ready') repeated in your mind to maintain and increase confidence and resolve, as well as undertaking checks and re-checks and making adjustments are all positive and required practices.

The brain-to-boot package allows for human error in selection and order of bodily reactive and turned on and up senses, as well as deliberate hard targeting and preparation actions to go combative or escape and evade, as long as control is gained or regained by tactical respiration immediately or as soon as possible. To enable a regaining of control by fast mapping decision making tactics and skills employment.

There are variations to the number of components deliberately switched on in relation to whether the situation is expected or unexpected. Expected situations require constant fast mapping processing of information, and initiating adjustments to ensure the combatant is best ready to deal with the changing threat situation in real time. Inclusion of self-reassurance is one such important practice, and a constant reminder that when going tactical you must ensure you self-reassure, combined with constant checks and re-checks of every aspect of yourself and your enemy threat and situation.

Often I have observed that exponents on battle handling exercises in unexpected unknown threat category situations performed better than they did in expected threat situations, where the time and distance created stresses of their own. The enemy actions-on unexpected threat left no time for anything other than the post autonomic subconscious reaction employment of pre-learnt skills to combat or counter the specific threat, powered by important psychological and physical performance requirements beginning with tactical combative respiration.

I can remember watching an early edition of the Rugby League Footy show on DVD where the host, Paul Vautin, took a mystery envelope from a numbered box on the show, and as he did so it exploded. His immediate action was one of an autonomic flinch, or more of a spontaneous crouch in relation to the intensity of the blast and the shock it provided. The immediate flinch crouch reaction followed a simultaneous away from the threat decentralization, and this bulky, red-haired former footy player reactively turned to look at where the threat originated from. When he regained his footing, his face said it all; shock, horror and a look of anger.

When taken by surprise, especially from the rear flanks, trained combatants in the brain-to-boot package should immediately employ resistance, tactical combative respiration, vision alignment, assessment and decision-making simultaneously, including adjustments set up, and making range, all within several seconds. The importance of skills having commonality with natural human reactions in high risk high stress aggressive shock action situations is reiterated throughout this program, and for a very good reason.

I have evaluated myself and my senior assistants under training, battle handling exercises and under testing conditions, and have identified the importance of such practices as self-preservation and hard targeting. I personally slightly crouch (CQC squat) before I execute any physical combative skill, no matter how minor or insignificant the skill may be. This practice has commonality with flinching, which is a mechanism of preservation that lowers your centre of gravity, reduces your target mass, increases your stability and increases your ready status to go combative.

In a deliberate unarmed offensive assault or counter-offensive assault skills employment, I will always employ deliberate combative respiration, and a slight deliberate CQC squat to reduce or move my bodily targets, as well as assuming a definite ground affinity and ready status to go combative. The achieved positive outcomes by employing these practices were considerable in relation to safety, timing, deception and importantly, achieving the objective.

Take the example of an evasive counter engagement action executed from an upright stance. The reality is that, in the upright stance, a combatant produces more target mass when they have to transition from a flat-footed status to a definite ground affinity expedient action footwork status. In contrast, a combatant who utilises syncronised combative respiration and a crouched ready status is a less static target and immediately ready to go combative. A CQC squat also causes an enemy reaction, and is deceptive, changing the position of your top 20 cm or 8 inches (i.e., your head). This may cause your enemy to miss, or at the least, ensure you reduce target mass and assume a more loaded and ready status to go combative.

Exploiting autonomic reactions and psychological effects of specific targets

Understanding the anatomy and medical aspects, including psychological automatic reactions and psychological reactions to targeting specific bodily vitals, provides increased capabilities.

Autonomic reactions to the targeting of various bodily vitals, out of self-preservation, specific bodily vital protection and general self-protection, can be exploited in the employment of combative skills. Such combative skills employments may require the enemy to be doubled over, bent backwards, or simply forced into a false reaction.

Automated autonomic reactions to specific bodily vitals targeting include groin attacks that bend the enemy forward, throat and head attacks that bend or move the enemy backwards or back and to one side, and leg attacks that can cause the enemy to bend forward and simultaneously hyperextend their knee joint, or if employed with a fake or deliberate action at the upper quadrants can cause the enemy to lean back and hyperextend their leg.

Having an understanding of how to exploit such autonomic reactions and biomechanical leverage provides advantages in combative offensive assault action employments and counter engagement skills employments.

Some reactionary responses provide an initial and then changed responses, such as when a deliberate fake action directed at the upper quadrants is followed by an immediate mid-section/groin attack or lower quadrants stamp kick. Your enemy's first look reaction will be to move or protect their head and upper quadrants, and when and if a second look is possible, and they realise the groin or lower leg is being targeted, they will try to change their initial reaction to provide increased safety and protection of the groin or lower leg.

Having a knowledge of how to employ combative offensive and counteroffensive actions to create psychological reactionary enemy responses will increase your combative skills employments, by providing that small but important dirty tricks brigade skill employment enhancement.

To understand how to exploit such involuntary psychological human reactions, you must first know the specific targets that will achieve the involuntary reaction in relation to the required change in bodily position, to aid and enhance your specific combative skill employment. In particular, bodily targets that are physically and psychologically delicate, such as the eyes and genitals, provide common sympathetic reactions and responses.

I can remember in my early days learning of the medical aspects and implications of CQC and CQB, being informed of groin attacks creating reactions and responses because of an embedded psychological means of protection of the genitals to ensure reproductive capabilities survive, and as such the protection of the family and the future of the family. This could be part of the reasoning, combined with the pain related aspects of physical contact with the genitals deep in our psychological mechanisms of self-protection and self-preservation.

Not all of the autonomic reactions and responses to targeted specific bodily vitals produce the best means of protection and risk reduction in relation to those bodily vitals. Low quadrant defensive actions, including in reaction to below the knee joint offensive actions can cause an involuntary bending of the torso forward over the waist and hyper extending the lower leg, increasing the effect of stamp kicks. Such reactions are emergency reactions, when, by the nature of the offensive action employment, the first awareness of the specific targeting of the bodily vital is immediately before contact. This removes the ability to move the targeted bodily vital off the offensive action contact line.

Combative psychological tactics

Understanding how to cause psychological confusion, interference or knowing how to exploit human reactions to definite or fake actions can provide major advantages. This includes maintaining a grey status and situational silence. Often the unknown and unexpected response to threat and intimidation can have negative effects on the enemy aggressor. Threatening actions, intimidation and verbal threats are a common means of causing severe and psychological stress. An enemy using such threatening measures expects the subject of their threats to respond and react predictably under the circumstances. An aggressive response, a submissive response or an attempt at reasoning with the enemy are common expected responses.

When you break a 2 meter reactionary range, stand neutral, look your aggressor in the eyes, meeting them on even ground present yourself in a neutral grey status while remaining silent; you are not responding in a predictable manner. No matter how vile the verbal threats may be, by remaining silent and focused on the enemy, you appear both neutral and formidable by remaining ready and vigilant to the enemy. Such tactical actions can play on the enemy's own mental toughness through fear of the unknown and unexpected means of responding to their menacing threats.

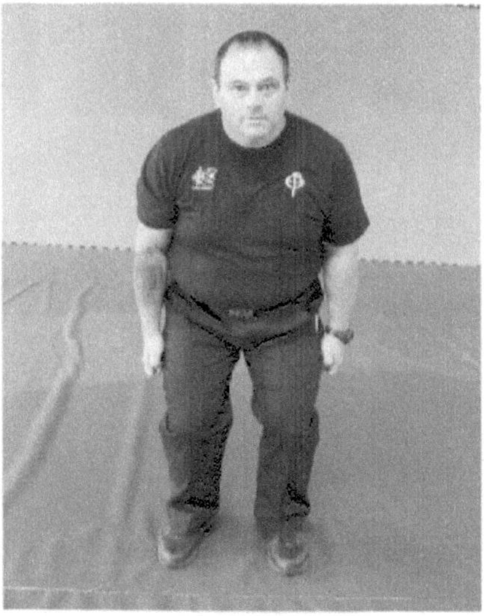

CQC squat to initiate breaking a reactionary range

First pace of breaking a 2 meter reactionary range

2nd pace of breaking a 2 meter reactionary range

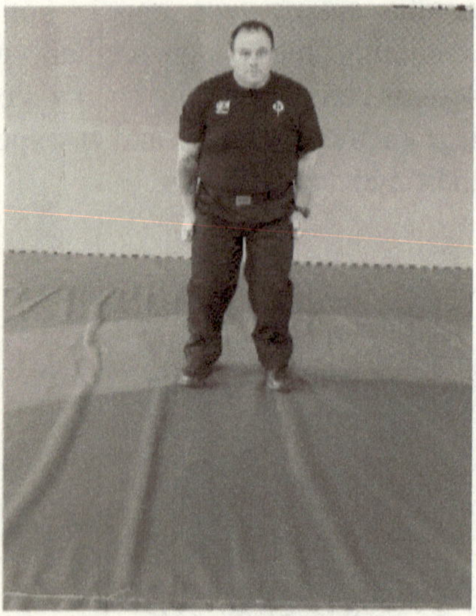

Post breaking reactionary range neutral ready status when uncompromised

Thoughts of you being armed, capable and ready to deal with their aggression are common in relation to such a tactical response to their threats. Two meters is a considerable distance to cover against a ready and willing adversary. They may well consider covering such a range to be risky against the unknown.

Often you can psych an aggressor out by using tactics such as remaining vigilant, breaking a safe reactionary range, combined with not responding in an expected predictable manner and by keeping the element of surprise on your side by maintaining situational silence. Utilising tactically correct safety ranges combined with maintaining a vigilant but neutral unknown quantity combative capabilities persona, can weaken an aggressor's resolve and desire to assault. Such tactics increase your hard target status. If your enemy attacks by means of deliberate evasive moving off the confrontation line fast mapping post evasion assessment and setting up and executing counter engagement you have the best chance of threat neutralisation under the circumstances.

Fake and deliberate actions such as a fake head punch, or deliberately throwing objects in the enemy's face, create defensive upper quadrant reactions leaving the lower quadrants exposed and vulnerable to attack.

The previous methods of employing element-of-surprise grey status tactics to maintain the element of surprise, while presenting oneself as vigilant and ready, cause confusion by unpredictable action and can weaken an enemy's commitment to going combative. Hard targeting by controlling range utilising angle, or putting barriers between yourself and the enemy, can be perceived as an indication of combative smarts and tactically savvy capabilities making you a hard target and unknown quantity. Weakening an aggressor's resolve using tactics that present a persona of the unknown, a persona that is unpredictable and unexpected but vigilant, are all definite means of outsmarting an enemy and preventing a physical actions-on encounter.

Using deception, including deliberate or fake actions, are a means of interfering with an aggressor's point and line of vision as well as mental focus and conviction in the execution of their intended option prior to employing their intended actions. The reality is humans are predictable in relation to specific tactics and actions that prey on human reactions, responses and interpretations of such tactics and actions. Use your brain and tactically savvy options to outsmart, confuse or weaken your aggressor's resolve. Every advantage and edge that interferes with an aggressor's intentions and actions increases your chance of threat neutralization.

Primary option training is a priority

In training a combatant's primary option, skills that provide quick kills or quick threat neutralisation should be practiced first, and far more extensively than contingency options.

Human nature is predictable, and if you give most human beings contingency options early in the training or in high enough percentages, they will often under-commit with their primary option executions, believing that if their primary options are ineffective they can rely on their contingency options.

The reality is that, often the reason for the ineffective outcome by means of their primary options is simply because they did not commit to it to a high enough level, because of their tactically flawed belief in having backup contingency options. Every second longer that an actions-on encounter is prolonged increases risk and drains physical capabilities as well as affecting mental toughness. Combine this with fears of failure, self-injury or being counter engaged through high level controlled aggressive commitment, and the undesirable practice of under-commitment and relying on contingency options if unsuccessful can be a reality.

Given the above, in order to develop and enhance psychological confidence, it is important to identify the individual combatant's physical skills that fit their physical attributes and capabilities, as well as identifying their psychological makeup. Then the selected primary skills should be practiced in high repetition until proficiency is achieved—before the practice of any contingency options. When the contingency options are introduced they should be practiced in low percentages compared to primary options repetitions. This means approximately 90 percent or more primary options practice compared to 10 percent or less contingency option practice.

The exception to the rule is the contingency option employed if engaged while stalking into range. The stalking into range contingency option, if engaged, is vital to develop in the combatant the confidence in capability to be able to, in a controlled calculated and deliberate manner, stalk into the specific skill execution range with confidence knowing they can, if engaged, stop the enemy in their tracks.

Military CQC ranges are extremely close, and taking into account battle dress, webbing and body armour, load bearing and difficult terrain combined with fatigue, they need to be close. The need for a battle-proven, stalking into range contingency option to physically neutralise any enemy assault, will only stand to enhance the combatant's decided skills setup by enabling them to be psychologically confident to stalk into range knowing if engaged they have a primary contingency option.

Psychological confidence maintenance by having a Plan B

The reality is that some skills simply will not achieve objectives on some individuals. Physical attributes, body types, battle dress and body armour makes some skills less than guaranteed to achieve the objective. Some individuals, simply through tolerance to pain or their biological makeup, can resist the effects of some physical skills or not be affected at all.

Recently, on a combative course, an advanced exponent felt little or no effect to carotid strangulation applied by both his training partners and instructors alike. The reality is that with less or non-lethal skills, where a subject is not affected and your laws of self-defence and where the rules of engagement do not permit the employment of lethal means, you need to have a Plan B that is cohesive in transition and application. It is vital that you maintain situational security and control of the enemy and that through prior training you be proficient in cohesively transitional skills that will enable you to achieve the objective. Understanding that no skill works on all subjects, and that you need to be able to fast map on the move and employ another option to achieve your objective, will allow you to maintain psychological confidence.

The fault can sometimes be not only that the enemy has a tolerance to pain or the effects of the employed skill, but that your physical attributes such as your arms do not fit with the requirements to achieve the objective by the selected means, and simply using a more fine-point means of target contact pressure will achieve a much greater effect. Large forearms and an enemy with a bull neck, in strangulation, can affect objective achievement. More pointed, penetrative, squeezing or crushing web of hand fingers and thumb methods of objective achievement as a first-up option or transitional option, against an enemy that is unaffected by a larger extremity employed option, are known as being more effective against tough and formidable aggressors. Employing the most proven primary and deliberate options of objective achievement as a first option is a psychologically maximising CQC modus operandi.

The blackspot

Unarmed evasive counter engagement's primary evasive option is evading diagonally forward. Evading diagonally rearward or horizontally enables your foe to maintain a target visual.

There are situations and circumstances where a horizontal or diagonally rearward evasion is required to increase safety, such as when your enemy is too close, too fast, fully committed or when you are taken by surprise.

Such practices as a horizontal or diagonally rearward evasion require confidence in post-evasion hardcover guarding capabilities as your enemy will be capable of maintaining a full visual on you the target, and can continue to engage you during and post your evasion.

Evading diagonally forward, when timed correctly, will cause your enemy to lose visual focus on you, their intended target, momentarily. The Todd Systems refer to this as creating a blackspot.

Timing your diagonally forward evasion when your enemy is fully committed and beyond the point of no return is a primary means of evading an incoming unarmed offensive assault threat.

Utilising unarmed counter offensive assault evasive sighting, dropping your primary point of vision from your enemy's eyes to their midsection when they are fully committed to their assault, enables vision of all four quadrants of your enemy's body. High right and high left as well as low right and low left vision is achieved through dropping your visual focus from your enemy's eyes to their belt line. This will enable you to identify not only the attacking limb, but also its incoming travel line and direction.

Threat specifics such as the type of strike or kick can also be effectively identified using evasive CQC sighting.

The CQC squat ready set to go status is employed simultaneously with your visual focus change from looking your enemy in the eyes to their belt line when the enemy is fully committed to the employment of the assault entry. The CQC squat interferes with the enemy's line and point of sight as well as their mental focus and is detailed in the brain to boot.

The CQC squat has a slowing effect on the enemy's incoming assault entry which in turn provides increased evasion and threat neutralisation time.

The primary diagonally forward sidestep evasion increases the chances of your enemy losing visual focus of you by means of a combination of your diagonally forward evasive movement and their committed entry assault.

Their speed and commitment will for that moment in time cause them to pass you, their intended target, as you evade diagonally forward and outside their incoming line of assault entry. You will effectively end up to the side rear flank of your enemy and outside their 140° to 180° of peripheral vision capability. This requires your enemy to have to visually scan for your post-evasion position and then have to orientate to you in order to continue with their unarmed offensive assault. This provides immediate unprotected access to your enemy's side and rear flank targets.

Evasive counter engagement competency through drilling in training and battle handling exercises will increase not only your diagonally forward sidestep evasion capabilities but also your fast mapping assessment, making the D and actioning the required adjustments to execute your counter engagement option.

Psychological confidence is increased through training in such unarmed counter offensive assault actions against willing committed enemy pers, even though they have prior knowledge of your primary skills.

Mental confidence in your capabilities to effectively evade diagonally forward and fast map assess to identify available enemy targets and combined with making adjustments in range position stance, guard and employing your decided counter engagement creates increased psychological confidence.

Timing your evasion so as to create a blackspot, where your enemy cannot visually locate you at that moment in time, stands to increase your enemy's combative confusion and stress levels.

Causing increased stress and confusion under committed assault entry for your enemy can induce hesitation or panic and can certainly invoke fear of the immediate unknown in relation to losing a visual on you their intended target. This is like the hunter becoming the hunted.

A correctly executed diagonally forward sidestep evasion being around 20 cm diagonally forward in distance will ensure you are within contact range of your enemy.

Knowing that your CQC squat will interfere with your enemy's mental focus as well as their line and point of vision, slowing their entry, and that your visual focus drop from your enemy's eyes to their belt line will provide a full combative threat visual makes you more confident in the execution of your sidestep evasion. Knowing that the 20 cm diagonally forward evasive maneuver can create a black spot where your enemy loses a visual of your post-evasion position, providing time and opportunity to quickly quietly and as safely as possible neutralise the threat, will increase your evasive side step employment confidence.

If adjustments in range position, stance and guard are required, then by means of being proficient in economical and safe adjustments, the chances of objective achievement are maximised and mental toughness can be maintained at the highest possible level in relation to the individual combatant.

Pivoting and sliding methods of post-evasion making range as well as changes in stance are 50percent more economical than maneuvers that require transfers of both feet.

Such advantages increase post-evasion counter engagement employments chances of threat neutralisation before your enemy can detect align and again go on the offensive.

The sidestep evasion diagonally forward comprising of the CQC squat ready set go and evasive sighting visual capabilities, timed correctly, will interfere with your enemy's visual and mental focus and can provide unimpeded post-evasion threat neutralisation as a result of creating a black spot.

These battle-proven combative trade craft practices are tested and proven in training and as such are primary decided options in actions-on encounters.

Every edge and advantage over your enemy is psychologically enhancing and the black spot provides an increased advantage and opportunity by evasive concealment outside your enemy's visual capabilities to exploit exposed bodily targets.

The black spot evasive combative capability, including the prior knowledge of the black spot advantages, amounts to increased psychological confidence for the combatant.

The black spot lost target visual for the enemy, when fully committed to their assault entry, will certainly increase their combative stress level and can invoke negative responses.

Going out in a blaze of glory

The unfortunate reality of battlefield close combat is that there may be situations that simply cannot be countered, combated or escaped through the enemy's massive advantages in personnel and firepower. The decision to take out as many of the enemy before they take you out is truly a last resort option and must be based on a life or death situation. Fortunately this is a rare situation in urban self-defence.

The mentality required to accept probable death defies the basic human instinct of wanting to live as long as possible. If this is combined with the need to 'go combative,' the result can be the ability to take as many of the enemy with you as possible. This outcome is a testament to the special mind-set and skill set of the individual concerned. In most CQC and self-defence encounters where you are faced with extreme unarmed aggressors, terrible odds and dire situations, undertaking a factual assessment to identify the threat realities and deciding on the best option to ensure you have the best combative chance of objective achievement (which may well be escape and evasion), is the best option and best means of winning and not merely surviving. Such decisions must factor in the highest levels of tactical self-protection and hard targeting, and you must be prepared to fast map on the move and make changes in relation to changes in threat situation and terrain-related obstacles, hazards, advantages and disadvantages.

You must be a realist and take control and responsibility for doing everything to reduce risk, increase likelihood of objective achievement and ensure a positive outcome. Remain flexible and be prepared to adjust and change to achieve your objectives. Use everything at your disposal. Maintain the assault momentum, and be unpredictable and deceptive in your actions.

Such a demeanour is preferred over psychologically accepting that you will certainly be killed or lose. The latter is a psychological negative, and possibly could weaken your resolve to neutralise the threat, or escape and evade. The reality is while there is a breath left in you, and the will to win and live, you must do everything in your physical and psychological powers to do so. Accepting anything less can weaken your capabilities, and may lessen your combative chance of victory. It can also increase the extent of wounds and injuries.

It is important that combative actions are decided and initiated before rather than later. Never go combative as a result of being assaulted and overwhelmed. Waiting until you are wounded or injured and enduring ongoing assault and injury to the point of desperation, or realisation that you are injured, wounded, and have reduced capabilities is life threatening. Take control, choose how and when to go combative or escape and evade, and cause confusion in your aggressor or aggressors by having a plan and being prepared to fast map on the move, making changes and adjustments when and where required. No one can live forever, but you can go combative against the odds using every dirty trick, tactic and skill possible, powered by a ruthless, controlled aggressive mentality and the best of self-preservation hard cover skills and deceptive deliberate actions.

Psychological enhancement provided by weapons

Having a weapon capability at your disposal not only can increase your chances of defeating a formidable aggressor, but also can boost your confidence prior to any actions-on encounter.

Many law enforcement officers I have trained are very honest when it comes to the admission that their duty weapons give them the confidence required to deal with aggressive offenders.

The realities of carrying, brandishing and employing weapons are very serious. The lawful carrying of concealed or visible weapons is not a license for reckless use, and comes with considerable responsibilities in relation to conditions of usage. Carrying a weapon without the mind-set required to use it can put the individual in a dangerous situation if the weapon is taken from them and used against them. A weapon is an inanimate object that requires a user to be prepared to use it.

The CQB and CQC operators I train, in addition to their high level of proficiency in armed combat, are also trained in the prevention of their weapon being taken from them, the retention of their weapon if compromised and the 'regention', or regaining control, of their weapon if seized when drawn. They are also trained in weapon disarming under an incoming assault and when ambushed at weapon point.

Brandishing weapons in a threatening manner is unwise and undesirable. The most effective weapon is the weapon which the target never sees prior to falling victim to its effects. Understanding how to employ weapons covertly with deception increases the likelihood of objective achievement, and by having knowledge of the effectiveness of the weapon and its covert employment, increases your psychological confidence.

Any purpose made or improvised weapon that is robust and made of materials harder than human unarmed assault capabilities provides advantages in physical effect and psychological confidence. Understanding human anatomy and biomechanics in relation to close combat empowers the combatant with enemy neutralisation capabilities and enhanced psychological confidence provided by the employment of weapons. Proficiency in the employment of the weapon, as well as weapon security and the disarming of such a weapon if taken from you, is a must to ensure mental toughness can be maintained during all aspects of the ownership of the weapon. Sound basic principles in relation to unarmed combat and military self-defence are the foundations that go hand in hand with the employment, security and disarming of a personal weapon. Any psychological advantages of a personal weapon would be lost in an instant, if the weapon was taken from its owner and used against that owner, through a lack of weapon security and disarming capabilities of the owner.

Sound unarmed combative basic principles, tactics and skills should have commonality with armed combative employments. Having a covert or concealed weapon capability that would enable the user to neutralise an armed threat if required, provides capabilities in relation to holding a ready status, or using de-escalation or negotiation to prevent a physical actions-on encounter. Complete familiarisation with any weapon is essential to increase and maintain confidence in weapon security the drawing, making ready and utilisation of the weapon.

Weapon proficiency requires personal custom setup carry positioning as well as weapon or accessories consideration. High repetition practice in the required means of drawing and making ready of the weapon is essential, as well as in any expected and probable actions-on encounter with constant mental and physical checks of the weapon's position, state of readiness and your intended means of drawing, making ready and using it. Psychological mind's eye confirmation and visualisation make and keep the combatant ready.

I reiterate the most effective and guaranteed threat neutralisation weapon is the one the target does not see, and when utilised covertly or from outside or under their peripheral vision, or with deceptive distractions or dirty tricks, increases the likelihood of threat neutralisation and the user's psychological confidence enhancement and maintenance. Every contingency imaginable in relation to weapons security, carriage and employment, both orthodox and unorthodox, should have been extensively practiced in training.

Combative positive and proactive mind-set

It is very important that the combatant is aware of the potential of probable threats and has the means to neutralise such threats. The level of awareness, and importantly arousal, must be in relation to maintaining a state of readiness with senses alert, and must be able to be enhanced in relation to escalation and changes in threat.

Combative primary performance levels must be adjusted in relation to the immediate threat as well as the degree of threat. This also applies to threat duration in relation to pre-actions-on, actions-on and post actions-on. Conducting oneself at a maximum level of combative arousal pre-actions-on, especially for any extended period of time—and we are talking seconds not minutes—can have extreme negative effects on outcomes and objective achievement. We need to be able to turn our combative physical and psychological capabilities on, commensurate with the threat, and be able to adjust them thereby increasing or decreasing them in relation to threat escalation or de-escalation.

Maintaining an overly high level of state of combative readiness, including utilising methods to psych oneself up, can reduce the individual combatant's capabilities of being in control of the required combination of combative skills and combative mind-set. We are all human beings, and those that are highly trained responsible combatants have emotions and instincts that play major roles in pre-, mid-,and post-combative actions-on encounters. Operating combatively on emotion and instinct as a result of setting and maintaining such a high level of heightened awareness or over-psyching oneself up can reduce combative capabilities considerably. To operate on impulses, instinct and emotions rather than definite and deliberate, combined, combative physical and psychological proven practices reduces the chance of defeating the enemy, neutralising the threat and objective achievement. When you turn on the combative physical and psychological requirements in unison, they must stay online, and in tune.

While knowledge through prior training practice and experience will give you an insight into the likely outcomes, it is important that the combatant is focused on the immediate offensive or counteroffensive action, so as to be able to make primary real-time decisions based on immediate information, and not on distractive thoughts of the likely outcome.

Maintaining the required levels of all the physical and psychological components executed in the correct order and in unison is critical to preventing the over employment of a single component. Over employment reduces performance capabilities, and increase risk through decreasing awareness and decreases the ability to fast map, decide on the move and execute the required skills to neutralise the real-time threat.

The combatant possesses basic instincts as well as the capability to assess and decide on pre-learnt options to neutralise the threat, and often the important ingredient of emotion is not taken into account. Emotion is something that gives us the ability to make responsible and proper decisions, combatively, in relation to rules of engagement and the laws of self-defence. Relying on overly high levels of emotion and instinct can affect your proven combative capabilities considerably. This can invoke an over-emphasis on human decency and reduce the desire to incapacitate or eliminate the enemy by reducing deliberate combative capabilities levels of employment. It can also cause over-thinking, stalling, or hesitation out of wanting or believing the threat will disappear, or decrease, and that there is no need for primary combative actions employments. The opposite is removing or dramatically reducing one's levels of human emotion and natural human instinct from the combative employment, and as such, running on over-ruthless aggression that can cause dire outcomes in relation to objective achievement, and can invoke a total disregard for human life.

This maximum mental and physical status, or majority killer instinct mentality can, through over physical commitment, cause skills telegraphing and slow down deliberate cohesive speed of entry and skills employment required to defeat an alert enemy ready to counter engage. It can also cause self-injury through over-commitment or loss of stability and decentralization. It reduces fast mapping, contingency option employment capabilities by being one dimensional, and unable to operate at anything less than a fully committed unconcerned for safety status. It also invokes enemy desensitization that can reduce the individual to killer animal instincts, regardless of the specific situation threat level, rules of engagement or laws of self-defence.

Staying on a connected line of controlled aggression incorporating all the required components in their primary execution order, by means of incorporating all major and minor components at the required controlled levels, is in line with high proficiency immediate combative skills employments. This controlled and calculated means of maintaining a physical and psychological optimum status in relation to pre-actions-on and actions-on requirements provides total focus on the immediate threat, threat neutralisation requirements and safety, over allowing the mind to become over aroused through psyching or being overly concerned with perceived outcomes. The combative controlled aggressive mind-set status must be maintained and controlled at all times, including being switched on as part of threat identification maintained during actions-on encounters and then being switched off post actions-on when the threat has been confirmed neutralised.

The danger of allowing over-promotion or excessive psyching is that mental focus and physical skills capabilities are compromised. Another danger is that allowing over-emotion to take effect or employing excessive psyching up, is that returning to a state of optimum combative readiness or performance is not immediate. Military combative and military self-defence tactics and skills employments are very different to your common sports martial arts and fighting arts physical and psychological practices in relation to pre-actions-on, actions-on and post-actions-on. Because military skills promote incapacitation and elimination by dirty and deadly means, they usually require considerably less physical capabilities. Obviously the combatant requires mental toughness and physical skills of self-preservation and hard cover guarding to enable them to achieve their objective against a formidable enemy foe, but unlike marital arts, military skills are not predominately based on taking an enemy on but rather are based on taking the enemy out.

Going combatively tactical has far less physical attributes required than that of the fighting fitness required for combat sports and martial arts. The reality is the knowledge of the risks and dangers of wounding and trying to take out the enemy before they take you out increases psychological stresses considerably. Under such conditions the physical skills must be supported by maximum psychological enhancement capabilities, and must consist of very ruthless controlled aggression that requires physical capabilities that ensure the combatant can achieve the objective by means of overkill but not maximum physical output capabilities.

Everything must be very controlled and calculated, and ensure the combatant maintains the highest possible levels of physical capabilities and mental toughness to meet considerations in relation to threat continuation, additional threats, or the requirements to escape and evade.

In many sports, the fitness achieved through training and practice naturally increases one's capabilities without constant deliberate thought. For primary combative output and capability, however, everything must be deliberate, controlled and calculated.

In military combative actions-on encounters, every action and reaction and skills execution, minor and major, is controlled by definite and deliberate combative respiration and physical and psychological components that ensure the combatant can maintain the highest level of capabilities for extended periods of time if required. While maintaining the highest level of psychological and physical capabilities as always planned for, it is important to understand that the combatant knows the importance of defeating the enemy and neutralising the threat in the first three seconds, and certainly less than 10 seconds against a formidable enemy. The very nature of kill-or-die CQC and CQB increases psychological stress considerably, and as such immediate or quick threat neutralisation is essential.

Deceptive or covert combative actions increase psychological combative confidence and the chance of objective achievement. Covert and deceptive offensive actions and counter-offensive actions increase the effect of contact and objective achievement. Swift cohesive deceptive execution lines to the target increase the likelihood of uninterrupted target contact.

Just as a twig flicks you in the eye as a result of unexpected unannounced entry line contact, combative offensive and counter engagement skills executions that are deceptive in relation to visual detection are combative smart. The last line of protection against the unexpected twig flicking you in the eye is your ability to blink, providing the last means of eyeball protection. Clearly the unexpected twig flicking you in the eye is far from a deliberate action, but it achieves contact by surprise, speed and a difficult-to-detect entry line to the target.

Employing combative skills that exploit visual blind spots, where the combative action is initiated outside the peripheral vision, reduces the enemy's opportunity to counter the action from the time it enters their peripheral vision and contacts with the intended target. The practice of proven combative actions that exploit blind spots and reduce enemy counter capabilities, psychologically builds confidence in the combatant, and helps them understand the difficulty in detecting and countering such combative options. Covert and deceptive initiation of combative actions from under or outside the enemy's peripheral vision not only increases objective achievement chances, but also increases psychological confidence through understanding the degree of difficulty the enemy requires to counter such combative actions.

Any advantage or edge that is known to enhance objective achievement by the combatant will increase the combatant's psychological confidence. Dirty and deadly, battle-proven practices are truly confidence building and boosting.

Distractive fake or definite actions that interfere with the enemy's vision, visual focus or point and line of vision—including fake or deliberate actions directed at another quadrant of the enemy's body other than the intended target quadrant— exploit human weaknesses in relation to definite or deceptive actions, and so increase combative confidence in the level or chance of objective achievement.

Combative or conflict resolution

The reality is that, against a formidable goal- driven enemy combatant bent on causing grievous bodily harm or death, the best of tactics and battle-proven skills are required to neutralise the threat. Conflict resolution, de-escalation and negotiation has its place in law enforcement, security operations and civilian self-defence, but it can be a fatal decision in a high risk combative encounter. Verbiage slows reaction time, and coming across as condescending, authoritative, aggressive or unconfident can lead to greater dangers.

There is a fine line between providing non-lethal or less lethal skills for military roles that require them, and reducing the controlled, aggressive, combative capabilities that are the primary requirements in battlefield kill or get killed situations. Military combative tactics provide hard target and hard cover tactical capabilities for crisis management and CQC non-lethal or less lethal roles and duties. These tactics and skills include remaining vigilant and constantly assessing threats, environments and situations in real time, adjusting tactics and procedures to maintain security and safety.

Using barriers, angles, being alert to deception, and familiar with body language masking aggressive intentions, all combined with maintaining role and situation specific primary ranges, reduces risk by presenting oneself as ready, willing and able to combat or counter in any actions-on encounters.

Utilising definite verbiage and hand signals, including the presence of the combatant's weapons, are great means of deterring situations. Conflict resolution and de-escalation using verbiage in high risk, high stress situations can create increased dangers by slowing reaction time and unless the verbiage is controlled, careful and calculated, it may well escalate the situation and increase risk and danger. There is a considerable difference between police or peace officer duties and tactics, and neutralising a volatile combative threat presented by a formidable enemy combatant. While roles require specific tactics and skills in relation to rules of engagement, it must never be forgotten that controlled aggression, including ruthless, controlled aggression is a major life-saving capability in battlefield CQC and CQB that a trained combatant requires to neutralise threats, achieve objectives and be victorious in life-and-death encounters.

Overly training combatants in de-escalation or conflict resolution tactics and skills may affect a combatant's decision making, and getting it wrong could be fatal. Highly trained combatants have a respect for life and an understanding of the importance of rules of engagement. They are highly trained in a wide range of skills applicable to wide ranging roles and requirements.

Being armed in a combat environment and carrying primary and secondary weapons is a great deterrent in its own right, and a signal that the individual is combat capable. Tactics and skills must enforce the combatant's status and role in situations where maintaining security and control is required. Signs of weakness, being prepared to go back on orders or instructions, and making exceptions or changes to conditions, portray the perception of, and give the subject a sense of being able to manipulate the combatant. Non-lethal roles for combatants require a firm, fair and impartial, tactically safe and correct modus operandi. Sound tactics, primary, proven skills, and a vigilant, confident, definite and deliberate demeanour that shows who is in control, will generally reduce risk considerably and increase the chance of objective achievement; this is in contrast to an over attempt to de-escalate high risk combative situations by conflict resolution.

Psychological enhancement in training

Having a sound cover guard and confident, competent training partners that can test and true up your cover guard and deflection capabilities will increase psychological confidence levels considerably.

The cover guard allows for combative sighting between the cover guard, for the deflection of strikes that are straight-line or uppercut and for the absorption of the impact of round house strikes. Understanding this and truing up the cover guard through high repetition and varied training, including unexpected actions-on encounters, increases the individual combatant's mental toughness considerably.

Understanding the importance of specific primary ranges for decided options executions to reduce risk and increase the chance of object achievement is very important to psychological confidence and enhancement.

To me a reactionary gap for evasive counter engagement will allow for the evasion of the most formidable enemy combatant even if you are fatigued or carrying injuries.

When engaged inside the kill zone sound hard cover guard and deflection capabilities combined with point-blank range closing timed footwork will enable the combatant to reduce the enemy's unarmed combat capabilities. This is done by pressing forward to point blank body contact range and counter engaging after jamming them up body to body and shutting them down or by seizing, securing and combative clinching to set up combative skills to neutralise the threat.

Exposure to increased levels of bodily compression in ground combat will identify the need to employ combative respiration and psychological confidence enhancement to overcome the effects of panic, pressure or pain and be able to identify the dangers of pain and or pressure and effectively take control and neutralise the threat. Inoculation against such mental and physical effects is achieved by introducing small doses of threat initially and employing proven, controlled physical and mental means to overcome the effects and neutralise the threat. The doses can be increased as proficiency to endure and employ the required means to neutralise the threat are achieved.

The same applies to enemy techniques that when applied create pain and the even greater risk factor of pressure. Understanding how to resist and yield as part of the relief of pressure, or how to escape and counter engage will, if practiced under controlled conditions with increased force and pressure employment, increase physical and mental capabilities.

Your mind follows pain. So, you need to be able to identify the nature of the pain and employ tactics and skills to relieve and reduce the dangers as part of the escape and enemy neutralisation process. 'Pressure is considered considerably more dangerous than pain' is a general rule in CQC as it is an indicator of the danger of potential fracture, dislocation or ligament damage or destruction, whereas pain in CQC is more an indicator of the fact that you are alive and need to go combative, stopping the pain and neutralising the threat.

Battle-proven tactics and skills that reduce the risk of injury, including preventing the enemy from applying pain or pressure, are primary practices in maintaining mental toughness.

Flat hand configurations in guarding reduce the likelihood of finger injuries or fingers being seized and dislocated. Keeping the thumb tucked inside the flat hand configuration reduces the risk of the thumb becoming seized and secured, dislocated or caught in battle dress or webbing. As such, this removes a physical weakness and psychological concern in relation to the possible effects of extreme pressure pain and loss of capabilities in skills employment through injuries or if the fingers and thumbs are deliberately targeted and fractured or dislocated.

Psychologically maintaining vision is very important in relation to combative capabilities. As with game birds and wild animals when a bag is put over their head, they lose a lot of fight or escape capabilities. Humans when blindfolded, hooded or having to defend themselves in darkness may initially panic, but the reality is that without vision to detect and engage the enemy the common likelihood is inaction. This is why it is essential that the trained combatant is proficient in utilising all senses including the sense of touch, and in how to use heightened senses to identify and neutralise risk as part of self-protection. Tactically correct methods of escape are also essential, require specific skill sets, and all senses heightened and utilised to reduce risk and assist in self-protection and escape.

We all know that medical attention is important in relation to wounds and injuries, however, in the middle of an actions-on encounter when a wound or injury is received it is important to neutralise the threat or escape and evade prior to first aid, assessment and treatment. The reality is that stopping to check one's wounds or injuries in an actions-on encounter means you lose momentum, makes you a static target, and takes valuable time away from neutralising the threat. If you are still able to go combative to neutralise the threat or escape and evade this is important in relation to life-saving enhancement. Depending on the individual combatant's level of mental toughness, the extent of the wounds or injuries could cause the onset of shock and reduce combative neutralisation or escape and evasion capabilities.

Trained combatants must have an understanding of risk reduction when capabilities are reduced as a result of injuries, wounds or being restrained with mechanical restraints.

Understanding how to improvise to increase self-preservation capabilities when restricted through injury, wounding or being a restrained prisoner is a required means to maintain mental toughness, increase self-preservation capabilities and neutralise the threat. I have had, prior to undergoing my instructor qualification, my senior combatants assault me while my hands were tied behind my back as a means of increasing physical tactics, skills and mental toughness as part of restricted situational self-preservation and combative threat neutralization. As part of combative conditioning training and under phase test conditions candidates have their wrists tied behind their backs and with reduced capabilities must evade, stationary evade or employ stationary hard cover deflection against single and multiple enemy pers. This reduced capability training increases mental toughness against adversity and requires the combatant to maintain control while making fast map decisions and employing the most effective means of threat neutralisation. They learn to appreciate their full combative capabilities and increase in confidence.

Restrained stationary hard target cover and deflection.

Restrained counter engagement.

In dire situations such as knife combat or knife disarming, when penetration or slashing is unavoidable, it is essential that you know how to reduce risk and lessen the effects of injuries by ensuring penetration or slashing is to muscle and tissue rather than arteries and tendons. Understanding the reality of the situation and the need to reduce risk to enable counter engagement to neutralise the threat will ensure, psychologically, that the combatant is prepared for the reality of wounding and psychologically prepared to, post wounding, neutralise the threat. Through such training to deal with the realities of risk reduction and wounding and setting up the incapacitation or elimination of the enemy threat, confidence is developed that will enable the combatant to save their own life and neutralise the enemy.

Military combative battle-proven primary methods provide psychological enhancement

There is a considerable difference between military combative skills and those used in combat sports including in no-holds-barred martial arts. Military combative skills provide deadly methods of threat neutralisation and as such empower the combatant with confidence to achieve their objective.

The combat boot provides not only protection for the combatants foot, but also when used in unarmed offensive or counteroffensive assault provides a means of safe and destructive capabilities. The combat boot is far more resilient than bare hands, and provides a high level of protection to the vital bones of the feet. When you consider there are more bones in the feet that any part of the body, and how delicate and vulnerable they can be, boots are an effective means of protection, which in turn provides enhanced destructive capabilities and psychological enhancement through understanding the outcomes that can be achieved using boots for stamp kicking.

Military self-defence skills that employ primary or secondary weapons to escape seizure in the clinch or escape secure holds, including ground combat, take away a formidable enemy's combat sports, martial arts or fighting arts capabilities. The reality of a ballistic or edged weapon employed at close quarters point-blank range to counter wrestling or grappling threat situations makes easy work of even a highly trained formidable adversary.

Battle-proven overkill destruction of the spinal cord and airway as well as targeting the eyes and other delicate bodily targets, including the use of weapons via orifices in deadly take out kill-or-die military CQC, are terminal practices that provide the highly trained combatant with deadly capabilities that have no preference to the enemy's fighting prowess, and as such, psychologically empower the highly trained combatant.

War requires dirty and deadly battle-proven tactics and skills that provide overkill means of threat neutralisation, that the highly trained combatant has total confidence in. Fully understanding the medical aspects of military CQC and military self-defence as well as the primary most proven skills of targeting and destroying the human anatomy provides psychological confidence.

The most dirty and deadly skills of human destruction are worthless if the individual trained in such methods does not possess the intestinal fortitude and inner resolve required to employ such skills. When facing a formidable enemy, being able to reduce the effects of a barrage of unarmed assault by means of sound hard cover guarding and shutting down or reducing your enemy's unarmed offensive assault capabilities in the setup of your enemy stopping employment, as well as being psychologically prepared to cause them grievous bodily harm or take your enemy out, are equally or even more important that the battle-proven means of threat neutralisation itself.

The previous provides a glimpse of some of the terminal methods of threat and enemy neutralisation by means of military close quarter's combat and military self-defence.

Military combative deadly take out skills are considerably different to fighting styles take-on skills. When the combatant has confidence in the combative skills they have been trained in, knowing they have been battle proven and adopted for the maximum destructive capabilities they provide, then this is psychologically empowering. Combine deadly capabilities with individuals that have been selected for their very special psychological and physical capabilities and the combative chances of quick and quiet objective achievement are increased considerably.

CQC/ SELF-DEFENCE TACTICS AND SKILLS

The order of execution of vital components to hard target the combatant and increase combative actions-on performance is critical. I believe human responses other than initial autonomic self-preservation reactions in unexpected sudden aggressive shock actions-on encounters are deliberate actions based on prior training and supported by muscle memory. In expected actions-on encounters where there is prior knowledge or warning of an imminent assault, and hard target tactics are being employed, it must be deliberate, decided combative actions to threat neutralise. In unexpected actions encounters, initially, through situation, it is more about self-preservation than immediate offensive or counter-offensive skills executions.

My working life instructing military CQC has identified some human actions and reactions that are counter-productive to combating or counter-engaging one's enemy. The two critical components that need changing in skill or order of execution are combative respiration and cover guarding. My research has identified that in an unexpected actions-on situation the normal first reaction is to flinch. This is followed by visual threat assessment and alignment to the enemy threat. Then comes decision-making post-assessment followed by adjustments and skills execution. Adjustments are normal preparatory requirements for skills executions to make ready, by means of minor actions that can make all the difference in relation to the effect of the employed skill.

The reality is that too often tactical combative respiration is not a consideration until skills have been or are being executed. Unfortunately the reality is also that many proponents, when going tactical and combative, never employ tactical combative respiration but just rely on normal breathing.

The time between going tactical and combative actions-on in an expected combative encounter can range from seconds to a minute or more. In unexpected actions-on or close to point-blank range expected combative encounters, where a flash of movement or contact is the first indicator of an actions-on encounter, there is little to no warning time initially to undertake anything other than self-preservation. If tactical combative respiration is not employed immediately from the point of threat recognition, or in an unexpected threat situation immediately at the realisation you are under assault, the combatant will in a very short period of time suffer the effects of rapidly diminishing physical and psychological capabilities. Often those that have not been trained in combative respiration, or that have been trained in it but fail to employ this single most important component in regards to combative psychological and skills enhancement, also fail to maintain normal life support respiration by holding their breath.

Their lips are puckered together as if they are super glued while they are under immediate threat or assault. When the realisation that they are falling victim to either fully restricted or partially restricted respiration takes hold, they open their mouth and gasp for air, but they are already disadvantaged and probably already defeated.

I see all too often individuals that are oblivious to such a dangerous fault in training. They do not believe you when you point it out and I have seen some confused expressions when they see themselves on video.

Another problem identified frequently in training is they quickly get tunnel vision, audio exclusion and their recollection of their combative employments and situational awareness is reduced considerably.

Failing to employ combative respiration from the immediate point of going tactical under threat or threat recognition in an expected actions-on encounter, or first indication or realisation in an unexpected actions-on assault, will result in struggling to maintain CQC required controlled respiration levels and may see the combatant reduced to hyperventilation when up against a formidable enemy.

Failing to employ combative respiration can cause rapid reductions in physical capabilities leading to psychological inner resolve deterioration. Tactical respiration from the outset will also keep the adverse effects of high stress, high risk human reaction to the stimuli of sudden aggressive combative shock action in check and under control.

Tactical combative respiration can reduce or prevent the effects of audio exclusion and tunnel vision, as well as ensure the highest skill level is maintained. When you consider that primary proven military combative and self-defence skills are gross motor skills, your chances of threat neutralisation as a result of correct combative respiration are enhanced.

Maintaining the capability to assess and decide under stress comes from confidence, competence and familiarity of operating under such threat situations in training and operationally. Maintaining the highest levels of fine motor skills through tactical combative respiration will certainly enhance the effectiveness and objective achievement outcomes of the execution of battle-proven skills that are predominantly gross motor skill orientated.

Going tactical in expected actions-on encounters and employing deliberate offensive or counteroffensive pre-decided combative actions is required to take combative control. In unexpected actions-on encounters first identified by autonomic initial incoming actions or actual contact reactionary responses, mechanisms of self-preservation combined with pre-trained hard cover guarding, must be simultaneously employed with CQC respiration, real time assessment, decision making and combative employments giving you your best chance of threat neutralisation.

Note there must be room for human error factored into combative tactics and skills, as well as fast mapping decision-making on the move to combat or counter a changing threat situation, or to reduce the effects of incorrect options employment or failed options employment. That said, the order of execution is as follows to ensure optimum combative levels are achieved and maintained, both physically and psychologically.

Immediately you are aware of a pending actions-on encounter, or are in an actions-on encounter, commence tactical combative respiration and maintain it until all threats are neutralised. Shallow, controlled, cycled respiration by inhaling via the nostrils and exhaling via the mouth is the respiration pattern required.

Combative respiration timing is essential; the exhalation is initiated and timed with the execution of any physical offensive or counteroffensive action. The shallow inhalation via the nostrils will feel as if the inhaled air is passing somewhere between the base of the nasal passages and the roof of your mouth.

Allow the inhaled air to cycle by means of low level, controlled flow from entry to exhaling via the mouth. Every inhale/exhale cycle will be approximately 1 to 2 seconds, and you must time your CQC respiration to exhale with every employed combative action as previously stipulated.

Note that in any actions-on combative encounter, keeping your jaw clenched reduces physical injury and the effects of contact impact. Combative respiration exhaling is easily performed with a clenched jaw via the gaps between the upper and lower teeth. Training with a combined upper and lower protection mouth guard promotes good combative respiration practices, as you must exhale via the vents in the mouth guard in CQC respiration practice.

When cover guarding, or cover guarding and deflecting, every enemy unarmed offensive action that is cover guarded or cover guarded and deflected must be synchronised with the exhaling component of combative respiration. Timing your defensive hard cover guarding and deflection with your exhaling will ensure your defensive capabilities are deliberate actions, in the same way your offensive actions are powered by exhaling. Synchronising your respiration with your combative actions not only increases performance and provides combative endurance, but against enemy unarmed contact it will also reduce the effects of impact. Inhaling or holding your breath during combative skills executions can, however, increase the effects of contact.

Adverse consequences can include respiration difficulties after holding your breath under assault in relation to forced catch-up respiration to recover, which is very difficult under assault. The effects of being winded as a consequence of abdominal contact are intensified considerably if you are holding your breath, or when contact is made on the inhalation component of the combative respiration cycle.

Employing controlled aggression of 75 percent plus of your maximum output capabilities, combined with your CQC tactical respiration, will increase your CQC high range performance capabilities outcomes and endurance capabilities considerably. If, however, you go at 100 percent your performance capabilities for 15 to 30 seconds can be reduced by 50percent upwards. CQC being a means to incapacitate or eliminate one's enemy by targeting major human senses and life-support vitals requires less power and more ruthless controlled aggression for objective achievement. Over 75 percent and under 95 percent controlled aggressive skills output employments provide maximum required human destructive capabilities physically, while keeping you in full psychological control including in dire situations, where combative endurance capabilities may be required for extended duration. The reality of 100 percent executions is the level of physical commitment can cause errors such as missing the target or balance loss. Combine this with having to recover when spent against a formidable enemy and the objective becomes unnecessarily considerably harder to achieve.

100 percent committed combative actions can also cause self-injuries through over extension and other target miss realities. You can compromise yourself and lose any element of surprise; as such, over committed actions tend to telegraph the intention and any formidable wired enemy will pick up on minor indicators, let alone major indicators of an incoming assault such as 100 percent over committed telegraphed actions.

Every action no matter how minor (such as stalking into range) requires you to inhale immediately prior to the physical skill execution, and exhale on initiation and throughout the skill employment. In the brain-to-boot exercise phases you will, with every skill employment, hear the commands for combative respiration (respire) first up, or in an unexpected actions-on encounter where contact is the first indicator, simultaneously with self-protection hard cover guarding commands.

Immediately on initiating combative respiration the further employment of the most important human sense in relation to close combat—being vision—must be utilised to determine the threat in relation to location, threat type and threat danger level, range, and all required specific threat and situational considerations.

Cover guarding immediately prior to aligning to your enemy, which is also referred to as 'orientating' or 'centering' to your enemy post visual, is an important aspect of making yourself as safe as humanly possible and a hard target especially when compromised.

In unexpected actions-on situations, out of self-preservation requirements, cover guarding is initiated simultaneously with combative respiration prior to or during visual assessment of the threat, its position and line of incoming assault. This cover guarding and alignment phase will usually require combined cover guarding and target mass reduction by dropping your centre of gravity to a CQC squat ready position, from which further adjustments can be made to increase stability, reduce target mass, set a ready status to combat or counter engage, and generally increase your personal hard target status.

Combative respiration must be a first consideration with all combative actions, or at least as soon as the actions-on is realised and your hard cover guarding protection is in place. Ideally, through combative competency and proficiency, your CQC respiration should be simultaneous with your hard cover guarding.

'Slow is fast' in training to perfect primary combative physical and psychological practices; this includes CQC respiration and CQC squat target mass reduction, and setting a stable ready status for expedient combative actions.

Time your CQC respiration with every minor and major combative action employment, and with the CQC squat when the downward squat component is initiated first, simultaneously followed by the blocking back motion with your master boot to maximise stability and expedient action from a ready, set to go stance and status.

Then to initiate expedient combative actions-on inhale on the small squat downward ready set component and exhale throughout the combative skill employment.

Front stance

Anti-clockwise front foot pivoting alignment

Front foot pivoting alignment ready status

Clockwise front foot pivoting continued alignment

Hard cover, hard targeting combined with CQC respiration is essential in unexpected actions-on counter engagement, combined with all other components executed in the correct order of execution to maximise safety and objective achievement.

Your enemy alignment execution must be a swift, stable, controlled movement and based on maximum economy of movement. Pivoting on your lead boot, and moving your rear boot only is 50 percent more economical than double-stepping enemy alignment.

Continued transitional assessment of the enemy threat and situation, during and post the alignment transition, is vital to be able to fast map and decide on your combat or counter measures and execute them as quickly, safely and discreetly as possible. Your senses will be on high alert from the moment you go tactical or are targeted in an unexpected actions-on encounter, and will be utilised in unison, and in the required primary order of execution, to maintain your highest levels of maintained tactical combative readiness, until the threat is neutralised.

You must maintain a state of controlled readiness and, under skills employment, controlled aggression.

Combative Respiration

The first required deliberate physical component to ensure a positive psychological controlled status is initiated and maintained respiration the combative way. When you go about everyday activities (e.g., walking), you don't have to focus on respiration or breath control, and unless the physical activity increases in intensity you do not have to give respiration a second thought. Combative respiration reduces, eliminates or keeps in check the effects of stress and fear, including controlling or stopping the effects of adrenalin dumping.

In a close combat encounter you must always presume your enemy is formidable and bent on killing you. Bearing this in mind and taking into account that you may be fatigued or suffering from dehydration or starvation, not to mention wounded, injured or affected by psychological concerns, you must conserve your energy and go tactical by taking control combatively; this starts by employing combative respiration.

Over the years I have observed and assessed many combatants and combat sports fighters that in the mid to full commitment range have a face that resembles a knotted balloon ready to explode or brain fart. They are red faced and their power and velocity decreases considerably with every additional action. They will struggle for breath and their actions will diminish rapidly in effectiveness. Psychologically their inner resolve and mental toughness is being eroded by their lack of effectiveness and the reality is that self-doubt and defeat could quickly follow.

Inhaling via the nose prior to any offensive or counter-offensive action, including any footwork, and exhaling via the mouth with and throughout any physical action will ensure you do not hold your breath and lose physical effect, and as a result risk being psychologically affected. You inhale via the nose and exhale via the mouth, and the controlled breathing is by means of low intensity but full cycled respiration.

Respiration is the most important aspect of close combat when you consider you must never underestimate your enemy and must be prepared to operate when you are at your actual physical and psychological worst. To maintain committed performance levels and ensure 75percent plus physical output in close combat you must employ tactical respiration.

Whenever you go tactical or combative at close quarters every step, every action, and every reactionary response must be a product of controlled tactical respiration to maintain the highest levels and status of combative readiness and capabilities. Tactical CQC respiration is a trained action in an expected actions-on encounter, and a deliberate response post flinch or contact factor in an unexpected actions-on encounter, to ensure your decided combative option has the best chance of objective achievement.

Extreme flinch factor decentralization recovery can be increased considerably by employing your second wind practice as it is known in CQC, exhaling on ground impact reducing the effects of being winded and then inhaling in preparation of re-gaining your footing and exhaling immediately prior to and throughout recovery. Every combative action post recovery will be employed with CQC respiration. CQC respiration is very much a physical component of close combat that will aid in maintaining not only physical capabilities but also mental toughness.

Utilising timed tactical CQC respiration cycles, commenced by inhaling through your nose immediately prior to any physical action with low intensity, full upper abdomen, cycled respiration and exhaling by your mouth on and throughout your CQC skills employments will aid in maintaining not only physical capabilities but also mental toughness.

This definite and deliberate combative respiration process provides wide ranging additional benefits and advantages apart from controlling or eliminating autonomic adverse reactionary effects. It enables you to overcome psychological threat and situational effects, as well as the physical effects of extreme aggressive shock actions encounters, and enables you to go combative. It not only enables you to take control or regain control in CQC or self-defence, but it provides high level combative destructive physical output. This high intensity combative destructive output can be extended for a prolonged combative duration through CQC respiration.

Through CQC respiration you can maintain sound assessment and decision making in real time. You will enable a clear thought process in real time to be available to you and a clear post actions-on recollection. Combative breathing also considerably reduces the adverse effects of combative abdominal contact including impact with the ground. Every executed physical action from stalking into range to offensive and evasive foot work, and the employment of armed or unarmed offensive or counter-offensive assault must be employed with tactical CQC respiration. I reiterate, this includes when you are decentralized, exhaling as you go to the ground and, as you recover, inhaling immediately before regaining your footing and exhaling throughout footing recovery. This will reduce being incapacitated (through being winded on ground contact) and to ensure you recover, will include controlled expedient counter engagement. Once you have employed combative respiration in training practice you can focus instead only on inhaling immediately prior to any physical action or response. This will reduce the required physical focus, mental focus and application by 50 percent because if you are inhaling as part of your set up initiation you will naturally exhale throughout the execution phase of your skill employment as a result of your prior training muscle memory.

Focusing on the CQC skill inhaling set up respiration component first is logical and correct as set up comes before execution. The execution phase of the skill will be enhanced by the controlled continuous output respiration exhaling via the mouth throughout the skill employment.

I have researched, developed, practiced and instructed CQB and CQC tactical respiration practices that promote delivering and maintaining performance intensity and endurance at peak combative output levels for more than two decades as a military CQB/CQC Master Instructor. From controlling the effects of adrenaline and the effects of fear risk and sudden aggressive shock action, through to achieving high levels of required physical capabilities for extended periods in the execution of combinations and repetition combative skills employments, tactical combative respiration is the difference between success and failure

My adopted respiration tactics principles and skills have been proven in training and in actions-on encounters. I have developed skills that have proven their worth and been adopted as primary practices in my military packages and programs as a result of being a hands on Military Master-Chief CQB/CQC instructor with a lifetime's working commitment to military CQB/CQC

There is a very real difference between the single repetition, strength required, athletic applied suspended breathing, and combative respiration requirements, where there is the need to employ continued combative respiration in relation to continuous combative skills employments.

For the past 40 years I have been a keen shooter and hunter, starting back with small-bore rifle shooting at primary school and continuing to hunt and shoot all my life. The method I was taught in shooting and have seen taught regularly in relation to inhaling, exhaling partially and then holding your breath is very different to the requirements for unarmed combat skills execution respiration. In fact that form of breathing for combat shooting on the move would be completely negative and non-applicable.

Under test conditions the brain-to-boot combative method of respiration proved very effective in relation to combat shooting accuracy, physical fitness and endurance requirements associated with continued shooting on the move.

During my development, evaluation, testing, proving and selecting of practices in relation to tactical combative respiration, the following method proved very effective in relation to accuracy and achieving time reductions in relation to bursts of fire: Inhaling via the nose while achieving your sight picture, and exhaling by means of continuous, low intensity, cycled respiration by the mouth as you squeeze the trigger. The number of rounds able to be fired per single respiration cycle would be determined in relation to the individual's physical fitness and respiration capabilities. Most physically fit combatants could empty their clip in one respiration cycle. For extended magazines, or if more rounds need to be fired than one respiration cycle can provide, then the process would be repeated by simply inhaling again and exhaling as the trigger is squeezed.

In relation to unarmed combat, the commitment level should be around 75percent to maintain accuracy and skill proficiency as well as ensure you operate at a level that allows for endurance by means of continued individual or combination skills executions.

Physically fit combatants will be able to execute two strikes per single tactical combative respiration cycle if required; however, combative kicks executions to achieve and maintain performance and proficiency would require one tactical combative respiration cycle per kick. Even individuals that are lacking in physical fitness capabilities but possess the combative skills capabilities can execute unarmed offensive and counter-offensive assault skills for extended periods by employing the previous tactical combative respiration practices.

No matter how insignificant the component or action, it must be initiated and powered by the exhale phase of your tactical combative respiration. I have observed thousands of exponents holding their breath during combative training, battle handling exercises and testing without realising it and the results have been as follows: From an evidential perspective their faces look like a knotted balloon or a sealed envelope, their lips change in colour as does the colour of their face with continued skills employments. They lose power and velocity as well as skills proficiency including accuracy with additional skills employments. They have difficulty in thinking on the move or recalling their exact actions, including being aware of the mistakes they have made in relation to failing to employ CQC respiration.

They become unaware very quickly of their surroundings including environmental and training related obstacles and dangers. They fail to hear commands, instructions and orders (including a megaphone or whistle) and as such in activities like crowd fighting, pugil stick fighting or combat milling they may not stop on the whistle or command.

Importantly if you ask them to outline exactly how they executed their chosen skills they find difficulty in providing an honest and accurate recollection. Effective programs such as silicone coachTM provide the ability to play back recorded footage by means of a time warp and are great tools in identifying and proving the faults of incorrect respiration or suspended respiration. While flinching is an autonomic response to sudden aggressive shock action, tactical combative respiration is the first deliberate action taken to ensure the combatant initiates, and maintains, the correct level of commitment in relation to individual and continued skills executions so as to maintain the proficiency and intensity levels required to achieve the objective under adversity and with the requirement for combative endurance.

One of the most physically demanding actions for a combatant, especially when they are stressed and fatigued is the ability to regain one's footing when decentralised. By employing tactical combative respiration, every action will be powered by tactical controlled respiration. By exhaling when decentralised by forced or deliberate decision, the risk of incapacitation by being winded in relation to ground contact impact is reduced. Immediately post combative falling, by inhaling and exhaling to achieve footing recovery, the combatant will have maintained cycled respiration and as such will improve their capabilities to continue at a high combative performance level. Counter-offensively, when cover guarding against enemy unarmed offensive assault by employing cycled tactical combative respiration, timing the exhaling phase with the execution of the cover guarding or deflection of enemy strikes will reduce the effects in the event of abdominal contact (in relation to being winded) if the cover guard or deflection fails to achieve its full objective. For effectively cover guarded or deflected enemy strikes the CQC tactical respiration cycle will enable controlled aggressive 75 percent plus counter engagement with expediency.

Stationary evasion and counter stamp kicking to combat an enemy kick with a stamp kick requires the same CQC respiration method exhaling via the mouth with the employment of the counter stamp kick.

I am in my 50s now and still involved in full-time CQB/CQC instructing. After several decades of doing so with the expected wear and tear that goes with the territory, my body has taken its share of use and abuse. While I may not be able to run a marathon in any record time, I find training, instructing and demonstrating combative skills utilising my developed tactical combative respiration, low intensity cycled respiration, provides the necessary capabilities to perform combative skills for extended periods of time maintaining the 75 percent plus performance levels. Combative respiration is the single most deliberate individual combatant employed practice to ensure psychological and physical optimum levels are maintained.

Mental and physical CQC timing

Definite and deliberate timing combined with all the brain to boot, physical and mental combative components major and minor increase the chances of threat neutralisation. From the instant of threat identification by means of CQC respiration initiation you have a primary means of control in the timing and employment of skills.

Correctly timed evasive counter engagement when your enemy is beyond the point of no return creates advantages in post evasion timing to adjust and execute threat neutralisation counter engagement.

Evasive respiration in groundcover evasive timing can be effectively timed not only by visual capabilities but also by inhaling immediately prior to the evasive action as part of the CQC squat ready set to go phase and exhaling throughout the evasive action to increase expedient action reduce risk and as such maintain maximum mental toughness.

Unarmed offensive assault skills employments are initiated by means of the same respiratory inhaling set up cycle and exhale cycle throughout the assault. Once range has been made combining cycled respiration timing practices promotes controlled cohesion and the highest level of control and maintenance of physical capabilities.

While timing in relation to physical combative capabilities may well be dictated by your enemies actions, the execution of combative skills can certainly be employed with cycled respiration timing to achieve maximum output while maintaining physical capabilities.

The old adage fail to prepare and prepare to fail is very true in relation to planning and preparation of which timing and timed respiration in relation to skills executions are primary practices in combative skills employments.

The brain to boot state of readiness practices from the ground up to the top of the head and everything in between have been developed on setting and maintaining a state of ready willingness. This state of ready and willingness senses at high alert and all physical and mental capabilities switched on provides the means to identify threats as early as possible and employ skills to reduce risk and increase combative threat neutralisation.

Timing and placement of combative skills combined with CQC cycled respiration timing increases both responsive actions, contact accuracy and combative skills capabilities.

Timing dirty tricks and distractions then exploiting enemy autonomic reactions to such actions by visually determined timing and respiration cycled skills employment timing increases chances of threat neutralisation.

Timing seizure prevention or escapes in relation to the set up of physical preventative or escape skills respectively that are initiated and powered by respiratory timed cycles increases chances of threat neutralisation and objective achievement.

Cycled respiration timing applies to the execution of all combative skills from unarmed offensive assault to unarmed counter offensive assault as well as close quarters combat in the clinch, ground combat and weapon disarming including ambush phase weapon disarming.

While human sensory visual capabilities are predominantly responsible for combative skills decision making and contact accuracy combining respiratory cycled timing will increase control output and the maintaining of combative physical capabilities.

The employment of combative skills by a single respiratory cycle or by multiple strikes per respiration cycle is an effective means of reducing risk during entry and the execution of skills.

Physical combative skills timing and CQC respiration timing employed in the correct order of execution with cohesion provide maximum combative capabilities.

The CQC squat develops confidence in CQC skills employment by gaining proficiency in its usage to make yourself a difficult target. Understanding and trusting in CQC respiration and CQC squatting to cause your enemy to miss you their intended target combined with increasing expedient action is a definite mental confidence booster. Timing CQC squatting to initiate CQC actions causing interference with your enemies line and point of vision as well as mental focus is advantageous in the execution of CQC skills. Timing static unarmed offensive assault and unarmed counter offensive assault off of a CQC squat increases safety and CQC skills physical output levels. Confidence and mental conviction in respiration and CQC squatting timing is achieved in training and testing increasing combatants mental resolve in the capabilities of such timed CQC actions.

Endurance and recovery breathing

Combative respiration comprising of deliberate inhaling prior to the execution of individual skills, or at most, two or three combative action repetitions per respiration cycled on the exhale phase is considerably different to the requirements of physical endurance activities respiration. Running, power walking and pack marching requires a far less deliberate, individual action form of respiration. Performance and distance as well as load bearing will be governed by the individual's physical fitness levels combined with mental toughness. Increasing gradient, distance and load bearing weight will all increase such extreme physical activity performance needs, and requires continuous physical fitness respiration over combative individual or low repetition skills execution specific cycled respiration.

Combative respiration can be employed in the execution of repetitious physical fitness exercising by employing the combative cycled respiration process per repetition. It can also be employed when training with weights especially in high repetition practice by the employment of combative cycled respiration per weightlifting repetition.

When it comes to long distance endurance type activities, the requirement is one's highest possible levels of physical fitness. One means of continuous practice of CQC respiration to become proficient and provide exposure to using CQC respiration under endurance requirements is to simply use it when on a treadmill as your form of respiration. You can switch on your CQC respiration for bursts and then switch it off, reverting to normal respiration and repeat the process many times over, changing the duration of the CQC respiration and intensity of the treadmill running or walking by increasing the speed or incline. While you will not be able to time the CQC respiration cycle with individual running strides you will be able to see the control you have over respiration.

The same means of practicing CQC respiration on a treadmill can be employed on staircases timing the exhaling component with the step up.

Recovery breathing post physical exertion, when the heart is racing and you are breathing heavily, requires the slowing of respiration and as such the reduction of the heart rate. This can be achieved by utilising combative breathing, slowing and reducing the intensity of respiration with every respiration recycle. For recovery, when extremely affected by heavy breathing and a racing heartbeat, inhaling and exhaling simultaneously via the nose and the mouth can reduce the effects of such physical fatigue more rapidly. This is achieved best by reducing the intensity with every inhale-exhale respiratory cycle.

Combining this with maintaining an open, upright posture, head-up, shoulders spread, chest out in order to allow a non-restricted non-compressed respiratory path and cycle will shorten the duration required to drop your heart rate and reduce heavy respiration. Then when your breathing and heart rate reduce you can employ a relaxed neutral status version of your CQC cycled respiration to recover and return to a normal resting status.

Decentralisation contact and impact respiration

Decentralisation, whether it be when you are knocked down in CQC, accidentally fall or you deliberately self-decentralise (as in escape and evasion, making it to cover or concealment) is an important capability, and ensuring you are not injured in the process to the point that you are unable to recover and achieve your objective is crucial.

Often referred to as gaining your second wind in regards to being decentralised in a combative situation, the reality is you are not introducing or requiring any new means of recovery in relation to CQC respiration.

You are utilising the same CQC respiration exhaling in relation to any physical combative skill being executed. The same cycled respiration is employed with your counter-offensive assault options (evasive or stationary) including exhaling under hard cover guarding, or cover and deflection under enemy assault, or in this case in relation to ground impact.

Understanding proper, safe combative falling for emergency decentralisation, combined with immediate ground or recovery counter engagement action movement and power and velocity generation through the employment of CQC respiration will ensure expedient, economic recovery and employment of threat neutralisation options. In any actions-on assault where you find yourself dropped to the ground with no chance of maintaining your footing or employing combative rolling to reduce ground impact, CQC respiration will increase safety and reduce the delay between falling and counter engagement. Seconds count when you are decked and static on the ground under assault. So having a cohesive option that enables recovery and counter engagement in one complete deliberate continued action reduces risk, increases safety and is tactically CQC correct.

Through your training and practice combining your combative respiration with your combative falling you will reduce the risk of physical bodily injury especially to your major life-support bodily vitals. You will also be able to exhale on impact with the ground and so reduce the likelihood of being winded and incapacitated.

CQC falling is a modified version of the para fall/roll and the major difference is that the height of the fall is comparatively low with CQC falling, changing the need for hard locked compressed legs.

Exhaling on falling and ground contact, ending in your combative side fall position will allow for immediate recovery ground protection or moving off the ground confrontation line, while remaining centered to any upright threat with your boots or barrel rolling away combined with recovery or a ground counter-offensive and recovery.

Remember every action on the ground such as adjusting to orientate to your upright enemy, the execution of ground counter stamp kicks, barrel rolling away or footing recovery is initiated and powered by CQC respiration.

A friend of mine fought bare knuckle on the street and in pubs all his life. Many years ago he told me of what he called his second wind; he described it as breathing out when dropped in street fights and then breathing in and out again as part of immediate recovery and getting right back into the blue with vengeance. In other words, a man that fought often and where there were no rules on the street knew the value of fight-specific respiration.

The reality is that it is continuous, controlled combative respiration in relation to offensive actions, counter-offensive actions, cover guarding, deflection and reducing the effects of impact that ensures the combatant maintains priority physical capabilities and is mentally prepared for the realities of CQC.

The level of shock and surprise, and of course impact, is considerably lessened when you are ready, willing and able and employing the very best of battle-proven tactics and skills to make yourself a hard target, and importantly the best combatant you possibly can be giving you the highest chance of achieving your objective.

No matter how minor or insignificant any physical actions or responses may be considered in CQC, they must be employed with controlled, combative respiration to ensure not only the best possible performance and objective achievement levels are provided and maintained, but also to minimise the effect of contact and impact.

Combative respiration aids many skills: controlled calculated stalking into range inch by inch, centimeter by centimeter, cover guarding and deflection, employing unarmed offensive assault, unarmed counter-offensive assault, during seizure prevention as well as in secured seizure escapes and weapon disarming employments.

Low intensity controlled cycled respiration—inhaling via the nose and exhaling on the execution of any physical action via the mouth—will make you physically more capable and committed, as well as mentally stronger by maintaining high levels of awareness recognition, and the ability to fast map on the move dealing with changes in threat and situation in real time.

Tactical Combative Visual Sighting

One of the most important skills I have developed for CQC against both unarmed and armed threats is specific threat and role related tactical visual sighting.

I have combative sighting for unarmed counter-offensive assault and unarmed offensive assault employments, armed combative offensive and counter-offensive employments, close personal protection and covert environment scanning to identify changes in threat or situation including identification of additional dangers.

In unarmed offensive assault decided employments, prior to initiating your offensive engagement, remain focused on your enemy's eyes to provide the earliest possible warning of any enemy engagement and utilize your 140 degrees of peripheral vision to identify additional threats or terrain obstacles or dangers. The Todd Systems terminology for this enemy and environment tactical visual focus is 'Point and Place' sighting.

Then like any good tradesman, focus on the target and skill in question at that immediate point in time to ensure maximum accuracy. Never operate on auto-pilot with accuracy-required, deliberate action skills employments.

Counter-offensively, when in the ready position to employ evasive or stationary unarmed counter engagement decided deliberate options, prior to any actions-on, it is a priority to remain focused on the enemy's eyes as well as on maintaining your 140 degrees of peripheral vision. Looking your enemy in the eyes promotes and projects self-confidence and provides the earliest possible warning of entry and engagement. Identifying head movement will certainly give you the earliest warning of enemy movement.

However, maintaining focus on your enemy's head and possibly being fixed on facial expression or the war cry will see you becoming unnecessarily concerned with target detail and locked on the upper quadrants only.

I developed, tested and adopted my combative sighting system over 25 years ago and it has produced the best possible results in high stress situations. Immediately after your enemy is committed to engaging you, you should combine the CQC squat preparatory ready set for expedient action status with nodding your head slightly downward to focus on your enemy's midsection belt line. This provides vision of the upper and lower, right and left quadrants of their body and will enable better identification of the direction and angle of the incoming attack. This increases your capabilities of employing primary orthodox evasion and counter engagement.

In an armed threat disarming situation between long and close range, your attention will be focused on the weapon point, and the place being your immediate surroundings using your peripheral vision. The weapon is the most immediate and greatest danger and will get your primary point vision. Focusing on the weapon point gives you immediate information on the enemy making ready or employment of the weapon, and gives you the earliest warning, and thus an opportunity to employ disarming tactics or escape and evasion. Always look at the most forward tip or point of the weapon; that is the closest and most immediate danger.

In close personal protection, your visual will be on the principal or 'point' (as I refer to the principal) and your 140 degrees plus of peripheral vision will be focused on the surroundings or 'place' (as I refer to the immediate environment) in CPP; point and place visual sighting.

These practices provide sound physical skills to maintain a state of readiness, employing factual assessment, and the earliest possible recognition decision-making combined with the best of battle-proven options employment to neutralise the threat. They reduce psychological stress and the dangers of entry into self-doubt, anticipating attack specifics and perceiving lines and types of attack over basing your plan on clear factual assessment. Always believe your enemy or assailant is formidable, cunning and deceptive in their assault employments. Never guess, always assess and let the threat be your decider. Having tactically correct proven tactics keeps your mind positively occupied with tasks that must be undertaken and as such removes time for negative thoughts, anticipating, perceiving or guessing.

Once you have employed any combative action and your senses are on and at the most alert state of recognition, the Todd Systems promote fast mapping—a term and practice I developed—so combatants on the move and under skills execution status continue to assess and decide on contingency options to address changes in situation and threat.

By employing previously trained and practiced options in relation to enemy position, range and threat specifics, as well as situational changes, the trained combatant can reduce hesitation and maintain momentum, reducing enemy recovery and counter offence, In the event of situational and threat changes, by fast mapping they can employ primary practices to neutralise the threat on the move in real time.

Hand-eye-foot coordination is something I enforce in my training to ensure combatants have an affinity with the ground via the balls of their feet (through the soles of their boots) combined with tactical combative sighting to identify enemy actions or additional threats, and the utilization of their arms and hands to provide hard cover guarding and deflection capabilities in the employment of CQC armed or unarmed options.

Your hand-eye-foot coordination combined with your heightened senses provide real time capabilities to detect immediate threats. Your senses of hearing, smell and touch are valuable assets in identifying additional threats or changes in threat. Then your actions-on required physical capabilities of hand-eye-foot coordination take over as part of the physical threat neutralization capabilities. Your eyes will identify threat and provide CQC visual capabilities, your feet will enable CQC movement executions and your hands and arms will enable offensive and defensive capabilities.

Employing all actions and counter actions off of a small to half squat set up will increase safety by making you a moving, not static target interfering with your enemy's line and point of sight and breaking their mental focus.

This causes reduction in their speed of execution and also makes them second guess if their decided option is still right and the best means to causing you their target bodily harm.

You have interfered with their initial decision making and the execution of that decided option weakening their confidence to achieve their objective and their resolve.

Your actions by means of the small to half squat set up initiation at real time under assault can cause enemy confusion panic and their immediate thought to wander into perception and self-doubt.

You may think as a result of your objective achievement under such circumstances that you were simply faster than your enemy but the truth is that you made them slow their actions down by your small or half squat causing confusion visually and by breaking their mental focus.

The final physical and psychological involved practice in making yourself-ready willing and set in a state of readiness is the employment of positive thought by means of self-reassurance. In your mind's eye, by continuously psychologically conducting situational, personal and kit checks and re-checks ensures your time is occupied with positive proactive practices. To avoid any chance of self-doubt say to yourself in your mind's eye that you are 'ready, willing able', or 'willing, able ready'; repeat to reconfirm and strengthen your resolve and believe in yourself and your capabilities.

You may be alone and as such can only rely on one person—yourself—and so to self-reassure and self-confirm prior to any actions-on or in any lull is a positive practice.

As part of a team under pre-actions-on or lulls, to self-reassure and self-confirm in your mind's eye through silent self-reassurance repeat: WAR—willing, able, ready to remind you that you are prepared, capable and committed to going combative for yourself and your team's sake. Ready, willing, able; willing, able, ready.

Remember you must not over-psyche yourself up as you may become so anxious, agitated or excited that you lose focus of the threat, and your respiration and heart rate can increase with anticipation to the point where you get tunnel vision, audio exclusion, a racing heart and heavy respiration that will affect your decision making skills execution and recollection capabilities.

The opposite of over anxious, agitated and over excited through allowing the threat and situation to overwhelm you, is to stall and freeze. Being unable to control the effects of fear, danger and stress will dramatically reduce your senses or shut them down completely, your heart racing, your respiration out of control, your capabilities to defend yourself lost and all you can think of is of your helplessness and the hopelessness of the faced threat situation. The unfortunate reality is that you feel you have no other option but to accept you will lose, be injured, wounded or killed. Your self-preservation capabilities will be ineffective or non-existent and you will practically shut down through fear to the point of freezing in place and being a static target.

I have covered the basic realities of fear and stress situations and provided information on physical practices and procedures, combined with psychological practices and procedures to reduce risk, make you a hard target and maintain a status of combative readiness. These principles and practices are employed in this package as part of mental toughening practical exercises. You must drill them until they are deliberate, decided primary options in self-defence and CQC any and every time you defend yourself or go combative. Practice them until you simply cannot get them wrong.

.

Combative sighting between hard cover guard

Tactical sighting front stance and guard

Neutral stance looking enemy in eyes

Small squat pre evasion setup combined with CQC respiration

Combined small squat vision transfer to enemy midsection belt line

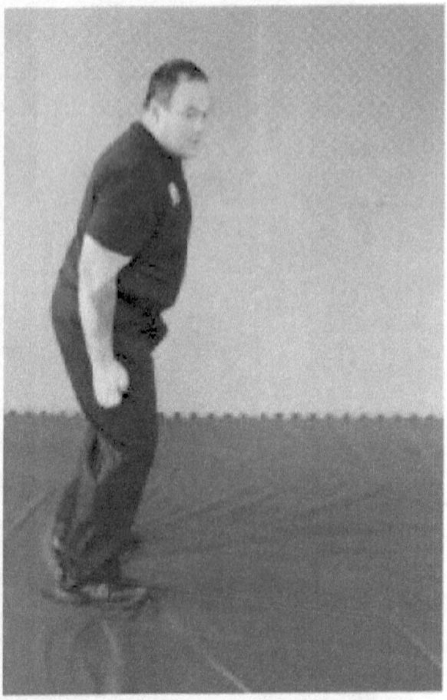

Diagonal forward side step evasion employment

Post side step evasion cover guarding

Twig-in-the-eye blinking

The twig that flicks you in the eye in the bush does so without intent and as a result of you either not expecting it or because its incoming travel is not detectable (possibly because it comes on a travel path line or angle from outside or under your peripheral vision). Your eyelid is your last means of protection.

Exploiting lines of attack outside your enemy's peripheral vision provides definite threat neutralization advantages and such lines and openings should be exploited. In a self-defence or combative situation in low to no light, or when your vision is obstructed or impaired through injury you need to be able to employ your additional senses to make yourself safe, recover and counter engage your enemy.

Blinking under assault is common and can be reduced by employing CQC respiration combined with initially facing and dealing with slow attacks in training:

- By having a deliberate and definite means of dealing with the threat while remaining focused on it can reduce involuntary blinking.
- Inoculation, by providing a reduced control measure of the stimuli that causes the blinking and providing a positive means of focusing on and dealing with the threat.
- Increased speed and deception only with proficiency and confidence increases to ensure the problem is resolved not made worse.
- As previously detailed the inclusion of a ball in cover guarding and deflection is beneficial

Although your sense of vision is the primary sense in most combative skills employments, all senses are important and have important roles to play in close combat.

Immediately when you identify or recognise a possible or probable threat visually by turning your sense of sight on, your additional senses are also switched on to varying degrees in relation to the situational specifics and the individual senses requirements. You have between 140 and 180 degrees of peripheral vision, and when your vision is switched on combatively, your sense of hearing is enhanced. Increases in your touch and feel senses, including your affinity with the ground, also all kick in to increase stability and a ready status to go combative. Obviously with heightened senses your sense of smell would be increased more than if you were unaware of any imminent threat.

Individual senses can also be enhanced to detect threats or threat levels.

Subtle but obvious identification of an individual's increased utilisation of the sense of hearing to eavesdrop can sometimes be detected by observing their head being turned so the ear is in line with subject they want to eavesdrop on. This is also used for detecting or locating the whereabouts of the enemy or unidentifiable threatening sounds.

The flinch reaction in relation to unexpected sudden aggressive shock action as well as the execution of resistance and continued CQC squatting to prevent being moved, lifted or decentralised requires utilisation of the sense of touch and feel via the boots in relation to ground contact.

In low to no light combative encounters, the sense of touch to locate and target enemy bodily vitals is essential. For example, use your hand to follow the sternum and locate the sternal notch and thyroid cartilage.

In low to no light, or when vision is obscured in a combative clinch by battledress and/or belt order or body armor, targeting enemy bodily vitals or changing seizure and securing positioning as part of the execution of combative actions requires utilisation of your sense of touch. Your sense of touch also applies to increasing balance and stability when there is a lack of visibility or your balance is compromised by seizing and securing objects that assist in maintaining or regaining balance and stability. You may well have to use your sense of touch and feel to find your way or regain your footing.

When combative vision is impaired or lost through injury or darkness, an untrained combatant's ability to go combative or escape and evade is lost and they can slip into despair and desperation. The trained combatant however, through training in such situations with realism and the utilisation of their other senses and situational required tactics and skills can take control of the situation and exploit any avenues and advantages available.

The loss of vision through impact effects can be reduced, and recovery time enhanced by proficiency in hard cover guarding and using one's sense of touch at close to point-blank body contact range by means of enemy seizure and securing as part of visual recovery. From point-blank body contact range, by means of utilising your sense of touch, enemy seizure, securing and bodily targets can also be located, setting up both striking and stamp kicking skills to neutralise the threat.

Being able to blind seize, secure, contain, control and set up and employ combative skills to neutralise a formidable enemy threat is psychologically empowering. I train my combatants in blind folded or hooded training exercises in wide ranging CQB/CQC skills including stand-up and ground combat, enemy seizure, containment, and unarmed and armed threat neutralisation. There are important principles of going blind such as never releasing a grip with one hand until the other hand has a secure grip for continued controlled containment and threat neutralisation.

Turning on your primary sense in a high stress high risk situation, and having additional senses automatically turned on (providing increased means of recognition of threat and changes in threat and situation) is essential to increased risk reduction and combative capabilities in relation to wide and varied threat neutralisation under adversity. When your primary sense is not available to you then using an enhanced additional sense relevant to the threat or situation provides the means to confidently continue with your threat neutralisation objective achievement. This ensures you maintain a psychologically strong attitude through having secondary alternative and emergency capabilities.

The Blur

Understanding the blur effect of vision in relation to unarmed offensive assault targeting and unarmed counter offensive assault evasive and stationary counter engagement is essential to increase your chances of combative threat neutralisation and to reduce increased risk through effective accuracy.

Under an unarmed offensive assault when 75percent plus committed to both entry and your combative skill employment, accurate and detailed vision can be difficult to maintain.

Being millimeters off in set up and in execution initiation can cause missed targeting by centimeters.

There are many factors that can contribute to combative blurred visuals including reduced eyesight capabilities as a result of age and health reasons or eye injuries.

Simply by the combatant knowing that their blurred vision increases risk by reducing target contact accuracy can weaken the combatant's confidence in their capabilities to achieve the objective. Through training or prior experience they may consider they do not have the required visual capabilities under committed entry against a possible moving target to achieve target contact at speed with power and velocity. To increase visual accuracy the combatant may well reduce speed and commitment and this only reduces target contact against a formidable foe and increases risk.

Prior awareness of impaired vision can certainly develop a disposition in relation to a lack of confidence and even lead to a combatant executing combative skills at greatly reduced speed and commitment levels in an effort to improve visual targeting.

This practice of matching speed and intensity of combative skills execution with reduced eyesight capabilities will only provide increased opportunity for the enemy to counter engage the combatant's reduced capabilities in unarmed offensive assault employments.

It is very important that the individual combatant understands weaknesses such as in their eyesight required for combative skills employments and seeks medical treatment or utilises methods to enhance combative capabilities by skills selection and methods of execution.

The Todd systems provides two primary methods of increasing enemy targeting contact capabilities at 75percent plus entry and skills employments levels.

The first is stamp kicking or striking right through the enemy target to a point or line approximately half a meter to the rear flank of the enemy target by visual specific target confirmation at the final fraction of a second prior to striking or stamp kicking execution.

Under training conditions have the enemy training partner stand on a shoulder width line with a vertical center line extending rearwards so it ends half a meter behind them meeting with a horizontal line over a meter across that can clearly be seen outside the enemy's body line on both sides.

Having the combatant aim right through the target and towards the rear most cross line will increase the likelihood of not only contact being achieved but also body line point blank range contact being made reducing the enemy partner's counter engagement capabilities at point-blank range under the added safety of a hard cover guarding status. The enemy per will be distracted and occupied with maintaining stability and resisting the body line and cover guard impact force as a first priority.

Stamp kicks would be directed diagonally downward with contact being made on or below the knee joint and continuing diagonally downward towards the rear horizontal line.

This would increase entry and execution commitment and as such increase the chance of target contact. However if contact was not made the chances are it was because the enemy training partner would most likely have been forced to clear the confrontation line possibly on the back foot losing ground and being forced into a defensive status.

Striking skills especially hand edge striking skills that also provide increased contact capabilities by means of the combined forearm to elbow length should be aimed right across and through the target to the horizontal line to the enemy partner's rear and should be employed in multiple entry strikes setting up the master hand or master boot finishing skill.

Short to medium length committed steps and hard cover guard capabilities with a single entry strike executed at the end of every entry step, using your torso cocking and forward body line commitment, will not only enhance your striking output but will also interfere with your enemy training partner's balance maintenance by forcing them backwards.

Using a line of vision completely through the target past the enemy point of vision increases targeting capabilities considerably and as such enhances psychological combative confidence.

The length of the combat boot and the combined hand edge and forearm as part of combative gross motor skills employments compensate for visual impairments and enhance confidence.

The second method the Todd Group employs to compensate for impaired or reduced vision capabilities under combative entry employment executions is the utilisation of two-part assaults.

Two-part assaults begin with a highly committed entry foot work component including hard cover guarding. This first component also includes high commitment body line contact impact with the enemy target.

This body line contact impact with the side of your hip and buttock as well as your hardcover guard promotes enemy distraction by contact interference that requires focus on self-preservation in relation to balance and stability maintenance as well as defence against the contact impact.

Being a gross motor skill entry capability under the increased safety of hardcover guarding requires considerably less eyesight visual targeting capabilities.

The entry impact contact not only creates the need for enemy self-preservation defensive capabilities but it also causes them to increase resistance to reduce loss of stability or possible forced decentralization.

While your enemy is contending with these negative concerns you can execute your second component: stamp kick or striking skills from point blank body contact range statically with maximum force and velocity.

Employing such skills from a stationary position making your enemy wear your weight. Masking your intentions by your body line increases objective achievement. In the case of employing stamp kicks your target, the lower leg from the knee joint down, will be concealed by your body and from the safety of your hard cover guard position you can enhance objective achievement and as such threat neutralization.

Being able to safely and effectively enter under hard cover guard causing the desired reactions from your enemy and putting you in a position to make any minor adjustments and employ your two-part unarmed offensive assault action from stationary will compensate for eyesight deficiencies.

Your hard cover guard should include keeping your chin locked inside your shoulder joint, protecting your jaw.

Your side cover guarding lead arm with the palm protecting from number one cervical vertebrae down as far as it will reach will provide maximum safety for the vulnerable nape of the neck as well as primary cover guard and deflection capabilities by means of your inner forearm elbow joint and upper arm.

A crouched hard cover guard status with your chin tucked inside your shoulder under a two-part unarmed offensive assault option employment with the nape of your neck protected will reduces risk considerably and in turn increase confidence with your entry commitment.

Your head being slightly tipped forward combined with the egg shape of the apex of your forehead will aid in contact by deflection in the event that hardcover deflection capabilities were not utilised in time.

While you may not consider contact with the apex of your head to be favorable, it very much is acceptable under risk reduction when no other immediate option is practical or available.

While a forehead cut may be the outcome there is also increased likelihood of your enemy injuring their hands on this most tough and resilient of human bones.

Understanding of risk reduction by the employment of secondary alternative or emergency options to neutralise a formidable or rapid changing threat at real time in an actions-on encounter ensures the highest level of mental toughness can be maintained. Execution of two-part close range unarmed offensive assault striking skills under deceptive hardcover guarding, including aggressive raising of the hard cover guard from outside or under the enemy's peripheral vision combined with body line contact impact can be an effective offensive action on its own. This is so even prior to the second part striking skills from point blank body contact being employed to neutralise the threat.

Having a high level of competency in such skills increases objective achievement capabilities under reduced or impaired visual capabilities, and as such will ensure psychological confidence is maintained.

Under unarmed counter offensive assault evasive maneuvers by means of employing evasive combative sighting you will reduce your need for high-level visual accuracy.

Combining your small to half squat ready set go status with a nodding of your head transferring your vision from the enemy's head to the midline section will provide centralized visual capabilities of the four quadrants of the enemy's full body mass and will provide increased opportunity to identify the striking or kicking extremity.

In military combative evasive disarming of an edged or bludgeon type weapon under incoming assault it is critical that the combatant does not initiate the small squat set up and evasive footwork execution until the weapon is on its final incoming travel at you its intended target and beyond the point of immediate directional change. Under blurred edged weapon or bludgeon type weapon incoming assault the evasion should be timed and executed before the immediate forward point of the blur reaches the kill zone.

Fast mind mapping including mind commands in relation to holding a ready status by giving yourself silent mind orders or instructions. For example hold, hold, hold or miss, miss, miss in relation to multiple swings or slashes and then go, go, go to command or order the initiation of the evasive action. This is extremely proactive by focusing sensory capabilities, and mind and physical body readiness and setting expedient action capabilities in unison.

The Todd Systems refer to it as mind orders and mind instructions undertaken by hand-eye-foot coordination. Eyes determining your timing and direction of evading the physical weapon or the weapon blur, your boots pushing off and clearing the contact zone in a timed primary evasive clearance movement, your arms and hands capabilities employed for disarming or self-protection.

Having enhancement capabilities in relation to reducing the effects of physical disabilities such as eyesight and mobility weaknesses or for the requirements of emergency contingency options employments ensures the combatant can maintain mental focus and psychological control without losing momentum and as such ensures the combatant is able to remain committed to threat neutralization.

The eyes in life and death

Our eyes are our greatest sensory capabilities in close quarters combat. They enable us to take in primary information and deliver accurate combative threat neutralisation capabilities.

Our eyes can pick up high speed incoming threats, the most covert deceptive actions, and transmit pieces of information to our central nervous system for evaluation and threat neutralisation decision-making before the incoming threat makes contact.

Our eyes can be utilised for multiple tasks including focusing on the primary threat while maintaining peripheral vision to identify any additional threats or situation changes including additional introduced threats and dangers.

The capability and efficiency in executing accurate combative unarmed offensive assault actions as well as counter offensive vision in stationary or evasive unarmed counter offensive assault options employment is truly incredible.

While our eyesight is our primary sense in close quarters combat and often our first utilised sense both in threat detection and identification as well as in combative actions employments, it is also a final indication of the end of life.

I never stop learning and several years ago on a course at Camp Todd I went for a hunt with 'Big Jim' a very experienced combatant and outdoorsman.

Jim took a rifle he had never fired before and under the spotlight shot a wild pig with accuracy. When we reached the animal I prepared to stick it when Jim told me it was already dead. I asked how he knew that and he told me its last ability to show existence of life was its ability to blink its eyes. He had simply touched its eyeball and there was no blinking of the eye lid proving it was dead. This was something I had not heard of before and it interested me.

The eyes in close quarters combat truly provide reaction capabilities that can be the difference between life and death winning and losing. In close quarters combat targeting the delicate eyes to impair vision and incapacitate your foe leaving them vulnerable to further assault is a primary combative practice. In kill or die military battle field encounters penetrating the frontal lobes of the brain via the eyeballs and thin delicate orbits of the eye socket bone is a brutally fatal reality.

In close quarters combat eyesight is a primary sense and first means of detecting and transmitting threat related information to our brain. It is also the last means of proving life or death as with the wild pig.

Thinking about this means of checking life or death status reminded me of a skill I learnt many years ago for defensive tactics training when checking if a suspect was conscious or playing possum. You simply lifted their hand dropped it towards their eyes to see if they would blink, redirect the dropped hand or move their head from harm's way.

Our eyes are truly a primary means of ensuring combative capabilities as well as detecting life or death and must be at all times given maximum protection by sound hard cover guarding and deflection capabilities to ensure our vision is not compromised in combative encounters so post encounters we do not suffer the effects of eye injuries and blindness.

Excessive blinking of the eyes under threat

Excessive blinking under threat is very much a nervous reaction and is a result of a combination of conscious and unconscious thought and memory.

Prior negative recollections can flow back and overload an individual that is not fully mentally and physically focused and prepared.

Our conscious sensory capabilities if not trained and focused can be overwhelmed by the negatives of prior experiences. Once a threatening situation, or even the thought of prior exposure to or an actual prior threat encounter, is allowed to be connected with an immediate faced threatening situation negative responses such as excessive blinking can result.

While we learn from prior exposure and previous experiences both positive and negative for training purposes, this must be done in a non-immediate threatening environment under controlled training.

If the training is undertaken post facing a real life actions on deadly encounter then the first step of overcoming the previous experience by the act of seeking to undertake such training is a positive. The fact that the individual was not killed and is wanting to achieve knowledge and capabilities on how to neutralise extreme violence threats is proactive and positive.

The training must be low intensity slow speed tactically correct and based on the best of battle proven skills with threat intensity increases gradually in relation to increased competency and proficiency. Slow is fast and less is more always when neutralising extremely high risk dangerous threats under training conditions. One of the most important things I learnt from my expert military Pioneer instructors was how to problem solve by tactically correct assessment and decision-making confirming not only the best means of threat neutralisation but how to make any changes and adjustments to tactics and skills that increase safety and the chance of threat neutralization.

Principle based skills and tactics are a must for neutralising unpredictable extreme violence where unconventional specific threat and situational means are required.

Allowing past negative thoughts and present non-factual and non-primary essential considerations to interfere with fast mapping factual assessment and best means decision making under threat is a complete negative and can increase adverse reactions such as excessive blinking.

Do not overload or overwhelm yourself with non-immediate required methods of increasing safety and threat neutralization.

Just as with increased heart rate, trembling thighs, chattering teeth and a feeling of sickness to the stomach when faced with a formidable threat of violence, excessive blinking of the eyes is just another means of your brains and autonomic nervous system warning you that you are in a potentially dangerous environment and threat and situation.

Our mind is a primary tool in threat neutralisation decision making that would not be utilising all or its best capabilities if it did not draw from its memory bank of prior experiences as well as factual assessment of the immediate faced threat.

The combatant's requirement is to ensure that when the brain, by means of electrical signals and chemical releases and reactions, initiates warnings in the form of physical reactions such as excessive blinking of the eyes you can reduce or eliminate such adverse effects by employing the brain-to-boot primary practices.

By doing so the combatant accepts the realities of the threat situation and sets in place a course of positive assessment decision making and threat neutralisation actions shutting out unnecessary over-thinking or consideration of previous negative experiences.

I have trained a small number of CQC exponents that when in a threatening situation develop compulsive increased blinking. These individuals under normal circumstances do not blink excessively and are not suffering from any illness or medical condition that ordinarily causes them to blink excessively. They had no diagnosed compulsive disorders and were not suffering from post-traumatic stress disorder. There were no obvious reasons such as chemical irritation of the eyes or dust and dirt present causing their blinking. The blinking was nothing like normal natural blinking related to automatic eye cleansing or lubricating.

I have identified that a small percentage of individuals in the face of danger and as a result of fear and stress will suffer from increased and excessive blinking.

Often in threatening situations when faced with a formidable foe an individual that is not ready willing and able by being totally focused and completely prepared will allow their mind to wander into focusing on negatives in relation to perceived threat levels and outcomes. For some people the effects of such negative thoughts include involuntary repetitious blinking. One of the reasons why prior to any actions on encounter I insist on exponents looking their unarmed enemy in the eyes or looking at the point or muzzle of the weapon in armed threat situations is to consolidate their inner resolve and state of readiness by being able to face and focus on the threat. If a combatant cannot both look at the actual threat and be able to employ positive thought in relation to what needs to be done to neutralise the threat then they can be psychologically weakened and such a weakening of resolve can increase involuntary reactions such as compulsive excessive blinking. Those that are not prepared to face and focus on the threat and through positive tactical assessment information processing and the best decision making in relation to threat neutralisation are prone to adverse effects of fear and stress such as excessive blinking.

If you face an enemy that is continuously excessively blinking then you know they are fearful and adversely affected by the stress of the faced situation you present.

It is important that the combatant is completely alert and aware and prepared for any and every threat but is not focused on prior negative experience and outcomes to the point of weakening the combatant's resolve and becoming locked into obsessive negative prior considerations that can reduce their required immediate combative capabilities. As part of psychological enhancement and conditioning I encourage my combatants to understand that we learn from our prior successes and failures but we must not dwell on them and certainly must not recall them and become locked into historic focus under immediate threat.

I instill in them that every immediate threatening situation is a new situation that can be neutralised by the best of battle-proven combative skills when combined with the brain-to-boot mental toughness and enhancement package.

When you allow obsessive thought to interfere with sensory assessment and immediate required decision making then adverse effects such as compulsive repetitive blinking are a reality.

Throughout the brain-to-boot package you are constantly reminded of the importance of the initial deliberate action of combative respiration to set a status of readiness and willingness to achieve and enhance psychological and physical combative performance. This must be your first and most important deliberate response or undertaking as soon as the threat has been recognized.

The reason why this is as important as a first deliberate undertaking is to prevent adverse effects related to fear and stress or to at least reduce them to the lowest level possible.

Autonomic nervous system reactions such as increased heart rate and increased respiration tremors and sickness to the stomach as well as excessive compulsive blinking are warning signs of the possible danger faced and can be stopped before they even start by the initiation of combative respiration immediately on threat recognition.

These subconsciously initiated warning signs only become adverse reactions when they are allowed to continue and increase.

Such reactionary effects must be reduced or eliminated as soon as they are experienced. The brain-to-boot package provides you with a simple proven means of psychological enhancement including the means to reduce or eliminate reactions to facing fear and as a result of stress. You must, however, drill and practice under realistic training conditions including expected and unexpected sudden aggressive shock action battle handling exercises until the making ready and delivery process is employed in every situation faced with competency and confidence and in the correct order of execution.

Some individuals show increased blinking when fatigued or tired just like they do when they are stressed or fearful.

To reduce uncontrolled blinking when you are tired you need to sleep and rest. To reduce uncontrolled blinking when facing a dangerous threat you need to go tactical and employ your brain-to-boot principles in the correct order of execution.

I have determined that blinking is increased when you lose visual and mental focus. For example when facing a formidable foe and looking them in the eyes meeting them on even ground combined with your brain-to-boot physical and psychological practices, blinking is minimised. However if distracted or breaking from tactically correct mental toughness practices, blinking rates can be increased.

Take your eyes off your foe and in the blink of an eye, as the saying goes, a savvy foe will attack.

I've also determined that the threat level can determine increases in blinking. Under low-level threat increased blinking is less likely even in affected individuals however under medium to high threat situations increased blinking was identified.

Human beings have become far more competitively orientated and verbal in relation to dealing with conflict over being more tactical or combative. I have determined this is one of the reasons why today individuals will try and reason and negotiate their way out of a threatening situation over employing methods of anti-counter or combat measures.

Verbiage, however, slows reaction time and for an individual prone to stress and fear adverse reactions can increase risk, danger and the extent of the reactions.

Over the years I have identified similarities between study and combative training in relation to blinking repetitions. Students that are not that interested in the subject tend to blink more however students that are extremely interested in the subject and are striving to achieve the highest understanding and examination results in the subject tend to blink less.

The connection with self defence and close quarters combat training is not only the interest, focus and commitment of the exponent but also that they are occupied with utilising the physical and mental practices correctly.

This mental and physical focus can produce reduced blinking over exponents that are not employing primary practices or are doing so with reduced attention to detail and limited focus and commitment. I have identified that there is a variance average range of between 1 and 10 blinks of the eyes per minute in combative exponents. The higher skilled the proponent and the mentally tougher, combined with utilising the brain-to-boot physical and psychological practices in the correct order of execution, has achieved considerably lower rates of blinking per minute. Usually less than five per minute and in a highly competent confident and focused proponent, blinking can be prevented for the duration of the situation.

Individuals lacking in commitment and that tend to not employ physical and psychological enhancement practices correctly or at all and that are affected by fear and stress by increased blinking have been recorded at rates of 15 to 20 repetitions of blinking per minute.

There are also differences in blinking in relation to the duration and speed of blinking. This is greatly determined by the individual's inner resolve and capabilities to control stress and fear as well as their capabilities to neutralise the threat.

The other important factor is the danger and risk level of the faced threat and the time and distance realities before the actions-on encounter materializes.

A threatening situation pre-actions on can weaken an individual's inner resolve if they are not resolute in their practices to overcome the effects of stress and fear. Employing the brain-to-boot practices starting with combative respiration on threat identification and employing hard targeting tactics such as controlling range, angle and alignment and utilising barriers, safe backdrops and escape routes is proactive and confidence enhancing.

In an unexpected actions on encounter there is little or no time for compulsive continuous reactions as all attention must be on immediate required self-protection and threat neutralization thought and employment under assault.

Normal levels of blinking are considerably higher for adults than for infants and this may well be a result of having a greater exposure and understanding of threats, dangers and related stress and fear.

Combatants understand how sensitive and delicate their eyes are and how they are the most important sensory capability in close quarters combat and close quarters battle.

Sudden movements especially directed at the face at close to point blank range increase the likelihood of involuntary blinking out of protection of this most delicate sensory capability. Even the most skilled and determined combatant under threat of eye contact as part of the protection of their eyes as a last line of protection will blink involuntarily.

This is normal automatic self-preservation and self-protection. However, compulsive continuous blinking under such threat increases risk and danger and is a definite determination of the individual falling victim to the effects of stress and fear.

Both rapid continuous blinking and an increased duration of the shut eyes component of blinking are highly risky under threat or assault.

Some individuals with minimal inner resolve against adversity will close their eyes and turn away or if decentralised assume a foetal position accepting a state of helplessness and hopelessness. A formidable foe will identify such weakness and exploit them to time their assault just like timing an attack when someone is distracted looking to their side or rear flanks.

Do not confuse normal physiological blinking in relation to automatic human lubrication or cleansing of the eyes with involuntary compulsive excessive blinking under threat stress and fear.

Never confuse subconscious blinking as a means of self-protection of the eyes under targeting or contact as well as blinking when surprised by sudden aggressive shock actions including loud or frightening sounds such as gunfire with compulsive blinking.

The brain-to-boot primary practices made up of major and minor components employed immediately the threat is identified and continuously employed until the threat is completely neutralised will reduce the likelihood of compulsive excessive blinking of the eyes. Combative mental focus combined with the required physical undertakings eliminate the time for allowing fear and stress to produce repetitious blinking.

Under training conditions by going combative you will achieve reduced levels of blinking.

The individuals that I have observed that are prone to blinking when stressed and fearful under training conditions also have a tendency when they execute skills with faults and errors to initiate increased repetition blinking.

I can remember spending time in the Middle East and the effects of fine particles of sand in relation to coughing and blinking of the eyes. Under such conditions blinking is an involuntary normal means of protection and maintenance of the eyes. Blinking under stress and fear is an obsessive sensory action initiated and increased by the faced threat and perceived possible risks and dangers.

I like to advise individuals that are prone to excessive blinking that the involuntary act of excessive blinking is not a life-threatening danger however the formidable foe bent on doing them grievous bodily harm can exploit their uncontrolled excessive blinking, reducing their combative capabilities and as such increasing the danger levels under threat. Understanding the negative effects of compulsive continuous blinking under threat is very much a reality check in relation to the need to learn how to prevent compulsive repetitive blinking.

Utilising a mirror for shadow check training by setting a state of uncompromised readiness in a neutral stance on initiating your combative respiration and all other brain to boot major and minor components while remaining focused on your mirror image is a great means of training and recognition of negative compulsive reactions such as blinking. Look in the mirror, and if you identify reactionary excessive blinking, then by ensuring you maintain constant combative respiration as well as focusing on your brain-to-boot state of readiness and conducting continuous checks and rechecks physically and psychologically combined with self-reassurance (silently in your mind's eye: willing able ready) you will find you can reduce or completely eliminate excessive blinking.

Again in the mirror, but this time under the reality of being compromised, practice all your brain to boot major and minor components starting with CQC respiration to reduce all adverse and negative effects of immediate real time fear and stress which are increased when setting and maintaining a combative stance and guard capability.

This is why practicing in a neutral uncompromised status first is recommended so the dose of the threat 'virus' can be controlled.

The combatant should always be looking at setting a grey status and neutral facial expression and focusing on this grey status facial expression will aid in reducing involuntary blinking.

Under inoculation training the counter means must be greater than the level of the threat stimuli or virus to ensure the exponent has the capability to neutralise the threat and maintain a mental state that provides superiority over the threat.

There are many professions where individuals have to keep a straight face or show little or no expression proving that this is a skill that can be learnt but requires practice.

I personally instruct combatants on how to attack the eyes with deception by means of eye targeting from under or outside the peripheral vision using direct lines to achieve not only eye contact but also target the throat or jaw. This form of deceptive straight line contact by outsmarting the eye's capability to detect the offensive action in time to be able to effectively react is confidence enhancing in relation to employing unarmed offensive assault.

Once an exponent has achieved increased levels of confidence and competency and any previous subconscious reactions to fear and stress have been eliminated or reduced the intensity and degree of threat can be increased to further boost and enhance psychological strength.

Under such assault the blinking eyelids are very much the eyes last means of protection. Being able to resist natural last line means of protection of the eyes under direct targeting can only be achieved by high level of awareness and readiness to employ pre-trained and muscle memory self-protection skills while remaining visually focused. Offensive assault skills executed at the eyes with maximum deception and the highest levels of speed and accuracy will, however, invoke a subconscious involuntary blinking reaction and this is important and cannot or should not be prevented.

Once an individual that previously was prone to excessive blinking under threat has, by means of the brain-to-boot tactics and skills, eliminated such reactive blinking the virus can be increased to the level of the previously described masked direct line targeting of the eyes from outside or under the peripheral vision.

Once again initiating this unexpected deceptive direct line the eyes in a slow but swift action and having the individual counter it in a controlled focused and deliberate manner will increase confidence and reduce excessive blinking.

With counter competency proficiency increased, the speed, intensity and closer range targeting of the eyes can be stepped up, being mindful to always ensure safety by accuracy.

I have spoken with some individuals prone to excessive blinking and identified another reason behind their excessive blinking it is over thinking especially in relation to prior incidents where they were not able to protect themselves under assault.

The mind is a powerful human computer capable of storing considerable information based on prior experiences both positive and negative.

The human brains especially our Homo sapiens brain provides high level capabilities in relation to problem solving including methods to neutralise threats of violence.

The dangerous realm of perception and anticipation in relation to threat as well as the negative realities of self-doubt increase effects of fear and stress considerably.

This is why when faced with a violent threat, over thinking or irrelevant thinking must be eliminated and only the brain-to-boot primary practices executed in the correct order of execution and in unison to set and maintain the highest levels of mental toughness combined with a state of constant readiness and complete willingness must be the definitive orders from your Homo sapiens brain. This must be combined with your primary CQC or self-defense skill decision making setting up and employment.

Controlled aggression not anger

Trained combatants must conduct themselves by means of a state of tactical readiness and in actions-on encounters they must operate under controlled aggression and never uncontrolled anger.

Individuals going combative or defending themselves by means of uncontrolled temper, rage and anger are simply not utilising their Homo sapiens neocortex brain to assess and evaluate and employ controlled means of threat neutralization.

The reptilian primitive brain is a reactionary brain that does not have a thought or problem solving capability and will out of self-preservation in a threatening situation endeavor to neutralise the situation by means of primitive reaction. The trained combatant must override primitive reactions and if that fails escape and evasion becomes the required option.

When an individual simply reacts or overreacts by losing their temper it is the combined reptilian and mammalian limbic brain that is usually responsible.

The reason behind this is that the mammalian brain draws on its memory bank of previous exposure to similar threatening situations. Being an emotive non-thinking brain influenced by the reptilian brain, it may well overreact to the threat simply out of self-preservation. This is especially true if there is no out option or escape and evasion option available.

The mammalian brain being a non-problem solving or thinking brain only has limited stored information from prior experiences to base its reactionary response on.

There is no place for out of control anger and rage when up against a formidable foe. While a bully may get away with this against an unwilling victim it certainly is negative and problematic when facing a formidable foe.

Apart from the lack of proper assessment, thought and decision-making and controlled aggressive skills employment, there is also the fact that rage reduces sensory capabilities, and uses excessive physical capabilities. Once the subject is psychologically demoralised by failure to achieve threat neutralisation, even if they realize the error of their ways, normally they are also physically spent and as such their combative capabilities may not be enough to neutralise the threat.

Uncontrolled anger has a tendency to cause a chain reaction of one error and mistake after the other, jeopardizing safety diminishing and depleting capabilities, both psychological and physical, and often ending in self-harm.

Simply by utilising the brain-to-boot tactics and skills beginning with combative respiration and neither under or overreacting but remaining in a state of controlled readiness remaining constantly alert and aware of threat and environment risk can be reduced to the lowest level humanly possible. Brain-to-Boot practices combined with primary proven CQC or self-defense skills employment at 75percent plus commitment can achieve the objective and provide the capability to continue at this primary level for extended periods of combative action time if required.

A highly trained formidable combatant up against an uncontrolled angry foe that is considerably bigger, stronger and more physically capable, by means of tactically correct engagement and counter engagement hard targeting and hard cover guarding capabilities can endure adversity, weathering the storm and when an opening is identified or the angry enemy has defeated himself out of rage they can neutralise their now vulnerable foe.

Uncontrolled anger identifies an individual that is not highly trained in the required psychological and physical tactics and skills needed to neutralise violent threats, or is simply uncontrolled in their actions.

Angry demeanour

Controlled aggression demeanour

CQC squat

Practicing offensive actions in slow motion, initiated with combative respiration and focusing on a slight squat to get set and also act as a means of deception (and as such cause confusion to your enemy) is a primary hard targeting practice. Slightly lowering your center of gravity to get set makes your upper quadrant vitals moving targets rather than static targets.

The set go components of the small to half squat are two-part cohesive actions. The first action is a direct vertical downward squat action to drop your center of gravity and reduce your target mass, making you a deceptive hard target. The second action is a diagonally backward and downward component to get you into a set-to expediently go combative status. Both components are performed simultaneously and cohesively.

From the slight crouched, cocked small squat set position you will power off by means of the rear ball of the sole of the boot, ground affinity with the toes of the rear boot being grounded immediately before pushing off for stability and the ball of the sole of the boot providing expedient action powering off from the ground upwards and outwards. In the execution of close range striking skills, straight line velocity will be generated in a natural outward, upward, downward or parallel progressive direct line to the target from the ball of the sole of the boot through the ankle, calf, knee, thigh, hip, torso, shoulder, arm, neck and head, and then retracting in the reverse order. This practice, with proficiency, will allow for the introduction of increased speed which will create increased velocity.

Roundhouse skills deliveries will involve the previous actions combined with pivoting to ensure proper target alignment and for master hand round house strikes from an orthodox stance pivoting to the lead leg closed stance side will require master foot footing stability adjustments to ensure maximum velocity.

The same small to half squat or in extreme resistance close quarters clinching the full squat, set up for stamp kicking skills applies, but with employment set up variations and the line of committed velocity transfers that provide the most economical efficient and powerful destructive transfer of velocity impact down through the target to the ground.

An alert enemy will identify and react to the most minuscule action, and the slight ready-set-go CQC squat cocking action will often draw a reaction, causing them to react prematurely thus attacking and missing. It will certainly break their visual point and line of focus on you, their enemy, and can bring on reductions in commitment, speed or even stalling, hesitation or a rushed reaction which will provide opportunity to exploit any failed responsive action.

When an aggressor has kicked off and is fully committed to the assault, even a subtle ready set small squat set up action will interfere with their mental focus, line and point of visual focus, and most likely cause them to reconsider if their decided option is still their best option under the circumstances. Your ready set CQC squat action increases your safety by lowering your center of gravity and moving your head in a downward direction a greater distance than the size of a large clenched fist. This stands a good chance of making a head punch miss you, the intended target, and leaving them exposed to an expedient, committed counter engagement.

Breaking your enemy's mental focus, reducing their conviction in their pre-decided assault option by tactical distraction, interfering with or breaking their point or line of visual sight is distractive and creates adverse reactions including slowing down their assault. This provides increased time and opportunity to counter engage. All this is made possible by initiating a well-timed deliberate small to half squat when the enemy is fully committed and beyond the point of no return. Such interference causes confusion and requires change in tack which requires a slowing of execution speed in the assault. The CQC squat deliberate set up action immediately prior to unarmed offensive assault employments as part of the offensive action set up also interferes with your foe's visual and mental focus, causing confusion and the need for threat re-evaluation. Not only is it distractive but it also reduces target mass, increases safety and sets up your primary initiation ready-set-go status for the execution of expedient combative offensive actions.

There are some human minor but deliberate actions that are very difficult to ignore in a high stress, high risk combative environment, and the CQC squat ready-set-go action is one of the most proven methods.

Another means of distractive interference of the enemy line and point of vision is a set up with a deliberate or fake action, delivered usually at the upper quadrants when the assault target is actually in the lower quadrants. Such upper quadrant distractive actions cause confusion and responses such as premature counter-offensive responses, leaving the lower quadrants such as the knee joint vulnerable to stamp kick targeting.

Fake upper quadrant deception, as in a feint or fake jab or cross, or definite distractions as in throwing something in your enemy's face to provide unprotected access to their exposed lower quadrants targets are definite and deliberate methods of breaking your enemy's mental focus as well as their visual line and point of focus.

The reverse could also be employed by attacking lower quadrants with deceptive or distractive actions to set up upper quadrants targeting.

To increase your safety the upper quadrant distraction is best done as part of an aggressive employment of a cover guard. This provides entry hard cover guard protection as well as upper quadrants distractive deception.

The Todd Systems primary offensive assault actions based on proven practices and combative smarts and logic are stamp kicks. Stamp kicks utilize the longest limb and the robust boot sole over the hand. Rather than athleticism, stamp kicks are reliant on making range and employing stamp kick, destructive velocity, set up by dirty tricks and deceptive, distractive, deliberate set up actions that prey on human reactions to such set up actions.

Battle dress, as with restrictive type civilian clothing, and load bearing, make stamp kicks the highest kick you should consider for CQC, and the best and safest most proven means of threat neutralization. CQC is not an exact science, but it is a military science based on battle-proven fact in skills selection, that provide over-kill with minimum effort and maximum safety. Dirty tricks distractions that break mental and visual focus as part of the setup of a close to point-blank range executed stamp kick are as guaranteed as it gets in unarmed combat in regards to primary practice maximum unarmed enemy incapacitation threat neutralisation. All my former instructors who were pioneers in military CQC considered stamp kicks the best, most proven and as such primary offensive and counter engagement means of enemy incapacitation.

The leg stamp with a definite or fake action is a primary option stamp kick that through upper quadrant interference and distraction breaks the enemy's mental and visual focus and provides lower quadrant exposure. Even after thousands of repetitions practicing stamp kicks and facing them in training, if performed with commitment and realism, it is difficult not to fall victim to it. Understanding how to use tactics and skills that prey on mental and visual focus, combative commitment and decided option conviction, psychologically affect your enemy's resolve.

My status as a military elite forces CQC Master-Chief instructor has allowed for some very privileged and special access and exposure to the combative elite of elite training and testing for my research and development of CQC tactics and skills. I have a responsibility to provide combatants with the very best and most proven combative capabilities and the stamp kick employed the military combative way either in a one part or two part employment has proven to provide the best and safest means of threat neutralisation.

I can report also that not a single combatant I have trained who has used the Todd special usage CQC tactics and skills employments has ever lost in an actions-on encounter.

While CQC options in special usage roles may be a last resort or special requirement option the fact of the matter is over more than two decades when required they have defeated all comers. The combat boot and military stamp kick provide maximum psychological confidence in unarmed threat neutralisation. Executed by highly committed elite forces pers maximise the chance of threat neutralisation.

True military CQC incorporates very definite ranges, deceptive movements such as the slight small squat to get ready and set, as well as definite length of ground cover movement in evasive actions that end in a primary counter engagement range. As I have always enforced and reiterated, military CQC and CQB may not be an exact science, but they are military sciences and includes definite, deliberate skills-specific offensive and counteroffensive employment ranges, distraction actions, dirty tricks and the utilization of tactics that prey on human reaction to deliberate deceptive actions.

Deliberate fake or definite actions including masked intentions exploit the human reality of being in a high stress situation and reacting to such actions. Deliberate, believable actions, even if it is nothing more than a fake action, cause confusion, hesitation, slowing of execution speed, error of decision-making and premature responses.

The primary evasive ranges and specific methods of evasion for unarmed and armed threats based on a formidable enemy combatant's capabilities to cover ground against even a wounded, injured and load-bearing combatant on difficult terrain requires evasive capabilities that must provide time and distance to effectively evade incoming unarmed and armed assaults. Combative respiration, ground affinity, combative visual sighting, senses at high alert, hard cover guarding, control of the primary reactionary distance, all combined with the inclusion of the small to medium squat immediately prior to evasion increases the chance of clearing the confrontation line and threat neutralization. Threat specific evasive options are definite primary methods in relation to providing threat neutralization in the military science of CQC.

Close-in CQC means just that; extremely close. If they just miss you through your small squat set up and evasion or small through full squat, as in stationary counter-offensive actions then you can contact with them, or make small positional or range adjustments and make contact.

The last thing you want is to make your enemy miss you by moving so far off the kill zone that you cannot make contact before they can recover, re-focus and hard target themselves, or reset, re-align and re-engage you. Psychological confidence is increased by knowing that your combative practices are the best of battle proven and provide safety and ease of employment and as such enable the best chance of objective achievement. This is an important component of psychological levels enhancement as it is employing the best and safest battle-proven options.

I include the CQC squat (or minor or mini crouch as it is also known) as part of my personal combative skills executions in employments of wide ranging skills. I use it in everything from unarmed offensive assault through to unarmed counter-offensive assault, hold prevention and hold escapes, weapon disarming and armed combative skills employments because it provides definite advantages, as discussed below. I have always, prior to initiating any of the previous actions, automatically employed a CQC squat initiation action. This is a habit I have developed through combative training and real-life employment of the skills I possess.

At 5’7” and 125kgs, now 112kgs I have often been up against adversaries that towered over me and possessed an arm’s reach close to as long as my leg length. This required, out of necessity, that I employed every advantage and dirty trick to ensure I achieved my objective. Preying on human reaction to deliberate deceptive actions, as in my CQC squat combined with hard target cover guarding myself, has provided multiple advantages. The small squat means your top 20 cm will be lowered by approximately 4 inches or 10 cm. through situational requirements this can be increased to a half or full squat.

I refer to the normal compromised expected actions-on stance and guard as a ready guard status and the simultaneous small to half squat prior to the employment of combative skills as a ready set to go status.

This combative pre-employment minor, but definite deliberate action, in the form of a slight small to half squat to a ready set for expedient action position status, may be no more than 10 to 15 cm (4 to 6in) in height reduction, but in reality this could be the difference between a fist finding its target and being made to miss it. Drawing an enemy reaction by such a simple means combined with every combative employment will increase the likelihood of forcing enemy reaction out of self-preservation or confusion, and as such create an opening for the initiation of a timed, deliberate, decided and primary ready-set-go executed combative engagement or counter engagement.

When combatants are in a state of high alertness and awareness in an expected actions-on encounter, they will identify the most insignificant movement; a twitch, change in enemy expression, visual focus physical adjustment and will out of self-preservation respond.

Interestingly, after identifying the small squat as a primary component, along with combative respiration, of my personal combative skills employments, I measured timings in relation to initiating the same combative skills from an upright status, both in a neutral stance and in a combative stance and guard without the CQC squat component included. My ready-set-go CQC squat method of skills employment in relation to entry or evasion duration, safety and importantly, objective achievement was more efficient and provided higher levels of objective achievement. The timings, but more importantly, the objective achievement when the ready-set-go CQC squat method was used to set up the combative skills increased objective achievement considerably, even with the additional inclusion of a CQC squat set up.

The reasoning was a combination of deceptive action distraction of the enemy's visual point and line of sight, as well as their mental focus. This affects conviction in their decided offensive option or defensive capabilities causing slowing or hesitation. By means of reducing your target mass, increasing stability, making ready for expedient offensive or counter-offensive actions, setting a ready to go ground affinity, may be minor in movement but it is major in increasing threat neutralization and objective achievement.

CQC small squat, half squat, full squat

Flinching, as detailed in this brain-to-boot package, is an unconscious reaction to reduce risk and increase safety under threat. The small squat is a deliberate action that further increases safety. By dropping one's center of gravity to increase stability and reduce target mass, the cover guard is made more effective by providing hard cover protection of the upper quadrants from head to waistline.

An unarmed attack directed at the head is considered a high percentage shot, and the small squat can make your attacker miss their intended target by deliberately reducing your stand up height. Tight body line cover guarding also reduces bodily mass, tightening and closing up gaps in your bodily cover. A 10 to 15 cm small to half squat reduction from your standing height is an effective means of causing enemy target miss.

The lower quadrants can effectively be protected from the small squat position by employing a stationary evasion, turning your body line from front on to side on to your open stance rear boot side. This has the effect of maintaining the highest level of stability. This also turns your frontal bodily vitals away from the frontal incoming threat, and sets up your lead stamp kick from a side on front stance and guard status to counter engage your foe.

There are varying degrees of the squatting actions that the combatant will employ, commensurate with the threat level in relation to safety, stability maintenance, and counter engagement requirements. From the flinch, the small squat is the most common means of static, deliberate self-protection, setting up a ready status to go combative. Continuation from a small squat to a half squat, or as it is also known as a medium squat, can enhance stability, and expedite unarmed offensive assault and evasive unarmed counter offensive assault capabilities. The level of downward continuation from the small squat to the half squat would depend on the appropriate threat neutralisation option, as well as the individual combatant's physical attributes, combined with terrain and footing considerations. The full squat or 'poo position' is a downward continuation from the half squat and is actually a three quarter squat. (The 'poo' terminology came from finding an efficient way to ensure large military exponent courses could quickly learn their maximum lowered level stability regardless of body type; giving them a colourful description of taking their e-tool, digging a field toilet, then squatting over it at a height outside splatter range but not low enough to risk slipping or landing in it achieves this). The full squat is employed in situations where maximum stability is required for balance recovery and maintenance, and it is especially important as part of enemy resistance in close quarters encounters. The full squat would put you in a powerlifting deep squat position i.e. 'just on or below parallel'.

Employing the half and full squat is also very important if deliberate or forced decentralisation is required; it ensures you fall or roll from the lowest and closest point to the ground, reducing the effects of excessive ground impact. Combining timed combative respiration with ground contact will reduce the risk of injury, and adverse effects such as being winded. Combining combative squatting with combative respiration, and a pivoting action, will ensure ground contact when falling and rolling is with the side of your body (as in your leg, buttocks and back of your shoulder blade). The primary purpose of safety in combative falling and rolling is the protection of your brain and spinal column and cord.

The full squat, combined with combative respiration and stationary pivoting footwork maximises safety, recovery, expedient counter engagement, or escape and evasion capabilities.

From the half squat, utilising your sense of feel you will be able to identify the requirement and degree of depth to regain and maintain stability, and will set a primary status of ready set to go positioning for expedient action.

Under CQC close to point-blank range actions-on, the small, half and full squat provide a range of capabilities; this enables maximum static target mass reduction, hardcover guard safety capabilities, and the setting of a ready set to go combative threat neutralisation status.

It is analogous to driving a car; changes in driving conditions are experienced through the sense of sight and sound, and the sense of touch conveyed through the hands and feet. Adjustments are then made by turning the wheel, applying the brakes or taking the foot off the accelerator. Similarly, in CQC encounters you will sense the need to reduce target mass, increase hardcover guarding capabilities, maximise stability, and increase resistance under threat. This is all synchronised with combative respiration timing, and achieving a ready set to go combative status, making any adjustments required to maintain a primary ready capability status. Increased proficiency through high repetition drilling, and practicing under factor of confusion, sudden aggressive shock actions-on conditions, will enhance capabilities of making minor adjustment by feel, aided by muscle memory.

Increased mental toughness under adversity is enhanced when the combatant is able to make adjustments in stance, guard and position, all the while achieving this with economy of movement. Simple transitions and adjustments to hold position can be achieved by transferring bodily weight downward, or by transferring force in a direction that increases the combatant's momentum or resistance. This keeps the combatant in a mental and physical combative positive status, by maintaining or increasing control and dominance.

In an actions-on encounter, performing deliberate minor through major actions (through assessment and feel), such as the small, half and full squat, will enable you to maintain your highest levels of combative capabilities, safety and mental toughness. This will enhance threat neutralisation capabilities by deliberately naturally assuming a primary ready set to go status. This ready set to go status must have commonality with your combative or escape and evasion skills execution requirements. You will have increased time to fast map, assess, and decide on your combative or escape and evasion option, without having to overly focus on your self-preservation and self-protection. You will be able to make adjustments in relation to change in threat, or situation, by visual assessment and by feel, in real time, without having to overthink under threat.

Being competent in the employment of varied squatting safety, stability, combative or escape and evasion set up positions, as a primary tactic in any actions-on encounter, means you can focus predominately on your best means, and execution of, threat neutralisation.

While the small squat, half squat, and full squat are descriptions in relation to the degree or range of the squatting action, the reality is you will simply employ the required depth of squat to meet the threat through assessment and feel, as part of your threat neutralisation.

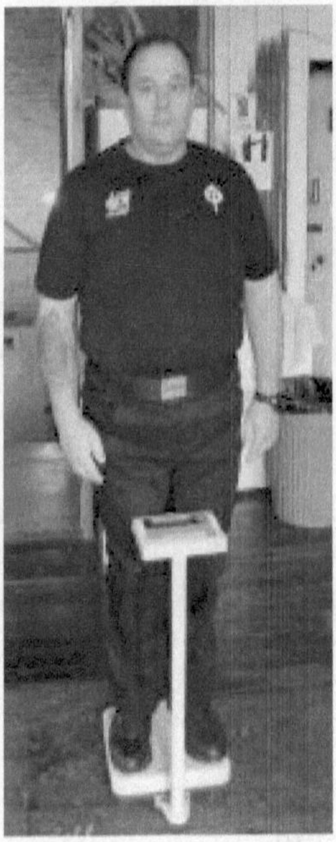

Standing weight 112kg

Full squat weight drop "poo position" 183.9kg

Interfering psychologically with your enemy's point of sight / line of vision and mental focus

Maintaining a ready position, controlling range, senses at high alert and employing counter-offensive combative sighting to provide a visual that enables you to identify the incoming limb involved with the offensive action and its line of travel towards you, its intended target, makes you ready to counter engage such physical offensive threats.

You can psychologically prey on your aggressor's fully committed offensive action simply by employing the CQC squat when your aggressor is fully committed and visually and mentally focused on a pre-decided offensive action that includes zeroing in on a specific bodily target with a specific skill.

The CQC squat will not only make you more ready to execute an expedient offensive or counter-offensive action from a ready-set-go combative status, but like a sprinter out of the blocks it will provide the best of physical capabilities. Ground affinity combined with reducing your target mass, making enemy upper quadrant responses or offensive actions more likely to miss you, their intended target, by employing your CQC skill from a cocked, loaded, CQC squat status provides a considerable edge.

Another equally important aspect of the CQC squat is the psychological interference with your enemy's point of aim. This interference usually causes decreased entry speed and requires the enemy to re-evaluate the situation in real time as a result of your preparatory action interfering with their decided option and target selection. This all becomes apparent to your enemy between skill execution range and previously identified target contact range. Such interference can produce not only confusion but additionally reduction in physical capabilities and psychological confidence. This confusion can convince your enemy that you are in a strong position to counter their initiated offensive action and as such, in real time, it can instill a fear of failure, defeat, injury or even death in even a committed enemy.

In CQB and CQC training, often counter engagement is an easy option through holding position and counter engaging or evading and counter engaging the incoming enemy. This is the reality of being psychologically prepared and ready as well as employing proven tactics in relation to range and position that provide time and distance to initiate ready-set-go counter engagement skills. Such ready-set-go counter engagement skills comprising of the CQC squat set up action increase safety and improve your state of readiness as well as increasing your expedient action. They also psychologically interfere with your enemy's point of aim and line of vision causing them to slow, hesitate or even stall, as well as having to re-evaluate the situation and their options.

The amount of information the eyes can take in and transmit at even real time actions-on speed is incredible and it can feel like everything is happening in slow motion—but it is not. Your enemy's re-evaluation undertaken in a fraction of a second, via their sense of vision picking up on your ready-set-go CQC squat employment, can achieve various reactions ranging from flinching when fully committed to slowing, stalling, hesitating or even aborting a decided executed offensive assault action.

Deciding to change a pre-decided offensive action amidst a fully committed execution entry, or changing one's decided target selection at full commitment will require at the minimum a decrease in entry execution speed. Imagine initiating a sprint for a close finish line and all of a sudden the finish line moves laterally, as identified by your visual sense. The identified changed situation information may well cause an immediate reduction in commitment and speed. The processed information by your central nervous system will certainly cause a change in commitment speed and tack if you want to cross the changed-position finish line. The returned processed information will include a definite decision that may include the option to continue with the initially decided offensive action option, or employing a replacement option at the same zeroed target or possibly a completely new target selected as a result of the CQC squat interference. There is also the consideration that the committed enemy may abort the execution of their offensive action and even completely resign from any further hostilities.

All these outcomes are subject to the mental confidence and physical capabilities of the aggressor and their perceived evaluation of their target's combative capabilities. The same can be said of evaluating and identifying their target's controlled state of readiness, and timing.

At least such slowing of the incoming action will ensure that you require less speed and have more time to engage or counter engage the incoming threat.

Interfering with a fully committed enemy's point of aim is a psychologically positive means of gaining an edge. The enemy must react, break their point of aim, decide on the nature of your subtle, minor initiated action and as such make a decision on their next and best replacement action. All this will create time and execution advantages in relation to your engagement or counter engagement.

Hard cover- hard target

Hard cover guarding applies to most, if not all, aspects of CQC against a formidable enemy. In the brain-to-boot psychological conditioning preparation for CQC and CQB and self-defence, hard cover guarding is essential in risk reduction and objective achievement.

As I've explained throughout the brain-to-boot package, combative respiration as soon as the threat has been identified is a priority in the correct order of execution of primary major and minor physical and psychological combat and counter components.

In an unexpected actions-on encounter where your first knowledge of the threat is when it is right upon you inside the kill zone, or when contact has been made with you, this is when hard cover is essential. Under such compromised immediate actions-on or first actions-on awareness being contact impact, then the order of execution becomes based on self-preservation combined with simultaneous combative respiration.

Hard cover guarding can be employed statically, or if time and situation allows, evasively.

Your autonomic reactions to immediate shock action include a flinch and visual response to determine the incoming direction of the threat, and immediate threat specifics required to neutralise the threat, defend against, or escape and evade it.

The flinch reaction reduces target mass and increases stability, and must have commonality and cohesion with your hard cover guarding.

Soft guarding refers to maintaining a state of pre-actions-on readiness in a combative stance and guard, prior to any actions-on encounter that will require the soft stance and guard to be changed to a hard cover stance and guard status. This will improve stability and the capability to cover and absorb against impact, or hard cover guard deflect against straight line or upper cut offensive assault.

Ideally, immediately on flinching and upon your senses, specifically your sense of vision, identifying the incoming line and type of assault, simultaneously employing a cover guard combined with a CQC squat execution will reduce target mass and improve stability—reducing risk and increasing personal safety. If time, distance and situation allow, by means of fast map decision making, then the CQC squat, cover guard status cohesively allows for continuation into a ready set status for expedient evasive action.

In unexpected first awareness combative contact actions-on situations, hard cover guarding including the required squat, target mass reduction and increased stability would be simultaneous with the employment of combative respiration the degree of the squat depth will be determined by situational specifics. The sooner combative respiration is initiated the better will be the decision making, setting up and execution of the skill to neutralise the threat.

Often the force of the contact/impact will determine the capability to not only employ hard cover guarding, but also evasion off of the confrontation line, especially if incapacitated or decentralised.

High force contact impact may well cause incapacitation where no deliberate means of hard cover guarding or stability maintenance is possible.

In some situations the initial contact impact will force movement off the confrontation line and point. Being forced by contact impact off of the confrontation point can provide time and distance to hard cover guard, as well as recovery time and space for fast mapping, assessment, decision making and the capability to adjust, make ready, get set and execute your counter engagement.

Changing from a front hard cover guard to a side hard cover guard, from stationary or with evasion, is a simple straight line transition.

Sound hard cover guarding will provide protection from the highest level of your skull down to your pelvic bowl. Your arms locked onto your side of your head above your ears and in a hard cover guard position will reduce the effects of round house impact, and any straight-line or uppercut strikes between your combative sighting cover guard can be deflected.

Your lower quadrants, from stationary, can be protected by pivoting to the rear boot open stance side, where strikes and kicks can be countered with your lead boot stamp kick to either the kicking leg or the stability leg, whichever presents itself first and is closest.

This form of stationery evasive counter engagement is especially applicable to an unexpected surprise flash of movement, shape, colour or sound -all warnings of an incoming assault.

In situations where you are compromised by an unexpected attack, but detect the line of the attack prior to it making it into the kill zone, you may be able to employ a combined CQC squat and hard cover guard ready-set-go and get off the confrontation line.

Unorthodox closed stance stationary evasion pivoting to the lead boot side will require rear boot adjustment to regain stability. Such adjustments ensure not only regained physical stability, but also ensure maintained or regained psychological confidence in your combative skill execution.

Stability and balance loss requires an immediate, real time, contingency response to avoid being decentralised, which in a self-defence or combative actions-on encounter means increased risk and danger. This known reality will make the trained combatant make any adjustment or employ any contingency option to prevent decentralisation.

Autonomic self-preservation reactions aid in prevention of decentralisation, by ensuring the arms are used to assist with stability maintenance if necessary, as well as changes in stance and footing. Note that in an actions-on assault, removing your cover guarding arms to assist with maintaining stability leaves you open to unprotected assault. As such there are some autonomic reactions in assault situations that reduce CQC safety and as such increase risk.

To maintain effective hard cover guarding in situations such as unorthodox closed stance stationary evasion by pivoting and adjusting of footing to regain balance and stability, ending side on to the enemy in a front stance a single cover guard can be employed for cover or deflection of strikes. This is a trained primary deliberate transition to regain and maintain stability and maintain hard cover guard protection.

Using your enemy for balance and stability recovery or maintenance by pushing forward against them with body line contact is a primary practice. This practice increases safety by restricting enemy capabilities. It also promotes enemy resistance, aiding in you balance and stability recovery and maintenance.

Utilising the rear-most guarding arm in relation to the enemy in amphibious CQC and all other military employments of a stamp kicks, is a balance maintenance or recovery contingency in military CQC. By extending the rearmost arm during the execution of a stamp kick, where stability and balance has been compromised diagonally backward and downward, the effects of forward downward balance and stability loss can be countered.

Such training in combatively proven contingencies is psychologically enhancing. It is often a required trained response to ensure human autonomic self-preservation reactionary responses are adjusted or changed to provide not only self-preservation and safety, but also combative required capabilities.

Trained combative capabilities and contingencies to maintain or regain a primary combative status, including hard cover guarding and recovery capabilities that have commonality with autonomic human reactions by minor changes and adjustments, provide psychological strength and combative capabilities confidence.

In evasive counter engagement, depending on time, distance, your immediate environment and the threat situation, the best available evasive line will be evident and selected. Evasive lines include diagonally forward, diagonally rearward and horizontal evasive lines off of the confrontation line.

Through prior training, your deliberate actions will be decided, or as it is known in CQC, 'your training kicks in', initiated with either combative respiration or hard cover and simultaneous combative respiration.

The importance of contingency capabilities that make you force protect under assault as a result of realistic prior combative training and that have general major component commonality with your autonomic reactions is that you need not lose mental confidence under assault when things go wrong.

If incapacitated and decentralised, or your stability and footing is compromised as a result of contact impact, then your forced protection combative side falling and respiration are very important to reduce risk in relation to hard ground contact. Your combative side fall must include sound hard cover guarding to reduce ground or solid back drop impact contact with the nape of your neck. 'You can replace your wish bone but not your neck bone', as the saying goes.

In ground combat your boots are a major source of forced protection counter engagement to neutralise your stand up kicking and stomping aggressor.

In ground combat when your enemy is employing unarmed assault from a straddle, your cover guard capabilities are again a forced protection requirement.

The sooner that combative respiration is undertaken, the better control you will have over the situation in relation to reducing the effect of contact, and maintaining your capabilities to go combative from your hard cover guard.

In ground combat or when taken by surprise and decentralised, the importance of risk reduction in relation to identifying, avoiding or reducing risk by hard cover guarding to force protect against ground and terrain related hazards contact impact, makes sure your best combative chance under the circumstances is employed. Combative side falling or combative rolling and expedient footing recovery, or ground counter engagement all require effective employment of hard cover guarding and combative respiration.

You should not only power every skill execution with combative respiration, but also time your respiration in relation to covering against, or cover and deflection of, unarmed offensive assault. This will ensure you maintain your constant state of readiness and do not hold your breath, and as a consequence, face the dangers of such a tactically flawed and dangerous practice.

Hard cover guarding combined with combative respiration, when compromised in an unexpected incoming actions-on or first indication contact situation, must be employed and maintained until the threat is neutralised.

The hard cover status to absorb or deflect high impact strikes usually requires the extended small squat to the half or full squat poo position. This is combined with a hard cover guard, with the palms of both hands grasping the highest sections of the skull above the ears. Your forearms and upper arms in line with your immediate outer body line must be locked rigid to absorb impact shock force.

Combative sighting (looking between the cover guard) must be employed to identify type and direction of incoming assault.

Combative respiration must be timed to exhale on every executed combative action, and also to exhale on every absorbed or deflected enemy assault combative action.

Any lower quadrant assault can be countered by pivoting from a front on cover stance and guard position, to the open stance rear boot side, turning your body mass from front-on to side-on, reducing target exposure and increasing cover guard capabilities by reducing the target window of opportunity.

From this position a lead boot stamp kick can be utilised to neutralise the threat.

In high-risk high-stress immediate actions-on situations having a single primary physical capability to counter wide-ranging unarmed offensive assault threats increases confidence and provides increased time and primary range to counter engage.

However, if such important force protection primary practices are not cohesively initiated to self-protect, and as part of going combative, then safety will be compromised and the physical effects will soon reduce your psychological capabilities. Sound combative training in high repetition practice, as well as high intensity combative training with the factor of confusion ever present, will ensure your primary skills are tested and proven in training. Under the unknown exact whereabouts and unknown threat category of CQC battle handling exercises, and in real-life actions-on encounters, your CQC training should kick in, as you have trained the combative way and are familiar with the threat and how to neutralise it. Psychologically you will be strong of mind through familiarity with the threat, and having trained in how to neutralise it under combative extreme actions-on training conditions. Your belief in yourself and your best of battle-proven combative capabilities, supported by primary contingency options including hard cover guarding, ensure your best combative chance of threat neutralisation.

Cover guarding and deflection over blocking

Mental confidence through a knowledge that your means of self-protection in relation to neutralising strikes and kicks, especially from stationary, is as close as humanly possible to fool proof is critical to ensure the highest levels of self-confidence.

In the real world of combative dirty tricks and deception, feints, cheats and set ups of combative skills, blocking comes down to a 50-50 chance of success or failure. This is unacceptable in kill-or-die military CQC, and the same applies to military self-defence.

The autonomic reactive flinch is a self-preservation reaction under assault and especially under unexpected immediate actions-on encounter assault. The flinch reduces your bodily target mass, and increases your stability by means of a reactive slight crouch and dropping of your centre of gravity.

Any reactive skills to unexpected sudden aggressive shock action must have commonality with the autonomic flinch reaction. Continuing the flinch to a CQC squat cover guard provides even further reduced target mass, and as such a considerably smaller window of opportunity for enemy contact.

By utilising your arms in a cover guard in relation to the direction of the incoming enemy threat, you are keeping your extremities close, tight and reducing exposed bodily target areas by not employing upward, downward or outward blocking actions.

Effective crouching and hard cover guarding will provide full upper quadrants cover guard protection, from the top of the head to the waist, while not breaking the rectangular form of the outer body line.

Round house strikes can be caused to miss by the CQC squat component, or absorbed on the forearms or upper arms which provide shock absorber capabilities.

Straight line or cross line strikes or upper cuts can effectively be deflected between the cover guard, with the directly opposite inner forearm to the enemy striking arm.

Combative sighting between your forearms in a cover guard provides the capability to effectively identify the specific limb, and that specific limb's incoming travel line. As such, you will be able to effectively deflect the strike, making it miss you, its intended target, this will in turn provide you with the capability to make range, adjust and counter engage.

Employing your lead boot post crouching and cover guarding to combat an enemy kicking leg or the enemy's stability leg, whichever is closest, will enable you from stationary to cover guard and counter not only kicks but all unarmed offensive actions.

Combating a kick with a stamp kick requires from the crouch cover guard position a stationery evasion to the open stance rear boot side, which will also reduce target exposure by changing your bodily position from front on to side on. Employing a lead stamp counter kick will remove your lead leg, which is the most exposed and the closest limb to the incoming enemy, and utilising it as a counter engagement unarmed weapon will ensure it is not a static target.

Being proficient in battle-proven skills that are as simple and safe as humanly possible requires minimal output, but can provide maximum combative destructive results and is a definite means of psychological enhancement when faced with a formidable threat.

Hard cover guard

Enemy left arm deflection

Enemy right arm deflection

Side stance and guard

Side stance hard cover guard against right roundhouse strike

Side stance and hard cover guard and deflection against inside cover guard strike

Self-reassurance

Self-reassurance is a critical aspect of maintaining the highest state of readiness, and ensures you do not enter into the negatives of anticipation or perception over physical assessment and threat determination based on fact. I have previously covered the critical practice of self-reassurance in relation to expected actions-on threat situations where, as part of your setting and maintaining a state of readiness, you will self-reassure by silently, mentally in your mind's eye self-reassuring. The Todd military CQB/CQC/MSD systems use the silent self-reassurance, 'ready, willing, able', or 'willing, able, ready'.

Another important aspect of self-reassurance is silent self-instruction to ensure that the timing of combative actions employments is as correct as you can possibly make it.

One such important usage of silent self-instruction is the timing of evading multiple knife slashes. Often focus can be lost on the weapon through fear and stress, and as such, at the last critical instant before contact the combatant may hesitate, freeze or be left with no other option than employing an emergency contingency disarming option.

Emergency contingency disarming options are important in a situation where by the very nature of the situation you are unable to determine the final incoming weapon direction of travel, and so cannot safely evade its incoming travel line. Under such situations emergency disarming contingency options are a must.

Your eyes will determine the incoming weapon, important information in relation to weapon type and direction, and line of incoming weapon travel and timing in real time. This identified and processed information can be utilised to provide self-instruction as to the incoming weapon's range and the primary timing of pre-disarming evasion.

Visually recognizing threat characteristics, transmitting information to your central nervous system, and silently from your mind's eye relaying information in the form of self-commands combined with the 'Go' command to initiate your evasive disarming action, optimises levels of timing, proficiency, safety, objective achievement and importantly threat neutralisation.

In the case of the multiple slashes knife threat, maintaining a ready status, ground affinity, employing combative respiration and keeping your extremities in close to reduce target mass will decrease unnecessary injury. Maintain your vision on the weapon's point, and with every out of range incoming slashing action, silently from your mind's eye, give the self-commands 'no, no, no' and then 'go' when the knife is on its final incoming travel at you, it's intended target. By using mind's eye self-commands you have improved your combative chance of correct timing, and evasive direction away the weapon's incoming travel. By means of commanding yourself as to the primary timing and direction in relation to executing your evasive pre-disarming counteraction you are increasing control of your dire situation, and using positive self-reassurance, ensuring there is no time for self-doubt or anticipation over factual assessment and definite deliberate silent commands.

In unarmed evasive counter-offensive assault utilising the same principles, with commands like 'evade, assess, execute' or 'evade, assess, adjust, engage' ensures timing, decision-making and correctional footing and range adjustments are made post evasion.

This is a form of fast mapping combined with mind mapping that provides critical threat information, including determining priority timing in relation to skills execution. Always remember, the verbal information and instruction commands are a silent transmission and are really more like deliberate positive thought commands than verbiage—which can slow down physical skills executions when both are combined.

Silently, by fast mapping assessment of threat information and decision making, recall from your memory bank the required command instructions to best ensure the primary components of timing and evasive direction are utilized as silent mind's eye self-commands.

There are varied silent command terms such as no, no, no; go or hold, hold, hold, go, and of course stand by, stand by, go. Whatever command terms you use make sure for brevity they are short and to the point

Life or death military self defence
Specialist CQB/CQC proponents at the highest level should be competent through prior training in the last resort options to neutralise deadly specific situational threats. Such threats are usually related to being wounded or taken prisoner and facing immediate execution. They require life or death specialist principle-based military self defence tactics and skills as the last and only means of threat neutralization.
This form of training prepares the combatant when faced with the most deadly and dire close combat situations where the difference between life and death is the individual combatant's intestinal fortitude, inner resolve and commitment combined with best specialist last line of self-protection and threat neutralisation capabilities to save their life by combative means and neutralise the threat.

Crowd combat when grossly outnumbered by armed enemy combatants, when you only have your unarmed or improvised weapon capabilities, as well as being taken prisoner by an enemy that considers the best prisoner to be a dead prisoner, or an enemy intending to torture the prisoner, make last line of threat neutralisation capabilities the difference between the chance of threat neutralization versus no hope and no chance.

There are civilian situations where such capabilities are the only option possible for self-preservation and threat neutralization.

We have seen civilians beheaded in recent years and terrorist killings by means of using non-ballistic weapons. Family violence ending in murder and suicide and armed robbery are threat types where knowing when and how to take threat neutralization action can be the only chance of saving your life. Threat neutralization by escape and evasion would be a safer option if available.

By employing constant threat assessment fast mapping from the moment of threat recognition, a decision may be able to be made and employed before the lines of threat neutralization are shut down.

The occurrence of such threats is statistically low among all categories of all violent threats but they do happen and finding out you have no capabilities under threat is terminal.

Civilian street fight situations are a more common threat to civilians where you are outnumbered on the end of a major beating, possibly decentralised and being kicked and stomped by multiple assailants. This specialist last resort methods of self-protection combative counter engagement or escape and evasion.

Make sure you are a mentally tough and physically prepared combatant armed with the best specialist battle-proven capabilities and be a formidable force to be reckoned with.

Worst-case situations scenario training for the specialist combative proponent level provides a capability that is simply a last line of threat neutralisation best chance option when faced with extreme and overwhelming violence.

I can remember before my instructor qualification course not only preparing physically but also practicing everything from basic level close quarters combat through to advanced as well as specialist kill-or-die tactics and skills that give you the best chance you can expect, a combative chance in life-threatening odds against you extreme combative encounters. I would never want to find myself without the tactics and skills required to neutralise the threat. I have always trained the combative way and the same way I will go combative under threat, whether it be in training under qualification testing or in real life actions-on situations.

I personally practiced emergency risk reduction and best means of threat neutralisation under being taken prisoner conditions facing unarmed as well as armed enemy threats. This included when gagged and tied.

Understanding your combative medical implications and how to protect life-support vitals and more delicate bodily parts by positioning and constantly adjusting to make yourself as hard a target as possible is very important.

Timing your combative respiration, not only when you are executing physical skills but also to ensure you are exhaling immediately prior to and throughout assault contact, is important to reduce the effects of impact contact. This reduces the likelihood of being incapacitated to the point of helplessness or hopelessness.

Practicing disarming skills where you are restricted including being tied up against edged weapons and bludgeon type weapons as well as in situations like being pistol whipped is important if you are to reduce the risk as much as possible. Avoid penetration or blunt force trauma impact. If, however, if there is no avoiding it making sure contact is directed at a non-fatal part of the human body in relation to being able to still neutralise the enemy threat by combative or escape and evasion means.

Understand that first aid is important when injured or wounded, but in an actions-on encounter, stopping to check your wounds or injuries will only make you more vulnerable as a static target to further wounding or death.

If you are still in control of all or some of your capabilities and can feel pain then you are alive and capable of some form of self-protection.

Your self-protection must ensure you reduce risk to the lowest possible level. You must know how under such extreme assaults to not only reduce risk but to neutralise the threat. Never have only a self-protection plan. It must always include a threat neutralization plan. Do not stop until the threat has been neutralised.

You must be able to identify improvised weapons at your disposal then utilise such improvised weapons to neutralise the threat.

In knife combat where you are going to be stabbed or slashed keep your tendons and arteries in against your body use your outer arm muscle and tissue to protect your airway carotid arteries, including covering your heart with your arm reduce the effect of the wounding dramatically.

Employing stationary evasive angling of your body by pivoting and crouching in the last line of protection covering and guarding of your delicate bodily vitals increases your chances of threat neutralisation considerably.

The previously explained crouched cover guarding and using angle in a side on positioning to reduce target mass and target access will provide last line of protection reduced risk of your major vitals being exposed. Under such extremes the importance of stamp kicking to neutralise the threat while maintaining your risk reduction best option bodily vitals cover guard protection is your best chance of threat neutralization even when wounded.

Specialist combative training combined with a never give up or give in psychological demeanor is the difference between life and death when facing the most extreme calculated violence.

In realistic crowd combat practice when you have been decentralised and have multiple assailants kicking and stomping you on the ground, you must make yourself as safe as humanly possible and as quickly as possible recover footing. Alternatively, combat the kicking and stomping from the ground by executing stamp kicking options of your own maximised dire situation safety and counter engagement capabilities.

Understanding how to adjust on the ground in an effort to keep your boots facing the immediate threat and how to ground pivot or barrel roll away or use your body mass and momentum to decentralise and possibly incapacitate your enemy by impacting below the knee joint in an effort to destroy the integrity of the knee cap and knee joint ligaments increases your combative chance of threat neutralisation.

Practicing such terminal gross motor skills to aid in footing recovery, escape and evasion or enemy neutralisation will increase confidence by know-how and familiarization.

Pivoting and sliding footwork are two of the most important means of economically and effectively changing position and safely covering ground.

Pivoting provides an immediate stationary means of clearing the contact zone and sliding footwork allows you to maintain ground affinity contact with slippery terrain.

In situations where you need immediate contact zone clearance being able to do so without having to evasively move one or both boots provides maximum dire situation stationary clearance capabilities.

Contact zone evasive capabilities for unarmed combat as a rule should provide a primary means of directional evasion being diagonally forward, secondary means being diagonally rearward. Alternative means for specific situations including horizontal side evasion and emergency means such a stationery evasion or reversed diagonally forward evasion. All of these are combined with fast mapping assessment decision making and threat neutralisation employment.

Under actions-on assault where emergency contact zone clearance is required, pivoting both boots to reduce target mass and clear the contact zone is far more economical and safe than having to move one or both boots off the immediate contact zone combined with adjustment footwork.

In military firearms disarming phase ambush threat or in weapon seizure prevention retention of a weapon or regention (a Todd Systems term for regaining control of a drawn seized and secured weapon) pivoting clearance foot work as part of disarming and threat neutralisation are primary practices.

A formidable willing combatant must be armed with the best of battle-proven knowledge from basic level through advanced level to specialist level in order to have the widest ranging capabilities to neutralise unpredictable unexpected and often unconventional extreme violence.

Through high level combative knowledge including competency in primary, secondary, alternative and emergency options employments, the individual combatant can maintain a high level of mental toughness under extreme adversity.

The most important factors are the individual's intestinal fortitude and inner resolve and their high level of specialist prior combative training.

CHECKLIST

Important physical practices to be ready and willing

Hard targeting simply means reducing risk by making yourself a hard target. Being trained in the best principles that arm the combatant with tactically correct, battle-proven knowledge of objective achievement, by various means in relation to the threat category and specific threat situation, will provide options in relation to required objective achievement. Early recognition, and if applicable, threat avoidance will certainly be the safest option. Immediately initiating combative respiration and simultaneously employing all your senses, especially an immediate visual assessment to ensure sound decision making based on factual information, will provide the best chance of achieving the objective. Factual assessment and tactical decision making will not only reduce risk and enhance objective achievement and the chance of victory, but also will ensure combatants are occupied with positive practices. Additional hard targeting practices that are common continuation practices are by means of physical and psychological checks and assessments, maintaining a state of complete readiness. This constant, maintained state of readiness will occupy all available time, and as such prevent veering into the dangerous realm of self-doubt, anticipation and perception. Hard targeting begins in training with preparation and practice long before any situation is encountered.

Tunnel vision and audio exclusion reduce or eliminate your ability to see or hear. This applies not only to dangers, but also to friendlies. Failing to be capable of hearing instructions, warnings and orders, or being unable to visually see hand signals not only reduces you combative ability, but also may affect your safety and that of your fellow combatants.

Remaining constantly ready is a priority, and this requires a combination of psychological and physical skills working in unison to stay in the primary combative zone.

The key to reducing the risk of the enemy threat is to make yourself a hard target, by controlling distance and protecting your rear and side flanks, and in turn reducing the likelihood of falling victim to a sudden shock attack from an identified or unidentified enemy.

Employing layers of security, effective cover, early detection devices and having confidence in your team members to protect your back will make you psychologically stronger.

In an escape and evasion requirement you need to ensure your escape route is in line with your position and plan. When you are going to engage the enemy you need to reduce risk by reducing your mass, making the window of opportunity for attack as slight as possible. You must understand that psychological strength and physical preparation are linked, and one without the other would see the combatant less than ready, willing and capable. This is why in the Todd Systems, skills, principles and tactics are selected because they are proven, and make the combatant as confident and competent as possible.

Remember you are only human, and certain threats are best avoided, escaped and evaded, and that is often the best option to keep you alive. Always use your brains to outsmart your enemy and don't become a victim unnecessarily. If there is no escape or way out, then take the best combative option under the circumstances, and do everything and anything to be victorious.

Never be suicidal in your attitude or execution but realise you must be aggressively, ruthlessly committed to your objective achievement. If you have no option other than a combative option, then this is all the added incentive you need to ensure controlled, aggressive, ruthless commitment. If you do not employ such a committed combative action, you stand to be a victim, but if you take your chances by means of calculated, controlled, committed, aggressive combative actions you increase your chance of victory.

When faced with extreme adversity, silently, in your mind reiterate that you can and will win and will never quit ('ready, willing, able—willing, able, ready'). This reduces the risk of failure, and gives the combatant the best chance of victory through psychological and physical readiness, and a belief in your skills capabilities being the best and most proven, combined with your maximum intestinal fortitude and inner resolve to achieve your objective.

Becoming completely familiar with equipment, weapons and battle dress, or for civilian situations, your state of readiness, and by identifying or making ready any improvised object that could aid in your combative or self-defence skills employments is a proactive definite physical requirement. Psychologically this will aid in maintaining or increasing your confidence and resolve. Achieving a state of such readiness means that in an instant you can locate and draw, or arm yourself, through familiarity with equipment and weapon placement. You must be able to identify environmentally provided improvised weapons, secure them and make them ready in the blink of an eye. Such competencies reduce error, arming time and as such increase additional capabilities that provide physical advantages that are definite confidence boosters which will improve the combatant psychologically. This must be second nature as well as physical combative conditioning and practice of skills, principles, tactics and procedures. When operational or in a civilian situation, when confronted, by checking and rechecking your person, weapons, communications, devices and equipment as well as your immediate situation and surroundings, you are taking a very proactive approach to maintaining a high level of alertness and readiness, and this in turn reduces risk and eliminates time for self-doubt, anticipation or perception.

When doing your checks of the situation and of your kit and person, take into account your physical readiness from the ground up. Ground affinity, stance, guard, and your kit carried on your person including weapons are all necessary considerations. Tactical carry of weapons and equipment, making yourself a hard target and remaining in the ready status is of paramount importance.

Primary, secondary and emergency improvised weapons do provide physical advantages and as such are likely to increase psychological confidence and resolve, but you must never allow armed capabilities to make you underestimate your enemy or assailant. Even a coward when cornered or facing a formidable threat can increase their commitment level.

Danger has the effect of providing an instant reality check. If there is no out option then it's either be a static target, or attack your attacker, or attempt to disarm and neutralise the threat.

Never be so confident that you underestimate your enemy or adversary as it may lead to your demise. Always remain quietly confident, alert, ready, constantly fast mapping to identify change in threat or situation, and be able to assess, decide, adjust and combat or counter changes in real time.

The amount of time and distance you will have at your disposal will determine the extent of your checks and re-checks when faced with an immediate or imminent threat situation. When the luxury of time and distance are at your disposal, I reiterate that you should constantly scan your environment for changes in situation or threat, and perform physical and mental checks and re-checks of yourself and your equipment and weapons.

This practice is not only very proactive but it also reduces the risk of self-doubt. It avoids negative influences that can affect your resolve and ultimately your combative performance and chance of achieving your objective and dictating the outcome.

During training, select skills that enable you to neutralise your enemy, make sure you have confidence and competence in the physical skills allowing you to never underestimate your enemy and also know and believe you have the capabilities to neutralise the threat. I reiterate, never underestimate your enemy or be overconfident to the point that the target is incapable of engaging or defeating you.

Be honest with yourself and evaluate your inner resolve and mental toughness when faced with the likelihood or reality of extreme violence. Think about your first thoughts, actions and reactions when faced with the danger of physical violence or other dangers (such as the fear of heights, speed, etc.). Ask yourself, "What would I do if faced by every imaginable threat of violence?" Don't leave any combative threat out; ask yourself how you would react to an unknown subject threatening you with unarmed violence.

Don't stop at common threats. Cover non-specific unarmed and armed threats, work your way through threat categories and enemies of all ethnicities, physical appearances and attributes.

Imagine in your mind's eye every conceivable physical stature, physical capability, threatening appearance and consider what situations, individuals, or weapons cause you to panic or create the most concern fear or stress and weaken your resolve.

If properly prepared for a situation where ambushed or confronted, you'll certainly go into making yourself a hard target mode by assessing your immediate situation, and reducing risk in relation to the specific situation by protecting your rear flanks against a solid backdrop or an open area or escape route depending on situational specifics and on your intended actions. You'll scan the area and the enemy to identify increased dangers, chinks in the enemy's armor and situational advantages that can be exploited. You'll identify any possible terrain related advantages or dangers and any potential improvised weapons. Take for example the use of an empty jerry can as an improvised weapon; hold the jerry can in such a manner and employ it so that target contact is with an edge or corner and not the flat surfaces. Always achieve maximum advantages by primary employment.

Going tactical includes both physical and mental familiarity with your kit and weapons and is a proficiency gained through continuous practice of high repetition usage drills.

Again, exact positioning and placement of kit carried devices and weapons will improve your ability to draw and allow for slick employment without hesitation or fault. For high-stress, high-risk employments this is essential. In low to no light, being ready and completely familiar and proficient with the locating, drawing and employment of weapons and equipment can be the difference between victory and defeat.

The sense of touch competency applies not only to weapon or accessories location and drawing but also to enemy or assailant bodily target location by feel in low to no light situations. I instruct my CQC proponents in not only enemy target locating by the sense of feel but also enemy seizure securing and containment without vision.

There are many other combative unarmed and armed practices that I instruct blind employment of. I do so to ensure that under such reduced capabilities panic is not the response, but rather that through prior exposure and practice, the execution of the required tactics and skills are definite, deliberate, decisions and executions.

Prepare yourself well psychologically, perform checks and re-checks and stay mentally alert

After hard targeting, your next concern in relation to psychological preparation for battle is to assess the situation and threat, including your environment. You do this by controlling distance, position, ensuring your rear flanks are as safe as possible, and being aware of your terrain and ensuring any advantage or improvised weapon belongs to you.

Maintain the element of surprise and give nothing away. Be ready to employ every dirty trick, distraction, and feint tactic, element of cunning and advantage you can imagine that is at your disposal. Remember you may have to mask your intentions or use verbiage to provide an edge or opening to ensure you achieve your objectives. Be aware that verbiage use has risk in the sense that it slows down your reactions and interferes with your mental focus, and can also provoke or escalate the situation. It is normally used only to get a verbal response that will cause the same effects, plus hesitation, for your enemy immediately prior to you going combative. This including in ambush or mugging threats and weapon disarming as part of your skills execution enhancement.

Assess all aspects of the enemy threat situation and means of achieving your objectives and decide on the best plan of attack. Once you have decided on your plan of attack remember range plus tactics, skills and ruthless commitment equals your best combative chance. Remain ready for anything and everything always, and be prepared to fast map on the move employing contingency options to deal with changes in threat or situation. Presume, anticipate or perceive nothing, only assess and decide your combative actions based on assessed and decided real time facts.

Setting a stance and guard is only recommended if you have already been compromised and have lost the element of surprise, as it increases tension and stress, as well as requiring more physical effort to maintain. It also builds up lactic acid in the muscles.

The best option is to employ your skills from neutral where you have the advantage of the element of surprise. When combined with aggressive, controlled over-kill shock actions increases your odds of achieving your objectives. You should be mentally focusing on required physical and psychological requirements and factual observations, and never anticipation, perception or guesswork.

Mental checks should cover and recover your combative readiness in the presented and current situation. This way you can assess, decide and execute your specific plan based on fact. Planning, preparation and practice to prevent pretty poor performance. You'll decide on your plan of attack getting into the optimum range and position, set it up and execute it with ruthless, controlled commitment and aggression.

Psychologically ready for CQB

The first phase of this combative psychologically-ready-for-CQB/CQC/MSD enhancing program is to ensure that you are honest with yourself in relation to your combative physical attributes, abilities, strengths, capabilities, weaknesses and handicaps. You need to take a look at yourself in the mirror honestly and objectively, and combine what you see with what you know.

Height, weight, reach, speed, power, strength, and stability as well as fast or slow twitch fiber predominance, explosive power, coordination, reaction time, endurance, recovery time, flexibility, prior injuries or physical handicaps as well as your ability or lack of to think quickly on your feet are all important factors in capability. Physical attributes include combative weaknesses such as a glass jaw or poor balance and stability. Be very critical of yourself to identify your every weakness and every strength, including attributes that could be exploited by your enemy. Physical fitness state of health is a very important consideration.

During this research phase you must evaluate your combative skills, principles and systems to ensure a factual record of physical capabilities and physical attributes relevant to achieving your objectives as quickly quietly and safely as humanly possible.

Ask yourself if your physical attributes and skills provide the best means of achieving your objectives. Assess your skills and ask yourself are they the best skills for CQB, CQC, MSD.

Could you employ these skills as primary options against an enemy that is bigger, stronger, faster, fitter, possibly armed and committed to killing you?

Would your skills provide the best, safest and most battle-proven means to victory if you were load bearing, wounded, injured, suffering from starvation and dehydration, stripped of all weapons capabilities and left with only your bodily weapons such as in a prisoner of war situation?

This program of instruction will require you to not only evaluate your physical attributes and capabilities as well as your inner resolve and mental toughness but also your skills, principles and tactics capabilities.

It's very much a case of the right tools for the job to make the outcome as predictable as humanly possible under extreme circumstances and with the factor of confusion ever present.

Evaluate your height and weight in relation to the average physical height and weight of the individual enemy you consider most formidable and you are likely to face. Expand on the most likely physical attributes of your envisioned enemy and extend the physical attributes of a perceived enemy to that of the most fearsome, extreme and dangerous of human threats.

Now identify in the most deadly of specific close combat situations, that being unarmed combat, what primary option would be best to neutralise the threat.

Once you have identified your physical strengths and weaknesses you can enhance your capabilities in the required areas and if required expand on your knowledge base to ensure you make yourself as physically competent, confident, proficient and capable as you can.

Evaluate your stability, stance and guard, footwork, speed of entry and of evasion as well as your physical strength, and the power and velocity of your strikes and kicks. Work on improving your reaction time and train the way you intend to operate by ensuring your training environment is as far removed from a studio or dojo environment as possible, and as close to a combative environment as you can make it.

Ask yourself, what are your strengths, physically? Are you fast, or strong? Do you have a chin made of granite? Do you have good footwork? Does your posture, stance, balance and ability to move or hold ground make you formidable? Is your reaction time at its peak? Do you physically commit to employment of skills producing maximum velocity, power and destruction confidently and competently?

Ask yourself, is your knowledge what it should be, and are your skills the best options for you personally and the best of battle proven. Do you have confidence in your physical skills or do you think that the skills that you have learned may not be the best of battle proven to conquer likely threats?

In your mind's eye identify whether or not you have the means to combat all the threats you may face and the capabilities to employ skills to achieve operational objectives in all the roles required. Identify any and all your physical combative weaknesses and ensure you employ measures and put into progress undertakings to achieve your maximum physical and skills capabilities.

Psychological training advantages

Decent responsible citizens, being what they are, have a tendency to be reluctant to go combative or defend themselves unless there is no other option open to them. Bearing this in mind I have determined that when training combatants it is far better to instruct offensive unarmed assault first up.

Even if the individual is defensive by nature, introduction of unarmed offensive assault, and especially the most effective, safest and proven means of unarmed offensive assault first up, is a primary option of threat neutralization and is proactive with confidence and competency development.

Primary unarmed offensive assault instruction in relation to military CQC in the Todd System is based on the reality that the individual combatant may require the skills immediately after the current training session as part of their duties, and for civilians as part of self-defence. Not only is the subject order important but also that the skills of the subject are the primary most proven, most effective and safest options. The leg being longer than the arm and the boot being far more resilient than the hand ensures that long-range stamp kicks below the knee joint are the first instructed unarmed offensive assault option.

Once the individual combatant has selected and gained proficiency in their decided stamp kick option, close range unarmed offensive assault strikes are introduced.

The reality of a formidable enemy requires that close range unarmed offensive assault striking skills comprise of entry strikes to injure, distract, off-balance, incapacitate or eliminate, followed by finishing skills once the enemy is vulnerable.

Close range unarmed offensive assault combinations executed with entry strikes from side-on reduce target mass and the window of opportunity open to your enemy to counter engage you. However, once your enemy is adversely affected by your entry strikes from a side stance and guard position your transition to a front stance and guard combined with your finishing strikes or oblique stamp kick, executed in cohesive combination provide the proven means of threat neutralization.

Achievement of the competency level above an enabling level and working towards a combative level of achievement, the individual combatant would be instructed in a primary and secondary means of unarmed offensive assault.

The primary and secondary means of unarmed counter-offensive assault are evasive options to ensure that the combatant has the unarmed counter offensive assault employments capability in relation to the specific threat level of entry speed, range of execution, deception and commitment of the enemy.

The reasoning behind instructing the previous unarmed offensive assault primary options and unarmed counter-offensive assault primary options combined with the required stances, guards and footwork executed from the correct range is to ensure the individual combatants develop the mentality to end an encounter in 1 to 3 seconds; in other words achieve quick kills in military terms.

The only contingency option provided at this early level of training is the stalking contingency option to allow the combatant the contingency capability to neutralise the enemy if they attack during the stalking into range phase.

Counter-offensively, stationary unarmed counter-offensive assault is not introduced until a later stage so that the combatants will not get lazy and try and hold ground, meeting the enemy assault head-on, but will employ the considerably safer primary or secondary evasive unarmed counter-offensive assault options.

As soon as the combatants have gained proficiency in relation to the previous skills employments and required safety training aspects, they are a drilled in the employment of their chosen primary unarmed offensive and counter-offensive assault options with the objective of achieving immediate threat neutralization.

I have discovered over many years of instructing that to introduce multiple contingency options immediately or early in the entry-level exponent's training commonly reduces the level of controlled aggression and commitment applied to the execution of primary offensive or counteroffensive options. When human beings, being the decent responsible citizens that they are, have contingency options, often they will initiate less than fully mentally and physically committed skills employments out of a belief that if the objective is not achieved they have contingency capabilities.

The reality is anything less than 75 percent plus physical commitment and total psychological commitment may well lead to the individual combatant's defeat.

Later, when the contingency options in relation to threat and situation changes are introduced, the training ratios are approximately 90 percent primary unarmed offensive and counter-offensive assault options and 10percent contingency options applicable to failed primary option employment.

I believe after decades of involvement with training, observing and assessing combatants, that less is more in relation to providing contingency practices training. The order of instruction is also critical as first learnt skills, especially if there is a high emphasis on them being primary proven options, are best retained and utilised when they are most needed.

The employment of unarmed offensive assault and unarmed counter-offensive assault skills initially from a neutral stance is the preferred option, over stance and guard employed skills that tend to create more psychological and physical stress.

Obviously if compromised, a combined stance and guard may be essential; however, if uncompromised, maintaining a grey neutral status, being the unknown quantity, keeping the element of surprise on your side, and creating the factor of confusion when initiating your combative options from neutral is the preferred method.

Target identification consideration selection

I am not in favor of enemy or target de-humanization or desensitisation. For example considering the target to be unworthy of human existence, lower than a sewer rat, or totally responsible for mass death, disease and destruction or the like. I believe such hatred-inspired combative or self-defence evaluations can only interfere with controlled aggression and a combatant's ability to operate within the laws of the land and rules of engagement.

Equally, I instill in the combatants I train the advice that they should not concentrate on enemy specific features that may intimidate or distract them psychologically out of fear, or conversely, because they feel empathy for the enemy.

I instruct combatants to predominantly focus on the enemy bodily form and extremities in relation to outline, but lacking specific individual detail.

I also instruct the importance of employing not only target but also immediate environment sighting. This method of visual focus and scanning in the Todd Systems is referred to as point and place sighting. The target is the point and the immediate environment is the place.

Effectively you have 140 plus degrees of peripheral vision of the immediate surroundings and the enemy target will be included in this.

This is also an important point of sight and vision means for close personal protection, where you must be able to keep a visual on the principal, as well as vision of your immediate surroundings and any potential or actual threats.

Employing such maximum open visual awareness will reduce the chance of falling victim to tunnel vision on the threat only, or a single point of sight visual on one aspect of the situation or threat. It is very important that you never fall victim to target fixation only, as this will leave you unable to recognise additional threats or changes in threat.

Combative respiration is essential to ensure you maintain your vision and all senses at high alert. I employ in combative training methods of visual audio and deceptive distraction when a combatant is committed to executing combative actions in order to determine if they can identify the additional actions and distractions to the primary enemy threat. Most exponents that are unknowing subjects of these experiments are completely surprised at the important bigger picture aspects that they are unable to identify and as such recall. During the execution of an unarmed combative skill, for example, I will make changes to the immediate threat situation clearly inside their peripheral vision with the addition of one or more subjects, or have stationary subjects undertake suspicious or unusual actions. This includes verbiage as well as physical movements and actions, and the usual outcome is that the exponent fixated on the target with single point of sight vision is oblivious to the situation. A combination of single point visual fixation and holding one's breath not only can lead to tunnel vision and audio exclusion, but also a lack of recollection of not only the threat and situation but also the exponent's specific combative actions. Combine this with the dire effects of failing to respire combatively during the execution of unarmed combat skills and the exponent is performing dramatically below their optimum combative capabilities; as such they increase the risk and danger, as well as reducing the likelihood of safe quick and quiet combative objective achievement.

There is a high likelihood that a combatant that is holding their breath will have difficulty in identifying any distraction or additional threats and will fail to achieve the desired physical performance. In fact, holding their breath which is very apparent where their face looks like a knotted balloon, combined with a reddening of the face and an appearance that they are about to have a cranial explosion, is all descriptive of a lack of combative respiration. Employing a combative action without combative respiration and under a deprived respiration execution will decrease the effect of the power and velocity considerably, and a secondary employed physical skill with deprived respiration or after a skill executed with deprived respiration will additionally decrease the effect of that action considerably. If the encounter requires continued combative actions, the combatant will have difficulty in respiration, may hyperventilate and as a result will physically and psychologically decrease their capability. I have measured combatants' combative actions when withholding their breath against their combative respiratory, correctly executed options, and the difference in power and velocity has been up to 40percent, with additional non-combative respiratory executed actions dropping their output in power and velocity by as much as 60percent. Combine this with an inability to visually detect additional threats or dangers including situational changes as well as audio exclusion reducing or eliminating the ability to hear warnings, orders or instructions, and this is a dangerous practice.

When not breathing properly, the ability to adjust is also compromised. This in turn affects balance and stability, and being unable to think clearly affects assessment and decision making in real time as well as post encounter recollection. Throughout the brain-to-boot package you will note that combative respiration is the most important practice in relation to combative requirements in the sense it is the first required combative component in an expected actions-on situation and immediately when engaged in an unexpected actions-on situation. It is not only the first required action, but it must be maintained and employed with the execution of every combative skill, no matter how minor or major, to ensure you can achieve committed high-performance outputs for an extended period of time when up against a formidable enemy.

So immediately when going tactical or combative, respire and continue to do so until the threat is neutralised to ensure you are at your combative best psychologically and physically. Combative smarts starts with respiration.

Personal Checklists

Working from the top of your head to the soles of your feet, evaluate the following physical bodily strengths and weaknesses, rating them as follows:

5 = Excellent

4 = Above average

3 = Average

2 = Below average

1 = Poor.

Consider every strength and weakness giving an overall rating; for example, hair (could it be seized and used to contain you in close quarters unarmed combat?) or shoulders (are they strong and developed for clinching and striking, or through an injury to the AC joint and scar tissue, is one shoulder restricted and/or painful thus reducing performance?).

The following checklists include your body, your skills and your mind. You need to think carefully as well as thinking outside the circle in relation to your bodily strengths and weaknesses and how any weaknesses could be exploited by a formidable foe. Your bodily parts should be rated in relation to their condition strengths and weaknesses. Any bodily part that rates below 4 will require careful consideration as to how you can improve the rating, if possible. This may require talking to your health professionals in relation to medical treatments. Physiotherapy or surgery may be required and you need to speak to your doctor to determine this. If the problem cannot be fixed, then you need to look at your tactics and skills to reduce risk and improve safety to the affected bodily part.

Evaluate your skills and rate each skill category honestly. Remember do not hope or wish your current skills to work, but rather evaluate them and physically test them in realistic situations against formidable training threats to destruction.

Don't let blind loyalty or stupidity determine your accepting of skills capabilities if there are safer and more effective options.

Seek advice from experts in relation to specific threats and your best means of neutralising them to determine if your capabilities are in fact safe proven and effective. If you require up skilling to be able to safely and effectively neutralise any threat with the most current and proven methods then it's a no-brainer and you should do so. Your combative and self-protection skills are a very personal thing in relation to fitting with your psychological and physical capabilities. Never settle for anything less than the best when it comes to protecting yourself or your loved ones. If you need to up skill then do so.

Your mind helps in relation to identifying recognising and facing wide ranging threats. Work through the checklist carefully, being honest with yourself in relation to the listed threats. In your mind's eye envision the listed threats and variations of them under different conditions including the dark of night and be honest with yourself in relation to what effects such threats would have on you. Rate your capabilities in relation to being able to effectively deal with such threats including being prepared and willing to neutralise them. Threat categories that rate below four will require careful gradual inoculation training in order for you to effectively become familiar with coping with and dealing with such threats.

By introducing low intensity slow speed small doses of the threat stimuli and ensuring your threat neutralisation capabilities are far superior to the threat stimuli gradually build up confidence to neutralise the threat in relation to the threat and the threat specifics.

Be aware that psychological effects in relation to threat may be a result of physical bodily weaknesses or a lack of confidence in skills. Skills weaknesses where you do not have confidence in your skills under sudden aggressive violent shock actions against a formidable foe will certainly weaken you psychologically. A lack of physical capabilities would certainly affect your combative capabilities to neutralise threats and as such psychologically weaken your resolve.

Make sure body, skills and mind checklists are answered honestly and that the required actions are taken including seeking professional assistance to ensure any weaknesses are addressed and your body, skills and mind are improved to the highest level personally possible.

My Body

Body Part	Rating	Body Part	Rating
Hair		Knuckles	
Skull		Fingers	
Brain		Heart	
Jaw		Lungs	
Teeth		Kidneys	
Ears		Spleen	
Eyes		Liver	
Chin		Bladder	
Cheekbone		Abdomen	
Throat/Airway		Genitals	
Neck		Hips/Pelvis	
Side of neck		Thighs	
Clavicle		Knee joints	
Sternum		Shins	
Ribs		Calves	
Spine		Achilles	
Shoulders		Instep	
Biceps and Triceps		Toes	
Elbow joints		Heel	
Forearms		Sole of the foot	
Wrists		Any nerve damage	
Hands			

Log any medical conditions and prior injuries that may affect your combative capability.

My Skills

Now to physical combative skills that need to also be assessed.

Select the skills you need and evaluate your competency.

Skills possessed	Rating
Unarmed offensive assault	
Unarmed counter-offensive assault	
Stance	
Guard	
Cover guard and deflection	
Seizure, clinch, grab and hold prevention	
Grab and hold escapes	
Edged weapon disarming	
Long weapon disarming	
Combat multiple armed and unarmed attackers	
Point-blank range firearm disarming	
Military ground combat	
Knife combatives	
Improvised weapons	
Combat aimed and point shooting	
Riot breaking/ Crowd control, Crowd Combat	
Sentry take-outs	
Detainee handling	
Weapon Retention	
Canine Neutralisation	
Ambush/Mugging Threat Neutralisation	

Now compile your list of areas you need to improve or focus on and decide on your plan to achieve this. This may require medical expertise, physical training or skills training.

If you are really honest with yourself with this identification process, you will by now have identified your requirements and the lengths and extents you need to go to so you can improve skills and performance.

Sometimes through age or injury it's a matter of changing your skills to suit your condition and abilities, and there are no better options than the best of dirty tricks brigade battle-proven practices to reduce the physical requirements.

The previous findings will identify your needs and you can employ a plan to achieve this.

Now that you have established what you require to work on physically to ensure you are best prepared in relation to your physical attributes capabilities and requirements, it's time to identify your psychological strengths and weaknesses.

My Mind

Following are some of the common stimuli of suspicious and sudden aggressive shock action that through prior contact and familiarity will activate the human automated reactions to such stimulus. Rate the following in relation to your fears; 5 minimum, 4 minor, 3 major, 2 extreme, 1 terrifying.

	Rating
Aggressors of different nationalities	
Gangsters	
Individuals reputations	
Physical attributes	
Physical size	
Dress and foot wear	
Multiple assailants	
Being unable to see an aggressors hands	
Canine threats	

edged weapons	
Opposite gender threats	
Kicks	
Punches	
Grappling	
Wrestling	
Strangles and chokes	
Bear hugs	
Throws	
Ground fighting	
Throat attacks	
Facial contact	
Unarmed mugging	
Armed mugging	
Threatening verbiage	
Verbal profanities	
Threatening gestures	
Suspicious approaches	
Aggressive demeanors	
War cry	
Flash of aggressive action	
Firearms	
Gleam of stainless steel	
Muzzle flash	
Firearms cocking action	
The dark of night	
Confined spaces	
Biting	
Eye gouging	
Head-butting	
Kneeing	
Genitals attacks	

While the reaction may be automatic and spontaneous in relation to human beings, generally the earliest recognition and decision making in relation to the threat post automatic reactionary response will reduce reaction time and ensure the most immediate response is employed. While prior exposure to the sounds and sensations related to common threats may not be honed to the point that the exact weapon or threat could be identified, it certainly would identify the category of threat and other important information such as enemy location and direction of the threat.

Some stand out: Explosions, gunfire, running footsteps and the subtle sounds of stalking footwork, the sound of foot contact with the terrain, the sound of vehicles including the screech of brakes.

More subtle discrete sounds relating to the setup or execution of unarmed combat skills, employment of non-ballistic weapons include the sound of a lunge, release of the safety catch or the drawing, cocking, loading or reloading of a weapon.

The sound of heavy breathing includes the exhaling associated with boxing or fighting. The war cry is a definite indicator of immediate danger and through prior knowledge of this the combatant's initial response and continued actions will ensure the best combative chance.

Visual stimuli including a shadow, reflection, a flash of aggressive colour, action or movement, muzzle flash or gleam of stainless steel.

The individual combatant's sense of smell is not useful in an immediate actions-on situation but you can identify close imminent threats by scent at close quarters. These include tobacco, perspiration, chemicals, fuels etc.

Once you have developed your combative skills and principles, individually and in combination, you should practice with the factor of confusion ever present and with the element of surprise at its highest possible level.

Begin with stands where the factor of confusion and element of surprise is low to moderate, and progress to battle handling exercises where the factor of confusion is high.

Never try and change natural human reaction to sudden shock aggressive action with techniques that oppose natural human reaction to an actions-on situation.

If you are practicing techniques that are based on traditional or sporting codes that have been developed around a definite requirement such as ring fighting, mat sports, or full contact martial arts, where the opponents' techniques are no surprise and the conditions have been formulated around the competitors' safety, then you are not practicing battle-proven primary combative options under battlefield conditions. The fear and stress of what an enemy can subject you to and inflict on you is only one side of the combative psychological coin. The other is the reality that you may have to employ deadly force against your enemy.

You may have to do the unthinkable, operate under ruthless, controlled aggression and execute options that will for that moment in time see you operate outside the boundaries of a normal civilised human being. Such terminal and fatal actions will only be employed as a must and in the execution of one's duties. The effects of deadly force must never be taken lightly and the psychological consequences of the use of deadly force must be well understood.

The professional combatant must be able to assess the situation, decide on the best and proper action and employ it with total control, commitment and aggression, increasing the levels of commitment and aggression when required and then decreasing the levels and returning to a normal civilized human state just as quickly. Not just anyone can for a moment in time, in a controlled calculated manner be completely ruthless. It takes a very special individual to undertake such actions in a controlled manner and not only return to civilized reality but also deal with the consequences of the actions for the rest of their life.

Once you have identified your physical capabilities and weaknesses and attended to improving your physical capabilities you must now evaluate your psychological strengths and weaknesses.

Before you do, however, in your mind's eye choose a specific enemy combatant based on physical size and abilities as well as their specific combative or fighting style or system. Now in your mind's eye practice your imaginary assessment of the combatant and situation, and decide on a plan to neutralise your enemy based on your rules of engagement, SOPs, laws of self-defence and your beliefs, morals and principles. Use your powers of imagination to combat your enemy, covering every possibility, from achieving your objective immediately according to plan, through to every possible scenario and the employment of every contingency option. Once you have exhausted all your situational and threat-related changes then select a new enemy threat and start again.

This is a positive process to ensure you can effectively assess, decide and execute primary combative options and may well self-identify your levels of skills capabilities that require up skilling if you are brutally honest with yourself. You need to take a look at yourself and be brutally truthful in your evaluation of yourself. Get a notebook and write down the honest facts.

Based on your lifetime experiences ask yourself honestly what your reactions and responses as well as actions have been in high-stress situations previously. What are your pain thresholds and reactions and responses to environmental conditions such as the dark of night or the extremes of heat or freezing cold? Do not restrict your evaluation to that of only threats of physical violence but also any stress or fear situations you may have encountered

If you are ruthlessly honest with yourself you will identify general enemy assailant types that you fear most or more than others. You must also identify other enemy derived factors that psychologically affect you such as race, appearance, and reputation.

An individual's association with or affiliation to extreme organizations, or elements of society, are also factors that may psychologically affect you. Specific weapons threats can also create more fear or stress than others and also different environments, places, times of day or night.

The next stage of your psychological evaluation is to identify the physical effects related to psychological stress you experience as a result of one or more of the previous factors. These factors are not restricted to only the individual themselves and their appearance and reputation but also identified additional threats or weapons. While you may not overly fear an individual that is unarmed, with the reality of a presented or perceived weapon your stress levels may well be increased considerably and your fear of injury or death a reality. Dangerous situations and thoughts of personal risk or injury, as well as objects and weapons, are all triggers that can cause physical reactions through psychological stress.

Chattering teeth, trembling thighs, hands and arms, sweaty palms, abdominal butterflies, increased heart rate, a feeling of physical weakness or freezing in position, and breathing difficulties are all physical reactions and realities of stress and fear. I consider any of these physical reactions as a positive and not a negative as they are a very real warning sign of the impending or immediate danger you are in.

Too much of anything can be dangerous; so too the warnings of stress and fear. Immediately upon being affected by such symptoms of fear and stress, you must address them, keeping them in check and eliminating the physical effect on you. Doing so means that you do not find yourself overcome by these effects and unable to engage your enemy or escape and evade effectively. The moment you either identify any risk or are affected by the effects of the situation, you need to be proactive in not only stopping or reducing such effects but also by employing sound principles of assessment and hard targeting.

Control your breathing, which will reduce your heart rate and reduce the physical effects of stress and fear. This is your first priority. Through prior training, practice and preparation for such effects of high stress and fear you will quickly identify the symptoms and employ controlled breathing to quickly reduce and eliminate the effects.

Breathe in through your nose and out through your mouth in a low intensity full and uninterrupted respiration cycle. Anticipation and perception are dangerous and you should never allow your mind to wander into the realm of perceived threats or the anticipation of an expected type of attack. Time and distance being on your side, always assess and decide on the facts of the threat and situation.

If you find yourself in an actions-on situation without prior knowledge or warning then you must rely on your initial reaction to sudden shock action. You will react initially to flashes of aggressive sound, colour and movement, but as soon as you have subconsciously reacted to the first onslaught, you must begin employing your skills, tactics and procedures to make yourself safe and take control of the situation. Starting with CQC respiration and hard cover guarding.

'Fast mapping' is a Todd Systems term for assessing on the move and deciding and employing skills to achieve your objective. When fast mapping you must rely on and maintain all your physical senses to ensure you can detect and counter or combat any threat or change in threat or situation in an instant, on the move. You must also be correct at the end of any entry, retreat or evasive footwork movement, to avoid being caught mid-flight or left in a stretched stance with a lack of immediate mobility.

Never allow your senses to become overloaded or locked onto one specific threat or aspect or get into a take-on mentality; always think 'take out'. Tunnel vision or audio exclusion are realities of high-stress situations where the individual combatant has allowed the situation or the actual or considered threat to occupy all their attention to the point where they can no longer focus on or hear additional threats or factors that may be the difference between life and death.

If you allow yourself to be overwhelmed or lose control through an out of control or overzealous get even, get after, take-on mentality, you may well enter the less than ready and less than tactically alert zone you need to maintain to be the best combatant you can be.

Combative fitness.

Fighters require a high level of physical fitness specific to their combat sports requirements. We all know that being physically fit is an advantage in any situation where you require strength speed, power, velocity and endurance. Dirty and deadly CQC requires less of this, but still does require CQC physical capabilities specific to skills execution employment requirements and being able to withstand the rigors of close quarters encounters.

Against a physically formidable enemy threat, a trained combatant employing dirty and deadly CQC or MSD options will still need to be able to maintain position, make range and adjustments, as well as hard target themselves and execute their dirty and deadly options to neutralise the threat.

As an exponent I was taught that combat sports at a peak performance level are for young athletes in top condition; however the best of battle-proven dirty tricks brigade military self-defence and close combat are for life as they provide the best chance to neutralise a formidable determined foe. I have seen many individuals with considerably higher levels of physical capabilities defeated by means of dirty fighting that knows no rules.

Having a controlled aggressive demeanor and high level of intestinal fortitude combined with skills that prey on your enemy's most vulnerable delicate vitals can stop the most physically capable in their tracks. Battle proven skills that require less physical capabilities are certainly a primary means of destroying your aggressor's physical prowess and taking their superior physical capabilities out of the equation. If your practices arc dirty or deadly military combative means of enemy destruction then your chances of winning are increased.

Being proficient in dirty and deadly military CQC and MSD methods of human destruction capable of formidable foe neutralisation will also psychologically increase your resolve and confidence in achieving your objective.

Soft, Medium and Hard Footing

'Soft footing' versus 'medium footing' and 'hard footing' refers to your ground affinity in relation to your state of readiness. It can be further broken down to describe the limbs and joints of your body in relation to their non-physical skills employment resting status, and when they are made ready and set to go, as well as the go status in relation to expedient and resistance requirements in actions-on executions.

Soft to medium footing, toes and heels marginally off the ground

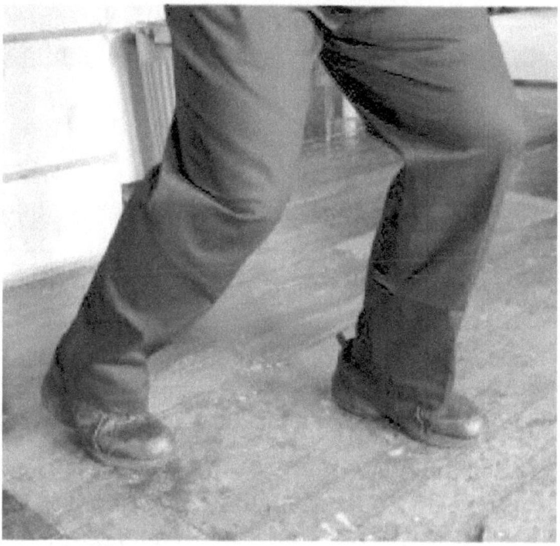

Front foot flat full resistance, knee over toes. Rear foot heel off the ground ball of foot pushing forward

Soft footing or soft boots refers to a non-CQC footing rested easy footing status.

Medium footing or medium boots refers to a controlled CQC ready status being set and maintained as well as the execution of committed footwork and skills employments executed under negative resistance.

Hard footing, hard boots refers to high level forced expedient action and enemy resistance requirements in combative actions-on encounters.

Hard, medium and soft footing and the same bodily terminology applies to many bodily parts in relation to combative skills employments as part of skills execution and objective achievement requirements. Soft, medium or hard footing and bodily parts and functions levels provide capabilities ranging from a rest status to expedient ground cover and fast fluid skills executions through to CQC high resistance situations capabilities requirements. Such terminology and principles are very important to meet actions-on requirements and are checked in CQC TOETs to ensure every component of the required action to maximise capabilities is utilised correctly. In order to achieve an execution of a combative skill that is as close as humanly possible to correct, giving you the maximum chance of threat neutralisation, being able to transition from a soft through hard status, maximising safety and destructive capabilities is essential.

For example, angling of the right hand to 10 o'clock with the fingers and thumb locked in against the palm, and with the left hand employing the same practices with the hand pointing to 2 o'clock, will reduce the risk of injury during flat hand status palm heel strikes by correct hard hand and arm execution, which in turn increases the chance of objective achievement.

Soft-hard-soft striking by initiating the striking action at between a soft to medium status on outward extension, and immediately before and on contact is made, ensuring the hand and arm is in a hard status followed by post contact soft to medium status retraction of the hand and arm ensures speed of execution, extension and retraction as well as increased safety.

Confidence is increased when you know that your speed of execution is at your maximum and that your involved extremities are as safe as is possible, reducing the risk of execution injury.

Stamp kicks are another example of the need for changing from a soft boot pre-combative actions-on status through a medium expedient action entry status to a hard boot and hard leg stamp kick employment status.

Hard status stamp kick executions also require the alignment of the foot and ankle, shin and knee joints to achieve maximum safety and destructive velocity force transferred from the head through the body and hips down the leg to the sole of the boot with the arch of the boot encapsulating the shin below the knee joint.

Like the alignment of the hand to reduce the risk of injuries during palm heel strikes, and the slight upward rotation of the side of the heel of the palm for flat hand edge strikes to reduce the risk of injury to the bones of the little finger, so too does the foot need to be directly aligned to the fibula and tibia for the execution of powerful destructive stamp kicks.

Under the previous and wide ranging CQC skills employments not only does the body need to be target aligned but also skills executions need to be initiated soft through hard to increase safety and ensure your best combative chances of threat neutralisation.

In the execution of oblique kicks, pivoting towards the oblique stamp kicking leg will align you to the target ensuring maximum destructive velocity can be achieved. Having your wheels and chassis aligned to the target is essential to enhance performance destructive physical capabilities and reduce the risk of injury.

Pivoting footwork is the best footwork to achieve static target alignment and footwork transitions, it provides increased safety and performance, and as such, increased chance of objective achievement.

Pivoting footwork enables maintaining footing ground contact at all times and is important for maintaining balance and stability.

Understanding the advantages of hard and soft anatomy aspects in relation to combative executions will increase confidence and mental toughness, and the capability to execute skills without the fear of bodily self-resistance or self-injury.

Skills employments executed at the correct soft, medium or hard status and under primary target alignment not only increase threat neutralisation chances but will feel right and are confidence boosting.

The term hard boot, hard ankle and hard knee also apply to training, practicing, battle handling exercises, combative stands and combative testing by increasing rigidity and resistance to reduce risk and increase safety.

The Todd System employs putdowns under training and test conditions that require a change for the enemy per target of the put down, from soft or medium status to a medium hard status, combined with enemy per cooperation to reduce the risk of injury. This will provide a realistic outcome in relation to the execution of the same skill as if employed in a real life destructive combative level execution. The same putdown practices can be utilised in situations where the nature of the threat or situation requires an option where the integrity of the subject's limbs are not deliberately compromised as in security or law enforcement subject handling.

Having an understanding of human anatomy and body mechanics in relation to CQC and MSD is another means of increasing mental confidence. When you know how to make yourself safer and more combative capable, as well as knowing that your skills will neutralise the most formidable enemy if properly employed, then you will be psychologically prepared to commit fully to the execution of your decided skills.

Tactical psychological practices

Psychological methods of increasing one's inner resolve and methods of self-reassurance to maintain one's maximum levels of readiness and preparedness to counter or combat enemy threats is just one type of combative psychological practice.

Another important psychological combative practice is utilising methods to weaken an enemy's psychological preparedness to engage you.

Having an understanding of how to create self-doubt, concern, fear and as a result, hesitation, in decision making or a change of mind, can prevent a physical actions-on encounter moving beyond a threatening situation. There are many practices that if employed in the right circumstances and situation against a less than fully confident and committed enemy can neutralise the threat before it turns physical.

Understanding how to use deception, a state of readiness, or how to maintain a grey neutral status can all psychologically affect an enemy's ability to initiate an actions-on against you. Likewise, in some situations, a show of confidence, force, intimidation or aggression can be utilised to weaken an enemy's resolve and convince them they have confronted a far more formidable adversary than they first considered. Employing methods of intimidation or aggression can escalate the threat level and lead to an immediate actions-on encounter.

Such practices require an understanding of reading signs of fear in one's enemy and exploiting such weaknesses to end an encounter before it starts, or to cause confusion, fear, stress and reconsideration. Such psychological tactics can weaken your enemy's resolve, affect their intestinal fortitude to go combative, and psychologically demoralize them to the state of looking for an out option, even though they were the aggressor. In reality, they have been affected by their psychological weaknesses to the point where self-doubt in their capabilities to defeat an enemy who was initially considered 'easy' has overcome them. The hunted has now become the hunter, and a superior psychological capability, combined with sound tactics and skills have exposed the initial aggressor's weaknesses, reversing the roles. Posturing, especially in a formidable stance and guard, remaining combatively focused on your enemy, presenting and constantly conveying a ready, controlled, aggressive capability can, against a less than formidable enemy combatant weaken their intestinal fortitude and inner resolve, and ultimately take the fight out of them or make them more exposed and vulnerable to your combative actions.

One has to be careful utilising such a definite show of combative willingness and confidence and the degree of such a show of willingness if the intention is to neutralise the threat without going physically combative, as even a bully-coward once convinced they are cornered, may lash out. In this case, an actions-on encounter will be initiated and leave you no option but to counter engage. Usually prior to any physical actions-on kicking off, maintaining a neutral status is the best and a tactically correct practice to maintain the element of surprise and increase the chance of preventing an actions-on encounter, through maintaining a grey status and as such being the unknown quantity you can weaken your enemy's inner resolve.

If uncompromised, maintaining a neutral stance and status is far better than initiating a combative stance and guard, where you lose the element of surprise. In addition, maintaining a combative stance and guard increases the physical stress and tension pre-actions-on.

In unarmed counter-offensive assault, for evasive counter engagement breaking a 2 meter reactionary distance between your enemy and you, and maintaining a neutral stance non-guard status will stand to cause your enemy to be unsure of your intentions and capabilities. Remaining centered to your enemy, preventing them from being able to exploit your sides and rear flank, will not only present you as a grey neutral subject but will also imply a state of readiness and an unknown quantity in relation to your combative capabilities.

One of the biggest fears in a combative encounter is the unknown nature and quantity of one's enemy. Presenting yourself in a neutral grey status, maintaining a safe reactionary range while continuously remaining centered to your enemy as well as maintaining verbal silence can psychologically weaken your enemy's willingness to cover ground and engage you out of fear of the unknown, and knowledge of the known, in regards to their own psychological weaknesses.

Maintaining combative operational silence is very important, especially if you want to prevent the threat from materialising by means of utilising a grey but ready status. Verbiage slows your decision making down, if, while going verbal you are engaged and have to make decisions and employ combat or counter measures against an enemy that has already targeted you. Your pre-decided actions executions are also less immediate when you have to break verbiage and go combative.

This is one of the dangers for law enforcement and security operators as part of their duties when they must verbally warn, caution, or interview suspects. If the suspect attacks them mid-sentence or while taking down details, they are forced to go defensive or counter-offensive. Such duties should be performed employing every proven tactical option and advantage to reduce the likelihood of being engaged unexpectedly.

Reactionary distance utilising angle, barriers or objects to make direct line engagement difficult or impossible are but some such recommended tactics. Looking one's enemy in the eyes when confronted, while maintaining a tactically correct reactionary distance and a neutral stance and status, combined with operational silence, is a definite means of promoting oneself as confident and ready. Maintaining such a status and not reacting to verbal threat, no matter how intimidating or offensive that verbiage is, just causes more self-doubt in your enemy who is trying to weaken your resolve or cause you to react adversely to their comment.

You must remember in civilian self-defense that if you hear comments like 'you're a coward, wimp' or the like, then you have psyched your aggressor out by means of the fear of the unknown. By presenting yourself as a neutral but also a ready unknown quantity you are simply not an easy target to engage.

You must remember that utilising such a grey ready status requires constant awareness, all your senses at high alert, and a definite plan. You also need proficiency in the employment of fast mapping contingency options if needed to neutralise unpredictable actions or changes in threat or situation.

Use the brain-to-boot major principles of combative respiration, combative sighting, heightened awareness, maintaining a positive ground affinity, combined with mind's eye, self-reassurance, and your combative capabilities will be enhanced. Your brain-to-boot minor components are also very important to maximizing your combative capabilities. They are often simultaneously executed with your primary components, and if minor components increases or decreases are required, real time adjustments can be made. You are staying ready and maintaining a high state of constant vigilance, continuously checking your state of readiness, as well as remaining confident in your combative capabilities to neutralise any actions-on encounter that may materialize. Then, through inner resolve, sound tactics, confidence and skills competency you will stand to prevent an encounter eventuating, or if it does you will be best ready prepared and willing to combat or counter such a threat.

Unexpected actions-on

In all immediate unexpected actions-on encounters, or reduced ready status preparation time frame encounters, generally the very first reactionary responses will be dictated by autonomic reactionary reactions to the shock or surprise, and/or first enemy contact, and these reactionary responses will be initiated out of immediate autonomic self-preservation.

In unexpected actions-on encounters, autonomic self-preservation reactive responses must be immediately followed by CQC respiration, or deliberate self-protective hard cover guarding and simultaneous CQC respiration if under assault, real time threat assessment and the execution of decided, deliberate combat or counter engagement measures. Reduced or no immediate situational assessment time may require post hard cover and combative respiration initiation, fast mapping assessment on the move, or, from a static reduced target mass, increased stability cover guard positioning.

Unexpected actions-on encounters depending on the surprise shock action and contact levels may also cause involuntary disengagement moving you out of the contact kill zone. This can be followed by a continuation, deliberate evasion out of or off the initial contact kill zone, or by deliberate closing in on close to point-blank body contact range in relation to fast map decided threat neutralisation options set ups.

The autonomic reaction of flinching has commonality with the combative CQC squat, and the trained combatant that employs the CQC squat ensures they are in a natural ready-set-go status to evade escape or go combative.

In some combative or dire self-defence situations, through low to no light or restricted or prevented visual capabilities, you will be required to use your sense of touch to increase safety, and locate bodily targets. Time, risk, threat and situational factors will greatly dictate your order and means of execution in an actions-on encounter post hard targeting. This will be combined with your combative respiration to ensure a primary CQC employment status is initiated and maintained in the execution of your primary combat or counter engagement skills employments.

Post respiration and hard targeting, multiple components must be employed without compromising stability or losing momentum, and must include skills cohesion to reduce execution breakdown through hesitation, stalling or a lack of components commonality and compatibility.

The military close quarters combat we instruct provides to a great extent single, simple, safe and as effective-as-it-gets principles to combat or counter entire specific threat categories.

This reduces hesitation and confusion in decision making and enables quick definite threat neutralization.

An example is that against any insecure hold or seizure by turning side on and raising your side cover guard, you narrow the window of target opportunity to your aggressor or enemy, increase the difficulty in them maintaining a dominant hold on you, and put yourself in a position where you can counter engage, break their grip and counter engage or seize and secure your aggressor or enemy and counter engage.

Your primary first human sense to be utilised is usually vision, and when you turn your combative vision on your sense of hearing, smell and touch are automatically turned on, as well to varying degrees in relation to the specific threat situation and post decision making counter threat requirements.

While other senses may not be engaged and utilised to as high a degree as your vision, they are certainly active and can be turned up if required to identify or monitor specific threats or threat characteristics, aiding in maintaining a state of combative alertness and readiness.

In an impending expected situation, after being confronted or becoming aware of a probable threat situation of extreme violence, and immediately having to deal with your initial autonomic human reactions as well as fears and concerns, you will need to reduce immediate risk by making yourself a hard target, threat assess, counter or combat option decide set up and execute your decided option.

Being familiar with sounds and any other means, your foe may compromise themselves by including moving in on their target covertly or an overt assault entry, and in an armed threat, making a weapon ready enables general threat recognition or specific threat identification, and when combined with heightened senses of awareness provides increased time and distance to go combative.

Maintaining a ready, willing and able status as well as being alert, aware and familiar with threat characteristics increases the chance of early threat recognition before any actions-on can be initiated. As such, this provides increased combat and counter opportunities and increased safety.

A subject that is not considered a threat or not an immediate threat by his appearance, actions or demeanor but is within the threat zone, or close to the threat zone, needs to be included in your place sighting along with the point sighting which is the primary threat.

Proven hard targeting tactics including maintaining safe counter engagement range, utilising solid back drops to protect your rear flanks, or keeping a line of escape open depending on situation will make you a more difficult target and psychologically stronger. Utilising angles that require the enemy to turn and cover ground, before they can attack provides increased time to identify the assault and neutralise it.

The requirement to support and enhance such tactics is belief in the capabilities they provide and self-belief. Tactics and skills without physical competency and employment commitment as well as psychological confidence, inner resolve and intestinal fortitude are like an unloaded weapon. Employing sound, hard target tactics will provide increased advantages to identify, fast map, assess and execute skills to neutralise dire threats initiated by a subject not considered a threat or not an immediate threat. Hard target, ready for anything and everything tactics enable you to identify covert or overt danger zone advances, as well as cunning masked actions under entry or discreet advancement. You can then neutralise threats by real time assessment and decision making based on prior training in threat recognition, hard targeting and deliberate threat neutralisation.

A covert calculated approach when you are distracted by a primary enemy threat, or a sudden aggressive entry unarmed assault, as well as a masked or concealed weapon being drawn immediately prior to or under entry will not only be detected as a threat but the specific threat can be determined. I reiterate, being familiar with armed and unarmed threat employment characteristics combined with hard targeting tactics and keeping all your senses at high alert will provide high level advantages in threat neutralisation. The shape and black colour of a hand gun, or the shape and gleam of a stainless steel blade can be easily identified under immediate actions-on threat initiation if you remain ready, alert and aware.

In a low to medium risk environment, a nuisance threat raises the threat level by making a grab attempt at you or your weapon. You should be hard targeting yourself in relation to prevention of weapon seizure, but if compromised and your un-drawn weapon is seized, retaining the weapon and neutralising the threat is vital as well as regention, that is regaining control of a seized drawn weapon and threat neutralising.

All these tactics and skills are made possible and more effective by preventative hard targeting tactics, realistic primary and emergency skills employments that have been practiced and perfected as much as is humanly possible in training, and mental conviction in your skills and your personal combative capabilities.

Having definite principles and deliberate skills that are battle proven and importantly can be adjusted to the specific threat characteristics in a threat situation or actions-on encounter at real time arm you with the required capabilities to best neutralise the most formidable of threats.

In multiple foes assaults, having primary proven yet adjustable skills that are easily decided under fast mapping threat assessment, provides maximum economy of time utilisation, removes skills selection confusion in decision making, and gives you the best combative chance of threat neutralisation. Under such a threat you can cause multiple enemy pers confusion and hesitation when you have a set principle based primary deliberate means of the specific threat neutralisation where you only have to think for yourself but your multiple aggressors have to consider each other's intentions and actions.

I leant in my early days of training with Harry Baldock that your tactics and skills must prepare and provide you with the required capabilities to neutralise specific threats by specific means that are principle based and allow for adjustment.

The military CQC expansive capability under wide ranging threat categories of having primary, secondary, alternate and emergency principle based skills truly provides wide ranging capabilities, and provides best and most applicable means of specific threat neutralisation.

Having such hard targeting tactics to increase safety, provide factual, real time, threat assessment and decision making, and enable expedient decided skills employments to combat or counter threat categories, as well the widest range of specific threats included in such threat categories is empowering physically and psychologically.

If you know how to set a ready status when under assault and how to neutralise such threats by means of combative competency in tactics and skills, and you combine this with psychological combative capabilities, then you have your best combative chance of threat neutralisation. Combine this with dirty tricks deception, as well as set up and skills initiation practices that interfere with human line and point of vision and mental focus, as well as provide expedient combative action, and your combative chances of threat neutralisation are maximised.

Ask yourself if you have the best tactics and skills and are mentally tough enough to utilise them to neutralise formidable foes bent on causing your grievous bodily harm. Read and be honest with yourself in regards to being confident and competent to neutralise the threats below:

* You are stunned by unexpected contact to the back of your head or an unseen punch to your jaw.

* An unexpected rear choke employed with force and increased pressure with every millisecond.

* In darkness in a bad place, you hear a suspicious sound emanating from your rear flanks.

* Blunt force trauma: a king hit from your side flank. You are down but not out.

* You are pounced upon and, out of self-preservation, are struggling to maintain your footing while your aggressor is pushing, pulling and lifting you with all his might.

* Your first sensation is that of a ligature around your throat from behind, and it is tightening as you are being pulled backward and downward.

* You are rushed from behind cover, and engaged in unarmed combat by an enemy that has the advantage of sudden shock action and momentum.

* At close quarters, after you have been stunned with strikes, your unarmed enemy clinches with you and attempts a take down.

* Under unarmed assault, while secured in the grapple, your aggressor pulls a knife on you.

* In a close quarters clinch you find yourself falling to the ground with your enemy.

* In an ambush or mugging the first thing you know is that you are being held at weapon point or edge.

* You are encircled by 6 or more aggressors.

* You have been knocked to the ground and several aggressors are stomping and kicking you.

To effectively neutralise such threats and many more, you must be trained in primary, proven practices, believe in yourself and your tactics and skills, and know how to adjust to the threat specifics and environment in real time. The brain-to-boot package provides the physical tactics, and psychological enhancement capabilities to effectively and safely increase your chances of threat neutralisation if your skills are the best of battle proven.

TRAINING SECTION

Training exercises

KISS: Keep it simple stupid

KISS; Keep it simple stupid was a common saying of my mentor the late great Col Rex Applegate, and is something I firmly believe in, in relation to CQC and MSD. The higher the stress level, the lower the skill level, and lesser the response time to the threat and as such the need for simple proven gross motor skills.

While true battle-proven military CQC, MSD and CQB may not be exact sciences they certainly are military sciences comprising of primary, secondary, alternative and emergency methods to achieve the objective.

The combatant mindset is critical in relation to enemy threat neutralisation and objective achievement. Train the way you intend to go combative to either combat or counter enemy threats—the military combative way. This means exponents must be able to use their combative smarts to evaluate specific situations and decide on the best tactics, principles and skills to achieve the objective of threat neutralisation.

They must enter into combative learning, training and practicing with genuine realist commitment and resolve to achieve their best possible combative capabilities. All too often in this modern era of perceived easy ways to achieve everything, individuals pay minimum attention to detail, minimum effort paper hounds, rather than realists committed to being the best combatant they can be; They need to evaluate teachings, confirming that they are the best options for the requirement, and put in committed high-repetition practice along with high-intensity battle handling exercises practice.

Many believe practicing a skill only several times equates to proficiency, but nothing is further from the truth. Often the instructor has barely got through giving the method of introducing a skill the military combative way of 'State, Explain, Demonstrate, Questions, Safety brief, Practice' and before the go to is given they are met with 'I already know that one' or after as little as one practice repetition you hear 'finished'. The assessment of their weak flawed attempts proves as much about the individual's attention to detail, perseverance and commitment as it does identify their pathetic show of the skill execution.

It takes thousands if not tens of thousands of repetitions to achieve a high level of proficiency of an individual skill and as such competency. Mastering skills takes considerably longer and requires the practice of employment of skills in wide, vast threat situations and encounters to ensure every aspect of the skill set up and employment follow-through, and the individual skills contingency options can be decided on the move in real time without hesitation or a break in confidence when executed under threat.

In combative training there are several ways of practicing individual combative skills and they include the following.

Shadow training

Shadow training is the practice of skills without any physical target, under controlled execution conditions with less than full extended limbs to avoid unnecessary ligament, tendon or joint injuries.

The individual skills execution during shadow training can be from slow speed, low intensity at an initial enabling level, and building up to high speed committed intensity once competent.

Shadow training can be used to practice wide ranging CQC and MSD tactics and skills statically or on the move silently, or walking and talking your way through such practice.

Low intensity slow speed shadow training practice is an excellent way to familiarise yourself with tactics and skills employments developing skills competency and proficiency.

You can give yourself silent mind's eye threat identification and recognition warnings or spoken word warnings followed by silent mind's eye or spoken threat neutralisation tactics and skills instructions.

The following are some examples of shadow training.

- Use your imagination to provide yourself with wide ranging challenging threat situations and best means threat neutralisation instructions.
- Start simple and basic and work your way up to challenging.
- Walking, walking, walking unarmed enemy 11 o'clock actions on armed incoming respire small squat evade go, go, go assess adjust counter engage go, go, go.
- Compromised 3 o'clock respire first look D attack your attacker target align stance and guard stalk into range respire small squat attack your attacker go, go, go.
- Subject approaching knife pulled respire eyes on weapon tip break reactionary evasive disarming range set neutral status actions on right thrust small squat evade go, go, go assess weapon retracted adjust leg stamp hand edge threat neutralisation go, go, go.
- Full nelson respire resist set stance assess set up and employ full nelson escape go, go, go.

You can make the threat information as brief or detailed as you wish and the same with your silent or spoken threat neutralisation instructions.

You must ensure all and any omitted major and minor required components are employed as needed to threat neutralise.

The brain-to-boot audio exercises to command will provide you with principles, terms and practices that will assist you with developing your own shadow training threat situations and best means shadow training threat neutralisation.

Impact Targets

Inanimate objects that are robust and safe to employ high levels of contact impact on, with safety to yourself and any assisting training partner, are a great means of developing physical output and psychological enhancement. Such objects include tackle bags or wedge-like super stamper targets, high density impact shields, combative dummies and the like.

Burying a car tyre in the ground with half the tyre exposed makes a great stamp kicking target.

Remember safety in relation to ensuring your training partner holding the tackle bag or shield has it braced against their upper quadrants, and their head is positioned on the side away from the direction of travel of the incoming striking skill.

Stamp kicking skills can be practiced with the tackle bag on the ground, horizontally against a solid backdrop, or held by a training partner upright with the tackle bag base firmly on the ground and the tackle bag angled diagonally up and back. This is to ensure the tackle bag, when stamp kicked diagonally downwards from below knee height bends and is not driven back into the holder's legs.

The training partner must always ensure they position their legs safely astride of the tackle bag. Training on such inanimate objects does build confidence through being able to heavily commit to the impact; however safety of not overextending joints is important.

Also it is important to understand that with striking skills practiced on foam filled impact targets; the targets can compress and can then cause wrist sprains or breaks. It is important that right handed palm heel strikes are angled to 10 o'clock, and left-handed palm heel strikes are angled to 2 o'clock, lining the heel of the palm up with the bones of the forearm to reduce the likelihood of injuries.

The clenched fist variation of the palm heel strike reduces wrist sprains through compacting and compressing the hand more. This is an option in gross motor skill palm heel striking and on soft compressive impact targets. The 10 o'clock right hander and 2 o'clock left hander hand angling as with the flat hand palm heel strike must be employed.

The clenched fist palm heel hand configuration has the thumbs positioned on top of the clenched fist index finger. Styles that promote clenched fists for striking must ensure that the fist is properly clenched and the top of the hand is flat in line with the forearm—to avoid boxer's fractures.

I have overseen CQC training of an entire military service, and one of the primary objectives was to develop combative confidence at an enabling competency level while minimising combative related training injuries. Utilisation of the tackle bag for high commitment impact was the chosen inanimate object to achieve this objective.

The human reality is that at an entry-level, on intensive courses of instruction where exponents are victims of soft tissue injuries, the effects of cumulative contact reduces the individual combatant's levels of commitment considerably.

However, the tackle bag inanimate safe training impact target has the opposite effect, and as the exponent grows in competency, the level of contact impact is increased considerably. This is the best means, at an enabling level, to achieve confidence and increase battlefield required competency so that if the exponent was deployed and used the same high level of commitment on an enemy combatant as they had on the impact target, this would increase the chance of the enemy threat being neutralised.

Putdowns

The putdown as a means of training in the Todd System has been adopted and further developed for its realism and safety in training. The Todd System also has a full range of putdowns for specialist roles where a non-harmful method of subject decentralization is required.

In training, utilising the buddy training partner system where both combatants have competency in the same skills and in the putdown method, controlled leverage from the combatant is required over destructive velocity, and cooperation is required by the enemy per in relation to not resisting the contact leverage but allowing decentralization to avoid compromising the integrity of their knee joints and knee caps. The end result will be that the enemy per will be decentralised, ending in the same position they would have ended if the strike or stamp kick was employed with ruthless controlled aggression.

This is an effective means of combative practice that develops increased confidence, through increased proficiency in competency of skills executions, in a controlled manner and environment.

Leg stamp putdown under Phase 1 test conditions

Military CQB/CQC drills

The Todd Systems have complete physical combative and psychological enhancement training drills packages.

We have been instructing CQC technique-to-command drills to the military for over two decades. They are a Todd Group developed military drills-to-command complete package. Also, the brain-to-boot psychological enhancement drills package provides a military-drills means of practicing the brain-to-boot major and minor components, in the correct order to command.

This valuable training exercises package is part of this manual and is available for downloading to purchasers of this manual.

The package provides initially basic static and marking time drills practice to command and later will be released movement drills practice to command, and partner training drills exercises to command in expected and unexpected actions-on encounters, for both unarmed offensive assault and unarmed counteroffensive assault options employments.

Enemy Take-outs

Range plus skill and commitment equals your best combative chance; nothing more and nothing less.

The take-out should incorporate every component of psychological and physical requirements in relation to the tactics and skills specifics, executed in unison at 75 percent plus controlled aggressive commitment from extreme close quarters.

Executing such skills out of a service duty in relation to rules of engagement, or knowing they are the right, best and a legal means of protecting oneself inside the laws of self-defence in a civilian self-defence situation, should support such actions from a moral, legal and decent responsible human being perspective, and knowing your actions are right and necessary is a psychological motivator. Knowing you are doing the rightful thing for the right reasons is just another important aspect of psychological enhancement through being right and just in your actions and options.

Shadow training, impact targets, putdowns and drills provide excellent training options for everyone from enabling level exponents, right through to specialist combative proponents. In operational CQC skills employments and in dire self-defence situations, the employment of combative dirty and deadly skills practices provide a primary means of incapacitation or elimination of the enemy.

Training kicks in

In order for training to kick in when it is needed in an expected or unexpected actions-on combat or counter employment, the combatant must have undergone not only intensive and extensive training, but also must have trained and practiced the tactics and skills in the correct order to achieve competency and proficiency. The brain-to-boot expected actions-on encounter principles, tactics and skills require constant checks and re-checks, and the maintaining of a state of readiness as well as sound tactical decision making and decided options confirmation.

This, combined with self-reassurance and emergency contingency options, best prepares and makes ready the combatant to deal with the realities of aggressive actions-on encounters. In unexpected actions-on encounters the combatant may only at the last instant identify the incoming actions-on threat. In this case, they must employ combative respiration, make a sound tactical options decision, and incorporate all the required components to effectively neutralise the threat in real time. If the first indication of the threat is physical contact, then the first priority is to employ hard cover guarding or combined hard cover guarding and clearing the contact zone simultaneously with combative respiration, and then assessment, decision making and threat neutralisation employment with all the required components included. In the brain-to-boot training drills, in expected actions-on encounters of both unarmed offensive assault and unarmed counteroffensive assault, long version whispered commands are given. This requires the combatant to ensure their senses are maintained at high alert in order to utilise them to take in the instructions, make decisions and effectively employ the decided options with competency, confidence, conviction and cohesion.

In the unexpected actions-on encounters drills training, the aim is that through minimal, necessary loud command instructions the combatant through gained competency in prior training will employ deliberate major components, and the minor but important components will then be employed out of necessity through skills retention, skills recollection and muscle memory. In real life actions-on encounters, the combatant is required to make deliberate definite decisions in relation to their combative actions, and through the brain-to-boot drills training to command, they will become proficient in their primary practices, their best and correct order of execution and ensure they are employed with cohesive unison.

These deliberate decisions and definite tactics and skills employments are comprised of major and minor components performed in a correct order of execution to best achieve threat neutralisation. Like turning on one of your senses to a higher degree than the others to identify the specific threat, your other senses' levels of awareness are also heightened.

When you utilise the required combative option, employed with the brain-to-boot psychological and physical enhancement components, you achieve your best combative chance of threat neutralization. This is all initiated with combative respiration, or in unexpected actions-on encounters, with combined hard cover guarding and combative respiration.

In the case of first awareness being physical contact in actions-on encounters, your training kicks in, from the moment of an unexpected actions-on encounter, you will respond as required subconsciously and deliberately out of self-preservation hard targeting, and employ your skills as you have trained, practiced and exercised. The correct or best order of execution in relation to situational and threat specifics, and the required major and minor components order of execution will be employed to psychologically and physically enhance your combative skills employment. Through combative training where all skills employments combine both the decided combative skill components and the brain-to-boot psychological enhancement components drilled through thousands of training and exercising repetitions, the logical order of employment will kick in through confidence, competency, retention, muscle memory, self-preservation and out of extreme desire to neutralise the threat.

So, one of the realities of training kicking in is the feeling of time standing still and enemy actions appearing to be in slow motion. Your awareness and the clarity of everything that is happening in real time, through being psychologically strong and primed, combined with having the combative tools and the confidence, competency and intent to use them can give you the perception that you have all the time and opportunity to neutralise a foe that is seen as moving at slow time.

On reflection post actions-on encounter you will be surprised at how clearly and accurately you can recall all details of the actions-on encounter.

Training kicking in is a result of not only mega drilling both your combined combative skills and psychological enhancement capabilities in unison at a high intensity combative level, but is also a consequence of high intensity, unpredictable, realistic battle handling exercises and training exercise combative encounters where sudden aggressive shock action is always the reality. Train the way you intend to go combative and real life actions-on encounters will not be foreign territory or overwhelming. They could well be considerably less threatening than your battle handling exercises training because you have trained the military combative way, and with highly skilled completely committed comrades conducting themselves as enemy parties doing their utmost to ensure you fail to achieve your objectives and they achieve theirs.

Effective range in relation to the length of your bodily extremities

To employ skills with confidence, the combatant must understand their capabilities in relation to the length of their striking or stamp kicking extremities relative to real life combative or self-defence employments.

They must take into account that a formidable enemy will employ any means of self-preservation to avoid the loss of limb or life. This reminds me of recently instructing a CQB course when I enquired into the background and whereabouts of an old veteran that I had not seen for some years. I did not find out about what had become of him, but I was told of one of his sayings. It went like this: "move aside or lose a limb"; very relevant, I thought, to the Todd Systems signature stamp kicks to destroy the integrity of the knee joint.

The reason why so many skills in self-defence and combat sports often fail to make contact, and as such achieve their objective, is often because they are executed outside the kill zone or contact range. This is often a result of a lack of confidence and competence to enter into the kill or contact zone, which is between close range and point-blank bodily contact range. Sometimes individuals simply believe their limbs are longer than they actually are, and that the target of the skills executions will remain static.

Practice in real life skills executions against formidable enemy targets will identify the need for range, skill and commitment. Generally speaking, to employ hand striking skills the combatant should stalk into a range between 20 cm and 30 cm (8 to 12 inches) from their lead boot to the enemy target's lead boot, prior to employing CQC squat initiated expedient entry action and the decided striking option.

Employing stamp kicking skills, you want to stalk into approximately between one meter and just over one meter from your lead boot to the enemy's lead target leg boot, prior to employing your CQC squat initiated expedient entry and setup of your stamp kick execution.

The actual contact range of a striking skill with the hands or a stamp kicking skill with the boot post expedient entry will be preferably with body to body contact.

Self-defence or deliberate action, deceptive or covert static stamp kick executions should be employed with boot-to-boot contact prior to the stamp kick execution. In situations of low to no light or where your vision is impaired, using your sense of touch with the toe of your boot to the arch of the enemy's boot, or the arch of your boot to the toes of the enemy's boot will provide directional point of aim contact by means of limited vision, and your sense of touch or no vision executions completely by your sense of touch.

The same stamp kick execution applies when the enemy is at your rear flanks and you have limited or no vision capability.

By using your boot-to-boot sense of touch with the toes of your boot to the enemy's arch of his boot or the arch of your boot to the enemy's toes of his boot you can effectively employ a rear flank stamp kick. Combine your sense of touch with your boot with leaning against your enemy making them wear your weight loading up the target leg for stamp kicking as well as masking your intention by bending at the waist concealing the targeted leg for stamp kicking, this all increases your chances of threat neutralisation.

Bodily contact hand striking skills in low or no light executions, or where your vision is impaired including being blindfolded, or executed by using your sense of touch both with your boots and with your hands to locate enemy bodily parts. This allows direct paths to follow to major vitals. As such, it is another means of maintaining mental toughness through prior learnt skills that provide competency and capabilities to achieve the objective under such adversity.

It is far better to be too close to a target than too far away to achieve effective contact and threat neutralization. You can always make adjustments at point-blank range; it is considerably more difficult and dangerous, however, to cover ground and make range when combined with executing effective skills

Tethering

Tethering is a means in training to ensure exponents execute skills from primary ranges. It also develops expedient entry competency and confidence the importance of CQC respiration and CQC squatting assault initiation becomes clear through primary range tethering. Tethering can be practiced for both unarmed offensive assault employments and unarmed counter offensive assault employments it promotes not only initiating actions from primary ranges but also continued closing on the enemy per. Confidence can be increased in training by testing and truing up the combatants hard cover guard capabilities by the enemy per pre, mid and post CQC action execution.

Tethered pre actions on.

Tethered unarmed offensive assault employment

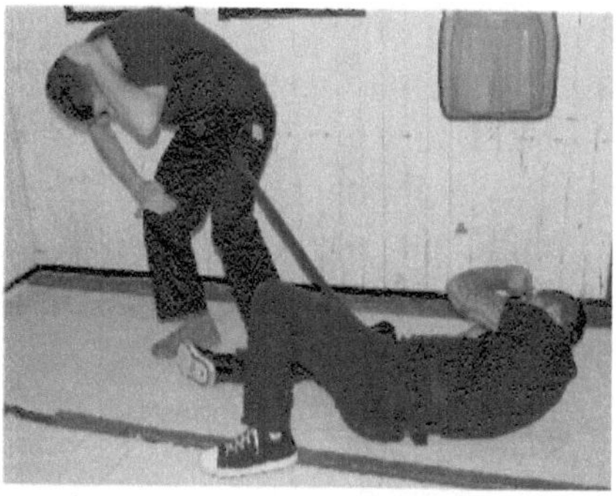

Post unarmed offensive assault training stamp kick put down.

PUTTING IT ALL TOGETHER

The following is the primary order of execution of components in relation to expected and unexpected combative actions-on encounters, for both unarmed offensive assault and unarmed counter-offensive assault threat neutralisation. While military CQC and military self-defence allows for human error, it is important to gain proficiency in competency in the execution of primary major and minor components in their correct order of execution to increase the chance of threat neutralisation.

Order of execution under expected and unexpected actions on

If compromised in an unexpected actions-on encounter, either immediately prior to contact or as a result of contact being made, if there is no chance of clearing the confrontation zone the following primary components order applies.
The following combatant and enemy per pictures are taken from an expected uncompromised covert neutral status and unexpected compromised neutral status.

Compromised unexpected actions-on pre-contact stationary counter engagement:

1. Hard cover guard and hard stance footing, employed simultaneously with combative respiration.
2. Real time actions-on threat assessment and decision-making of combat or counter-engagement options.
3. Alignment to the enemy and set ready status adjustments to go combative.
4. Decided option employment off of a small half or full squat combined with CQC respiration.
5. Threat neutralisation fast map assessment and threat neutralisation confirmation.

Incoming threat, Respire, Eyes on, D stationary counter engage

CQC squat, hard cover

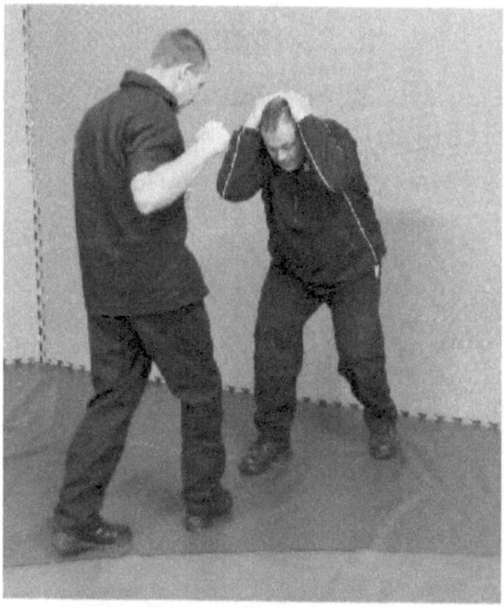

hard target, hard stance, hard cover guard, adjust

Counter engage

Unexpected actions-on, unarmed offensive assault skills employment attack the attacker:

1. Prior to contact last millisecond enemy threat identified in the kill zone.
2. Simultaneous hard cover guard and hard footing stance risk reduction combined with CQC respiration.

3. Fast map assessment, decision making and immediate combative pre-execution adjustments.
4. CQC squat combined with combative respiration employment of unarmed offensive assault decided option attack your attacker.
5. Fast map assessment confirmation threat neutralisation.

Actions on incoming, eyes on, respire

CQC squat, hard cover guard, fast map assess D attack your attacker

Adjust, make range, timing

Attack your attacker

Unexpected actions-on unarmed evasive or stationary counter-offensive assault skills employment prior to actions-on contact:

1. Self-preservation/flinch/deliberate CQC squat hard cover guarding and hard footing ready status stance combined with simultaneous CQC respiration.
2. Assessment, decision making, adjustments, CQC squat and CQC respiration initiated decided unarmed counter-offensive assault evasion if time and distance allow or if not stationary counter engagement or stationary evasive counter engagement, evade assess make adjustments and counter engagement employment.
3. Fast map assessment.
4. Confirm threat neutralised.

Incoming actions on, eyes on, respire

CQC squat, hard cover, fast map D evade, adjust, get set

Evade, hard cover, fast map D counter engage

Adjust, counter engage

Unexpected actions-on unarmed counter-offensive assault skills employment immediately post actions-on contact:

1. Self-preservation flinch/CQC squat, hard cover guarding resistance, hard stance footing ready status setting, simultaneous CQC respiration.
2. Fast mapping, assessment, decision making, adjustments small to full squat respire and employ stationary counter engagement.
3. Fast map assess confirm threat neutralised.

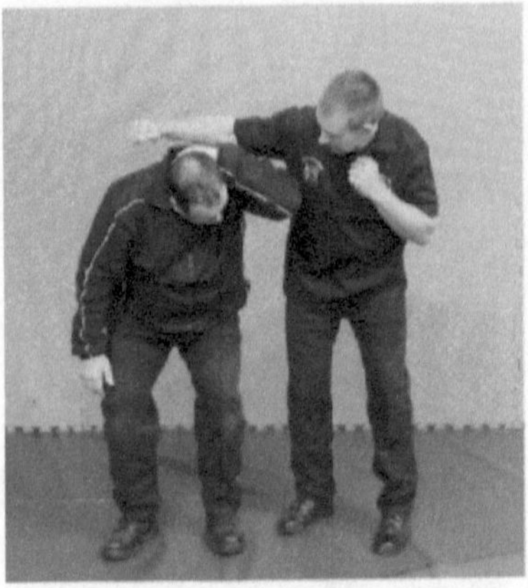

Contact, hard cover, respire, CQC squat, fast map D counter engage

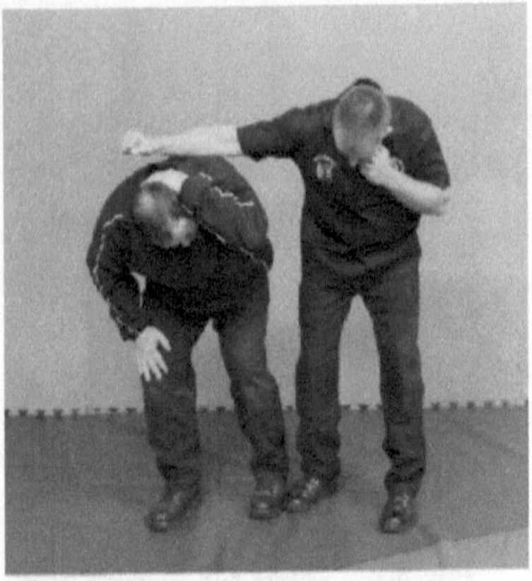

Adjust, make ready, make range

Counter engage

In an expected actions-on unarmed offensive assault skills option employment, the following is the correct major and minor components order of execution:

1. Threat identification and recognition.
2. CQC respiration.
3. First look visual threat assessment and initial decision making.
4. Enhanced senses.
5. If compromised, ready status medium to hard footing stance and hard cover guard setting.
6. Enemy alignment.
7. Ground affinity ready status set.
8. Continued assessment and unarmed offensive assault option decision-making and confirmation.
9. Decided option visualization.
10. Decided unarmed offensive assault option pre-employment adjustments.
11. Self-reassurance: Ready, Willing, Able; Willing, Able, Ready.
12. Emergency contingency option confirmation and visualisation to be ready if engaged prior to the decided confirmed combat option employment.
13. Constant checks and re-checks of the enemy, situation and environment as well as your ready status.
14. Constant adjustments at real time to maintain a primary ready status.
15. Controlled calculated stalking into range combined with constant fast mapping assessment to detect changes in threat and situation.
16. CQC squat and combative respiration ready-set-go unarmed offensive assault option employment to provide the highest level of expedient action, risk reduction, as well as enemy deception and confusion in combat actions on execution.
17. Continued fast mapping assessment throughout the execution of the decided unarmed offensive assault option, to detect changes in threat and situation, and

make decisions if contingency options employments are required.

18. Confirmed threat neutralised.

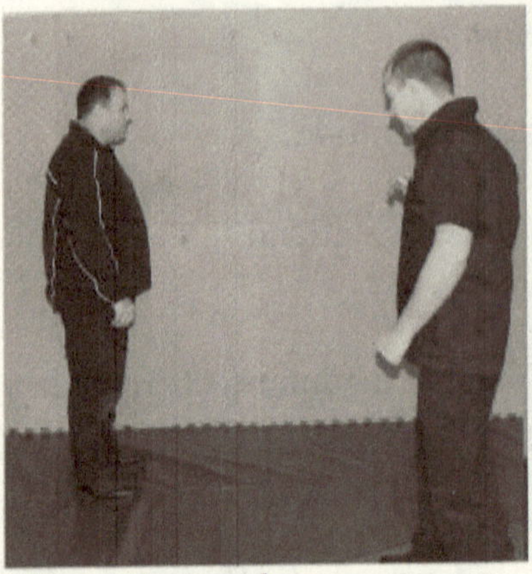

Threat detected, uncompromised, respire, senses on

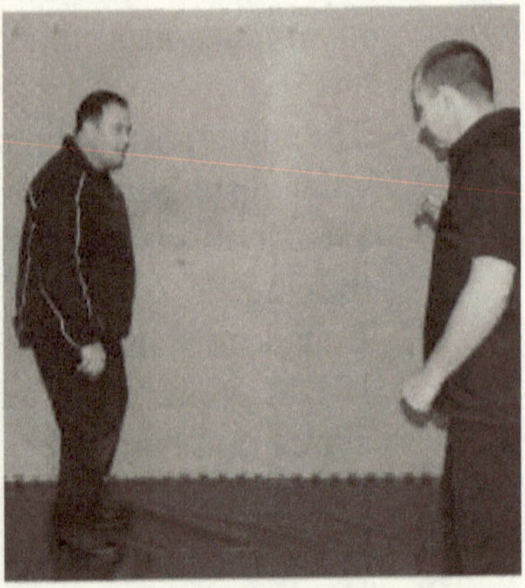

Fast map first look D covert attack your attacker

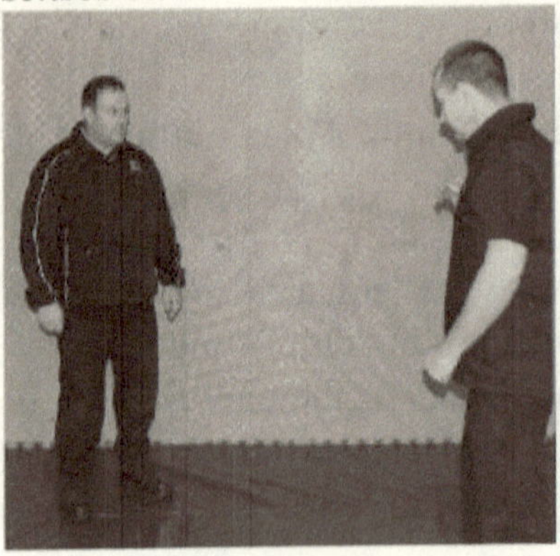

Neutral status covert assault make ready. Align and adjust. Second look D unarmed offensive assault option confirm and visualise.

Self-reassurance willing able ready. Stationary contingency confirm and visualise. Minds eye checks and rechecks

Range, Timing, commitment willing able ready. respire CQC squat, expedient entry, Hard cover setup

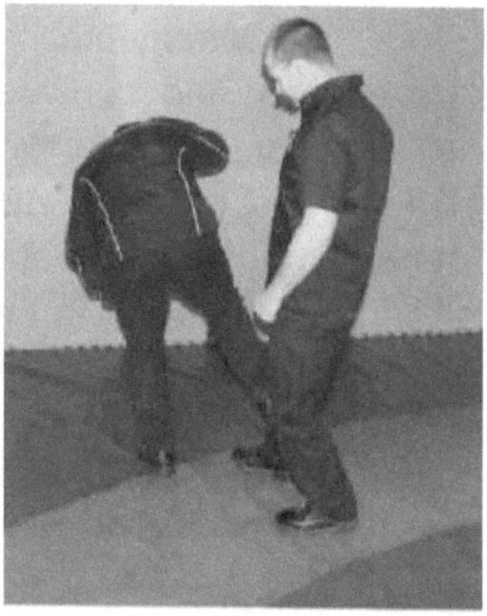

Attack your attacker

Expected unarmed evasive counter-offensive assault options order of execution:

1. Threat identification and recognition.
2. CQC tactical respiration.
3. First look visual threat assessment and initial decision making.
4. Enhanced senses.
5. If uncompromised maintain a neutral status.
6. Enemy alignment.
7. Break an evasive option primary reactionary range.
8. If compromised set a ready status, medium to hard footing stance and guard.
9. Ground affinity ready status set and hold ready.
10. Continued assessment, second look, unarmed evasive counter-offensive assault option decision making confirmation.
11. Decided option visualization, evade, assess, adjust, counter engage.
12. Maintained combative sighting between your pre-actions-on cover guard if compromised or un-compromised neutral status point being the enemy and place being the threat environment visual sighting.

13. Maintaining evasive counter engagement stability and expedient action ground affinity footing ready status.
14. Continued checks and re-checks of enemy threat situation and environment as well as your ready status.
15. Stationary emergency contingency option if engaged and unable to evade confirmation and visualization.
16. Self-reassurance: Ready, Willing, Able; Willing, Able, Ready.

Threat detected rear flanks, respire, eyes on, senses open

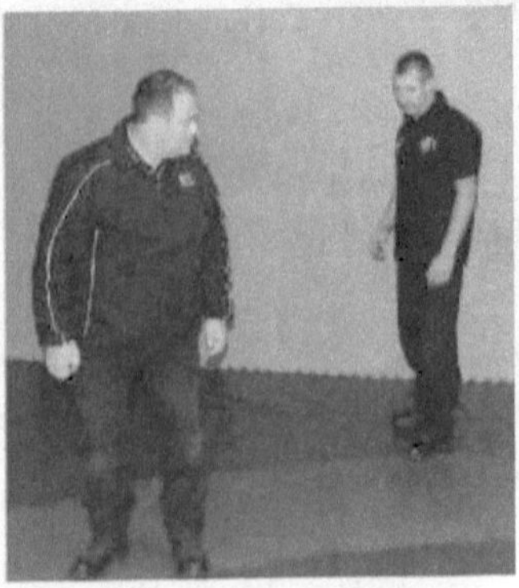

Fast map covert assessment, first look D evasive counter engagement

Orientate, neutral ready status set, second look D evade assess, adjust counter engage confirm and visualise, evasive initiation adjustments undertake. Willing able ready. Stationary counter engagement contingency confirm and visualise

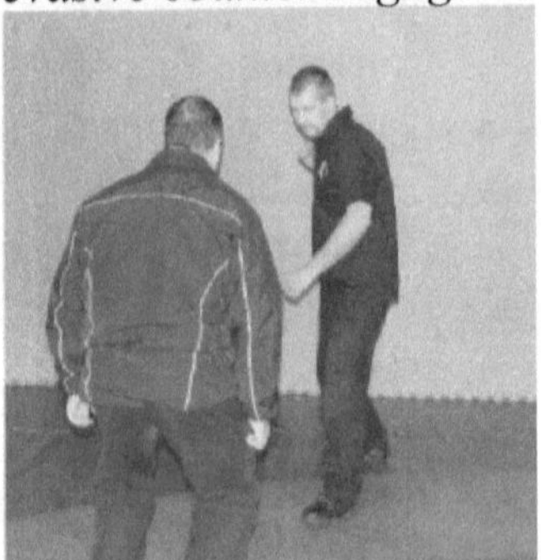

Willing able ready. Evasive footing set to evade. Actions on incoming, Respire, CQC squat, evasive sighting on, initiate evasive action

Timing, Evade GO GO GO

Post evasion, hard cover, fast map D counter engage, adjust, range position

Counter engage

Common required pre-actions on employed contingencies:

- If required, real time fast mapping assessment of changes in threat and employment of pre-actions-on contingency options, such as the maintaining of a primary evasive reactionary range, by controlling distance and edging back and away.
- If required prevention of enemy stalking inside your primary counter engagement evasive range by engaging your enemy before they can assault you with a being-stalked deceptive fake high attack low unarmed offensive assault option.

- Evasive counter engagement employment initiated off a small squat with combined combative respiration, post-evasion fast map assessment counter engagement decided option adjustments in position, range, stance and guard, and post counter engagement decided option employment. Confirm threat neutralised.

The following pictures depict a compromised expected actions-on CQC skills ready status.

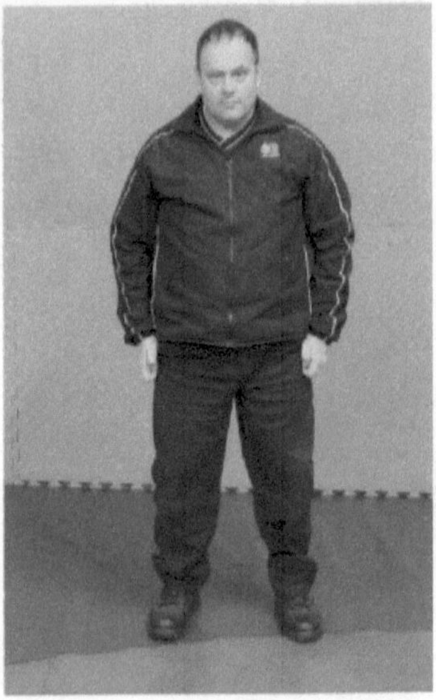

Compromised respire all senses on. First look D

Stance and guard enemy align adjust make ready to go combative CQC sighting on second look D decided option confirm and visualise. Emergency contingency stationary option confirm and visualise. Willing able ready. Checks and rechecks adjustments CQC action initiated off of CQC respiration and CQC squat.

CQC Mind training exercises and post actions-on encounters mind's eye evaluations

No matter how high tech warfare may become, the best of battle-proven skills and combatants with high-level, combative competency who are mentally tough will provide the best combative chance of defeating one's enemy when no other option is available.

Proficiency and competency can only be achieved by high repetition drilling and the most realistic battle handling exercises training. The mentally tough combative-skills-competent combatant must become accustomed and resilient to fear and stress in relation to facing and neutralising violence under such conditions. Fear and stress inoculation training as a result of low level, controlled doses of fear and stress stimuli being presented to the combatant who will use superior combative tactics and skills levels to neutralise the controlled level presented threat, will achieve psychological enhancement. The combatant becomes conditioned to conduct under such actions-on threat conditions and situations.

With increases in confidence, competency and proficiency the threat stimuli can be increased.

Post actions-on encounter debriefs, including honest factual actions-on recollections, reporting and recording is a positive means of determining both positives and negatives that can be learnt from for future actions-on encounters combative employments. We learn not only from our successes but also from our mistakes. Positively focusing on negatives is proactive in ensuring that when faced with similar future threats your actions will be superior. If we learn from mistakes by effectively evaluating errors in determining means of self-improvement then our errors and failures have provided positives.

It is important that when doing mind's eye evaluations that you do not dwell on negatives, but focus on methods of improving your decision-making and methods of threat neutralisation. Charles Nelson would say to me 'an imagination is worth more than a college education in self-defence'. He would go on to say 'you probably will not be fighting too many college professors, but if you do bash him with his books'.

An effective mind's eye capability to process information, evaluate strengths and weaknesses and solve problems will enhance combative capabilities for when you need them in real time, real-life actions-on encounters. Use your imagination to present yourself with dangerous and difficult threat situations, and then by means of the power of your mind's eye, evaluation and problem solving capabilities neutralise the threat by the best and safest means of threat neutralisation.

While it is not always possible to be training in physical combative skills, you will find considerably more time and opportunity to undertake combative mind's eye exercises. Our brain is flexible and innovative, capable of discarding prior information when more proven safe and effective information is obtained. Our brain has the ability to change to meet our life and living needs including our self-protection and combative requirements.

One of the negatives of human addictions of all kinds is that too much of many things can be dangerous. Too much fear, stress or over aggression, just like overtraining to the point of mental exhaustion or self-injury, are negatives.

Self-honesty is one of the most important attributes in the achievement of combative competency. Many practitioners of fighting arts must know that some of their techniques are far from safe and not the most effective means to neutralise threats. If they are not prepared to admit to themselves that their tactics and skills simply are not the most current primary and proven practices, they are fools prepared to overlook their personal safety and combative capabilities of threat neutralisation.

A combative smarts attitude and attributes that provide primary capabilities of threat neutralisation begins with mind's eye evaluation of the effectiveness and safety of one's tactics and skills.

The evolutionary pioneer military combative experts who were my former instructors possessed wisdom and high-level expertise. They earned that through training, testing and proving themselves as exponents and then being open-minded, instructors willing to ensure the skills they developed were the safest and best means of formidable threat neutralisation.

Wisdom, expertise and intestinal fortitude are all attributes and attitudes of expert military combative master chief instructors. These are learnt hands on and enhanced through maximum psychological capabilities. They are as much a state of mind as they are a state of body or physical condition in relation to combative capabilities. They can be enhanced by combative mind's eye exercises, living and reliving unpredictable, expected and unexpected actions-on combative encounters.

We learn from our successes and mistakes, and can ensure our successes are retained positive practices; our mistakes, however, are remembered but replaced by superior and safer combative capabilities by mind's eye combative training exercises. Combative expertise means the ability to do what needs to be done to neutralise a threat, using the best tools and means at your disposal, and not settling for less effective tools and means out of blind stupidity.

Blind stupidity in relation to your personal safety, self-protection and combative means of threat neutralisation as a result of personal preference to some traditional or sporting fight style equates to and identifies a flowing robe brigade follower as Col. Applegate would put it and not a military close combat proponent

A primary combative status and capability is achieved through being prepared to learn by experience, both positive and negative, and being committed to striving for combative excellence—not settling for anything less than the best and safest means of threat neutralisation.

A combative means of threat neutralisation requires a practical and realistic demeanor and attitude unaffected by personal preferences if they are not battle proven. Being able to assess and evaluate the immediate in relation to the threat, and make the best of battle-proven threat neutralisation decision-making, begins with having the combative smarts from the outset in relation to deciding on a training system and the tactics and skills of that training system being the safest and best means of objective achievement.

As previously mentioned I personally believe that many practitioners of less-than-primary fighting arts practices must know that their techniques are unsafe and would be ineffective against a formidable foe. Possibly their lifestyle is safe and their chances of having to fight for their life are extremely unlikely, so they are content with practicing ineffective skills in relation to self-defence or unarmed combat. They really need to perform an honest mind's eye evaluation of the self-defence and combative capabilities provided by their so called primary practices.

The competent combatant needs to be wise, smart and mentally tough, for without these qualities their personal safety and means of combative objective achievement is compromised. An important check for an individual that is not sure if their tactics and techniques are the best and safest means of objective achievement is to put them through a mind's eye evaluation, pitting them against formidable threats.

Combining this with performing physical testing of tactics and skills capabilities and objective achievement capabilities should be clear and apparent. The combatant must balance out training levels achieved in relation to available training time and training intensity to ensure primary outcomes are achieved.

Often the situation and environment where combative and self-defence skills are most required includes increased negative aspects through high levels of fear, stress and environmental risk and danger as well as individual combatant negative considerations such as fatigue, sleep deprivation, injury and wounding. To increase combative competency capabilities, proponents need to train with the goal of pursuit of combative excellence. Achieving as close as is humanly possible to combative excellence will enable the combatant to perform at higher levels of competency and maintain the highest possible levels of cognitive skills when facing extreme adversity.

Like training your musculoskeletal system and respiratory system to increase physical combative capabilities, your mind needs to be trained by drilling the brain-to-boot practices in high repetition as well as in unpredictable and unexpected actions-on encounters.

Training both expected situations, where you need to deal with the effects of maintaining a ready status for various durations, as well as contending with the element of surprise in unexpected sudden aggressive shock action situations, ensures psychological capabilities to provide the requirements to neutralise threats under various conditions and threat levels.

Walking and talking your way through employing the brain-to-boot components in the correct order of execution, and in unison, will increase proficiency and competency, reinforcing primary means of combined physical and psychological components usage. 'Walking, walking, walking, unarmed aggressor 4 o'clock, first look, decision, unarmed offensive assault, make ready, attack, attack, attack' and so on. Rehearsals by mind's eye mental combative training exercises is a most positive means of developing combative proficiency.

Training your mind by walking, and giving yourself verbal commands and instructions is proactive in developing confidence and competency just as is shadow training.

Fractions of seconds count and training your mind and body by means of mental combative exercises improves your decision-making capabilities including reducing time taken from threat detection through threat identification to threat neutralization. Being flexible and innovative in decision-making based on factual assessment not perception, including the deciding of contingency options to deal with changes in threat and situation in real time, is a vital part of combative competency achievement.

The brain-to-boot principles allow for human error and, being principles, provide a range of methods of threat neutralisation including primary, secondary, alternate and emergency methods.

The combatant being their own self master decision maker achieves increased confidence by the knowledge and capability provided by principle-based tactics and skills that can be changed and adjusted to meet threat and situational requirements in relation to threat neutralisation.

A responsive combative means of threat neutralisation is essential over a reactive means of threat neutralisation that is not thought out in regards to the best and safest means to neutralise the faced threat.

A controlled responsive combatant will take into account wide ranging considerations in relation to legality in relation to the laws of self-defence or rules of engagement, feelings and emotions as well as the best and safest means of objective achievement. This provides the best combative chance of threat neutralisation by the most intelligent means. Every individual is responsible for their own actions and the outcomes created by their actions, so it is important that the combatant, through being highly combative, confident and competent can employ tactics and skills commensurate with the faced threat, and within their rules of engagement or the laws of self-defence. This is best achieved through training to be the best combatant one possibly can be, by striving for combative excellence and to achieve an expert combative status.

The individual combatant must be quietly confident, cunning and capable of objective achievement by wide ranging means, from outsmarting their foe with non-physical cunning, through to wide ranging combative means of threat neutralisation to achieve the objective quickly, quietly and safely. The combatant that continuously evaluates and tests their capabilities by undertaking combative mind training and testing stands to increase their combative capabilities.

Neutralising threats in your mind's eye as part of psychological exercise training, high-level decision making, and mental capabilities enhancement to neutralise imaginary presented threats are all an important part of increasing combative confidence and competency. An important part of enhancing psychological confidence is factual assessment and decision-making which, with increased proficiency will provide reduction in the time frame from threat awareness through to threat neutralisation. As such, this is a positive means of confidence and competency boosting in combative assessment and decision-making.

Being able to neutralise wide ranging threats in your mind's eye, testing yourself by insisting on physical and psychological combative training methods to deal with extreme adversity requiring immediate contingency options, is an important means of mental fitness and training mental capacities required for the neutralisation of formidable foes. The professional sportsperson generally has superior capabilities to the amateur sportsperson, and these superior capabilities are both psychological and physical.

The close combatant that trains to achieve all means of combative excellence through both physical and psychological training stands to have superior psychological and physical combative capabilities to that of a combatant that settles for only an enabling level, or just beyond an enabling level, of combative competency. The lesser combatant may foolishly be training only physical skills and not training their combative mind.

Mental combative training exercises in your mind's eye can be conducted without equipment, while standing seated or lying down in your bunk, and are a positive way of enhancing combative competency.

Mind's eye combative threat neutralisation increases retention and recalling capabilities for when tactics and skills are required in actions-on encounters.

The brain-to-boot audio instructed exercises provide a valuable means of mind and body exercising combative training that reinforces the importance of a correct and effective order of execution of combined physical and psychological components employed with cohesion.

The brain-to-boot audio exercises provide a repetitive drills means of pursuing combative excellence that will provide the combatant with increased combative chances of objective achievement and threat neutralisation.

Just like the Todd Systems technique-to-command package, where exponents learn skills by name and application, increasing retention and reinforcing the skills' means of objective achievement, the brain-to-boot exercises provide an important means of psychological enhancement through mental exercises and conditioning, thereby enabling increased capabilities to enhance physical actions-on encounters capabilities.

The proponent that is prepared to commit to training outside service-provided combative training in both physical combative training and psychological mind's eye combative training exercises stands to increase their chance of threat neutralisation capabilities.

The importance of practicing mind's eye combative exercise training prior to any actions-on encounters as well as post actions-on encounters provides the best preparation and means of learning from previous actions-on encounters outcomes in relation to both positive and negative aspects. It is a positive practice to relive the combative actions-on encounter in your mind's eye by using hindsight to mentally provide more effective means of threat neutralisation, including safer options to neutralise the prior faced threat. This mental up skilling will ensure any same or similar threat future actions-on encounters can be neutralised by a superior means.

Military CQC has, and always will be, a living package to ensure it provides the best and most current means of threat neutralisation. As such can only benefit from post-encounter mental mind's eye training exercises. Mental combative inoculation training is a valuable way of increasing competency and confidence. Simply by mentally deciding on a threat situation, and walking and talking your way through the threat situation in your mind's eye, the threat and the best means of threat neutralisation become more familiar.

Mind's eye combative exercise training enhances competency and retention as well as speed of recalling and employment of combative tactics and skills. This training may be undertaken statically, or it may be combined with walking drills. In either case, mind's eye threat related decision-making can come in the form of silent mind's eye self-instructions and orders or mind's eye decided threat neutralisation tactics and skills spoken aloud by means of self-verbal orders and instructions.

Mind's eye combative exercises should be constructed to be challenging in regards to their provided mind's eye threats as well as in the level of threat and self-determined but unpredictable immediate changes in threat. Then these exercises will considerably enhance your capability to deal with multiple threats, utilise multiple senses, and multitask so as to increase personal safety and neutralise threats.

Challenge your mind to provide the most proven, safe and effective means of threat neutralisation as part of unpredictable irregular mind's eye threats that require deliberate, specific threat neutralisation capabilities. Make these mental combative exercises as real as possible and to do this keep your eyes open and all senses on and alert. Mind's eye mental exercises are best performed with your eyes open as this provides a combined visual sense and mind's eye capability in relation to threat recognition and identification. Utilising your human senses and mind capabilities for mental combative training exercises will increase realism especially in immediate environment and physical recognition specifics in relation to threat visualisation. You will find it considerably quicker and easier with your eyes open to visually identify the specific extremity and nature of threats as well as their line of travel. The level of visual information is considerably reduced when performing such mind's eye exercises with your eyes closed. Closed eye exercises require considerably more thought concentration and the use of your practical imagination.

Trying to see in darkness, and trying to visualise with your mind's eye without your sense of sight open and on, will reduce mind's eye combative training capabilities considerably, especially in speed of threat detail identification. Silent or spoken self-instruction walking or static mind's eye exercises combined with silent mind instructions or spoken instructions will enhance mental combative exercises. Even training in total darkness, keeping your eyes open, switches on all your senses and provides enhanced combative psychological exercises realism, as well as most effective decision-making in the execution of threat neutralisation capabilities in your mind's eye. Developing a link between your human senses and your mind's eye decision making capabilities has a direct connection with real life actions on threat recognition and primary threat neutralisation decision making. On achieving proficiency in conducting mind's eye exercises you can test yourself by performing mind's eye exercises with your eyes closed.

Recently as part of a Phase 1 test candidates were completely blindfolded and exposed to controlled unarmed offensive assault. Amazingly all candidates' hard cover guarding capabilities were performed at a higher level than they were with full vision. The reality was although they were blindfolded their eyes were open and all senses at high alert. The reality was the need to utilise additional senses once vision was removed and combine their senses with hard cover guard tactics.

The Todd System developed means of coming down and cooling off post actions-on encounters includes the closing of your eyes to remove combative stimulus and combative actions thought capabilities, as well as thoughts in relation to fear and stress. This is the opposite of what is required in combative decision making and skills employments, and is the only time the combatant should deliberately close their eyes in regards to CQC training. This will be detailed in the chapter on stopping physiological adverse effects post actions-on.

To test the difficulty in mental mind's eye combative exercises in darkness, simply close your eyes and mentally try and focus on a mind's eye threat, deciding on the best means of threat neutralisation, and mentally in your mind's eye with your senses switched off try and neutralise the threat. Then open your eyes, switching your senses on and perform the same mind's eye threat neutralisation of the same threat and compare the difference in visualisation and the ability to effectively psychologically assess, decision make, and threat neutralise.

Mind's eye combative exercises are extremely beneficial to increased physical combative competency, but must be practiced with attention to detail and under primary imaginary combative mind's eye training conditions.

The smart combatant will utilise every means of pursuing combative excellence. Given that mental toughness is the most essential combative attribute to ensuring the individual combatant is capable of neutralising formidable threats, they should understand and take advantage of mental mind's eye combative enhancement conditioning exercises. This is especially true given that they can be practiced anywhere, at any time and are an effective means of utilising available down time.

Training to objective achievement and threat neutralization

You will be best at your primary system and the tactics and skills provided through familiarity and intensive drilling, as well as utilising the tactics and skills in unpredictable, unorthodox, sudden aggressive shock action battle handling exercises and scenario training. You must treat all training with the same attention to detail and employment of battle-proven tactics and skills as in real life, real time actions-on employments to ensure the threat is neutralised.

Training in low-intensity, minimal-repetition, less than primary proven practices self-defence training is a dangerous means to prepare for the neutralization of formidable foes. Training in high-repetition self-defence techniques under training conditions, when the tactics and skills that would be used in real life, actions-on encounters to neutralise the threat are not being practiced is also a negative practice and can increase risk and danger.

Soft, fast, hand flicking or slapping, repetitive alternating partner self-defence training is tactically flawed and dangerous. Unfortunately, many people believe what they see in the movies and martial arts demonstrations, thinking that a formidable enemy can be neutralised by means of soft or fast hands, inner energy, soft option, low-powered techniques. Fortunately, statistically most will never face a formidable foe in a life-or-death encounter.

You need to understand that a formidable, goal driven, violent aggressor is capable of doing the unthinkable to you, and will kill you even in their final death gasp, if given the opportunity.

Tactics and skills employed in real life actions-on encounters must be the same tactics and skills used in realistic training. You have battle-proven tactics and SOPs in relation to serious threat neutralisation that must be adhered to in training in the same way as real-life actions-on encounters.

I remember showing a book that was supposedly about CQC to a former Vietnam veteran and Special Ops friend of mine. Obviously the instructor in the book had never trained and qualified on military CQB/CQC courses of instruction, but had come from a traditional martial arts background. The skills were suicidal, especially in the disarming of edged weapons. The instructor recommended rising bent arm blocks to defend against downward ice pick attacks and forearm-to-forearm blocking skills against an enemy's knife holding hand that, by its normal extension and retraction, would clearly slice through the tendons and arteries of the blocking forearm. There was no finality to any of the disarms, and often striking skills were utilised while the armed enemy had the knife still in hand, providing every opportunity for the combatant to be stabbed or slashed multiple times. Even when the book suggested the martial arts-based unarmed combat techniques were being used against an injured or incapacitated foe, there was still no security and control of the weapon holding hand and wrist, and clearly the enemy, if bent on killing you, could have done so before he expired.

I remember getting the book back from my Vietnam veteran friend who obviously had a real understanding of the realities of neutralizing formidable threats or paying the ultimate price. I say this because unbeknownst to me, he had written throughout the book in pencil comments like ‘get real such and such’ and ‘what about his free weapon holding hand’ etc. Well some years later a friend of the instructor in the book asked me if I had read the book, and I said yes and produced my copy. He looked through it and got a strange look on his face, obviously as a result of my friend’s penciled-in comments. Facts are facts to those that have been there and done that.

Another danger of high-repetition training that does not adhere to the tactics of threat neutralisation is that you are developing muscle memory. I was briefed on a situation where, in law enforcement, an officer keen on defensive tactics training off duty did, in the line of duty actually disarm a live weapon from an assailant and then hand it back to them. This is the danger of studio or dojo training that does not include terminal tactics to ensure the threat is neutralised and the entire situation is made safe. Sound law enforcement defensive tactics training, as part of SOP’s, require weapons disarmed or taken from suspects to be stowed safely in their belt order, or ensure it is given to a fellow officer to be secured in a vehicle.

In military combative training the weapon can be secured in your webbing, combat vests or body armor. Under realistic training, if not in battle dress, the weapon can be deposited in a designated safe area after neutralising the enemy threat. The important thing is that the training is in line with real life threat neutralisation skills, where the enemy is neutralised, and the weapon is removed from the situation and made safe.

In training and testing, having specific tactics post disarming such as always neutralising the decentralised enemy and then handing over the weapon, or depositioning the weapon in a designated safe area confirms the importance of removing weapon accessibility from the enemy or anyone else post disarming.

The terminal objective in training must be the same as in real life actions-on encounters, and whether it be CQC, CQB, defensive tactics or self-defence, regardless of the rules of engagement or laws of self-defence, threat neutralisation means all risk and danger has been completely eliminated. To effectively do this the enemy must be unable to pose any continuing threat and must have no access to any weapons capabilities.

Always remember the most dangerous weapon is the one you don't see but which you subsequently feel.

Never allow access to your own weapons. Use weapons seizure prevention, weapon security retention and in the event that you are compromised and your weapon is seized and secured by the enemy, employ weapon regention, regaining control of the weapon and neutralising the threat.

Be aware of available improvised weapons and ensure your foe has no means of getting access to them and utilising them against you.

Ensure in battle handling exercises, during scenario training, and in disarming training and practice that SOPs in relation to threat neutralisation include the disarming, making safe and securing of disarmed weapons are employed each and every time under tactically correct threat neutralisation conditions.

In self-defence and unarmed combat training, through the controlled employment or simulation of over-kill enemy neutralisation every time, as part of objective achievement, you are developing the required skills to ensure formidable foes are neutralised and present no continued threat.

I have seen under training and testing, exponents, especially from martial-arts-based self-defence backgrounds, who will simulate ground neutralisation skills and then step back and away from the enemy a meter or more. This is tactically flawed and provides recovery time and distance for the downed enemy to counter engage.

The old traditional martial arts tournament demonstration of finishing the decentralised opponent by bending or crouching over them and reversed punching is tactically flawed in self-defence defensive tactics and CQC. By crouching over the decentralised foe you are bringing your vulnerable bodily vitals within range of his boots, not to mention providing the opportunity for the downed enemy to tackle you, finish you on the ground, or get up and stomp on you. In unarmed combat the decentralised enemy should be finished with heel stomping, utilising your leg length and your resilient combat boot to neutralise your foe. Bare feet are for bathing, boots are for combat.

For law enforcement defensive tactics, C&R methods of subject handling and applying must be the same tactics and skills in training as on the job of mechanical restraint devices. There is no place for anything but realism in training and conducting oneself according to primary tactics and procedures to achieve deliberate, definite, permanent threat neutralization.

Always think like the bad guy and ask yourself what he would do to you if your tactics were loose, insecure, weak, or provided him with recovery and continuation opportunity or access to weapons.

Train the combative way, training the way you will go combative.

Understand the considerable difference between some traditional martial arts type self-defence under pre-determined, controlled, choreographed conditions and the realities of a violent, unorthodox aggressor who will do anything and everything to cause you grievous bodily harm.

You do not want to find out that your techniques and methods of training do not provide the most proven primary practices to neutralise the most high-risk dangerous threats of violence when it is too late and you are under assault in a real life-or-death actions-on encounter.

Never give or give back any advantage or opportunity to a formidable foe; the same applies to the enemy per in training. To give or give back any advantage or opportunity to a formidable foe will ensure the violent encounter is prolonged, and increases the risk and chance of you failing to achieve your threat neutralisation objective.

Primary dirty or deadly battle-proven methods of threat neutralisation are quick and easy gross motor skills that provide maximum destructive capabilities, and the best chance of threat neutralisation. These methods are a must to ensure your resolve is not tested through providing advantage or opportunity to your enemy.

Mental toughness and psychological strength means combative smarts in relation to ending an encounter quickly and quietly by removing any advantage or opportunity for your foe to cause you any harm. Employing anything less than the most proven means of threat neutralisation, employed in its correct and full execution, may well provide opportunity to your enemy to gain momentum—reducing your chance of threat neutralization.

Allowing the enemy to recover can reduce your chance of threat neutralisation, and can increase the risk of you being wounded or injured, as well as increasing combative fatigue, all of which are negative factors that can weaken you psychologically. Having to regain momentum, recover from injury or having to go combative when fatigued as a result of tactical errors and skills faults, can physically and psychologically reduce or destroy your capabilities to neutralise a formidable threat.

Multiple options to neutralise varied employments of the same threat type

There is a huge difference between a combative skill employed by a highly skilled combatant and an unskilled individual's employment of the same technique.

That is not saying that the unskilled individual's technique is not a danger to their foe. Highly committed unskilled aggressors employing less than primary skills are renowned for their effect and can by means of ruthless commitment over tactically correctly executed skills take out a formidable fighter.

For military CQC and military CQB the modus operandi is threat neutralisation by the best of battle-proven dirty and deadly combative means. Taking out the threat and never taking it on or engaging in fighting a formidable foe must be the mindset and means of neutralising formidable dangerous foes.

In street fighting the skilled bigger fighter does have the advantage over a skilled considerably smaller fighter. However, by means of dirty and deadly military combative threat neutralisation options physical attributes and fight skills capabilities do not present an insurmountable advantage.

However, you must always remember a highly trained combatant must have sound high-level competency in the basic principles of hard targeting and hard cover guarding and other methods of increasing safety by maximising self-protection under assault as part of achieving threat neutralization.

Against a superior physically capable and highly skilled foe, if unable to covertly or by means of maximum sudden aggressive shock action over-kill capabilities neutralise the threat, you will not only need maximum hard cover and related self-protection and self-preservation capabilities but also the highest levels of intestinal fortitude and inner resolve.

Highly committed and motivated skilled combatants will reduce the risk and increase safety to the highest levels humanly possible and are prepared to endure the rigors of a torrid close quarters combat encounter maintaining focus and fully committed to neutralising the threat.

Basic military close quarters combat instruction order of training begins with stamp kicking with the leg being longer than the arm and the boot being more resilient than the hand followed later by striking skills to incapacitate or eliminate the enemy.

This is important if the enemy is physically bigger, stronger and highly skilled, especially if they know how to fight.

Always presuming your enemy is bigger, stronger, faster, fitter and more skilled potentially armed and bent on causing grievous bodily harm makes clinching with such a foe and grappling them a negative practice.

Seizure prevention is a primary practice over being fully compromised and having to escape secure holds employed to incapacitate or take you out.

For military combative holds escapes, the primary means is by employing a weapon to stab, shoot or bludgeon your way out of any compromised hold position. However, in the reality of only having unarmed capabilities at your disposal, it is important that you can escape even the most securely employed painful holds or neutralise high level stand up punishment as part of your hard targeting and hard cover guard threat neutralization.

Against a formidable foe when compromised and completely vulnerable it is important that you have options other than your employed option if it is failing to achieve the objective. Secondary alternative and emergency options may be required and must be able to be called upon in an instant if required.

Neutralising difficult threats may require specific counter options from standing, crouched, kneeling or a self decentralised ground position.

Understanding what is required by constant fast mapping assessment and having the tools at your disposal provided through prior training will allow you to maintain your highest levels of mental toughness. As such your inner resolve will not be weakened by the effects of pain, pressure or inability to neutralise the threat by your first option employment.

You must be able to resist when required, yield when necessary, and change tack when your means is failing to achieve the objective with cohesion all while maintaining control.

You must command and control threatening situations by training your brains and autonomic nervous system to respond by the most intelligent means employed.

The combative mindset must be prepared and willing and when combined with primary combative skills give you the best combative chance of threat neutralization.

Don't give your enemy the response time to exploit any available weaknesses. Don't think like a fighter prepared to take on a willing enemy; think like a combatant that will neutralise a formidable enemy by battle-proven dirty and deadly means.

Under threat, human reactions amount to self-preservation and deliberate responses mean actions-on threat neutralization. Actions or responses require utilisation of sudden aggressive shock action, maintaining the element of surprise set up adjustments to achieve a primary status for the employment of dirty or deadly options powered by ruthless controlled aggression.

Calculated timing and smooth cohesive engagement action reduces the likelihood of you telegraphing your intentions.

Pick your time and opportunity to neutralise your enemy when they are least aware, distracted, not ready for what you are going to deliver, fatigued or fearful.

Exploit any weakness, maintain the momentum by committed controlled aggression, be relentless, ruthless and as accurate in targeting as possible.

Your mindset must be that of a trained combatant, always maintaining a primary ready status alert to anything that is going on around you and aware of everything, no matter how insignificant. You must be able to identify and neutralise changes in threat and situation. Maintain constant SitStat (situational status) factual awareness.

Combative competency and self-confidence must enhance your conviction and capabilities to neutralise even the most formidable threat decisively.

Your mind, when correctly utilised the combative way, is far faster than your combative skills and must be utilised from the moment of threat realisation in threat identification for threat assessment decision making and combative skills execution until the threat has been completely neutralised.

The combatant mindset takes longer to master control and utilise than the physical combative tactics and skills and must be drilled to even greater extent than your physical skills.

Challenge and test your mindset under realistic battle handling exercises and scenarios with the factor of confusion and element of surprise ever present. Ensure the actions-on training encounters comprise of surprise sudden aggressive shock action and are over-kill threats that required deliberate controlled aggressive neutralisation.

Your mind in a threat situation will be working at lightning speed and taking pieces of information and putting them through a high-speed thought process as part of threat evaluation and counter means determination.

If your mind is not commanded and controlled by you it can become a hindrance in relation to deciding on and employment of the most simple and proven means of threat neutralization.

The combative mindset just like the physical combative skill set is not a natural human capability and must be trained until you are its master. Then your personal safety and chances of formidable threat neutralisation will be at the highest possible level.

Your mind very much controls and commands your body but you must be aware that your body must protect your central nervous system and mind at all costs in order to be capable of formidable threat neutralisation.

The primary CQC mindset demands your control of unnecessary or unrelated non-CQC thoughts and considerations in high-risk imminent actions-on encounters and under real-time assault.

Your mindset must be strong, deliberate and built on the most robust mind and bodily foundations required to do the unthinkable and endure extreme adversity if required against a formidable threat as part of deliberate neutralisation of that formidable threat.

The word neutralise provides wide ranging means to put a stop to the threat or actions-on encounter in relation to military rules of engagement or for the civilian in relation to the laws of self defence.

Never start it but always finish it in relation to your self-protection or in close quarters combat actions-on encounters.

Never start it does not mean you have to wait until your aggressor engages you, it simply means do not abuse your skills and psychological capabilities by using them to promote, provoke or incite unnecessary violence.

If the best means of ending it is to attack your attacker and it is inside your rules of engagement or laws of self defence then this may be the best and safest means of threat neutralization.

We live in the most violent times but violence for the decent responsible citizen is not acceptable and as such decent responsible citizens to a large degree have been disarmed and dumbed down.

When society breaks down it is the mentally tough and combatively ready willing and capable that stand the best chance of defeating lawless foes.

Understanding that your mind and mental toughness requires more training than ruthlessly-simple basic combative threat neutralisation skills means you should take advantage of wide ranging means and methods of developing and enhancing your CQC mindset.

Be the master of your military combative and self defence mindset by knowing and understanding everything about it. Start with knowing all the principles and practices by title as well as by what they provide, can achieve and how to effectively employ them.

Practice what you learn and train the combative way always employing both the psychological and physical combative requirements in the correct order of execution in unison cohesively with controlled committed aggression.

Initial practice should ensure each component is employed in the correct order of execution to achieve threat neutralisation in the practiced expected or unexpected combative actions-on encounter.

Practice each component in high repetition before adding the next component and do so without high intensity or any stress factors.

Once you have locked into your combative memory bank the complete and correct order of execution of the required principles tactics and skills, in relation to both expected and unexpected actions-on encounters, both offensively and counter-offensively, then you can increase the speed of practice execution which will in turn increase your output in power and velocity.

Once you have mastered the brain-to-boot principles, tactics and skills then employ them under surprise element and factors of confusion situations such as battle handling exercises.

Increase the intensity and degree of surprise sudden aggressive shock action in relation to your confidence and competency.

Always remember the safety of your enemy training partners must be maintained through controlled aggression and safety training combative trade craft practices.

Vary your methods of testing your capabilities from drills, as in the audio brain-to-boot training exercises, through to employing your skills against safe and robust contact impact targets, and finally using controlled aggression in high competency enemy putdowns and ground neutralisation simulation.

Try and make your battle handling exercises and scenarios as unpredictable and as challenging as safely possible.

If you find problems with dealing with any part of sudden aggressive surprise shock action, go back to basics and through exposure and inoculation become familiar and confident to perform the requirements to neutralise the threat.

Slow is fast and less is more. So, for exposure inoculation a small amount at slow time and low intensity of the virus (as in the threat stimuli to be neutralised by a superior means and level of combative capability) is the correct method of training.

Always ensure your inoculation provides more than is required to neutralise the threat.

Through controlled exposure to a calculated threat and through a high level of competency and proficiency in the means to neutralise the threat you will become inoculated against the threat by familiarization.

When you have achieved this high level understanding and capability your training will kick in and everything will appear to be easily identified with plenty of time and opportunity to neutralise the threat. Achieving this primary combative status, known as when your training kicks in, will reduce your fear and stress factors by providing a ready, willing and capable attitude and demeanor for neutralising even the most formidable threat.

The high level of shock and surprise will be lessened considerably and it will be like time is standing still and actions are slow motion and obvious in their intention and means of execution.

In your downtime, when physical training is not possible or practical, use mind visualisation of wide and varied threats of violence employing your memory bank methods from your brain-to-boot and combative skills options training to neutralise the threat silently in your mind's eye, giving yourself silent mind commands and instructions. The silent mind's eye orders and instructions should clearly provide what you need to do in relation to the visualized threat and when to initiate the visualized combative options combined with mind instructions of every required component from your brain-to-boot tactics and skills in the correct order of execution.

Combine your tactics and psychological components with your primary unarmed offensive assault and unarmed counter offensive assault options in expected and unexpected actions-on encounters in your mind's eye to ensure you achieve highest level of competency in the correct order of execution of the required psychological and combative components.

Utilise any available time and combine any physical actions that are practical with your mind's eye orders and instructions.

Practice threat neutralisation visualisation with your eyes open in the quiet of your armchair or when you're lying in your bed, utilising your senses as well as you mind's eye capabilities to provide realistic threats and threat neutralisation.

This is a very proactive way (when you cannot fall asleep) to mentally exhaust yourself by combative employments to neutralise violence by controlled calculated visualisation threat neutralization. It is far more productive than counting sheep to get to sleep.

You may be seated watching television utilising the content of the program or the flashing from frame to frame of the television as the initiation trigger.

By initiating CQC respiration sitting there in your armchair setting your senses at high alert remaining visually focused on the threat and utilising your peripheral vision to detect additional threats you may take a first look assessment and decide on your means of threat neutralisation visualise that means or take a second look assessment changing your method of threat neutralization. Confirm and visualise your decided option, do checks and rechecks of your state of readiness, including deciding and confirming your emergency stationary or stalking into range means of threat neutralization. Visualise holding ground, breaking or covering ground required to effectively employ your decided option. Visualise alignment adjustments and give yourself mind's eye self-reassurance willing able ready, ready able willing then by means of your pre-decided trigger or a simple minds eye silent command actions-on visualise the employment of your means of threat neutralization. This may be combined with some physical components such as when seated raising a cover guard or the execution of a controlled strike or oblique stamp kick from your seat. You must be in total control of what you practice when you practice it and why you practice it. This means being flexible and innovative in your training environment and decision-making.

Regardless of whether you are practicing standing, seated or in bed lying down in your mind's eye undertake assessments of your imaginary threat situation and employ tactics and skills components to neutralise the threat. The important factor is you are training, utilising your combative psychological and physical skills capabilities in the correct order of execution.

The more proficient and higher level of competency achieved with assessment decision making and execution of your combative psychological and physical tactics and skills options employments the more capable and committed you will become to neutralise even the most formidable threats in actions on real life encounters.

The best means of practice once you have achieved a high level of competency and proficiency is under surprise sudden aggressive shock action battle handling exercises and scenario training. When this is not possible through situation or circumstances utilise your combative mindset to increase your memory bank retention and deliberate response capabilities.

There are wide and varied ways to practice the brain-to-boot threat neutralisation capabilities and when you do not have available an enemy party or a fitting training environment or equipment then simply use mind's eye training scenarios to neutralise wide and varied actions-on encounters. You can do static stand up, seated, while lying down mind's eye combative training or on the move walking drills mind's eye threat neutralization.

For static mind's eye silent commands and silent instructions combative threat neutralisation training exercises simply initiate all the required components in the correct order of execution. Begin with CQC respiration or in an unexpected actions on encounter hard cover guard stationary or evasive self-preservation combined with simultaneous CQC respiration assessment decision making adjustments and threat neutralization combative skills execution. For walking drills on the move silently in your mind's eye start by saying to yourself walking, walking, walking identifying the threat in this case a suspicious subject at 12 o'clock, CQC respiration, first look assessment and immediate decision making, second look decision unarmed offensive assault threat neutralization. Compromised stance guard, ready status, combative sighting, ground affinity, senses high alert, decided option reconfirmed and visualized emergency stationary contingency option if engaged by your enemy prior to executing your unarmed offensive assault decided option. Self-reassurance willing able ready, ready able willing. Range, skill and commitment, CQC squat initiation, go, go, go.

Follow these simple combative shadow training drill based training exercises from your brain-to-boot psychological and physical combative skills packages that can be practiced in any environment on your own to increase in competency and confidence. Practice expected as well as unexpected actions on encounters and neutralise them by means of unarmed offensive assault or unarmed counter offensive assault decided options.

These unexpected and expected drills can be practiced from stationary, or as part of expedient unarmed offensive assault forward entry engagement, or post breaking a reactionary range prior to unarmed counter offensive assault threat evasions and counter engagements options employments.

Start out with low intensity slow speed controlled aggressive employments increasing in expedient action speed intensity and velocity with proficiency. This will increase competency and reduce assessment and decision-making timings.

Always remember not to compromise your safety in relation to overextending limbs in the execution of the brain-to-boot shadow training.

Also a major fault with many fighters and combatants that have not achieved a high level of competency is their lack of awareness of their immediate surroundings, environment and terrain. Being aware of your immediate environment and terrain will enable you to identify hazards and dangers that need to be included in your risk reduction to increase your personal safety.

By wide and varied static and on the move brain-to-boot methods of shadow training practice you will train your combative mindset and be its master determining the threat and by silent mind's eye commands and instructions you will dictate the employment of all the brain-to-boot psychological and physical components in the correct order of execution, cohesively and in unison enhancing your combative capabilities by positive threat neutralization.

You should be able to in your mind's eye give yourself silent instructions in relation to both the expected and unexpected actions-on encounters in the proper order of execution without hesitation.

Remember to execute all your unarmed offensive assault and unarmed counter offensive assault decided options by means of the CQC squat ready set go increased hard target and expedient action capabilities.

Train your mind and your physical bodily capabilities will be enhanced. Ensure your physical combative capabilities are the best of battle-proven safest and most effective means of protecting your brain, nape of your neck, and delicate combative bodily vitals including your eyes and throat.

You can never do enough mental enhancement practice or combative tactics and skills combined with your psychological components practice.

As part of skills development I personally utilise mind's eye combat or counter actions methods of threat neutralization. Silently in my mind's eye assess and evaluate the threat to be neutralised confirming my combative plan including every component in the correct order of execution.

This process has proven invaluable for wide ranging courses of instruction when exponents or instructors request answers to questions in relation to some very difficult threat situations. Being able to mind map my way silently through the best means of threat neutralisation at quick time giving them a deliberate primary course of action is both appreciated by the proponent and a beneficial means of maintaining and enhancing my instructor combative competency.

I also utilise silent mind's eye mind mapping and a whiteboard or notebook to develop tactics and skills to combat or counter wide ranging threats.

As a military combative master instructor contract CQB/CQC training provider instructing wide ranging training for specialist role and specialist operator's requirements, being able to deliver full courses of instruction at little notice and without unnecessary training aids or copious amounts of resources is what is required.

Recently I was requested to provide a specialist course of instruction comprising of tactics and skills needed to neutralise threats under wide ranging and varied operational roles requirements.

I turned up as requested ready to go and the course manager commended me on my capability in relation to the complete course requirements being as he put it, and pointing to my head, stored up there.

Military CQC is a back-to-basics last resort means of threat neutralization and must be as proven as it gets. If the training requires copious amounts of equipment and cumbersome protective gear then it is becoming unrealistic and very much removed from what it is meant for.

Being able to deliver complete courses of instruction without programs, overhead projectors, laser pointers, lecterns, truckloads of training equipment and training aids is a primary and positive means of course delivery that reduces wasted time with setting up and suiting up.

Conducting the training in a realistic relevant environment whether on a training field, in the bush, on the beach in the water or in an urban environment is preferable to a sterilised environment.

The less protective equipment the better as this increases accuracy and safety in training and deliberate controlled aggression without wasting available training time suiting up. It also advocates that true CQC is unarmed and dangerous.

Utilise your environment to provide diverse and interesting realistic training. Never overcomplicate or sanitise military combative or military self defence training. The contact lumps and bumps are all part of combative conditioning and are character building.

Keep your combative mindset active by challenging it to neutralise wide ranging threat situations by means of your mind's eye mind mapping assessment and decision making in psychological and combative tactics and skills methods of threat neutralization. Post decision making introduce changes in threat and situation that require mind's eye fast mapping assessment and real time contingency option decision making. Challenge your combative mind's eye assessment and decision making contingency capabilities. Give yourself silent threat neutralization mind's eye orders and instructions required to effectively neutralise the changing threat including multiple contingency options required to neutralise a constantly changing threat and threat situation. Employ your brain-to-boot primary major and minor components cohesively in unison in the correct order of execution to maximize your decided threat neutralization capabilities.

I spend hours on long haul flights between multiple countries on combative courses circuits and when I am not working on my combative programmes and projects I focus on silent mind's eye combative training.

Always remember the general requirements to neutralise formidable threats combatively are more than 90percent mental toughness and less than 10percent combative gross motor over kill skills.

It takes a lot longer psychologically for a combatant to achieve increased mental toughness than it does to increase their physical combative skills capabilities.

All the physical attributes and combative training capabilities amount to a lot less than is required to neutralise a formidable foe if you cannot overcome your fears by means of the required combative psychological enhancement. Achieve a high level of psychological capabilities and you will positively power your combative threat neutralisation options employments.

Once you have mastered static and walking silent mind's eye threat neutralisation training make sure you regularly practice to increase proficiency competency and confidence to the maximum.

This must be undertaken in a non-public quiet environment.

Another means of silent mind's eye combative threat neutralisation training is to practice your silent mind's eye training to neutralise imaginary threats in various public places.

This could be in a restaurant or bar where you visualise likely threats and discreetly and silently in your mind's eye mind map methods to neutralise the threat. It could be in a busy shopping mall, walking in the street or while waiting for a bus.

You are now taking your mind's eye mind mapping threat and situational assessment capabilities out into wide-ranging environments utilising them to neutralise wide-ranging threats without any physical tactics and skills needing to be executed.

The more you practice this type of beneficial visualisation the more your mind and memory will increase in speed and accuracy of response.

When you combine your mind's eye capabilities with your combative physical tactics and skills methods of threat neutralisation performed in either walking or static drills training situations you are not only training your mind and memory bank capabilities but also developing connections between your central nervous system and the required bodily extremities to be ready to perform the physical threat neutralisation capabilities when needed.

This will achieve proficiency in assessment and decision-making as well as tactics and skills employment preparation through familiarity increased confidence and skills competency in mental memory.

COMING DOWN AND COOLING OFF

Just as there is combative respiration to enhance combative capabilities, there is a respiratory means for reducing the effects of physiological and to a lesser degree psychological stress post encounter.

I spent decades developing testing and proving ways to increase combative psychological and physical tactics and skills capabilities. Part of this research and development was on methods to reduce recovery times in order to return to a non-combative pre-actions on status. The method I have developed, tested and proven to be beneficial is specific to CQC post encounter coming down and cooling off requirements. It is simple and easy to execute, and the major focus is on anti-combative respiration.

This method is considerably different to combative respiration where you want to utilise controlled, level, low intensity cycled respiration inhaling via the nose immediately prior to skills employments, and exhaling via the mouth throughout the skills execution phase.

When coming down from an actions-on encounter, reducing and ultimately eliminating the flat line combative maintained controlled ready status can be achieved, or should I say reduced in duration, and effects reversed by finding a quiet place, closing your eyes and inhaling and exhaling via both your nose and mouth simultaneously, at a low intensity level. Starting with your eyes closed and head down, initiate the inhale phase as you raise your head and then the exhale phase as you lower your head.

The best means of undertaking this effects-reversing return recovery means is while seated, with all your weight supported by the chair and your entire body in a comfortable state. It can be done standing, but you must be relaxed, and the immediate feeling of a state of relaxed ease and nothingness is lessened to a degree by having to hold an upright position. Note also that the combined minimal head up and down movement coordinated with the respiration under a closed eyes status can affect balance and stability. If unable to perform the coming down and cooling off seated, then lean against a solid back drop instead.

When balance and stability are affected it interferes with maintaining a neutral controlled state and to a degree produces stress. However if the situation required an upright status be maintained, then this would still provide return status recovery benefits, especially if leaning against a solid back drop.

Through consciously and unconsciously focusing on your coordinated head raising and inhaling, and head lowering and exhaling, your mind will be cleared of any other thoughts. Inhaling on the head raising movement is the opposite of primary combative physical actions respiration, where you inhale pre-action and exhale throughout the physical skill execution phase to power the employment. This reverse cycled respiration is also important to set a state of non-combative familiar respiration when coming down and cooling off. This all promotes a state of relief under ease.

The head motion is not a full range motion but is only approximately 10 cm (4 inches) in each direction of movement. You must never hyperextend your neck by moving your head full range. Also, the movement should be smooth and slow in speed.

This technique produces a state of tiredness and sleepiness that is important to clearing the mind in a most restful and relaxed manner while coming down and cooling off post encounter. This can promote yawning which will encourage sleep time. This is positive to promoting safe coming down and cooling off while safely tucked away in your bed sleeping. It is a sound way to reduce the effects of being under the influence of a post actions-on encounter state of continued or lasting arousal and anxiety. It will promote a relaxed feeling and aid in achieving a sound sleep. Importantly if it makes you want to go to sleep it ensures you will not be subject to negative stimuli that could trigger adverse reactions.

I recommend doing this coming down cooling off practice for between 1 and 3 minutes or until you feel a sense of calmness. The coming down cooling off effects can be achieved in as little as 15 to 30 seconds. If you need to return to duties immediately after an actions-on encounter, I recommend 15 to 30 seconds duration only, to reduce the likelihood bringing on increased levels of tiredness and the desire to sleep. Perform it sitting on the side of your bed if possible prior to going to bed.

You will experience a gentle inner cranial inward and outward suction feeling and an internal sensation/feeling that your eyes want to stay shut. You will be aware of sounds around you. Your mind will be blank apart from being aware of your coming down and cooling off undertaking. Thinking of anything else to any focused degree is very difficult, if not impossible, which is important and why such effective and fast results can be achieved.

If you cannot or do not get sleep immediately after undertaking this practice you may still be psychologically under the effects of the actions-on encounter, but you will have reduced or most likely completely eliminated the physiological effects of actions-on hormone dumping.

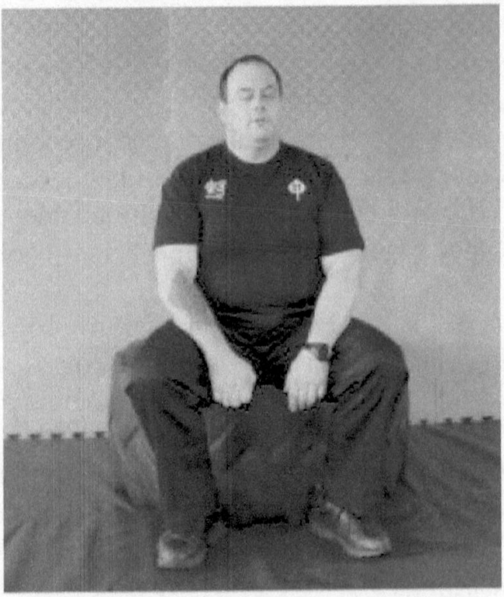

Coming down and cooling off closed eyes head raising inhaling via the nose and mouth

Coming down and cooling off head lowering exhaling via the nose and mouth

Chief instructor Todd Group since 1986. The Todd Group was formally the Baldock institute that began instructing military unarmed combat and military self defense in 1927. Harry Baldock trained and qualified Tank handing over the facility to him in 1986 and with the changing of the guard came the name change to the Todd Group. Geoff "Tank" Todd has instructor qualifications from 3 of the evolutionary pioneers from WWII: Sergeant Major Harry Baldock (NZ Army), Platoon Sergeant Charles Nelson (USMC), and Col Rex Applegate (OSS). He volunteered for his Special Forces hand to hand combat instructor qualification course in 1991 and has also been Special Forces hand to hand combat master instructor certified. Tank has also been trained and qualified by some of the next generation military elite forces master instructors and has the lineage of no other military Combative Master instructor. He is a civilian that has spent his working life training the regular force and elite forces military as a Combative Master instructor.

www.ingramcontent.com/pod-product-compliance
Lightning Source LLC
Chambersburg PA
CBHW022006300426
44117CB00005B/59
9780473674502